MODERN VIEWPOINTS IN THE CURRICULUM:
NATIONAL CONFERENCE ON CURRICULUM EXPERIMENTATION

MODERN VIEWPOINTS IN THE CURRICULUM:

NATIONAL CONFERENCE ON CURRICULUM EXPERIMENTATION
September 25–28, 1961

The Institute of Curriculum Experimentation
of the Center for Continuation Study
University of Minnesota

Edited by **Paul C. Rosenbloom**
*The University of Minnesota, and
The Minnesota State Department of Education;
with the assistance of* Paul C. Hillestad

McGraw-Hill Book Company

New York   San Francisco   Toronto   London

MODERN VIEWPOINTS IN THE CURRICULUM:
National Conference on Curriculum Experimentation

Copyright © 1964 by McGraw-Hill, Inc. All Rights Reserved.
Printed in the United States of America. This book, or parts thereof,
may not be reproduced in any form without permission of the publishers.

Library of Congress Catalog Card Number: 63–13163
53849

PREFACE

This symposium is the first to be concerned with the general substance of education. To keep the book to manageable proportions, we had to limit it to the academic subjects in the elementary and secondary school. Professional persons who have interest in other areas or levels of education will also find the articles in this book valuable.

Each paper was prepared by an outstanding leader in his field: the various sciences, languages, history, and the arts. This volume contains complete and authoritative reports of current progress and trends in education and its relation to the government, the economy, professional societies, and the private and public agencies which support experimentation and research. This book focuses attention on the importance of quality in education and of preparing today's school children for living in a rapidly changing future.

This book contains information on many aspects of the curriculum, not available in any other single source. It is supplemented by important reference material on educational projects and proposed legislation.

Although this symposium is not primarily intended as a textbook, it may be used as the basis for an undergraduate or graduate course in curriculum, or as a supplementary readings reference for courses on educational research, philosophy of education, and educational administration.

Paul C. Rosenbloom

FOREWORD

The world rests only upon the breath of the school children.   *The Talmud*

Our fundamental problem is that we are the first generation in history which must educate children for an unforeseeable, changing society. Many of the things they will need to know have not even been discovered yet. They will have to face problems for which we cannot specifically prepare them. Learning must be for them a lifelong process. We cannot foresee what use a child will have for any particular thing he learns. Any job he takes will change, perhaps even disappear, within a few years.

Our main effort, therefore, must be directed toward teaching the child how to learn new things and toward giving him the desire to keep on learning all his life. We must teach him elementary concepts and skills by methods which he can apply in further study.

The child must learn that learning itself is valuable even when he cannot predict the payoff in "practical" terms. For this he must acquire values beyond his immediate self-interest. One of the most serious practical problems in our educational system is to find an ideal powerful enough both to galvanize children with an urge to learn and to imbue an often underpaid, overworked, and unappreciated corps of teachers with a mission to inspire children.

Since sputnik, the general public has become more aware of the dependence of national defense on the development of our national resources of human talent. With the appropriation by Congress of $43,000,000 in 1961 for the retraining of workers, we have taken public notice of our economic stake in the quality of our educational system.

Belatedly, we are beginning to heed the warning of Norbert Wiener in 1950 that we are entering an era in which machines are cheap and plentiful, whereas human manpower is scarce and expensive. The demand for unskilled labor and routine work is disappearing. Shortages exist in every category of skilled labor and professional manpower.

Our society is much more complex than it was when Andrew Jackson asserted that any educated person was qualified for public office. Consider what one must know in order to make wise decisions with regard to disarmament, space exploration, juvenile delinquency, transportation networks, economic growth, and, indeed, education! Even when a public official knows what must be done, he cannot get the public support for the right decision unless he can discuss the issues with the voters. To manage our public affairs, we need a higher level of general education for all citizens than any previous society. This raises questions about the kind of quality control in education which we need and could accept.

Just as we find ourselves beset with the problem of teaching everybody more and better, the psychologists ride in to the rescue with exciting new discoveries about man's capacity to learn. A stupid child, in learning to speak without previous knowledge of any language, accomplishes an intellectual task far more difficult than any we set for the students in our schools. As von Neumann pointed out in the Hixon symposium, the human brain is far more complex than any computer ever conceived. We are just beginning to learn how to take advantage of the power and flexibility of this marvelous organ.

The ferment in our schools comes largely from the curriculum projects now in progress and those being planned. The reports in this volume represent a continuation of the conference sponsored by the National Academy of Sciences at Woods Hole in the summer of 1959, which was described by Bruner in his book *The Process of Education*. As we found at that conference, people in the various disciplines can profit from studying the common features of these different projects. Let us review them briefly.

A successful curriculum project:

1. Teaches an intellectual structure
2. Involves research scholars deeply
3. Abandons preconceived notions of "readiness"
4. Emphasizes intrinsic motives for learning
5. Provides for differences in ability
6. Builds a grass-roots movement in the schools
7. Must have adequate resources in manpower and budget
8. Develops an intuitive feeling for the subject
9. Brings out correlations between subjects
10. Strives for beauty as well as truth

We see a general attempt to teach a coherent pattern rather than isolated bits of knowledge. A person learns better and retains longer those ideas and skills which fit together. He can acquire new knowledge more effectively when he can relate what he learns to a structure already built up in his mind.

Workers in every field are finding that traditional ideas about readiness must be revised. My own experiments with teaching analytic geometry to eight-year-olds, O. K. Moore's with reading in nursery schools, and those of Karplus and Seeger with physics in the primary grades show that children, if taught properly, can learn undreamed-of things. The projects on foreign languages in elementary school and linguistics for adolescents are the most extensive in upsetting conventional concepts of readiness, which seems to be as much a function of the teacher's imagination as of the student's maturity. It appears to be more profitable to explore what human beings can do than to set dogmatic limits on what they cannot do.

We observe, both in the behavior of children and in the history of civilization, an intense curiosity about man and the cosmos and a delight in creative work. When we incorporate in the teaching of each subject the elements which have led people to devote their lives to it, we find that it is intrinsically fascinating to young people.

The leaders of each of the projects mentioned above have sought primarily for the ways in which their subjects could contribute to the general liberal education of all students. All have found it necessary to provide for differences in ability and interest. The School Mathematics Study Group has produced special materials for low-ability students. Most of the projects have prepared materials for general classroom use and supplementary materials for superior students.

No curriculum for American schools can or should be imposed from above. A reform, to be successful, must be a genuine cooperative effort of scholars, teachers, and schoolmen. These groups share in the policy making, in the creation of materials, and in the experimentation in the schools. An integral part of the planning must be the building of an *esprit de corps* among the teachers so that it becomes their project, too.

A successful curriculum project must have adequate resources for production of materials, experimentation, and dissemination of information. The needs in staff and budget are ordinarily beyond the resources of any one institution or school system. The Federal agencies have provided support for curriculum improvement and have avoided interference with local control as well as the danger of the imposition of a "national" curriculum. The competing projects in mathematics and chemistry supported by the National Science Foundation illustrate how national support can be managed without the imposition of uniformity.

At present, in schools, we devote a great deal of effort to the teaching of analytic methods of attacking problems. A striking common feature of the new developments is the attempt to impart an intuition for each subject, to enable students to guess what ought to be true even before they can demonstrate it. This goal is especially noticeable in mathematics, where the traditional emphasis has been almost entirely on algorisms, on mechanical rules for always getting the right answers. The development of *Sprachgefühl*, the feeling for form and idiom, has, of course, always been an aim of language teaching. Now we also see this striving for intuition in some of the new proposals in history.

Intuition is closely related to aesthetic considerations. We do not feel that we really understand something until it fits into a pattern. The physicist Zacharias speaks of building a cathedral of the mind. The mathematician wants to instill a sense of elegance. In each field, the reformers try to teach their subject not only as a body of knowledge but also as an art. When we turn to the attempts of musicians and painters to teach the appreciation and creation of beauty, we find some common elements. We see them trying to develop taste by teaching an understanding of the structure of a work of art and by giving firsthand experience in creative work.

Each subject is presented as a part of the totality of knowledge, and this part must be correlated with other disciplines. Some of the goals of the core curriculum are being achieved as a by-product. The problem of integrating many fields of knowledge has been especially acute for the earth scientists, who must draw upon basic research in mathematics, physics, chemistry, and biology to explain the phenomena of geology, meteorology, and astronomy. They must join with the ecologists in discussing the interaction between living organisms and their physical environment, and with the social scientists in teaching the implications for public policy.

A curriculum proposal, no matter how good it looks on paper, must be judged on the basis of experience rather than a priori opinion. Evaluation leads to both practical and scientific problems.

Practical problems arise from the disturbances we create when we experiment in schools. We must enlist the voluntary cooperation of teachers, school administrators, and parents. We add to the work loads of many schoolmen. The scientific problems require a variety of competences which has only rarely been brought together for this type of investigation—*expertise* in subject matter, pedagogy, psychology, and statistics. The scope of the problems requires an organization of some magnitude which must be administered with a sensitivity to the human and social problems which arise and must be financed adequately. It seems impossible to do what must be done without an institutional framework analogous to the agricultural experiment stations.

The professional organizations in the sciences, the humanities, and professional education have played an extremely important role in curriculum experimentation. They have served to identify urgent problems, mobilize national resources in manpower and money, and disseminate information.

Some of the pioneering efforts in curriculum experimentation were supported by the Carnegie Corporation, a private foundation. Since then, both the Ford and the Sloan Foundations, as well as several smaller foundations, have aided in this work. The National Science Foundation provided an enormous impetus to curriculum improvement in science and mathematics when it established its Course Content Improvement Section. The policies which have governed the administration of this Federal agency show that:

A modest investment in the quality of education can have a tremendous impact on schools.
Federal aid can be managed without interference with local control.
Federal aid can help all schools.
Federal aid can be managed without imposing uniformity in education.

Unhappily, these aspects of the program are not well understood.

The Cooperative Research Branch of the U.S. Office of Education has supported many projects which have implications for the curriculum. Some of this research has spanned many fields of knowledge, while other activities concern specific branches of the curriculum. Since 1958 the U.S. Office of Education has been supporting a major national effort in modern foreign languages, and recently has inaugurated "Project English," which has long been needed.[1]

The differences in policies between the Federal agencies and the private foundations in the support of curriculum improvement are interesting. For the immediate future, the private foundations can certainly play a role in the social sciences, the arts, and the classics. In the long run they can cut across some of the boundaries which have been marked out by the Federal agencies. For example, they can support research which involves simultaneous improvement in content and in pedagogy. They are also freer to establish the

---

[1] Since this was written the U.S. Office of Education has also initiated "Project Social Studies." The Cooperative Research Branch has been reorganized to include a section on curriculum and instruction.

kind of program which the Sloan Foundation has been conducting in the physical sciences—the support of creative individuals rather than projects.

The existence of governmental units—Federal agencies, state departments of education, and local boards of education—is a recognition of education as an integral part of public policy. Several papers at this conference deal with the interplay between the executive and legislative branches, and between Federal and state action.

The conference also brings into sharp focus several urgent national needs. First, there are no adequately supported major efforts in the social sciences, the arts, or the classics. There is no agency with specific responsibility for the support of curriculum improvement in the social sciences and the humanities, although some makeshifts have been created here.

Second, there exists no national mechanism for continuous study of the curriculum, both as a whole and in detail; for setting priorities on allocation of resources; and for initiating action where necessary. The Supplements to this book include some proposals for the creation of such a mechanism, whether by government action or not.

Third, there exist no adequate means for the dissemination of information to the schools and the general public. For the schools, we need an analog to the county agent in agriculture. We also must make it possible for local schoolmen to see, with their own eyes, children learning the best available curricular material under practical school conditions. We must work with the newspapers and the other mass media and learn how to tell the general public what is being done and what must be done. We must tell the story, not in fragments pegged to events of transient interest but in perspective and depth. Only when we take these two steps will schools all over the country teach the best that is known, even after it has been put into practical form and thoroughly tested.

Our society faces uncertain dangers from within and without. A rational analysis of the problem of what we must do and how to do it is not enough. Many people in all parts of the country and in all segments of the community must act without coercion. And they must move quickly, since neither the external enemy nor the social forces within will allow us much time. Our very survival is at stake.

For enough people to move fast enough to do what has to be done, the improvement of our schools must become a mass movement. It must become a holy mission for our schoolmen and our parents. They must take it as a sacred duty to know what youngsters need to know and can learn, and to teach it diligently to their children.

What must we do to create such a mass movement? The answer is ancient yet ever new. Each of us must wrestle with the problem, must learn, to the limit of his own capacity, what must be done, and must decide which aspects of the whole problem he can take as his personal responsibility. And once he understands what is needed, he must speak of it and think of it when he sits in his home, while he goes about his daily business, when he arises in the morning, and when he lies down at night.

Paul C. Rosenbloom

CONTENTS

Preface v

Foreword vii

I. THE STAKE OF SOCIETY IN EDUCATION

1 The Curriculum and the Economy   Luther H. Evans   1
2 Manpower and Education—The 1960s   Eli Ginzberg   7
3 National Planning and Quality Control in Education   Ralph W. Tyler   11

II. THE NATURE OF LEARNING

4 The Psychological Background for Curriculum Experimentation
  Lee J. Cronbach   19

III. CURRENT PROBLEMS IN VARIOUS FIELDS

5 The Physical Science Study Committee   Gilbert C. Finlay   38
6 Curriculum Experimentation in Foreign Languages   A. Bruce Gaarder   49
7 Curriculum Improvement in the Classics: Progress in Teaching—Motives of Learning
  Carolyn E. Bock   57
8 Wanted: Breakthrough for Better Social Studies Instruction
  John H. Haefner   66
9 The New Mathematics Programs   Edwin Moise   73
10 Current Progress in English   Harold B. Allen   88
11 A Possible Approach to High School Chemistry   Laurence E. Strong   95
12 The Chemical Education Material Study   Paul R. O'Connor   99
13 The Music Education Curriculum: Recent Development and Experimentation
   Marguerite V. Hood   103
14 Curriculum Experimentation in Art Education as Seen through Recent Research
   Kenneth R. Beittel   113
15 The Threshold of a Revolution in Biological Education
   Arnold B. Grobman   129
16 Curriculum Experimentation Problems in the Earth Sciences
   Robert C. Stephenson   143

xiii | Contents

IV. EXPERIMENTATION AND EVALUATION

17 The Minnesota National Laboratory   Paul C. Rosenbloom   149
18 Statistical Problems in Curriculum Experimentation and Evaluation   Rosedith Sitgreaves   157
19 The Practical Problems of Participating in Experimental Projects   Melvin W. Barnes   163

V. THE ROLE OF PROFESSIONAL SOCIETIES

20 The Changing Art of Science Teaching   Thornton Page   169
21 The Role of the American Council of Learned Societies in Secondary Education   Gordon B. Turner   173
22 The Role of the Association for Supervision and Curriculum Development in Curriculum Experimentation   William Van Til   181
23 The Role of the American Educational Research Association in Curriculum Experimentation and Improvement   Walter W. Cook   187
24 The American Association of Colleges for Teacher Education—A College-wide Approach to Improved Curriculum   Edward C. Pomeroy   193

VI. THE ROLE OF SUPPORTING AGENCIES

25 The Role of the National Science Foundation in Course Content Improvement   Bowen C. Dees   199
26 The Role of the Cooperative Research Program of the United States Office of Education in Curriculum Experimentation   David L. Clark   206
27 The Private Foundations   Frederick H. Jackson   211
28 The Role of the United States Office of Education in Curriculum Experimentation   J. Boyer Jarvis   216

VII. THE ROLE OF GOVERNMENT

29 The Role of Congress in Curriculum Development   Frank Thompson, Jr   223
30 The Role of Government in Education   Jennings Randolph   231
31 The Role of Government in Curriculum Research and Experimentation   Edgar C. Fuller   236

SUPPLEMENT

Introduction   244

1 The Contributors to This Volume (Identification of Participants)   244
2 Curriculum Projects Supported by the Cooperative Research Program of the U.S. Office of Education, July 1, 1956–September 30, 1961   246
3 Curriculum Projects in Science Education   249
4 "Project English," Reprinted from *School Life*, November–December, 1961   263
   "Project English: Its Implications for Colleges and Universities," by J. N. Hook. Reprinted from *Higher Education*, April, 1962

Contents | xiv

5   A letter from Prof. Paul C. Rosenbloom to Senator Hubert H. Humphrey regarding the National Science Foundation education programs in science and mathematics, with recommendations for the establishment of corresponding programs in the social sciences and humanities. Reprinted from the *Congressional Record*, March 3, 1961   273

6   "National Planning and Quality Control in Education," from a report of the Conference on Policies and Strategy for Strengthening the Curriculum of the American Public Schools, Stanford, California, January 24–27, 1959, by Ralph W. Tyler. Reprinted from *The Clearing House*, vol. 34, no. 3   276

7   *A Proposed Organization for Research in Education*, Report to the Advisory Board on Education of a Conference held at Madison, Wisconsin, July 9–11, 1958. Published by the National Academy of Sciences–National Research Council   278

8   "NEA Project on Instruction," by Ole Sand. Reprinted from the *NEA Journal*, May, 1961   285

9   *The Minnesota National Laboratory*. Reprint of a Minnesota State Department of Education bulletin   288

10 Text of the "Improvement of Educational Quality Act of 1962"   291

11 Text of the President's Message to Congress Relative to an Educational Program, February 6, 1962   296

THE STAKE OF SOCIETY
IN EDUCATION

part

i

In his inspiring opening address, President O. Meredith Wilson of the University of Minnesota posed the questions fundamental to the conference: "What to teach? How to teach? Whom to teach?" He presented our society's answer to the third question—"Everybody"—as a challenge to our deliberations. These first three papers tell why our society has made this decision. The benefits which we expect to derive from education serve as guides in making public policy with respect to the first two questions.

Drs. Evans and Ginzberg are concerned with the demands placed on our educational system by advancing technology. They note the shift to skilled, flexible manpower as machines take over routine operations of production and paper work. They refer to Schultz's estimate that about two-thirds of our economic growth since 1900 is due to the increase in productivity of our manpower resulting from our investment in education. They point to new patterns of education of adults, especially of women.

While they deal with the "practical" values of education which can be measured in dollars and cents, which can be understood even by a hardheaded budget maker, there are obviously others, some of which have economic implications as well. For example, reduction of the work week will affect the need for people in the arts, the humanities, and in education itself, to minister to our leisure time.

Dr. Tyler discusses the national interest in standards of quality. He points out ways in which this interest can be implemented in public policy while retaining our commitment of diversity and local control of education.

1 ❦ THE CURRICULUM AND THE ECONOMY
Luther H. Evans* *National Education Association*

I speak as a layman. My association with the NEA might mislead you into believing that I speak as a professional educator. But I have been a member of the staff for only a few months and do not pretend to be able to speak for it.

I do think I ought to report to you, however, that certain current NEA projects have a relationship to the subject and purpose of this conference.

The first is the Project on the Instructional Program of the Public Schools, under the leadership of Ole Sand. He and his staff have published a series of very useful papers and reports concerning what to teach, and organizing

---

* Luther H. Evans was Director of the Project on the Educational Implications of Automation of the National Education Association, Washington, D.C., 1961–1962.

instruction for the purpose of teaching it. They have not stated the categories quite the same way that President Wilson has, but I think you can see that the term *organizing instruction* would cover a number of the points that he mentioned. This project is concerned with many of the problems that are being discussed at this conference. The teaching program for various subjects comes first because the members of this project are interested in what to teach and how to teach it. Organizing the curriculum, and the techniques of education come into the second part of their study.

I would like to mention here, also, that there is another project which has a bearing on your work, which has been going on for some time in the NEA. This is the Technological Development Project. It is headed by Prof. James Finn of the School of Education at the University of Southern California. This project is financed by the U.S. Office of Education, and perhaps some of the representatives of that office can tell you more about it. The program is concerned with the role of different technological developments in the work that goes on in the classroom, including audio-visual techniques, teaching machines, programmed learning, and various other technical developments.

There is still another project which I think might be of interest, although it is not primarily a project dealing with the curriculum, namely, the Project on School Dropouts, which Mr. Daniel Schreiber of the Higher Horizons Program in New York City directs. His problem is to find out why there are dropouts and what to do about them. There are a good many relationships between the drop-out problem and the curriculum.

The last project I wish to mention is the new project on Educational Implications of Automation. There is an unfortunate parallelism of terminology between this project and the Technological Development Project, but there is no confusion between the work programs of the two projects. The Technological Development Project staff is interested in technologies in the classroom; the automation project staff is interested in what automation is doing to society that education might do something about. In other words, it is concerned with the new social situation produced by automation. This is of concern to educators, not only in the classroom but through the whole range of the educational activities of society. Thus, our work is largely in terms of social implications, with emphasis on the educational significance of the social implications.

I think the adult education staff of the NEA has a real role to play with regard to curricula because it is very interested in how, through programs of instruction, to make up for the fact that so many of our people need to supplement their education because they did not finish high school, or grammar school. It has become clear that this deficiency needs to be repaired after these people have reached adult life, if they are going to fit well into our economy. To repair the failure of these people to get all their schooling imposes on the high school the responsibility to produce specialized curricula, teaching materials, and methods for teaching adults things they should have learned when they were adolescents.

I feel that the NEA ought to coordinate the efforts of these separate projects somewhat more than it has done. All of them are struggling with certain data, all of them are interpreting the data somewhat differently, all of them are trying to arrive at certain conclusions, conclusions which may conflict as we deal with one aspect or the other of a particular problem. There ought to be the kind of coordination which would result finally in the presentation of a well-integrated picture of what all of us in the different projects think about the different problems and what we think the educational solutions should be. Otherwise, we are in danger of confusing the poor school teacher.

I was asked to speak on the curriculum and the economy. I do not want to be critical of my host, but I think I was a bad choice to speak on that subject. The matter could be covered in quite general terms by saying simply that education is certainly, next to natural resources, the foundation on which to build economic production. It is the foundation on which we must build our social structure and our democratic process. It is the foundation of our civilization as it moves from one stage to the next.

Before I give you a few statistics, I would like to say that I think the economists have been misguided, until quite recently, in not recognizing that human resources were the main element in a productive economy. I remember making a speech on this subject several years ago, as Director-General of UNESCO, in which I pulled together what my staff could find in the literature on the relation of education to national productivity. The material was not very extensive at that time, and I did not make a very good speech in point of content of statistical data. I did raise a question, however, by asking how one could explain that Denmark, with its scant natural resources, has one of the highest standards of living in the world. The answer, of course, is education. I asked how one could explain why Venezuela, with some of the richest resources in the world, has one of the lowest standards of living any place on the planet. I think the main explanation of the difference between these two countries is education. Economists today are recognizing this more and more. They did not recognize the economic importance of education sufficiently until quite recently, but Theodore Schultz at Chicago and others have been writing a great deal about it in recent years. The evidence is somewhat mixed, because not all the value of education, which is itself not easy to measure, reflects itself in economic production or in economic rewards. We therefore have to be cautious when we try to equate a particular amount of education with a particular amount of economic growth. Not only is quantity involved, but also quality, and, since we do not know much about measuring either of these, we have to be very cautious, and we have to recognize that we are dealing with rather crude measures and rather broad generalizations. An effort to be precise in this field at this stage would be, I think, misleading.

The recognition of the value of human resources in economic development has been brought into sharp focus recently by the questions people have been asking about the United States' aid program for the underdeveloped countries. Education has been too greatly neglected in this program. I was concerned with this when I was in UNESCO. I was fighting an uphill battle to have education recognized. I was told, "No, we need dams, we need machinery, we need power plants, we need transportation facilities."

And my rejoinder was, "Yes, and you do not have the mechanics in Uganda even to keep the present automobiles running, so how are you going to make these plants function unless you have education?" Well, my voice was not very loud, but President Eisenhower later called attention to the whole problem in his speech to the United Nations General Assembly in 1960 in which he said that in Africa the future would be determined by education.[1]

Now there is new thinking going on in Washington, and it has spurred the economists to do a lot more thinking. But even earlier, in 1945 and again in 1954, the United States Chamber of Commerce spoke of education and investment in people and indicated that education was in their view an essential instrument through which commerce, industry, and agriculture could be expanded. They said that the cost of adequate education is an investment that local citizens and business can well afford in increased measure because investment in education pays high returns to the community and to the individual.[2] Recent studies of some of the underdeveloped countries have shown that the return on the investment in education, measured purely in terms of the individual's receipt of income, is the highest possible rate of return that one can achieve in such a society unless one is running some kind of a racket.

In 1958, the average male American with an incomplete elementary education earned less than $2,000 a year. If he had a little high school education, his earnings went up to $3,600 a year. If he graduated from high school, he received $4,500 while college graduates earned an average of $6,400. These figures are for the men.[3] The women are a bit more difficult to gather statistics about because they dodge in and out of the labor market so much. I mentioned Theodore Schultz a while ago. He has said that it is far from easy to identify the fruits of education, but he makes a strong case, in general, for education's being the best-paying investment one can make.[4]

I wish now to give you just a few facts about the labor force, because they bear on the kind of curriculum we ought to have in the future. About four years ago, the number of white-collar workers in the United States became greater than the number of manual workers. At the end of World War I, the number of people in mining, agriculture, manufacturing, and construction greatly outnumbered the workers in the service industries, who by 1955 totaled 30 million, whereas those in mining, agriculture, manufacturing, and construction, who numbered 24 million right after World War I, totaled only 27 million in 1955. This figure of 27 million is a considerable decrease in terms of its relationship to the total population. Today over 55 per cent of the labor force is engaged in trade, finance, government, transportation,

---

[1] Dwight D. Eisenhower, "The Goal of Peace with Justice," Address to the 15th General Assembly of the United Nations, New York, September 22, 1960, in *Vital Speeches*, vol. 27, pp. 3–4, October 15, 1960.

[2] Chamber of Commerce of the United States, Education Committee, *Education: an Investment in People*, 1945. 55 pp. Revised Edition, 1954, 43 pp.

[3] U.S. Department of Commerce, Bureau of the Census, *Income of Families and Persons in the United States: 1958*, Current Population Reports, ser. P-60, no. 33, January 15, 1960, p. 38.

[4] Theodore W. Schultz, "Education and Economic Growth," *Social Forces Influencing American Education*, 60th Yearbook, Part II, National Society for the Study of Education, The University of Chicago Press, Chicago, 1961, Chapter III, pp. 46–88.

communication, and service, as contrasted with mining, agriculture, manufacturing, and construction.[5] A considerable acceleration is taking place at the present time in this trend. With the introduction of automation, productivity is skyrocketing and the number of workers is actually decreasing in some areas. For example, if the telephone industry had not introduced automation and other technological changes, there would not be enough women in this country to operate our telephone system at its present load of telephone calls. A responsible industrial leader has said that if we were to build today's large automobiles by the technological processes of 1908, each automobile would cost $64,000.

It is clear, therefore, that automation and other technical changes are decreasing the number of workers in manufacturing and increasing the number of workers engaged in other occupations, including office work. And now automation has also reached the office work field. Computers are beginning to handle enormous amounts of paper work, and low-grade office skills are being displaced. Part of this effect is covered up by the fact that there is total growth; the labor-saving impact of automation is not fully felt because of the skyrocketing growth in paper work. The skills that remain have to be, on the average, higher, just as in manufacturing. And this means that greater difficulties are going to be encountered by people without a good education, without training in mathematics and science, and without training in expressing themselves in the English language. A terrific squeeze is being exerted on people with low-level skills.

Simultaneously, we are experiencing the effect of another phenomenon that we have not fully appreciated, namely, the great increase in births right after World War II. The postwar babies are now beginning to enter the labor market, and the number of young people that will have to be absorbed in the next ten years will be about 50% more than the number that had to be absorbed in the past ten years. At a time when many experienced workers are unemployed, a new flood of workers, many of them with no skills, will hit the market. This is why the drop-out problem that Dan Schreiber is dealing with is becoming one of our most critical social problems.

To solve the drop-out problem thus becomes an urgent national objective. Our capacity for economic growth will be put to a severe test to provide jobs enough, but that is an issue outside of my competence. But a solution must be found, or else we will not be able to convince teenagers and their parents that education will produce a return. If the enormous loss of potential talent is to be stopped, students need to know that there are jobs available to them if they complete their education.

But the schools must face up to other reasons for dropouts. One of these is that to many children school is not challenging enough. There is too little relation between what today's children learn in school and what they learn outside it. School curricula and methods are frequently boring, and fail to nurture properly the desire to learn by making education an exciting adventure. It is clear that serious revisions in the school curriculum are called for. This conference will hear presentations of new developments in the curriculum of foreign language instruction and of biology, and perhaps other

[5] U.S. Bureau of the Census, *Historical Statistics of the United States, Colonial Times to 1957*, 1960, pp. 72–73.

presentations of encouraging experimentation. Much that is going on in science and mathematics teaching shows that subjects can be taught a great deal better and a great deal earlier.

One of the deficiencies in our method of curriculum making has surely been that we have tended too much to leave the job to the teachers at a particular level, such as the primary or the secondary level. We must not leave the task exclusively to the teachers; we must introduce much more expertness in content from the university level, and we must look at the educational process at all levels and design the curriculum for all of it as an integrated whole.

A good curriculum would need to be supported by significant improvements in teaching methods. To make such improvements, we need to know more about how children learn. Bruner, whose recent book[6] is frequently cited in this connection, is no doubt a master well-known to most of you. Certainly, it seems obvious that much progress lies ahead of us in adapting methods of teaching to the learning process. The result will no doubt be a combination of methods for meeting various learning problems and situations which may have little relation to orthodox methods.

If curriculum and method are revised in the light of present knowledge, this nation will go much farther in the direction of meeting its economic goals and strengthening our security and the security of the whole free world in these difficult times. Some of this work, of course, needs to be done on a national scale.

While curriculum problems in the schools are no doubt the main ones, these problems must also be faced elsewhere. It is obvious that rapid changes in technology involve the learning of new skills, many of which can best be learned in some environment other than the school, such as the factory. School people should take more interest in the educational programs of industrial concerns and should help more in the design of courses of study which are not suited for high school boys, but for adults whose skills have become outmoded and who want to learn new skills. Flexibility rather than rigidity of design and method must be brought to this task. Much of what should be done would not fit into any graded system, but the material might range all the way between primary school and the university.

Not only must new skills be learned, but it seems wise to assume that nearly the entire adult population should be engaged in some kind of learning throughout life. In our world of exploding knowledge, specialists of all kinds need to keep up, by constant effort, with what is going on in their own areas of knowledge, and even more, perhaps, in other areas where concepts may be emerging which require new approaches in their own. This updating process, could remove many of the causes of our present cultural lags, including some which slow down economic development. What a field here for imaginative curriculum making!

Nor is this the end. It is quite clear that in the decades ahead our lives are going to be spent, in increasing measure, away from the work by which we earn our livelihood. Our work-oriented lives must undergo a new orientation to give larger emphasis to the positive values of leisure as human fulfill-

[6] Jerome S. Bruner, *The Process of Education*, Harvard University Press, Cambridge, Mass., 1960.

ment. In that case, it seems clear that we ought, in our educational curricula, from preschool all the way through, to do a much better job of encouraging learning that fits people for the most beneficial use of leisure. Here is one of our most advanced challenges. Perhaps this conference can begin to formulate responses to it, as well as the more urgent problems we are considering.

2 ❈ MANPOWER AND EDUCATION—THE 1960s*
Eli Ginzberg** Columbia University

This presentation will deal with the following four facets of our subject:

1. Some general observations about the interrelations between manpower and education
2. Trend data on manpower and enrollments
3. Curriculum implications of manpower trends
4. Some policy directions

1. Some general observations about the interrelations between manpower and education

The following should be noted:

a. The period during which an individual obtains his basic education is the same period during which he is preparing for the world of work. The period may be long or short, but there is an inevitable implicit competition between the two objectives.

b. To cite extreme cases, neurosurgeons and psychoanalysts seldom complete their education and preparation for work until their late thirties or even early forties. This is an important reason for their high fees. They have very little time to recapture their investment!

c. In the preindustrial society of Western Europe, education was limited to the wealthy, and the wealthy, by and large, did not have to worry about making a living. This meant that education could be shaped largely without regard for manpower considerations.

d. There was an intermediate period during the nineteenth century when the education of a gentleman was postulated to be the best preparation for work—at least certain types of work, such as government service—with the result that those who carried the white man's burden were trained in classics and philosophy, rather than in economics and agriculture.

e. In a highly specialized industrial society, such as our own, such relaxed relations between education and manpower can no longer be justified. In

---

* Professor Ginzberg was, unfortunately, unable to present this paper in person at the conference, but he has kindly sent it to us for inclusion in these proceedings. It is based on a Presentation to the Staff Conference, Commissioner of Education, New York State, June, 1961.

** Eli Ginzberg is Professor of Economics and Director of Conservation of Human Resources, Columbia University.

7 | *Manpower and education—the 1960s*

fact, the long record of substantial public support for education in the United States has been made possible by the awareness of the public and the willingness of the schools to make a direct as well as an indirect contribution to preparing people for work.

2. Trend data on manpower and enrollments

a. It is important to remember that children born in one decade become the children who must be educated in the next decade and become members of the labor force in the third decade.

b. The great depression of the 1930s resulted in delayed marriages and a lower birth rate, which in turn was reflected in the 1950s in the relatively small numbers of young people in the age group eighteen to twenty-five. By the middle 1960s we will be faced with an increase of almost one million young people reaching eighteen every year; this reflects the high marriage and birth rate which got under way in 1946. The annual size of the eighteen-year-old group is already increasing; this means that in the absence of a very substantially increased rate of economic expansion, the relative labor shortages of the 1950s will be transformed into a relative surplus.

c. The relative shortages in manpower of World War II which continued through the 1950s were the background for the revolution in the employment of married women. There is no doubt that this is a permanent change in the American scene and that in the years ahead more and more of them will seek employment.

d. The extent to which young people are in school or in the labor market is suggested by recent data about Detroit. In 1953, the last boom year in Detroit's employment, about 25 per cent of all fifteen- and sixteen-year-olds had special full-time work permits. The comparable figure for 1958 was 9 per cent.

e. In short, the 1960s will see many more young people looking for work; more women will be looking for work; and there will be the continuing drift from the farms to the cities if the cities are able to offer employment opportunities. It is also likely that many older people in good health may prefer to continue to work.

f. With respect to school enrollments, I am venturesome enough to question the assumptions of the experts that the high schools will hold on to at least 90 per cent of all youngsters until they are eighteen years of age or until they graduate. On the contrary, I think that high schools, as presently constituted, will not have enough to offer many youngsters who have little interest in or aptitude for book learning. Moreover many experts are beginning to question the desperate efforts that are being made to reduce the drop-out rate without really facing up to the issue of what the youngsters should be taught, or whether, in fact, they can be taught.

g. I am also dubious about the straight-line projections concerning the future of college enrollments, because of the inevitable increases in the costs of getting a college degree; the stepped-up demands on students for higher performance; and the possible relative decline in the value of a college degree as the college-trained population increases rapidly.

h. I anticipate, however, a very substantial increase in enrollments in

The stake of society in education | 8

junior colleges. It may well be that an Associate in Arts degree will satisfy the social aspirations of many families at a cost that will be very much smaller since most young people will be able to attend junior colleges in their home towns.

i. Because of the trend toward an ever lower age of marriage in the United States and the concomitant trend of young couples to have their children early, many women will interrupt their education in their late teens or early twenties, but may be ready to pick it up again in their early or middle thirties when their child-rearing responsibilities lessen and they entertain the prospect of entering employment.

j. Parenthetically, it should be noted that Russian women comprise 80 per cent of Russian medical manpower. This has probably helped the Russians to obtain an adequate supply of scientists and engineers because it has freed the men for these professions.

k. What will happen to all the people who seek employment in the 1960s will depend, of course, in the first instance on the state of the American economy. This in turn will be substantially affected by what the Russians do. In the past, the Russians have frequently helped to stimulate a sagging American economy by making trouble to which we have responded by increasing our expenditures. They are likely to do this again. Second, the accelerated technological change that comes under the term *automation* will probably contribute to further imbalances between the demand for and the supply of jobs. I expect automation to make considerable headway in the clerical and service areas, which in the recent past have been very important in the absorption of new workers. Third, the labor market will be characterized by the fact that the older group of unemployed persons include a disproportionate number of the less educated and skilled, whose reabsorption would be difficult. I, for one, seriously question whether many unemployed miners with only four years of schooling who lose their jobs at fifty-five are going to be effectively retrained.

3. Curriculum implications of manpower trends

a. We are living in a period of accelerated obsolescence of knowledge and skill. Not only do machines become uneconomical more quickly, but much of what people have learned is being quickly superseded by new knowledge. For example, the Electrical Workers Union has found it necessary to spend 1 million dollars of its own funds each year to send journeymen back to school so that they can acquire new skills growing out of nuclear technology. Or, to use a favorite example of mine: What parent would want to have his children treated by an honor student of the Harvard Medical School, class of 1930, who has managed to learn nothing new about pediatrics since then?

b. This accelerated obsolescence of knowledge and skill suggests that education must be transformed from a one-time undertaking to a continuing process throughout life.

c. If this assumption is correct, then it follows that what students must acquire in school is a foundation on which skills can later be acquired and reacquired.

Manpower and education—the 1960s

d. I have a personal predilection, therefore, for a curriculum based on the the following essential ingredients: teaching all youngsters how to write effectively, introducing them to quantitative relationships, and providing them with some sense of the physical and social world.

e. It is distressing that for many years the educators have not kept their eye on these major issues. I do not question for a moment that it may be difficult to teach many children these fundamentals, but I see no escape from trying.

f. What I have said above has direct implication for vocational education. I believe that it will be increasingly difficult, if not totally impossible, in a rapidly changing and ever more complex technology, to provide the replicas of industry within the classroom. Nor do I see any real need, in light of industry's willingness and desire to do its own skill training, for the schools to carry this heavy burden. I would suspect that the real challenge in vocational education is how to translate the formal curriculum so that it becomes more interesting and meaningful to young people who have a greater aptitude for applied than for theoretical work.

g. Moreover, I think it is much more important for the high schools which are now stressing secretarial and distributive education to improve the ability of young women to write an English sentence correctly, to do sums quickly and correctly, to keep a set of books, and to know where and how to assemble information and abstract it.

h. Clearly, if the foregoing trends have been more or less correctly delineated, then it follows that we are in need of a major reform in adult education so that educational opportunities are provided for people who are already in the labor force and for those, particularly women, who would like to reenter the labor force.

4. Some policy directions

a. Since the schools, as they are now constituted or as they are likely to be reconstituted in the near future, cannot by themselves offer a meaningful curriculum to many adolescents aged sixteen and above, and since it is reprehensible for the community and injurious to individuals if the schools serve as detention pens, there is urgent need for the substantial expansion of work-study and related programs which would provide a sizable portion of the sixteen-year and older group with an opportunity to get a job, earn money, associate with adults, and learn on the job—in short, the type of developmental opportunities which they require and which the schools cannot effectively provide them. In my opinion, many of these youngsters would become more interested in school work once they saw the relevance of more knowledge and education to the world of work.

b. There is great need for the speedy development and expansion of community colleges with the flexibility to provide opportunities for the education and training of older women whose education has been interrupted. Moreover, many of the established universities and colleges can also do much more than they have yet begun to do to meet the needs of this sizable group.

c. Since education is expensive, and good education very expensive, and since the numbers to be educated are constantly being increased and the role of education in life is constantly being extended, it becomes necessary to broaden and deepen the channels of financial support. In my opinion, it will not long be practical for state universities and municipal colleges to continue to operate without sizable increases in tuition fees—that is, if they hope to provide a quality education. Nor do I see any reason why the taxpayer should be asked to contribute to the education of a child whose parents have a family income of $10,000 or more. There may even be merit in arranging that certain supplemental expenditures at the high school level be covered by parents who are able to do so, if only to strengthen the interest of the parent and the child in the undertaking. Americans have never had much respect for what they get free of charge.

d. While I am sympathetic, in general, with Dr. Conant's emphasis on the importance of improved guidance and counseling, I believe that the stress should definitely be on informational services, not on psychotherapy.

e. There is great need for establishing and raising standards so that the current semantic confusion about a high school diploma or a college degree can be reduced, if not eliminated. I have long been distressed by the fact that students graduating from good high schools are in every sense of the term better educated than a high proportion of the students graduating from poor colleges. There is need for much more standard-setting within localities, within states, within regions, and within the nation as a whole.

f. Finally, considering the scale and complexity of the educational effort, I do not think that one can look forward to much by way of significant improvement unless the resources devoted to research and experimentation are vastly extended.

3 ❊ NATIONAL PLANNING AND QUALITY CONTROL IN EDUCATION ❊ Ralph W. Tyler*
Stanford, California

Any discussion of national planning in education is likely to degenerate into a heated debate. To reduce the emotional conflict which might develop, I shall begin by defining the terms in our topic. National planning is not the same as national control. National planning in education is educational planning which goes beyond preoccupation with local and state matters and gives consideration to national interest, to national opportunities, and to national needs. Furthermore, "quality control" is not a centralized control of school operations. This term has been taken over from the field of manufacturing, where it refers to the testing of the product and the maintenance of desired standards for the product. When applied to education, quality control means that evidence is continuously being obtained regarding the extent to which

* Ralph W. Tyler is Executive Director, Center for Advanced Study in Behavioral Sciences, Stanford, California.

standards of quality in education are being met by the schools and that appropriate actions are being taken to reduce inadequacies in the products and processes of education in the schools.

What is the national interest in education?

Any recommendation that there should be national planning and quality control in education is based on the assumption that there is a substantial national interest in education. This I believe to be a valid assumption even though our Constitution leaves to the several states the responsibility of organizing and maintaining public schools. In two important areas, the nation has a vital interest in education.

The first of these is in providing for individual opportunity. Equality of individual opportunity has been of long historic concern to the nation. As economic, political, and social life has become more complex and more highly specialized, education has become the most important means by which an individual attains the opportunity for significant participation in every phase of life. Increasingly, opportunity for the individual involves moving across local and state boundaries to those places where he may find employment and may participate fully in the social and political affairs of the community, state, and nation.

These facts have two major implications. The attainment of our historic goal of equality of opportunity requires schools in every part of the nation which can provide an excellent educational program. Lack of resources in a particular state or locality, or shortsightedness in local or state planning, insofar as they result in an inferior educational program, prevent our reaching this national goal.

Furthermore, the fact of mobility means that a school program is not adequate for many of its pupils when it meets only the needs and opportunities available within the community or the state. The local educational program should aid the individual to realize his potential, and often this means preparing him for a life largely lived in other localities and states. Hence, educational planning which considers national needs and opportunities, and the maintenance of excellent educational programs in every part of the country are matters of national concern.

A second important basis for the national interest in education is the increasing role which education is playing in national development and survival. The continual development of our economy, and the increased productivity required to meet the consumption needs of our growing population and at the same time to provide for national defense, are primarily dependent upon education and research. For example, since 1925, and particularly since World War II, the rapid rate of technological development in industry and agriculture has so changed the occupational distribution of the total labor force that there is very limited demand for those who are without a high school education. Farmers and farm laborers, who made up 38 per cent of the labor force at the turn of the century, now comprise about one-tenth, and the Bureau of Labor Statistics predicts a further reduction, of nearly 20 per cent of the present figure, during the next ten years. Similarly, employment in unskilled occupations has dropped sharply and is continuing to diminish. But there are large increases in the percentage of people employed in science, engineering, health services, recreation, administration, accounting, and controlling, and the changes are accelerating. The Bureau of Labor Statistics estimates that during the next ten years the labor force will grow dramatically, increasing by 13.5 million; during this period, twenty-six million new workers will enter the labor force, 37 per cent more than during the 1950s. Not only is high school education essential for most employment in our economy, but the percentage of jobs requiring college education is increasing at a rapid rate.

This technological development which has so increased the production of our economy is largely based on research. The development of hybrid corn, the discovery of new forms of energy, and the development of plastics are three of hundreds of illustrations of the way in which our material survival and development depend on research and technological changes which in turn necessitate more education. These are matters of national concern, not merely of local interest. The central role of education in developing the economy of a modern nation is well recognized by the Soviet Union, where planning for education is conducted in concert with economic planning.

But the role of education in national development and survival is not limited to its central function in the economy. The goals we seek as a nation include nonmaterial as well as material attainments, and they require intelligent and responsible citizenship. From the time of the founding of the United States, the importance of a literate citizenry has been recognized. But the time has passed when the ability to read and write is sufficient preparation for the duties of the citizen. The range of matters with which government must deal, the interrelationship of factors in political affairs, nationally and internationally, the complexity of the issues confronting the citizen, and the high stakes involved, all contribute to the pressing need for a high level of understanding and commitment on the part of the people in a democratic country. Failures in this respect on the part of the school in any locality or state thereby weaken the nation. Hence, we have a national interest in the relevance, quality, and effectiveness of education for citizenship in every school.

Other aspects of American education have national implications, but these two are particularly significant. We have a national interest in education because it is chiefly the responsibility of the school to provide for individual opportunity and because the school plays a major role in national development and survival.

What is required to serve the national interest in education?

How to serve the national interest in education is the primary subject under discussion. Because this conference is devoted to the school curriculum I shall focus my remarks on the curriculum and not comment on facilities, funds, and the like, which are also important.

So far as the curriculum is concerned, the national interest in education requires continuous, sound decisions on what to teach in the schools. Such decisions cannot be made simply on the basis of what has traditionally been taught, nor by an effort to satisfy every articulate request or pressure from the public. Furthermore, sound decisions on what to teach cannot be made on an *ad hoc* basis by boards or committees who depend solely upon their experience and opinions in making their recommendations. A careful review of several kinds of pertinent information should precede the making of the necessary judgments.

Information is needed, and judgments need to be made about current conditions, demands, and opportunities in the international, national, state, and local arenas of life. Schoolchildren live in this world, they will live in it and contribute to it as they grow up. The tasks and opportunities of education are partly indicated by present and changing conditions. For example, the emergence of new nations and the shifting of areas of conflict and development suggest new emphases in the teaching of languages and geography. To cite another example, the changing occupational structure of America suggests a reexamination of vocational education. Unless a systematic review of such information is made, decisions about what to teach will reflect only the most obvious needs and the greatest pressures from interested groups.

Information is also required, and judgments must be made, about the student's needs, abilities, and readiness to engage in particular learning tasks. The curriculum should consider the talents and abilities of students, since one of the functions of education is to enable each student to realize his potential. Furthermore, the selection of what is to be taught should take into account the present knowledge, skills, and interests of students in order not to present again what they have already learned nor to attempt an educational task for which they do not have the requisite background and development. The latter is a serious problem for students who come from homes and communities in which their experiences have been sharply limited in such respects as language and reading. In these cases the school may need to provide for learning which other students, whose homes and communities have given them the needed background, do not require.

Information and judgments are also needed regarding the current states of the various academic disciplines and what each can contribute to the education of children and youth. This conference includes reports from most of the major academic divisions, such as science, mathematics, language and literature, the fine arts, and the social sciences, indicating the contributions they are making or are proposing to make through the school curriculum. In several cases, emphasis has been placed on the new concepts in the field and the nature of its intellectual structure. The natural sciences are being treated differently in the new courses because of the current conceptions of the sciences and the views which have developed regarding their structures. Similar changes are under way in other fields of instruction. Clearly, those who wish to make any adequate decisions about what should be taught must give careful ear to such developments within the several disciplines.

The information and judgments obtained from these three kinds of sources —contemporary conditions, demands, and opportunities; students' needs; abilities and backgrounds; and the current state of the academic disciplines— will suggest much more to be taught than time will permit. Some of the possible educational tasks may also be in conflict with others. Hence, before a selection can be made the list must be brought together, inconsistencies and conflicting goals eliminated, and a priority established among them. These decisions require an educational philosophy which deals with such matters as our conception of the dignity and worth of the individual, the importance of intelligent individual thought in relation to specific habits and predetermined responses, the proper roles of originality and individuality in relation to conformity and cooperation. In the absence of such a philosophy, decisions are being made about what is to be taught which are not in harmony with the basic beliefs and traditions of our country. Many of these issues are not easy to resolve, but some resolution is required in order to plan educational tasks which are in harmony with the best thought of our culture.

As a result of the several steps outlined above, it becomes possible to integrate these decisions into operational hypotheses about what to teach. These decisions need to be recognized as hypotheses, for they are not fixed and final. Changes should be made as new information is obtained and new judgments made in the areas outlined above, and as experience in teaching the curriculum provides more data regarding the appropriateness of these objectives for different age groups, their attainability, the time required to attain them, and the consequences of the learning.

The national interest in education requires not only sound decisions about what to teach in the schools, but also the development of effective means for the attainment of the objectives established. This calls for the acquisition of more knowledge about how learning takes place, especially about how pupils learn the kinds of tasks outlined above. At present, teachers are more likely to know how to aid students in memorizing material and in acquiring specific habits than they are to know such things as how to assist students to develop an understanding of concepts and principles and to conduct an inquiry. This means, too, the formulation of principles to guide the organization of courses and curricula so that learning can be sequential and better integrated. In a well-organized curriculum, the learning tasks of each month, semester, or year build upon the learning of the preceding months; and efforts are made to aid the student to comprehend the relations between what he is learning in one field and what he is learning in other fields. Instructional materials and instructional technology must also be developed, so that teachers have efficient tools with which to work.

The national interest in education also requires that there be continuous testing of the ends and means of education, both to throw light on which are sound and effective and which are not, and to indicate new "leads" on what to teach and how. Much of what is being done at present in all educational institutions has not been systematically and comprehensively evaluated. Practices are as likely to be based on custom as they are on evidences of efficacy. It is likely that great improvement in the quality of education can be attained if continued and systematic attention, guided by intelligent analysis, imaginative invention, and sound appraisal, is given to this task.

Finally, the national interest in education can be served by the dissemination and use of these ideas, materials, and the results of appraisal, in ways designed to stimulate and guide state and local schools. The Federal Extension Service, in cooperation with the land-grant colleges of agriculture, has played an important part in the tremendous increase in the effectiveness and efficiency of American agricultural production through the dissemination of knowledge and the demonstration of the use of the knowledge, the materials, and the tools developed. No comparable achievement is found in American education, yet the national interest requires it. Any adequate program of national planning and quality control in the field of education must provide for reaching the schools throughout the country. Otherwise, we can anticipate that there will continue to be many areas where our youth have little educational opportunity and our nation suffers from the lack of full development of our human resources.

What forms could be devised to meet these requirements?

The invention of institutions and organizations to provide for new functions has been part of the genius of America. Our history includes many illustrations of new political and social forms to meet new problems and to provide for new functions. I am confident that we can devise the instruments required when, as a nation, we become committed to serving adequately the national interest in education. Some of these forms have already been devised and employed.

Through the encouragement and support of the National Science Foundation, the Physical Science Study Committee and similar groups in chemistry, the biological sciences, and in mathematics have been formed. They are making decisions about what should be taught in these fields and are devising courses and producing instructional materials. We need at least two such national study committees in each school subject—at least two—in order to encourage originality and a variety of ideas rather than limit thought and development to a single channel. Each of these committees should include highly competent scholars in the field, teachers, and some who are involved in the education of teachers. Each of these kinds of competence has something to contribute to the total product.

We also need to establish several committees to study the interrelations of the several subjects and their organization. Each of these groups should be concerned with societal opportunities and demands, with student abilities, needs, interests, readiness for learning, and with a comprehensive educational philosophy so that the total school curriculum will not be a balance among opposing pressures of special interests but a more integrated and broadly conceived educational program.

One or more commissions on educational priorities would probably be a necessary part of the structure. At the Palo Alto Conference on Policies and Strategy for Strengthening the Curriculum of the American Public Schools[1] held in January, 1959, considerable discussion centered on the difficulties encountered by lay boards of education and by citizens, generally, in getting wise guidance about current educational issues when so many special interest groups are involved. Several lay members of the conference said that they were keenly aware that today most of the articulate groups seeking to give leadership to education are groups with only a partial or limited view of the total situation. The conferees directly involved in the administration of

[1] See Supplement 6, pp. 276.

public schools also spoke in support of the establishment of a commission of respected, public-spirited citizens who would study the current educational situation and make recommendations regarding policies and actions for boards of education which would be recognized as a more objective and impartial view than any currently available.

Centers for experimentation, demonstration, and teacher education are also necessary in order to test out ideas and materials, demonstrate the feasibility of new developments, and help teachers and prospective teachers acquire the necessary knowledge and skill to utilize new and promising innovations. These centers would be responsible not only for careful and systematic appraisal of individual developments but also for operations research involving systems of several elements. Some centers would provide quality control reports which would serve as guides for maintaining standards of excellence in local schools.

By demonstrating new educational inventions individually and in complex systems, these centers would provide concrete help to teachers from many schools. They would also demonstrate new educational enterprises to interested lay leaders and this would help stimulate local leadership to urge the adoption of new developments.

In the total structure, one or more agencies would be required to provide encouragement to private enterprise and to individual attacks on significant educational problems. Publishing companies and other firms which produce instructional materials and equipment render an important service to American education, both in production and in distribution. They represent resources of knowledge, of facilities, and organization which will be an important part of any effort to improve the school curriculum throughout the country. The means to effectively enlist them in the task must be found.

The forms suggested above are concerned with committees and groups working on aspects of the total task. In our society there is also an important place for the individual with ideas and initiative. This resource should also be enlisted. Funds for educational research and development should be available for promising individual efforts as well as for the work of groups. The total organization of committees, commissions, centers, business firms, and individuals should be devised and developed so as to utilize effectively all the available resources to serve the national interest in education.

What are the possible results?

These can be summarized very briefly. The kind of efforts outlined above should get the required groups and individuals into the work of improving American education. At present this task rests largely on the shoulders of the teaching staff and the schools of education. Scholars, scientists, other professionals, and lay people criticize and demand improvement, but they are not constructively involved.

The method of operation I have suggested would also make more widely available to aid schools throughout the country the resources of men, ideas, and materials which are now so scarce. The organization and the public attention given to it would encourage systematic efforts to improve education. It would stimulate a great deal of voluntary effort, without the resistance which is encountered when attempts are made to improve the schools by force. The proposal does not at this time require new legal authority and controls, but it does anticipate the channeling of a considerable amount of public and private funds into the total activity.

The improvement of the school curriculum is a matter of grave national concern. Not only our survival, but also the achievement of many of our national aspirations, depends on the immediate and continued development and improvement of education. If we continue at our present rate of improvement, we cannot attain our goal as a nation. Some of our youth will achieve their potential and parts of our country will be economically, politically, and socially strong, but many youths will have limited opportunities and many parts of our country will be relatively weak and ailing. New determination, new vision, and new avenues for national planning and for quality control in education are necessary.

THE NATURE OF LEARNING

part ii

Dr. Cronbach expounds in masterly fashion both the possibilities and the limitations of applying psychological research to education. Our new knowledge of the working of the mind suggests that we have hardly begun to tap man's capacity to learn. But we must beware of generalizing too broadly or applying on a large scale conclusions which are based on research into limited problems and conducted under strictly controlled laboratory conditions.

When we introduce changes which may affect a whole generation of schoolchildren, we must proceed cautiously and evaluate carefully. We must base our policy decisions on sound evidence rather than on a priori opinion.

The new curriculum problems challenge the psychologist to shift his attention from rats and pigeons to human beings and to the kinds of learning which are peculiar to our species.

4 ❦ THE PSYCHOLOGICAL BACKGROUND FOR CURRICULUM EXPERIMENTATION
Lee J. Cronbach* *University of Illinois*

This presentation reflects my conviction that curriculum developers will inevitably be working with psychologists. I have taken it as my role to try to mention some of the current topics of interest and lines of thought in psychology which are pertinent to educational learning, and perhaps also to give you some idea of how the psychologist looks at curriculum experimentation and the biases which—for good or evil—he will bring to your discussion.

The psychologist enters your work in several ways. The obvious entrée is that gained through the desire which curriculum developers express for psychological advice. The specialist developing a new curriculum expects the psychologist to know when a child can be taught certain subject matter or how one can best present some idea. This trust in psychology is a source of embarrassment, for we not only lack the answers to most of these questions, but we find that such questions are incapable of being given a general answer. One aim of my discourse, therefore, will be to clarify what psychologists can and cannot do.

You encounter the psychologist at another point in your efforts, when you seek to persuade educators to adopt a new scheme. Innovations meet

* Lee J. Cronbach is Professor of Education and Psychology at the University of Illinois.

with resistance, often justifiable. What requires mention here is that the resistance may be bolstered by an appeal to the authority of the psychologist. Both the protagonists of change and the conservatives are much too ready to aver that "modern psychological research has shown" that their sectarian belief is true. I hope that our research has drawn attention to some fundamental truths. But even a conclusion properly quoted may be quoted without adequate recognition that the psychologist's authority in these matters is limited. We are limited, first of all, to what we have investigated; most educational recommendations require considerable extrapolation from the data. We are limited by the immaturity of our theory; cherished principles collapse under us, on occasion, as a new investigator formulates a problem more incisively and leads us to a fresh conclusion. One of your primary motivations for curriculum change is your vivid sense that the natural sciences, mathematics, and the content available for the social studies are changing very rapidly under the impact of inquiry. Part of my aim is to remind you that psychology, too, is a growing and shifting field, offering you its present insights into man's nature but not a set of immutable principles.

You encounter the psychologist first, then, when you ask for his advice; you encounter him a second time when his authority is invoked by someone. In curriculum studies, the third and most suitable role of the psychologist is that of evaluator. School policy has to be guided by two things: our vision of the good life, and evidence concerning the change in pupils produced by alternative educational procedures. Each of us has a legitimate vision to contribute, but not every visionary has the empirical commitment needed for curriculum engineering. Judgment can be based only on detailed and objective comparison of the pupils. Insistence on behavioral evidence is not unique to the psychologist, but he can be counted upon to sound this note in every discussion. More than that, he is the one most likely to have experience in trying to measure these subtle changes, and hence the one most likely to help you collect the evidence you need.

I should make clear that I am using the term *psychologist* in a fairly inclusive sense. A great many educational research workers are close in spirit and training to the psychologist; indeed, my own training in this field was acquired under Ralph Tyler, who is technically outside the field of psychology even though his viewpoint is psychological. Likewise, I must acknowledge the contribution of sociologists, and even of the occasional mathematician or philosopher whose curiosity leads him to become sophisticated in the observation of behavioral change.

Psychological participation in curriculum revision

There is, of course, a wide range of interests within psychology. A man can investigate learning without coming near a school child and without forming an opinion about the teaching of anything more complex than nonsense syllables. The aim of such a psychologist is to establish rigorous and dependable theory, even if this means that he must confine himself to simple, easily controlled processes. At the other extreme of the research spectrum are those who perform operational studies, committing themselves to obtain the best answer possible in a short time, no matter how complex the practical question to be settled. The price they pay is that their evidence is invariably tentative and incomplete, their theories vague and messy. If we had only these two types in isolation, psychology would be a weak ally for curriculum development. But there is truly a spectrum. There are laboratory psychologists who move out a bit toward complex problems; there are applied psychologists whose controlled experiments put them in touch with theoretical systems.

E. L. Thorndike, the founder of American educational psychology, was equally noted for his development of an abstract theory of learning. In both World Wars psychologists of the purest hue worked, effectively and with satisfaction, on military problems which included development of curricula, teaching methods, and procedures for evaluation. But somehow experimental and theoretical psychologists broke away from education in the 1920s and only very recently have begun again to think of school problems. Many influences contributed to this schism, but two of them are significant for us. Educational theory, and the accompanying emphasis within educational psychology, moved in a direction antithetical to systematic research into the curriculum and intellectual learning. And psychological theory, under the influence of radical behaviorism, withdrew attention from cognitive processes. The natural interchange between laboratory work, theory, developmental work, and field observation was thus broken off.

The language of educational theory, from 1930 until recently, was influenced primarily by those branches of psychology concerned with personality, mental hygiene, and individual differences. The faults of education in the 1920s were insufficient recognition of the child as a unique individual, uniform attainment standards which discouraged weaker students from developing, and reliance on punishment and repetitive drill as teaching tactics. Learning was often verbalistic, incapable of influencing the child's life and thought. It was to these ills that reformers directed their attention. Hence teachers were urged to use curricular experiences which their pupils could fully comprehend, preferably starting with local resources. They were urged to develop units of work out of their pupils' interests and capabilities. Indeed, since the prevailing opinion was that both general and specialized aptitudes are largely fixed, they were advised that the principal changes to produce in pupils were in their feelings and their perceptions of specific situations. Teachers were urged to judge their success by the growth in the pupil's interests, self-assurance, and self-expression, giving less attention than formerly to formal achievement.

The insistence that the curriculum must fit the particular class and the particular pupil tended to discourage research about learning. Systematic work on the teaching of, say, geography, seemed to have little point when the subject matter and class organization was to be different in every school. If the ideal teacher was to use a project method, with a new activity for each new group of pupils, the research involved in any one project was unlikely to establish conclusions pertinent in another year or another place. Add to this damper the fact that few research workers can pursue a problem for long without a feedback of interest and intelligent criticism from colleagues, and you begin to see why work on the psychology of school subjects, on standardized achievement testing, and on intellectual learning ground very nearly to a halt.

These frank remarks imply no endorsement of the view that the educational psychologist ruined the schools, if ruined they have been. If it were necessary here I would cheerfully defend basing instruction on concrete and familiar experience, reducing blame and frustration, seeking desirable changes in attitude and feeling, and the other principles we have advocated. The sins we preached against *were* real and they *are* real; the failure of the psychologist during this period was not that he remade the schools but that his efforts reformed educational practice so little.

Meanwhile, experimental psychology, for its own reasons, turned away from the study of the intellect. The behavioristic program of Watson was a house-cleaning operation, dedicated to the elimination of mentalistic concepts from psychology. The program of Clark Hull and his disciples which followed was a highly successful demonstration that elaborate psychological theories can be developed and used to derive quantitative predictions. To achieve such rigor, most of the Hullian psychologists found it necessary to confine themselves to narrowly circumscribed phenomena. It is extremely difficult to express, within a rigorous theory, such a notion as *meaningfulness*; hence American learning theory had next to nothing to say on the aspect of instruction which the educational psychologist considers primary.

Only in the last eight years—dating more or less from the appearance of Osgood's presentation of mediation theory (1) and from the translation into English of Piaget's major works (2)—have Americans become actively concerned with symbolic processes and the organization of thought. Today, investigators of all origins are attacking complex processes with a remarkable community of view. The demand for better teaching of knowledge coincides with this reorientation of interests and of theories in the field of psychology. Consequently, when psychologists have been asked to join in discussions of educational problems, there has been a hearty response.

The most significant of many such conferences was the Woods Hole Conference of 1959. The National Academy of Sciences brought together directors of several of the national curriculum programs and a dozen psychologists. The ten days did not produce great new educational or psychological thoughts, but they demonstrated strong common interests. We can review these interests in the terms of the chapter headings in Bruner's report (3).

"The Importance of Structure"—the idea that in properly learning any discipline, one acquires a structure which is something beyond the aggregation of separate principles and skills and that it makes sense, for example, to talk of teaching the pupil to "think like a mathematician."

"Readiness for Learning"—the famous dictum, modestly disguised as a hypothesis, that "any subject can be taught to any child at any stage of development."

"Intuitive and Analytic Thinking"—the view that the process of hitting upon conclusions, inventions, theorems, or artistic designs is entirely different from the process by which these are subsequently verified or checked out and that education has unduly focused on the second process.

"Motives for Learning"—the classroom demonstrations of David Page, as much as any discussion, reminded the conferees that intellectual activities can be exciting adventures for the youngsters. Sharp questions were posed for those psychologists who saw motivation as arising out of life problems or out of the desire for "reinforcement" by authority.

There was unanimous agreement as to the significance of all four of these areas. To be sure, some participants seemed to value the teaching of up-to-the-minute scientific facts, while others saw facts as transient and only structure as enduring. To be sure, there was division of opinion as to whether abstract science and mathematics is the right educational diet for average as well as superior pupils. And some of us thought that the teaching methods most advocated at the conference would call for teachers with talents rarely to be found this side of paradise. But these disagreements were minor.

There was a fifth topic, "aids to learning," and on this there was no agreement. Speeches hailing the electronic revolution in education were made, but they found little audience. Any general statement that (for example) films are beneficial was rejected by both the psychologists and the curriculum designers. To every such contention the curriculum maker delivered the *coup de grâce* with: "Let me see the film and how it is used, and I'll decide if that particular bit of teaching is good." When we tried this tack, it seemed that each participant was convinced the films *he* had produced were good and those another center had made were terrible. Since no evaluative research had been done on any of the films, there was no way to escape a battle of prejudices. The controversy over films was a dead calm beside the storm brought on by Skinner's demonstration of teaching machines. It gets me ahead of my story to say more now than that there is a fundamental antagonism between the aims that have been most often mentioned as reasons for the teaching machines and the values sought in the new mathematics and physics curricula.

Before ending this preamble, I should refer to a conference of psychologists sponsored this summer (1961) by the Social Science Research Council. The final day saw the preparation of a recommendation to the SSRC that committees be appointed and assigned the mission of encouraging work on certain significant problems.

Three broad topics were drawn to the attention of the SSRC. The first was the need for reflection on strategies of research in instruction and dealt with such matters as who should do research and how it should be supported. The second topic was the need for development of a science of teaching, on the ground that the behavior of the teacher is governed by discoverable laws, just as is the behavior of the pupil. The third and largest section of the report is a recommendation "for the establishment of a committee[1] on the acquisition of formal knowledge in the classroom." One of the proposals it contained was for a job analysis, a careful determination of what "competent performance" in any subject area means, followed by an explanation in psychological terms.

With regard to learning itself, the problem which appeared most pressing

[1] This committee was appointed in May, 1962.

is transfer. One type of transfer which has been little studied in the classroom is the development of attitudes toward school learning. This conference, like the conference at Woods Hole, was impressed by the fact that willingness to use one's knowledge, pride in one's own ability to discover new knowledge, and interest in continued learning may be the most important outcomes of instruction in any field. "Some methods of instruction may impair such affective qualities as feeling, values, self-acceptance, ... even though they are highly effective in promoting factual knowledge." Even more central to the report is the discussion of intellectual outcomes: "The goals of a curriculum are to teach something beyond specific facts, generalizations, and techniques. Much is said about the teaching of systematized knowledge and about acquiring the habits of thought of a discipline. Until these can be measured, the effectiveness of proposed innovations cannot be judged, and the individual school will tend to put excessive emphasis on those outcomes—often less important—that can be measured" (4). This led to the recommendation that particular attention be given to the development of better methods of evaluation.

Some remarks on evaluation

Evaluation usually means one of two things to curriculum developers. It is either a matter of preparing some standardized tests to assist teachers in assigning grades, or a matter of comparing the new curriculum to its predecessors. Both of these are legitimate enough, but they miss the key function of evaluation, the improvement of instruction.

Too many people regard the "horse race" type of experiment as the prototype of educational research. You put two groups of pupils, one through instruction A and the other through instruction B, and ask which one wins on the final test. At best, these experiments give little information; often they lead to positively misleading conclusions. Most of the time, the final differences are small and insignificant. This is particularly true when the test is restricted to material which both instructional methods cover; such a plan necessarily handicaps whichever program has the more ambitious objectives. In some areas—notably comparisons of film or TV instruction with live instruction, and studies on class size—there have been hundreds of experiments, all leading essentially to the conclusion that one method of instruction is as good as the next, on the average. This is a patently unreasonable conclusion, and it comes from asking the wrong question.

Evaluation research should concentrate on mapping the outcomes of each program. We should be more interested in describing how the instruction modifies the student's thinking and attitudes than in assigning a total score to his performance. You can evaluate how much your experimental program moves the pupil in various desirable directions *without* using a control group—though sometimes you want comparisons. You are certain to find places where you accomplished less than you had hoped for. The main goal in this type of research is to learn where you should try to improve your program. You judge against your ideal, not against a wooden-legged competitor.

Your measuring devices and your treatment of data should be as analytic as you can make them. Let me recite a few anecdotes to show what I mean. One of the Eight-Year-Study schools had as a social studies objective to make pupils more liberal in their political views. An attitude scale was prepared by the evaluation staff, and pupils were asked to respond with "agree," "uncertain," or "disagree" to 200 opinions on significant matters. These statements were carefully balanced; for every liberal opinion there was an "equal and opposite" conservative statement elsewhere in the test. The results were gratifying; from tenth to twelfth grades, the average score moved impressively in the liberal direction. Instead of stopping there, we asked the further question: "Who changed, and in what way?" Most of the change, we found, consisted in the movement from "uncertain" to "agree" or "disagree"; i.e., to crystallization rather than reversal of opinions. A student-by-student breakdown showed that among those who started with liberal views the changes were from uncertainty to the liberal opinion, and that those who started with conservative views changed their uncertainties into a conservative attitude. The school (or the passage of time) was making the liberals more liberal and the conservatives more conservative. It was failing where it most wanted to succeed. The only reason the average score seemed to show movement toward liberality was that the liberals were a majority among entering students.

In the Navy, we had at one time the task of training submariners to classify ships whose propellors were heard through listening gear. There was an increase in total score on ability to classify recorded sounds. But we went further and studied changes item by item, and we found that there was a decrease on some items. The reason? We had so successfully trained people to classify type A ships as type A that when they heard a type C ship they also tended to call *it* type A. We were training, not discrimination, but a bias. This result demanded revision of the program, whereas the average score, and the instructor's opinion, had told us our course was fine.

Finally, let us look at a study which Crow and Hammond (5) made of a program of medical education which was supposed to give the student physician insight into the personality of patients. In the test, students judged patients after seeing a filmed interview with each one. The specially trained groups did *less well* than the control group. Analysis showed that training had made them so concerned with individual differences that they judged these people as far more divergent than they actually were. The control group, which conservatively regarded each patient as reasonably like the average, made smaller errors than the group which had been taught to see each patient as unique. There is a moral here for teacher training which I leave you to draw.

Included under the heading of evaluation are the problems of retention and transfer. Most of our studies investigate the student's performance immediately after training, but our real purpose in education is to produce lasting change. You probably are familiar with some of the studies suggesting that a great deal of academic learning is lost in the space of one or two years, particularly when the knowledge consists of detailed facts. Only recently have psychologists begun to be aware that our research into the problem of forgetting has failed to do justice to educational learning. We have been using the wrong technique of investigation, and as a result we have next-to-no pertinent information about how well ideas acquired in school can be used several years later. To make my point, it will be necessary to remind you of a distinction introduced in studies of rote memory sixty years ago. If I teach you to recite a list of words, I can test your retention by asking you to reproduce the list several weeks afterward. That is the *recall* method of testing. Or I can give you a longer list of words and ask you to tell me which ones were in the set originally studied; that is one form of the *recognition* method. The third and most significant method is the *savings* method, which measures how long it takes you to recapture your original knowledge. Say that it took you twenty trials to learn to recite the list without an error. Now I train you again, and you reach perfect performance on the seventh trial. There has been a saving of thirteen trials, or 65 per cent. For the theoretical psychologist, either method may be appropriate, depending upon the issue under discussion.

For most of education, the savings method is the only truly pertinent way to judge effectiveness. There are few situations in life when we must call forth knowledge impromptu at whatever moment somebody chooses to ask about a topic which has not recently entered our minds. Beneath the active knowledge that we are continually using is a larger fund that we can bring up into use as we become engaged with the topic. You could not today name the Plantagenet kings of England; the better question is, does your ancient knowledge about the Normans and Saxons come back to you, as you watch a new play about Thomas à Becket, in a way that enlarges your comprehension? You have long since forgotten the reaction that produces formaldehyde. The question is, when some technical problem makes it necessary for you once again to use this knowledge, does a brief review suffice to restore the process to its original clarity in your mind?

The position hitherto taken by educational psychologists, on the basis of research using recall and recognition tests, is represented by these quotations from my 1954 *Educational Psychology* (6): "Tests administered a year or more after students complete a unit of work usually show an extreme amount of forgetting. The teacher cannot hope students will remember most of the ideas they hear. When motivation is more casual than in college, learning is probably even thinner and quicker to vanish." There are some qualifying remarks in the book which brighten this gloomy view, but these statements reflect fairly the interpretation which educational psychologists have placed on studies of the forgetting of factual learning. I expect educational psychology to be more optimistic about retention, now that we have realized that savings are what count. Obviously, it is difficult to carry out a study of saving, because this means that one must recapture the student at a later date and retrain him. But studies of savings are needed and someone must go to the trouble of making them.

The savings method is equally pertinent to the study of transfer. The books explain that the way to investigate transfer from learning A to learning B is to provide educational experience A and then to measure how much more rapidly students so trained acquire material B. While this design has been used in the laboratory, it has virtually never been applied to the evaluation of educational programs. Instead, we have measured transfer by asking how well the trained person can solve problems not included in his instruction. These problems are usually short, allowing no time for the student to reorganize his knowledge or to exhibit the thought processes of mature scholarship. These short-term transfer tests have often provided important theoretical and practical insight, but they are insufficient.

My concern with the savings method arises out of considerable effort to define for myself what is meant by the phrase "learning a discipline." Everyone has agreed that this means something more than learning specific theorems, scientific laws, etc. But it has been quite unclear just how one is to observe whether the pupil has grown in "ability to think like a mathematician," for example. I conclude that the central objective of the mathematics and physics courses is to increase aptitude for further learning in mathematics and physics. Presumably a mathematician is more likely to solve a brand new mathematics problem and a physicist is more likely to ask pertinent theoretical and experimental questions regarding a new physical phenomenon. It is not to be hoped that the solution will come in forty-five minutes.

The hope is that there will be a saving, that it will take the well-trained mathematician or scientist fewer months to solve the problem than an equally intelligent person without such background. Similarly, it is hoped that the science courses taken by a nonscientist will make it possible for him to comprehend a new theory or an explanation of an unfamiliar topic more rapidly and penetratingly than if he were less well educated. This leads me to suggest that an elementary mathematics program, for example, might better be evaluated by the comprehension the pupils show during grade 7, when they study entirely new mathematical topics, than by any test we can quickly administer.

Readiness and aptitude

The phrase I used a moment ago, that the physics course is supposed to develop aptitude for physics, may be a bit startling, but it reflects the emerging view regarding mental abilities. A generation ago, psychologists saw mental abilities as unfolding according to a natural timetable. There were inquiries about the level of ability required to comprehend a given topic, and educators were left with the impression that it is fruitless to try to teach a topic ahead of nature's schedule. This wrong idea is to be found even in the writings of prominent educational psychologists; there is one current text for teachers which says flatly that "adding sums over ten is not grasped by most children until they have a mental age of about seven years, four months."

The psychologist has no grounds for quarreling with anyone who wants to try to teach some skill or idea at an earlier age than hitherto. To be sure, there are thoughtless statements, but the position of the leading writers, such as Brownell and Gates, has always been that readiness depends very much on the method of instruction. The hypothesis of the Bruner report is a thoroughly reasonable one, if we put it in this form: Whatever your ultimate objective, the child at any age is ready for some experience that will move him toward that objective more rapidly than if he is left to unguided activity.

The question is how to teach, not how early. The view of most psychologists, very much reinforced by experiments of the last ten years, is that of William James. James, you will recall, gave a public lecture, and afterward was accosted by an anxious mother with the question, "Dr. James, how soon can I begin the education of my child?" "Madam," he asked, "how old is your child?" "He is only a year old now." Said James, "Go home at once, madam! Don't waste another minute!"

The psychologist is not ready to say to you that you can teach anything you want when you want to. The most careful evaluation is necessary before you can be sure that you are not teaching a response in some essentially false form which will interfere with later development and transfer. I am reminded of my junior high school teacher who thought we should recognize great works of music by name and who overcame our apparent incapacity by teaching us to fit the title to the tune of the selection, as in "This is— the symphony—that Schubert wrote and never finished." To this day it is difficult for me to hear some of the pieces we studied without the intrusion of these unmusical syllables.

More seriously, let me tell you about Jan Smedslund's attempt (7) to teach the principle of conservation of weight to eight-year-olds. Piaget has shown that one important stage in the development of thought is achievement of the conservation principles—that volume, weight, and other properties remain unchanged when an object is superficially transformed. The famous test is with balls of plasticine. When two balls of obviously equal size are presented, and one of them is flattened into a pancake or pulled into a rope, the less mature thinker says that it is bigger and heavier. The older one knows better. Smedslund set out to convince children (around age seven) who had not attained the conservation principle that their impressionistic conclusion was false. He brought in a balance, and after each judgment he and the child weighed the objects to see if the child was correct in calling one heavier. After a modest number of trials, the child responded consistently according to the conservation principle. But Smedslund did not stop at the moment of triumph. He posed a further test by starting with two equal balls of plasticine, deforming one of them, and at the same time squeezing in an extra bit of clay that he had concealed in his palm. The child, properly trained, said that the two shapes were of the same weight. And when he saw that the lumps, put on the scale, were *not* equal, he simply responded, "How interesting!" On the other hand, the child who had achieved the conservation principle over a longer period immediately rejected the result. "Something is wrong. The scales aren't right. You cheated somehow!" These children believed in the conservation principle so firmly that it took precedence over the evidence of their senses. The children given hothouse treatment had been conditioned to make a formal response the teacher thought correct, but they really had learned only that they should trust the scales rather than their own judgment. Smedslund's work continues; he has developed further training methods in the hope of truly accelerating this learning, and is now testing them.

The Brownell-Moser study of subtraction (8) is a classic, well worth our attention because of what it shows about how you can and cannot generalize about curricular content and readiness. The question at issue was whether

The nature of learning | 28

subtraction of two-digit numbers should be introduced in terms of borrowing or of equal additions. Half the pupils (third-graders) were taught one technique, half were taught the other. Each group was split further, half of each group learning in a rote, mechanical fashion, and the other half being given careful explanations, as meaningful as the experimenters could devise. Accuracy and retention scores under the *rote* teaching favored equal additions slightly. The groups taught meaningfully did better, with the *borrowing* group especially successful. The teachers had very little success in explaining the equal addition method; they could not make it intuitively reasonable to the pupils. The borrowing method could be made clear, so that pupils learned it better and could better transfer it to three-digit numbers. Another significant finding was that meaningful teaching did not work well with third-graders whose previous teaching had been mechanical; these pupils could not comprehend the explanations. But in groups that had been taught meaningfully in preceding years, the pupils worked out their own explanations for the new process. Readiness is created, cumulatively, by a proper combination of content and method.

That was where the story rested—a clear victory for borrowing taught meaningfully—until 1961. Then Richard Griggs, engaged in the Illinois Arithmetic Project, started thinking about that old bugbear, the subtraction of negative numbers. In this subtraction, decomposition (borrowing) does not work, and an attempt to use it leads to hopeless confusion. On the other hand, the logic of equal additions fits very nicely into work with signed numbers. Thus motivated to teach introductory subtraction in a way that would build readiness for signed numbers instead of interfering with it, Griggs worked out a new explanation for equal additions. This explanation, making use of jumps along the number line, seems to be considerably clearer to children than the best explanation Brownell and Moser had been able to devise. Griggs and Page tell me that this new teaching method works. It sounds as if a new teaching tactic has reversed the earlier verdict, though nothing like systematic evidence to support this claim has been offered. The main point for us to notice is that what pupils can understand at any age depends upon how you explain it—upon that, and upon what their background has been. It is this that justifies my initial remark that no question about readiness can be given a general answer.

The view of aptitude as being created by experience has been supported by a veritable flood of research. Piaget's observations establish a picture, rather well supported by research using other techniques, of the growth of ability through a series of stages. There is first the establishment of sensorimotor coordinations; then an impressionistic, intuitive stage; then a refinement of concepts into controlled, operational thought. A regulating concept, such as the ability to match two ordered sets, grows slowly, through hundreds or thousands of experiences. Each problem—for instance, in matching two bead chains—solved by trial and correction leaves some residue of improved understanding, until ultimately the abstraction is fully mastered. Two sets of objects side by side can be compared a year or so before the child can compare two sets at opposite sides of the room; only the latter comparison shows that he can "carry the order in his head."

Most of the pertinent American studies have followed the pattern of

Harlow's research in "learning to learn." Harlow reported in 1949 (9) that a monkey who solves fifty or more problems of a given type becomes a much better problem solver. This was a radical extension of the psychology of learning, for researchers had previously used only a single test in any one experiment. [I cannot resist digressing to mention Underwood's recent report on memorization of nonsense syllables (10). He looks at that sort of learning in Harlow's fashion, having a single subject learn many different lists of syllables and study each list, in turn, to the point of perfect reproduction. He finds that the more such lists you study, the longer it takes to learn the next list. So the Harlow finding shows gains in aptitude for problem solving from extensive practice in problem solving, and Underwood finds losses in aptitude for rote memorization with practice. I don't know how far to extrapolate from Underwood's results, but it is worth remembering as another warning against teaching meaningless responses.]

I shall give just one example of the Harlow type of research. People form concepts better from positive instances than from negative instances. The usual concept-formation experiment presents cards with designs on them, and arbitrarily defines, say, all cards with red designs and black borders as being positive examples. On a problem where four positive examples are logically sufficient to indicate how to classify all the cards, four negative examples are also logically sufficient. But college students solve the problem faster when they learn from positive examples. Some Canadians recently presented a whole series of such problems to two groups of college students. The group which had positive examples every time started out with a median solution time of two minutes for the first problem; by the fifth problem they were down to a median solution time of ten seconds, which is evidently about as fast as the problem can be solved. Aptitude had increased. The group given all negative instances had great difficulty. Even on the fourth problem they needed three minutes to solve the problem. This time gradually decreased; by the time they had done twenty negative-instance problems, they were down to the same ten-second average as the other group (11).

This study has something important to say about psychological difficulty. *Logical* complexity certainly makes one problem more difficult than another; but the *psychological* differences in difficulty can, to a significant degree, be overcome by proper preparatory experiences. Sometimes the proper experience consists of a good explanation, sometimes it consists of extensive practice. To define the conditions where each is needed is a critical task for current psychology.

Programmed instruction and creativity: an antithesis

No talk on instruction by a psychologist today is complete without a discussion of teaching machines. This brave new idea burst upon the educational world in Skinner's famous 1954 paper (12), in which he argued that much of teaching consists of repetitive acts which could be programmed, once and for all, and taken off the teacher's shoulders. The key ideas were identifying the desired responses, demanding active response from the pupil, and immediately rewarding the correct response. A subordinate principle was that of "small steps"; if learning takes place through making correct responses, as Skinner believes, the way to produce learning is to ask questions in a sequence which is so carefully prepared and which advances in difficulty so slowly that the pupil can proceed from question to question with never an error.

The movement has been changing in shape and direction; we are seeing its hectic commercialization, we are seeing the beginnings of theoretically oriented research on the method, and we are awaiting with interest the reports from the trial marriage with programmers into which curriculum reformers Begle and Beberman[2] have entered. It is foolhardy to predict what we will learn in the next year or two, or even to say where we are today. But I have spent considerable time reading reports on this topic—not all that were produced, by any means; that would have been humanly impossible—and I am going to report where I think we stand. This year we begin to have a reasonable volume of evaluative studies, that embody questions that go beyond race-horse comparisons of machines with old-fashioned instruction.

The research I have read convinces me of three things:

1. Instruction by machine generally produces results that are neither better nor worse than instruction covering the same material in a traditional manner.

2. The machine and the principles upon which it rests are not fundamental to the improvement of instruction. The machine is a technique of school management. As such it will have its values, but it has no special psychological value.

3. The psychological innovation that is significant is the concept of programming. This is a theory regarding the presentation of ideas, and it is likely to have great impact upon all teaching, by machine or by any other method.

One type of study seems to me far more significant than all the others. Programmed material is presented to one group in the Skinner manner, either by machine or in a workbook. The student responds by filling in a blank, and the response is immediately reinforced by his seeing the correct answer. The control group sees the same programmed material in textbook form. All the blanks are filled in; they merely study from the intact text in the old-fashioned way. There are only a handful of these studies, but they all reach the same result. The group which reads the complete text does just as well on both immediate and delayed tests as the group which fills in blanks according to the active-response-with-reinforcement principles, and the reading group achieves these results in less time. [Krumboltz and Weisman (13) found that writing the word for each blank produced better retention even though it did not improve initial learning.] So the machine serves only as a way of controlling the attention of the learner, of keeping him at work. It also routinizes judgments about the adaptation of material to individual differences, and this is likely to be valuable, but for the student who wants to learn, the Skinner techniques have no evident advantage over a combination of texts and tests.

[2] See "The New Mathematics Programs," Edwin Moise, this volume.

I am making a sharp distinction between the practice features and the programming features of these innovations. In 1954, all the emphasis was on practice—and this was reasonable enough for a psychologist who had been developing his theories on pigeons. I saw somewhere an apt comment on these machines: "Students may be strange birds, but they're not pigeons." Skinner found this out quickly enough as he started writing questions for his machines; now he and all other psychologists stress the programming. What matters in teaching humans is meaning. It is an article of faith that anybody can learn anything if you can develop the meaning gradually enough—and if he lives so long.

Programming has two features which are highly significant for every curriculum venture. The first is the precise specification of the response desired at every moment in training, and the fact that evidence about failures and misunderstandings is collected for every sentence in the program. This means that educational materials are subject to quality control. We have never submitted our textbooks or our teaching films to this sort of scrutiny, but we should have. This type of tryout shows exactly when an explanation proceeds too rapidly or when an unfortunate illustration is leaving the student with a false impression. Cumulation of evidence on moment-by-moment learning is especially easy in automated instruction, and it therefore stimulates more careful analysis of learning than we obtain in the usual sort of experiment which includes only periodic tests. We can apply the same point of view to other instructional procedures. Our judgments as writers, and the impressions of teachers who try out our materials, are by no means sufficient to identify all the faults in the materials we write. For any mass-produced instructional material, the present judgmental editing processes should be supplemented by a full and detailed experimental analysis.

The second virtue of programming is its emphasis on meaningful explanation. The programmers, operating under the small-step principle, are trying hard to make knowledge so coherent that each blank can easily be filled in on the basis of previously accumulated understanding. Communication theorists have told us that redundancy is the secret of transmitting information in the presence of noise. The programmer is applying this principle, achieving redundancy through repetition, through logical connectedness, and through other devices. As the programmer learns more about how to build up ideas in the learner's mind, he will have much to say to any teacher about how to present information intelligibly. The principle of redundancy runs counter to much that we are taught about good writing; neither literature nor journalism accepts redundancy as desirable. From programming efforts should emerge the outlines of a new art of instructional writing, an art that will submit itself to a pragmatic test.

Programming is the art of eliciting certain good responses from the student. Such instruction is just what we want, when we know what the good response is. But we must ask seriously whether education consists entirely of teaching predetermined responses, and whether programming techniques can be used for instruction which aims to make the pupil more creative. Many of the new curricula are seeking to develop the pupil's intuitive understanding of phenomena and relations. There is some reason to think that the pupil learns best if during early exposure to a phenomenon he thinks about it in his own way, developing understanding at a nonverbal level, then gradually formulating explanations in his own words, and only later being required to reshape his explanations in an abstract, formal, correct language. The PSSC, using a ripple tank, is letting the student experience the phenomenon in his own way, sensing the dynamic waves at a nonverbal level before he makes formal responses. David Page, instructing pupils in arithmetic, presents them with some problem involving Cuisenaire blocks or an array of numbers, and has them reaching answers intuitively long before they have any formal machinery with which to solve the problem. He leads the pupil to create his own formal machinery. He is currently experimenting with a number game in which the pupils are given some parts of a mathematical system, and soon discover that there are gaps not covered by the rules. The class suggests alternative ways of filling the gaps; that is, they make up various rules and decide which they like best before continuing the game. Page is teaching something very fundamental about mathematics: that it is a man-made construction, and that one can invent any set of axioms he chooses so long as contradiction is avoided. The heart of his teaching lies in eliciting a response that is *not* predetermined by authority—and the pupil who is to become a creative writer or a true scientist must learn to make such a response.

Suchman's teaching of inquiry is an example of what cannot be done by teacher presentation, questioning, and reinforcement. It has been charged that the usual school procedures quench curiosity by allowing no one but the teacher to ask questions. This makes no place for spontaneous thought; indeed, the teacher tends to regard puzzling questions from the pupil as threatening and vaguely subversive. Suchman is out to foment curiosity and to promote skill in asking good questions. He is working with physical phenomena; for example, he shows fourth graders a brief demonstration of a metal strip which, when heated, curls, and always curls with the same side inward. Their task is to figure out why this happens. His technique is a highbrow version of Twenty Questions. The pupil has to ask questions which can be answered "yes" or "no," eliciting facts from the teacher. The questions, in effect, describe experiments that could be performed: "If we put the heated strip into a cool stream of air instead of water, would it straighten out?" The use of questions and answers rather than experiment is a time saver, and it also has the virtue of requiring more focused thought than does concrete laboratory work. Suchman says that children given this training ask better questions, and take better advantage of information to form theories. Suchman is developing additional training schemes to supplement the practice in question asking. The important point to notice is that in teaching creative performance we wish to reinforce any response that meets certain standards. There is no predetermined question the pupil should ask; the false hypotheses represent scientific thinking as much as the ones that prove valid.

In this connection, you should know about Maltzman's fascinating laboratory studies in which he seems to be training college students to be more original. His method could not be simpler. He presents a list of miscellaneous words and asks the student to give an association. The same list is repeated, and on each run through the list the student must give a different association to the word. Of course this makes the student reach for more unusual associations. Maltzman measures originality by giving Guilford's Unusual Uses test, which has questions of the form: "Give as many unusual uses as you can for a coat hanger." Any answer within the bounds of reason is acceptable: bookmark, wire to fasten something together, swing for a parakeet, etc. The score is the number of different uses offered. Maltzman's students, after very brief training with the word associations, greatly increase their scores on the Unusual Uses test. They gain more than a control group; and another group that is taught to give the *same* associations on each run through the word list actually decreases in ability to find unusual uses. It seems very likely from this that all of us have untapped potentials for diverse, imaginative thinking, and that these can be released rather rapidly by a training which makes us feel comfortable about giving offbeat responses.

But I don't see how instruction via teaching machine can possibly encourage diversity and unconventionality. It looks to me as if we will have continued tension between the programmer, with his view that there is a definite sequence of right answers to be elicited, and the student of creativity, who comes close to defining a response as creative if you don't know what it will be or when it will occur. This tension will produce stimulating questions both for the psychologist and the curriculum developer, and in the end we may clarify our philosophy as to the proper place of standardization and individuality in education.

This Cook's Tour has touched down at too many points for any summary to be possible and has probably left you with a blurred impression on any one topic. But my aim has not been to do justice to the topics as such, but rather to help you to understand the psychologist if he is to be your ally in curriculum studies. His ruling passion is data, data on changes in behavior. Like a prize graduate of Suchman's course, he may not know any of the answers you want, but he will overwhelm you with his questions and with plans for the experiments he is bursting to have you perform. He will come to your programs with pet enthusiasms and active interests, interests closely compatible with the ruling interests of current curriculum reform. Psychological views on education, and on the underlying theory of cognition and motivation, are in a state of upheaval. Old dogmas are lying in the dust or tottering on their bases. Oversimple theories are being remodeled to take disturbing new findings and insights into account. The curriculum studies, insofar as they produce reliable observations of pupils, have a contribution to make to psychology, and the psychologist, insofar as he can help you to make more viable proposals and gather sounder evidence about their worth, will be delighted to assist in your efforts as educational engineers.

References

1 C. Osgood, *Theory and Method in Experimental Psychology*, Oxford University Press, Fairlawn, N.J., 1953.
2 J. Piaget, *The Psychology of Intelligence*, Routledge & Kegan Paul, Ltd., 1950, London, and other volumes.

3 Jerome S. Bruner, *The Process of Education,* Harvard University Press, Cambridge, Mass., 1960.
4 Quotations are from draft of conference report, privately circulated and unpublished. Social Science Research Council, July, 1961.
5 Crow and Hammond, "The Effect of Training upon Accuracy and Variability in Interpersonal Perception," *Journal of Abnormal and Social Psychology,* vol. 55, pp. 355–359, 1957.
6 Lee J. Cronbach, *Educational Psychology,* Harcourt, Brace & World, Inc., New York, 1954. Revised edition, Harcourt, Brace, & World, Inc., N.Y., 1963.
7 Jan Smedslund, "The Acquisition of Conservation of Substance and Weight in Children. III. Extinction of conservation of weight acquired 'normally' and by means of empirical controls on a balance," *Scandinavian Journal of Psychology,* vol. 2, pp. 85–87, 1961.
8 W. A. Brownell and H. E. Moser, *Meaningful vs. Mechanical Learning: a Study in Grade III Subtraction,* The Duke University Press, Durham, N.C., 1949.
9 Harry F. Harlow, "The Formation of Learning Sets," *Psychological Review,* vol. 56, no. 1, pp. 51–65, January, 1949.
10 Benton J. Underwood, "Interference and Forgetting," *Psychological Review,* vol. 64, no. 1, pp. 49–69, January, 1957.
Benton J. Underwood, "A Graphical Description of Rote Learning," *Psychological Review,* vol. 64, no. 2, pp. 119–122, March, 1957.
11 Vaira Freibergs and Endel Tulving, "The Effect of Practice on Utilization of Information from Positive and Negative Instances in Concept Identification," *Canadian Journal of Psychology,* vol. 15, pp. 101–106, 1961.
12 B. F. Skinner, "The Science of Learning and the Art of Teaching," *The Harvard Educational Review,* vol. 24, no. 2, Spring, 1954.
13 John D. Krumboltz and Ronald G. Weisman, "The Effect of Overt vs. Covert Responding to Programmed Instruction on Immediate and Delayed Retention," *Journal of Educational Psychology,* vol. 53, pp. 89–92, April, 1962.

CURRENT PROBLEMS
IN VARIOUS FIELDS

part
iii

The oldest national curriculum project, the one which has inspired the others, is that of the Physical Science Study Committee (PSSC) to provide a new high school physics course. The PSSC aims at building up in the student's mind the structure of the modern conception of matter and energy. Rather than handing this structure, ready-made, to the student, the authors first build up the structure of the classical mechanics of particles. They lead the student to situations in which this picture of matter breaks down. But in a preliminary study of wave motion and light the students have acquired the conceptual tools to build up a new structure. Dean Finlay presents the strategy in his paper.

In Dr. Gaarder's discussion of the new language programs we see clearly the breakdown of traditional ideas of "readiness." This came about when linguists realized that a natural language is so designed that even stupid children can learn it; and the earlier the learning, the easier it is. He alludes to the fascinating question, now under investigation, of how soon adolescents can learn linguistic structure.

Dr. Bock shows how, in teaching the classics, we face the problem of intrinsic motivation in its purest form. What can we do when we have no visible "practical" goal to fall back on?

Dr. Haefner emphasizes the need, in the social studies, for viewing as a cohesive principle the methods of acquiring knowledge—the skills of gathering and analyzing data, of synthesizing isolated facts into patterns, of testing hypotheses against experience. Such a program requires the joint effort of research scholars and teachers.

Dr. Moise compares several new secondary mathematics curricula. He points out how each has struggled to achieve a proper balance between logic and intuition.

English, like mathematics and the social studies, is taught in all grades to all students. Dr. Allen tells how, in English teaching, teachers and scholars have joined forces to build up a grass-roots movement. Only in this way can "Project English" succeed in making the urgently needed reforms.

The Chemical Bonds Approach Project and the Chemical Education Materials Study (CHEMStudy) illustrate how Federal aid supports two competing national projects.

The papers of Hood and Beittel deal with the problem of how to develop taste. The experimentation on which they report seems far removed from the usual "appreciation" courses in schools and colleges.

The biologists, more than the chemists and physicists, face the problem of individual differences, since their course is taken by most high school students. Dr. Grobman reports on the imaginative device by means of which the Biological Sciences Curriculum Study has provided for differences in ability and interest among both teachers and students.

Dr. Stephenson, finally, tells how the earth scientists are coping with a discipline which must integrate expert knowledge from many different fields.

5 ❊ THE PHYSICAL SCIENCE STUDY COMMITTEE*
Gilbert C. Finlay** University of Illinois

The Physical Science Study Committee was formed in 1956 as a group of university and secondary-school physics teachers working to develop an improved introductory physics course. The committee is developing interrelated teaching materials for physics in the secondary school. Materials intended for direct instructional use include a textbook, laboratory apparatus and a laboratory guidebook for students, motion picture films, and a set of ten achievement tests. Supporting materials include a four-volume teacher's guide and resource book, and a series of paperback books that provide authoritative science literature for students and adults.

To help teachers who are considering the use of these materials, the committee has encouraged the development of instructional programs that enable teachers to study the new course in detail.

For its various activities, the committee organized teams of university and secondary-school physics teachers. These teams blended teaching experience at several levels with deep insight into the nature and meaning of physics. The materials developed by these teams were used in classes and subjected to close scrutiny by the teachers who used them and by the committee's staff observers. The course materials were tried, evaluated, and revised for three years before they were released for general use in the fall of 1960.

The committee, in the course of its work, thought it wise to establish a permanent organization to provide for revision and related development. A non-profit corporation, Educational Services Incorporated, was formed. This corporation now administers the program of the Physical Science Study Committee.

Science is becoming an increasingly consequential factor in the affairs of man. There are the practical goods: the hand-in-hand advance of science and technology continuously increases human potential for producing, transporting, communicating, healing. The attendant problems of social control and adaptation are pervasive and complex. In business, legislation, and statesmanship, the scientist increasingly is called upon to help unravel the social and economic implications of science. But beyond its technological goods and meanings, science as a humanistic study stands on its own terms as a dynamically stable system with its own ends and procedural styles. As a form of human expression, it is one of the triumphs of the intellect. It lends perspective and direction to other aspects of life. It is a system one can ill afford to ignore if one is to become a whole man in a world of whole men.

Physics, as a parent discipline, stands close to the center of our scientific milieu. What instruction in physics is appropriate for secondary-school students in the mid-twentieth century? The work of the Physical Science Study Committee is an attempt to answer this question operationally.

* Reprinted from *The School Review*, vol. 70, no. 1, pp. 63–81, The University of Chicago Press, Chicago, Spring, 1962, with permission.
  ** Gilbert C. Finlay is a Professor of Education at the College of Education, University of Illinois.

As an initial target, the committee chose to design a new course to fit into the current pattern of school curriculums. Physics is usually offered as a separate, elective subject for students in the eleventh or twelfth grade. In terms of prior measures of ability, these students are drawn mostly from the upper half of their classes, with the distribution of their abilities skewed toward the top levels. Some of these students will follow careers in science or science-related fields, and further work in science will be a part of their higher education, However, the careers of many secondary-school physics students will be in fields other than science, and they will do no further formal work in physics. The committee judged that the needs of both groups of students could be served with a single course.

The committee chose to plan a course dealing with physics as an explanatory system, a system that extends from the domain inside the atom to the distant galaxies. The course tells a unified story—one in which the successive topics are chosen and developed to lead toward an atomic picture of matter, its motions and interrelations. The aim was to present a view of physics that would bring a student close to the nature of modern physics and to the nature of physical inquiry. Finally, the committee sought to transmit the human character of the story of physics, not simply an up-to-date codification of the findings. The student should see physics as an unfinished and continuing activity. He should experience something of the satisfaction and challenge felt by the scientist when he reaches vantage points from which he can contemplate both charted and uncharted vistas.

Achieving these aims in a one-year course meant that coverage of the field of physics had to be sharply restricted in favor of a deeper development of ideas that are central to a comprehension of the fundamentals of contemporary physical thought. This deeper development meant carrying key concepts to higher levels than have been ordinarily reached in secondary-school courses. Deeper development also meant a more extensive exploration of the substructure of experiment and thought that underlies the basic physical principles.

The student is expected to be an active participant in this course. The textbook, laboratory experiments, and films were developed in a way that reflects this expectation. The course materials do not assert the ideas of physics, then illustrate their utility by exemplifying them in problems and in laboratory exercises. Instead, the student is expected to wrestle with a line (or with converging lines) of inquiry, including his own laboratory investigations, that leads to basic ideas. The power of the fundamental ideas is brought out partially in the student's work on carefully chosen end-of-chapter problems, but more important, the intellectual thrust of the basic ideas is brought out sequentially through using those which are introduced early to illuminate other ideas in a chain that comprises an introductory view of the structure of physics.

As one examines the changes that have occurred in secondary-school physics courses during the past few generations, one is likely to get the feeling that modern technology has found its way into the courses almost to the exclusion of modern physics. Such modern physics as has been worked into many courses is often limited to statements of some of the conclusions. There is little other choice without a preceding development of such subjects as dynamics, wave behavior, and fundamental electricity, that is sufficiently penetrating to permit seeing modern physics as a logical synthesis of ideas emerging from a related structure of experiment, principle, and theory.

No one-year course can give an adequate account of both an expanding physics and the related technology. Planning a course that concentrates on either of these subjects still poses a selection problem of large proportions. As the magnitude of what might be learned grows rapidly, it becomes increasingly clear that the school at any given level, indeed in its entirety, can do little more than provide a base for further learning. The development of a mind is never ending. The function of the school is to provide a fertile start—such a start that the end of formal schooling does not mark the end of further learning. The central problem is to transmit those ideas and styles of thought that have the broadest applicability, the greatest power for further thought and activity. To this end, the Physical Science Study Committee judged it wise to shift the emphasis in secondary-school physics away from technology toward a deeper exploration of the basic ideas of physics and the nature of inquiries that can lead to these ideas. This choice was based on the premise that, for the future scientist as well as for the non-scientist, an introductory course that provides a grasp of the central ideas of physics and the kind of thought that lies behind them is more useful and rewarding than a course that emphasizes a somewhat more ephemeral technology. Technological applications have not been eliminated from the course. But they have been cut back sharply from the role they play in many secondary-school courses. While the course was not specifically developed with college preparation in mind, the course is regarded as providing a sound base for further work in physics.

In this course, experiments—whether they are performed by the student, analyzed in the textbook, or shown on film—are not used simply to confirm an earlier assertion. The laboratory experiments are designed to supply firm rooting for the growth of ideas by providing direct, non-verbal contact with relevant data. Hence, the most common use of laboratory experiments is to introduce a topic or to contribute to the early stages of its development. The students' laboratory guidebook keeps specific instructions to a minimum, directing the students' attention to key points by raising questions. The student is responsible for thinking out the nature and the meaning of what he is to do. The purposes of the experiments vary. Some are qualitative and give general familiarity and introductory experience with a set of phenomena. Many experiments are quantitative but differ extensively in the degree of experimental accuracy that is sought. Students should understand that prior knowledge and experimental purpose influence the precision required to secure new knowledge. Experimentation is a great deal more than establishing the third decimal place. In all cases, students are encouraged to establish or approximate their experimental error.

Clearly a student can have direct laboratory experience with only some aspects of physics. Careful selection of experimental activities can advance the student's understanding of the more important physical ideas. Moreover, presenting these activities in the spirit of experiments rather than as exercises should enhance the student's ability to analyze and appreciate experiments that he reads about or sees on film. Still further, the emphasis in the course on experiment and experimental style is meant to foster insight into the role of experiment in the generation and refinement of physical ideas. While some demonstrations are suggested, more emphasis is placed on experiments performed by students. The apparatus and the laboratory guidebook provide for more than fifty experiments, many of which include optional extensions to provide for variability among students and classes.

A great deal of what might ordinarily be called demonstration is provided by the films produced by the committee. Basically, the films are built around experiments. Films are used to bring bring to the classroom certain key experiments and a range of experiments that are likely to be too difficult, too time consuming, or too costly for students to perform or for teachers to demonstrate. For many experiments, films can bring the purposes, techniques, data, and analysis more directly within the students' purview than any other approach can. The films are planned with attention to the general aims of the course and to the particular choices that have been made in the development of related ideas in the students' laboratory and in the textbook. Because the films articulate closely with these resources and because most of the films assume that the viewer is familiar with earlier parts of the course, the scheduling of the films is a matter of consequence. The films are intended as take-off points for teachers and students. They are not intended to replace a teacher. As of October, 1961, forty-four films were available, and sixteen more were being completed.

Some films—such as those on the Millikan experiment, the Rutherford atom, and the Franck-Hertz experiment—are concerned primarily with the presentation and the interpretation of a complex experiment. Other films are more general in purpose and may use a dozen or more experiments or models to develop a set of related ideas. Such films are intended to help integrate and summarize a field of study. Films on crystals, on the relation between mechanical and thermal energy, and on frames of reference are examples. Finally, a few films are intended as introductions to major areas of study. Such films are meant to give the viewer perspective by taking stock of the array of phenomena that require explanation and by suggesting some of the central questions.

The films do not glitter. There is no background music, and there are no elaborate stage settings. They are frankly teaching films. It should go without saying that the experiments presented are scrupulously honest. The films are not impersonal, neither are they stylized in a personal sense. They present a number of real scientists, speaking in their individual ways to students, directing their attention to key points. In this quiet way, the films bring students into closer contact with a group of scientists as persons.

As supplementary sources of authoritative, scientific information, the committee is developing a series of paperback books. These books are appearing as the "Science Study Series." Some deal with individual topics in science or technology. Some are biographical, some historical. As of October, 1961, twenty books had been published in the series. More than thirty were in preparation, and others were planned. An interesting side light on the pedagogical application of these books is the occasional use of some of the foreign-language translations of the series as reading material for science-oriented students in language classes.

The content of the course of the Physical Science Study Committee has been described in somewhat greater detail in other sources (1, 2, 3). The course is divided into four parts. Part I is an introduction to the principal actor in the physical drama—matter—and its setting, time and space. The course begins with a consideration of the dimensions of time and space and how they are sensed. Through laboratory work the student sees how his senses can be extended by instrumentation and begins to develop a perception of the role, nature, and limitations of measurement. This perception is extended through films that go beyond the usual facilities for measurement available in school laboratories. Familiarity with techniques of defining intervals of space and time leads to a study of motion through space in the course of time. The student learns the relation between distance, velocity, and acceleration and how to move from one to another through graphical differentiation and integration. The use of vectors to represent these quantities completes this introductory view of the descriptive tools of physics. The course then turns to an introduction to matter, the substance of the universe. Here, the ideas of mass and conservation of mass are considered. The student examines experimental evidence for the existence and the size of atoms. In the laboratory he establishes an upper limit for the size of a molecule and sees how extensions of his experiment can lead to determining the size of an atom. The combination of atoms in molecules is studied, and the ideas of atomicity are extended through a consideration of the arrangement of atoms in solids (crystals) and in gases. A beginning on the molecular interpretation of a gas makes it possible to deal specifically with the idea of a physical model.

In Part II the student begins the process of observation of, and abstraction from, a family of physical phenomena; in this case, light. The natural development of the subject leads to an examination of a particle theory of light. This section of the course illustrates how models are abstracted from experimental observation, how they illuminate further investigation, and how they are established, modified, or rejected. Study shows that a simple particle model does not fit the behavior of light, and the course turns to another model, waves. Extensive laboratory experience with waves—first in one dimension on ropes and springs, then in two dimensions on the surface of water—shows similarities between wave behavior and light. A detailed study of interference establishes the wave nature of light.

Part III returns to motion, this time from a dynamical point of view. Again depending heavily upon laboratory work, and extensively reinforced with films, the course moves through the relation between force and motion, the story of the discovery of universal gravitation, and the conservation of momentum and energy. The generality of the conservation laws is stressed. The use of the conservation laws in situations where detailed observation of the motion is not possible (as in the molecular turmoil in gases) and emphasis on two-body interactions lay groundwork for exploring the atom in Part IV.

The atomistic character of matter is introduced in Part I and carried further in the kinetic theory of gases in Part III. Part IV develops the nature

Current problems in various fields

of electrical forces and energy; begins to bind together dynamics, electricity, and waves in a consideration of electromagnetic radiation; and returns with all these tools to an exploration of the structure of matter, atoms. Analysis of scattering experiments establishes a simple Rutherford model. Some of the inadequacies of this model are pointed out. The particle-wave nature of both light and matter is shown. Experiment discloses the internal energy states in atoms. The energy levels are explained in terms of standing wave patterns, and the course comes to a close with a quantum mechanical view in which both wave and particle characteristics are essential to an understanding of the structure of matter. In this part of the course, because of the difficulty of many of the relevant experiments, films carry a large share of the burden of presenting experimental evidence.

The logical unity of physics has been emphasized in this course. As an alternative to covering the various fields of physics at the same level, the course employs earlier material to clarify that which follows. For example, ideas about waves and particles recur, each time to be carried further in a higher synthesis of ideas. This characteristic plus the exploration of concepts that are clearly unfinished, the tightly related student laboratory, the investigative approach in the films and the frequent analysis of experiments in the text all contribute to a perception of physics as a continuing search for order in a picture of the universe. This coherent, searching character of man's approach to building an explanatory structure of the physical world is one of the course's principal aims and chief pedagogical characteristics [1:292].

The Physical Science Study Committee had its beginning early in 1956 in exploratory discussions, held first at the Massachusetts Institute of Technology and later at other centers. These discussions, led by Jerrold R. Zacharias of the Massachusetts Institute of Technology, established the desirability of rethinking the secondary-school physics program and made it clear that an adequate number of able secondary-school and university physics teachers would be willing to join in such an effort. In November, 1956, an initial grant from the National Science Foundation marked the official beginning of the project. The National Science Foundation has provided the principal financial support. The Ford Foundation and the Alfred P. Sloan Foundation have contributed to the support of the program.

By the time of the initial grant, informal groups had been established at Cambridge, Massachusetts; the Bell Laboratories in New York; the California Institute of Technology; Cornell University; and the University of Illinois. Several of these groups developed tentative outlines for a new physics course. A meeting of most of the people who had participated in these groups, together with other interested individuals, was held in December, 1956 (4). The proposals of the several groups were presented and discussed. General agreement was reached on a broad outline and on the major pedagogical characteristics of the course. Following the December meeting, several of the centers began to prepare detailed outlines and preliminary drafts for a work conference to be held during the summer of 1957 at the Massachusetts Institute of Technology.

About fifty people participated in the 1957 summer work session. Most of this group were high-school and university physics teachers. In addition, there were specialists in such fields as testing, film-making, educational administration, and editorial production. Work was begun on all parts of the project: textbook, laboratory experiments, films, tests, teacher's guides, the "Science Study Series," and instructional programs for teachers. The textbook and the laboratory programs were given priority so that enough material would be ready by the end of the summer to make it possible to use a preliminary version of the course in a few schools during the following year. Early use of the course in schools permitted an almost immediate application of classroom feedback to the problems of revising existing materials and helping to shape materials yet to be developed.

During the 1957–58 school year, eight teachers used preliminary versions of the course with about three hundred students. These teachers had participated in the committee's summer project, and they and their schools were in a position to work closely with other members of the committee in evaluating their teaching experience. During that first year, it was possible to supply teachers with printed versions of Parts I and II of the course, mimeographed copies of Part III, and the materials from which preliminary designs of the laboratory apparatus could be built. Formal materials for Part IV of the course were not available that year. Because of the newness and the tentativeness of the materials, few classes moved fast enough that year to get into Part IV. For those that did, the teachers improvised from their knowledge of the plans for Part IV.

This first year of experience in teaching the course was extremely fruitful. Because the number of classes was small, the committee's staff was able to work intensively with the teachers. In some cases modifications of approach were discussed and tried out on the spot. The over-all evaluation was highly favorable. Teachers and students found the course stimulating and were enthusiastic. The close relation between the laboratory and the textbook and the premium on student initiative in the laboratory were well received. The results of the preliminary achievement tests used that year indicated that students attained the desired levels. The desirability of revising the textbook and the laboratory program was pinpointed at various places in Parts I and III. Part II was judged as markedly successful. In that part of the course, teachers found that the mutual reinforcement of the textbook and the laboratory program enabled them to bring students to a deep understanding of advanced ideas on wave behavior. The year's experience also suggested the desirability of a change in the way in which the committee had expected schools to acquire laboratory apparatus. Originally the committee hoped that the use of simple designs of apparatus to concentrate on fundamentals would not only clarify the subject but make it possible for schools to acquire most of the necessary laboratory material locally with construction to be done by students. While the local acquisition of materials and local construction of apparatus were shown to be possible and instructive, shopping and construction time was costly. This excessive time burden on students and teachers was confirmed in the following year, and the committee turned to the development of easily assembled kits of pre-formed apparatus.

During the summer of 1958, five universities offered institutes on the course. The institutes were from six to eight weeks in duration. These institutes were organized under the National Science Foundation's regular program of support to institutes for teachers of science and mathematics. The institutes enrolled a few more than three hundred teachers. As a part of the experimental development of the course, the preliminary course materials were supplied without cost to any of these teachers who wished to use them during the following year, 1958–59. The course was used by about 270 teachers and 11,000 students.

The course materials available for that school year were not complete, but represented a considerable advance over the year before. The preliminary textbook included a partially revised version of Part I, and the textbook extended through the first half of Part IV. The committee was able to supply preliminary laboratory guidebooks and apparatus for Parts I, II, and III and a partial laboratory program and apparatus for Part IV. A preliminary edition of the teacher's guidebook was distributed for all portions of the course except the latter half of Part IV. A complete set of ten achievement tests was used. Although a number of films had been completed during the year, only a few were available for use in the schools at the most appropriate times.

The feedback from the larger number of schools benefited all parts of the program. Intensive feedback relations were maintained with a few schools. From the rest, information was derived from periodic reports, questionnaires, and regional meetings. Results from the administration of the series of achievement tests also contributed helpful information. In one school, a few students who had gone through the first three parts of the course in the previous year studied Part IV in the fall. This experience contributed several key ideas to the further development that winter of Part IV, which was used by a large number of students in the spring.

During the summer of 1959, about seven hundred teachers studied the course in fifteen institutes. For the 1959–60 school year, the course materials were provided at cost to schools that wished to use them and whose teachers had already taught the course or had studied in one of the institutes. That year about 560 teachers used the course with 22,500 students. Some of the teachers who had taught the course during the year before had moved to administrative positions, enrolled in graduate study, or had otherwise withdrawn (in many cases temporarily) from physics teaching. Of those who continued to teach physics, 96 per cent elected to continue with the PSSC course.

Except for the films (about thirty were available for use at the appropriate showing times), a complete set of preliminary materials was on hand. Feedback arrangements were the same as for the 1958–59 school year. The information gleaned from the use of the course in earlier years had already been used as starting points for some revisions of the textbook and the laboratory experiments, and these were tried out and studied. During the 1959–60 school year, the committee's major effort was directed to a complete revision of all printed materials and the design changes appropriate to the commercial production of kits of laboratory apparatus. By the fall of 1960 the textbook, laboratory guidebook, apparatus, tests, films, and teacher's guidebook had been turned over to commercial suppliers and were available generally.

The institute programs have continued to provide opportunity for teachers to study the course in detail. During 1960–61, the course was used by about eleven hundred teachers with forty-four thousand students. As of October, 1961, a conservative approximation of the number using the course in 1961–62 was eighteen hundred teachers and seventy-two thousand students.

Evaluation of the course has several aspects. The committee's own evaluations are directed toward the improvement of the course, not comparisons with other courses. The course differs sharply from most secondary-school physics courses both in selection of content and in style of development. Comparison with other courses is not a matter of evaluating the relative merit of different methods of teaching toward the same objectives. Rather, such a comparison involves questions as to the choice of the objectives themselves. Close scrutiny of the courses is enough to confirm this fundamental difference. Further confirmation comes from the few instances in which standard examinations have been given to PSSC students and PSSC examinations have been given to students in standard courses. The results show that the students have studied different courses. The sharp difference between the PSSC course and other courses has been recognized by the College Entrance Examination Board, which has provided separate examinations in physics for PSSC and non-PSSC students. Certainly it is possible to design an examination on which matched groups of PSSC students and students from other physics courses would achieve equivalent score distributions. This procedure would hardly provide a comparison. It would prove only that such an examination can be prepared. Comparative evaluation requires common objectives—common with reference to fundamentals of substance and intellectual style.

In terms of its own objectives, the committee judges that its present course is successful in the sense that it provides a context for teachers and students through which students have reached the desired goals. Evidence comes from several sources. Performance on the PSSC achievement tests speaks of the students' understanding of content and their power to handle ideas, to apply them broadly. In preparing the achievement tests, the level of difficulty was set so that an average performance of answering half the questions correctly would be regarded as satisfactory achievement. This goal was attained. On the qualitative side, the preponderant testimony of teachers and students who have used the course indicates that it sharply stimulates the development of more powerful styles of inquiry.

The difficulty of the course and its adaptability to students of varying abilities have been the subject of a great deal of discussion by those who have used and/or studied the course and by some who have not. The results of the analysis of achievement test performance by students from various levels of academic aptitude, as measured by conventional aptitude tests, clearly suggest that success in handling the ideas of the PSSC course is not limited to a narrow band of what, by traditional measures, might be called high-aptitude students. The testimony of a majority of the teachers who have used the course supports this view. Most teachers who have used the course feel that it is appropriate for the range of student abilities that typically has been enrolled in physics. Some teachers make the point that, for the less facile student, an exposition based on experiment rather than assertion is especially helpful. Of the teachers who have used the course, a clear minority feel that the course is too difficult for average students and prefer to restrict the use of the course to high-ability students. On the difficulty of the course, the committee is inclined to agree with the student who wrote that "the course is not for those who have difficulty tying their shoelaces." The course was intended to provide a challenging experience. Students and teachers say that it does. Most of them also say that it is highly rewarding. The committee feels that the course is close to the intended mark. Certainly other course structures could be developed that would provide a satisfactory secondary-school physics course. The present course is simply a stage in the development of one satisfactory course. Indeed, through Educational Services Incorporated, the committee expects to give continuing attention to the improvement of secondary-school physics.

The committee fell a bit short of reaching its objective of providing a one-year course. The course as it stands was prepared so that teachers could omit several sections without seriously undermining the material that follows. These are, however, omissions that most teachers will make only with regret. Without cutting, many teachers feel that the course should extend for more than a year. This problem is being met in various ways. Some teachers are making the possible cuts. Some schools are lengthening the time given to physics by teaching it for more than two semesters or by giving it more class time during the year. Some schools are trying early parts of the course in earlier science courses. The development of improved science courses at lower levels will be one of the factors influencing revision of the current PSSC course.

As of the fall of 1961, the committee has a number of on-going projects. To get information on what and when revision should occur, study of the use of the course continues. In this connection, it is now apparent that improvements in laboratory experiments for Part IV will be sought. The "Science Study Series" is being extended at the rate of nearly a book each month. The film studio of Educational Services Incorporated is continuing its work on the series of films that are a part of the course.

Another current activity is the preparation of a second battery of achievement tests to augment the existing series. In the development of these new tests, techniques are being investigated that are expected to extend the information that can be obtained on the nature as well as the over-all quality of student performance.

In the general area of evaluation, other studies are planned. While the course was not planned specifically as preparation for college work in physics, it is natural to look at students' performance in college physics for one source of evidence on the effectiveness of the course. With growing numbers of students completing the PSSC course in secondary schools and continuing physics in college, it will be possible to look more definitively than before at their performance in college physics. To the extent that certain college courses and the PSSC course share common goals, such studies should be helpful in reflecting the contribution of the secondary-school work. There have been a few preliminary studies of this kind, necessarily with small numbers of students. These studies indicated that PSSC students were at no disadvantage and in several respects (grades in one study; flexibility of thought and procedure, particularly in the laboratory, in another) were at an advantage.

Another kind of investigation that is being formulated uses the extensive element of design in the PSSC course (over-all story line with closely related textbook, laboratory, and films) to provide a context for a clinical study of learning over a year-long span. Among other things, this plan contemplates the development of non-verbal as well as verbal measures of performance.

The PSSC course was planned to fit a pattern in which physics is offered as a one-year course during the eleventh or twelfth grades. The achievement of adequate depth in a one-year course required the omission of many topics that logically could have been included and for which the course as it stands lays a powerful base. Some schools are able to offer a somewhat more advanced course either because of the time they give to physics, the ability of their students, the teaching of some of the earlier parts of the PSSC course in earlier grades, or a combination of these reasons. For such courses the committee is developing supplementary textbook material, laboratory experiments, and films for a series of advanced topics.

In the development in the PSSC course of an atomic model, some teachers have found a convenient structure for moving toward the integration of their work in chemistry and physics. Several schools have developed an integrated, two-year sequence in physical science using the PSSC course and a chemistry course, either one of their own devising or one of the chemistry courses recently developed with the support of the National Science Foundation. These activities are worth further effort and support.

The development, including trial and evaluation, of a course such as that of the Physical Science Study Committee naturally leads to suggestions on the kinds of educational experiences that might logically precede and follow such a course. A number of related activities, some of them partially stimulated by the work of the Physical Science Study Committee, have come into being. Some of those who shared in the PSSC project are now working with the Commission on College Physics, which is concerned with the improvement of physics teaching at the college level. Some are working in individual university centers on the improvement of the physics courses taught at their university. Some are turning to the problems of science instruction in elementary and junior high schools.

A great deal of interest in the work of the committee has been shown by science teachers and scientists from other countries. From the beginning, many foreign visitors have come to observe and discuss the project. This interest has led to the translation of the "Science Study Series" into other languages. Publication rights have been granted in eighteen countries. The books are now appearing in seven languages other than English. As the course materials neared completion, the interest of other countries in the use of the course (in some cases translation and use) quickened. By special arrangement, several dozen educators from abroad have attended some of the regular summer institutes of the Physical Science Study Committee. During the summer of 1961, staff members of the committee accepted three invitations to conduct intensive institute programs in other countries. These institutes enrolled secondary-school teachers, university teachers, and, in some cases, science supervisors. Two of these institutes, in Israel and in New Zealand, were national in character. One, in England, enrolled teachers from half a dozen European countries. One outcome of these institutes was that the course will be used soon in several countries. Also, during the past summer, a planning conference was held in Japan to consider the problems of translation and use of the course in that country. At the invitation of the Australian College of Education, a staff member of the committee recently spent a week in Australia discussing the course with teachers who were convened for that purpose. Similar visits have been made to India and to some of the African and South American countries. These various explorations of the applicability of the course in other countries have been supported by the governments of New Zealand and Israel; the United Nations Educational, Scientific and Cultural Organization; the Carnegie Foundation; the Asia Foundation; the Organization for European Economic Cooperation; the Office of Information Services; and the Organization of American States.

The course of the Physical Science Study Committee has proved to be rewarding to a large number of teachers and students. Clearly, its applicability is not confined to highly selected students or to a particular culture. The several hundred men and women who have contributed directly to the course have derived a great deal of satisfaction from that work. The committee looks forward to continuous improvement of the course.

References

1 Gilbert C. Finlay, "Secondary School Physics: The Physical Science Study Committee," *American Journal of Physics*, vol. 28, pp. 286–293, March, 1960.
2 Physical Science Study Committee, *Physics*, D. C. Heath and Company, Boston, 1960, pp. v–vi.
3 Stephen White, "The Physical Science Study Committee (3) The Planning and Structure of the Course," *Contemporary Physics*, II, pp. 39–54, October, 1960.
4 This conference was reported in "Physical Science Study Committee, A Planning Conference Report," *Physics Today*, vol. 10, pp. 28–29, March, 1957.

6 ❀ CURRICULUM EXPERIMENTATION IN FOREIGN LANGUAGES ❀ A. Bruce Gaarder*
United States Office of Education

Any discussion of the new curricula is indivisible from an equally indivisible set of three M's which mark each course: the new *methods* of instruction, the new *materials,* and the new *machinery.* Foreign language teaching and learning, at all levels of instruction from the early grades through the university, is not what it used to be. A rigorous, unrelenting self-examination by the foreign language teachers themselves—begun six years before Sputnik as a concerted effort sparked by the Modern Language Association of America— led to the widespread conviction that we were not teaching enough to

* A. Bruce Gaarder is Chief, Language Research Section, Language Development Branch, U.S. Office of Education, Washington, D.C.

enough people. A combination of circumstances—traditions, national attitudes, conflicting interests, and our relative isolation—had brought much foreign language teaching to a point where it was no anomaly—at least no one seemed to object—that the French teacher could not speak French and that the Spanish teacher could speak no Spanish.

The extent to which it is considered anomalous today is the mark of the change that is taking place in our methods, materials, and machinery—and especially in our teachers. It is the mark of the reform, the revolutionary changes, that now characterize the foreign language curriculum.

With the reform now in its ninth year, we can plainly see two concurrent levels of curriculum experimentation: The first, fairly uniform, and nationwide in extent—although certainly not yet including a majority of teachers and schools; the second, made up of separate and diverse experimental situations bearing upon single features of methodology. The first level of experimentation, now in its third year as a national movement, is known by several different names. Dr. James Conant has called it the "American Method" of teaching foreign languages. Some call it "the new American method." Maybe the most widely used term is "the audio-lingual approach" to foreign language learning.

Whatever the name, honesty demands an avowal of the origin. A very few teachers have always possessed the insights embodied in this methodology. As a teaching system it derives from the "linguist-informant" method devised as an outgrowth of the science of structural or descriptive linguistics. This method reached the colleges during World War II in a few of the best foreign language schools set up for the Army, and has since prospered as the methodology of the Foreign Service Institute school of languages and in other government schools, and at such institutions as the Hartford Seminary Foundation and the Summer Institute of Linguistics—both of which are devoted largely to the preparation of missionaries.

Audio-lingual—pertaining to ear and tongue—suggests the basic principle of the method: that language is primarily a system of communication by sound from mouth to ear, and that it must be learned as such if the learner is ever to communicate by speech. This principle, with its corollaries, has a number of consequences for classroom teaching:

1. Instead of learning to talk about the language, the student and teacher must talk the language. A functional mastery of grammar is learned by analogy and induction through drills, and formal analysis of language is deferred to a later stage.

2. Language learning in its early stage—the first three or four hundred hours—is considered to be primarily the acquisition of a skill rather than the accumulation of a body of facts. Comprehension of the spoken word is the first skill to be mastered; speaking follows listening. During the first three or four hundred hours reading and writing are generally not taught, beyond the minimum needed to reinforce the student's ability to communicate by speech itself.

3. The recognition that language learning is the development of a skill rather than the intellectual mastery of a body of facts is extremely important.

It means that, just as he would if he were learning to play a musical instrument, the student of language must practice actively, aloud, until he achieves something like automatic control of the language patterns. Just as if he were learning to play a musical instrument, the student must be provided with the opportunity to practice by himself, outside of the expensive presence of the teacher. This is half of the explanation of the third M: the machinery. It explains the installation of over three thousand language "laboratories" in our schools and colleges. These installations of electronic equipment should, ideally, permit the student to practice hour after hour when the teacher is not present. Unfortunately, for administrative reasons, the laboratory work in most high schools must be limited to and combined with the regular class period. The other half of the explanation is that by using recordings made by native speakers of the languages, the student is provided with a perfect linguistic model to imitate.

4. Solving the problem of time—the time needed to master a very complicated skill—has resulted in the most notable change in the curriculum. It has required abandonment of the two-year high school sequence in favor of a minimum of four years in grades 9 through 12. Even this is not considered optimal. Many schools are now beginning their foreign language instruction in the seventh grade, to provide a six-year sequence. Most significant of all is the strong trend toward a ten-year plan which includes grades 3 through 12. Over eight thousand schools give foreign language instruction in the elementary grades. No fewer than three-fourths of these programs are in every sense curriculum experimentation. It is safe to say that *if properly trained teachers were available* hundreds of these schools would now be offering foreign languages on the ten-year plan.

This summary description of the audio-lingual approach to foreign language learning gives only a part of the story of what I have called the first level of curriculum experimentation, the nationwide experiment. The real strength of the experiment lies in the materials that implement it and the teacher-training institutes that sustain it. At the Modern Language Materials Development Center in New York City, under government sponsorship (1) a four- to six-year sequence of new audio-lingual teaching materials is being produced for French, German, Italian, Russian, and Spanish instruction at the secondary school level. For each language there is a complement of magnetic tape recordings for laboratory use, disc recordings for audio-lingual homework, student workbooks, and a teacher's manual. This package of materials was introduced into hundreds of high schools in the fall of 1961. The Federal government has attempted, through this project, to stimulate the development of new types of materials, and, in fact, leading commercial publishers are now vying with each other to produce other sets of teaching materials with a similar orientation.

The problem of evaluation, of testing, has not been overlooked. Standardized achievement tests of the listening and speaking skills—as well as the reading and writing skills—are being prepared for five languages by the Modern Language Association and the Educational Testing Service, under the direction of Dr. Nelson Brooks (1). This is an unprecedented step. For the first time in history there will be, for students in grades 7 to 14, a standardized, objective means of evaluating ability to speak a foreign tongue. A similar battery of tests—but embracing also other areas of professional preparation—have been produced for the purpose of evaluating the qualifications of the teacher himself. These teacher-proficiency tests are expected to exert a strong influence on the foreign language teacher-training curricula at the college level. Their use is already pointing up deficiencies in the college preparation of foreign language teachers, especially in the listening and speaking skills and in their understanding of the foreign culture. As a new basis for certifying foreign language teachers at both state and local levels, they can be expected soon to lessen the weight given to the mere accumulation of credit hours. The teacher-proficiency tests are also under the aegis of the Modern Language Association, and the direct guidance of Dr. Wilmarth Starr (1).

No less important than the two batteries of tests in reshaping the curriculum are the intensive teacher-training institutes. In addition to the special summer schools normally held for foreign language teachers, a total of 133 intensive summer and year-long institutes have been conducted, beginning in the summer of 1959 and supported with funds authorized by Title VI of the National Defense Education Act. Seven thousand secondary and elementary school foreign language teachers have attended these NDEA institutes, and it is estimated that no fewer than seven hundred thousand students have been directly affected. Finally, through the authorization of the NDEA (2) and aid from other sources between twenty-five hundred and three thousand secondary schools, it is estimated, have foreign language laboratory installations to reinforce their teaching, and many thousands of foreign language teachers have participated in state-sponsored in-service workshops and demonstrations.

The second level of experimentation also accepts and incorporates much of the theory of language and language learning which I have sketched as the audio-lingual approach. It is made up of an uncounted number of projects, most of them small, a few quite large, which are attempting to develop and evaluate special features of methodology or highly specialized teaching materials. The largest of these is probably the Modern Language Project of the Massachusetts Council for Public Schools. This project, a highly organized effort to present French at the elementary school level by a combination of telecasts, homework discs for the pupils, and printed text materials, began broadcasting through forty different television stations on August 1, 1961. This Massachusetts program, known as *Parlons français*, is typical in that it attempts to cope with the problem of the extreme scarcity of teachers on the assumption that the untrained or minimally prepared regular classroom teacher can learn along with her pupils and can herself begin to serve as a linguistic model to be imitated, supplementing the recorded materials on TV, tape, and disc (4).

Possibly one of the smallest experiments is that of a high school teacher in Chappaqua, New York. Evangeline Galas, assuming that youngsters' great imitative ability is vitiated by the speech of even the minimally prepared teacher, has been devising methods by which the untrained classroom teachers might guide their pupils' learning, without attempting to speak the foreign language or serve as models to be imitated by the pupils. In this experiment, conducted in some twenty fourth- and fifth-grade classes, phonograph recordings are the exclusive source of the foreign tongue (1).

Between the huge *Parlons français* TV project and the small Chappaqua experiment stand the thousands of elementary school projects noted above, *most* of them experimental in every sense, plus several score other projects at the school and college levels, all concerned in one way or another with those problems of foreign language teaching which can be solved only through curricular innovations:

New patterns of staff utilization—varied combinations of specialists, non-specialists, and native informants; large student groupings for analytic sessions, very small groupings for "display" sessions

Electromechanical aids (tapes, discs, TV, films, etc., which model the language) to supplement the work of the good teacher, to offset the shortcomings of the untrained teacher, to extend practice hours far beyond the limits of the class period

Adjustment to individual student differences by providing as many learning tracks as there are students; programming laboratory work for a maximum of self-instruction

Exploitation of that readiness to learn which varies inversely with age

Use of visual aids, especially films, to increase cultural and linguistic authenticity

Production and trial of new teaching materials, especially those designed in accord with the principles of scientific linguistics

Development of teacher-training procedures for colleges and later in-service training which are adequate to the demands now made of foreign language teachers

In Exeter, California, Ruth Sherred directs an experiment in which she presents high school biology in Spanish, in an ambitious attempt to exploit the fact that there is a greater readiness—call it motivation if you will—to acquire a language, whether native or foreign, if it is learned as a means to an end rather than as an end in itself. In this case, all students study biology in English, as usual, and the Spanish language course in biology is conceived as a supplement to that course. Thus far the hypothesis has been sustained that the two-language combination produces more knowledge of biology than the English course alone, and that it produces more skill in Spanish than if the tongue were merely studied, in the usual way, as an end in itself (1).

In St. Paul, Minnesota, Dr. Walter B. Leino has undertaken a three-year study of the time-allotment factor as it relates to pupil achievement in the elementary school where regular foreign language instruction has been introduced. He wants to determine whether decreasing the time normally allotted to certain other subject areas, to allow time for teaching a foreign language, results in measurably decreased or increased achievement in these subject areas (1).

Special mention must be made of the use of the film to provide at one and the same time increased cultural authenticity and an authentic linguistic model. Two notable examples of this work, now on trial in secondary schools and colleges, are the Otterbein College Film-text for French, and the Wayne State University Modern Language Audio-visual Project, also for French (4). The first is directed by Dr. Lavelle Rosselot, the second by Dr. George Borglum. Although differing in emphasis, both portend drastic changes in the curriculum: new patterns of staff utilization, new groupings of students, new equipment.

There are other, better-known types of experimentation with the curriculum which must be mentioned in passing. The Advanced Placement Program, using the College Entrance Examination Board tests, has found increasing favor, especially in the Northeastern states. In a number of elementary school programs, foreign language learning is reserved for the academically talented, although the more commonly held view is that all children should have some experience in learning a foreign language. Finally, there are increased efforts to reinforce the regular school offerings by adding a session of study abroad. The "junior year abroad" and the "summer study tour" are becoming more and more common at the college level. A recent large-scale adaptation of this at the high school level merits detailed mention. The Indiana University Honors Program Abroad for High School Students, which has Carnegie Foundation and other support, combines an honors program in French, German, and Spanish with local scholarship funds to make possible intensive summer study abroad for outstanding sophomores and juniors. Following the study abroad, each honors student continues his language work in his own high school. All high schools in Indiana may participate in this ten-year effort, which envisages a restructuring of the patterns of foreign language instruction at all levels.

We have been concerned thus far principally with the schools, elementary and secondary. The colleges are no less scenes of ferment. At least seven hundred installations of language learning equipment—foreign language laboratories—have been counted in the colleges. And it is at the college and university level that one finds most of the carefully controlled, rigorously designed research leading to improved methods of instruction. Five examples typify the lines of inquiry and show the extent to which curriculum reorganization is the goal. The first two are complementary: At Louisiana State University a teacher of German, Dr. Earl Lewis, has been attempting to use electromechanical aids to extend himself qualitatively, i.e., to give the same students more than would otherwise have been possible (1). At Oberlin College, Dr. Joseph Reichard has used much the same equipment to extend himself quantitatively, i.e., to teach nearly twice as many students as he could have handled without the equipment (1). In two other projects, under Drs. William Wood and William Smithers at Tulane University, and Prof. Klaus Mueller, foreign language coordinator for the ten Associated Colleges of the Midwest, the foreign language faculties have boldly undertaken a program designed to refine and strengthen their foreign language curricula to the end that their foreign language majors and teaching majors will be able to meet the challenge of the new Modern Language Association's teacher proficiency tests being developed under Dr. Starr's direction.

The fifth experiment, conducted at Indiana University by Dr. Albert

Valdman, attempts, via a complete restructuring of the curriculum for French, to reach a solution to most of the problems which beset language teaching. Dr. Valdman, working within the overall curricular and fiscal limitations of the College of Arts and Sciences, has planned a program with these features:

1. It provides the student fifteen contact hours per week with the stream of speech of the new language. Of these hours, one is devoted to "language analysis" in large groups under the guidance of a scientific linguist. During two half-hour periods the students, in groups of three, *display* their knowledge and skill to an instructor. Thirteen hours go to drill on materials programmed through electronic equipment to facilitate a maximum of self-instruction.

2. The instructors not only are required to have a good command of the language, but are carefully taught how to conduct the "display sessions" and are under close direct supervision throughout the term.

3. Of equal significance is the grading and credit system, under which each student is allowed to proceed at his own optimum pace, without loss of prestige, credit, or time (1).

Were this a report on research, a score of different projects dealing with problems of methodology would merit prime attention. All are potential shapers of the new curriculum. Especially ominous, or heartening—as you choose—are the implications of the so-called "programmed" presentation techniques for the foreign language curriculum. Such programs are in the making—at least seven for French, four for German, five for Russian, five for Spanish, and one for Thai. These foreign language programs have not yet demonstrated their complete effectiveness. Suffice it to say that the nature of language learning is such (requiring of the student much more drill and repetition with a model than can be paid for in the presence of the teacher), and the present development of language-learning equipment is such, that even if it fulfills only half its promise, the Skinnerian programming principle will bring significant changes to the foreign language curriculum at every level. At least the problem of multiple tracks to accommodate individual differences will have disappeared.

All of this has a strong bearing upon, and even derives in part from, our changing concepts of the readiness of the child and the young adult for learning. First of all, Penfield (5) and other psychologists have confirmed the folk conviction that beginning the teaching of foreign languages at twelve or sixteen years of age, or later, is as contrary to "the unfolding nature" of man as would be a government fiat to postpone marriage until the age of forty. The optimum age at which to begin seems to be between four and ten. Add to this the indication from various researchers such as Penfield (5), Carroll (6), and Garry and Mauriello (7) that success in foreign language learning is not correlated with high measures of general intelligence. Finally, consider the fact that the methodology which we call here the "audio-lingual approach" conceives the acquisition of language as the conditioning of verbal behavior achieved through drill, and dependence on the student's ability to analogize rather than upon his ability to analyze. The conclusion is overwhelming: beginning earlier facilitates learning, and superior intelligence is not required for learning; hence the average child and the academically talented child are equally ready for foreign languages, and the earlier the better.

Finally, looking to the future, there is another kind of natural readiness which foreign language learning *of the proper kind* builds into the youngster and which researchers are seeking ways to exploit. It is the puzzling, unquestioned, but uncomprehended readiness to learn a third or fourth language. Secondary school teaching materials are now being produced for Chinese, Arabic, and other languages. Scholars have been at work producing basic materials of one sort or another for at least 116 of the hitherto neglected languages: Gio, Quechua, Kabyle, Bengali, Tamil, Somali, etc. (1). Despite all this, the American youngster will for many years to come study French, Spanish, or German in school and then reach adulthood to find that he needs badly to know Gio, Quechua, Kabyle, Tamil, or Somali. Or perhaps Twi. The problem is that not all kinds of foreign language study will produce this readiness. With ordinary teaching, such as now goes on, four years of French in college contributes too little to the learning of Quechua, Chinese, or Twi. Researchers are seeking to isolate the natural factors which produce this kind of special readiness to learn a third language, and then induce those factors as part of the process of learning the first foreign language. The importance of devising new methods, materials, and a new curricular structure to exploit this kind of linguistic readiness becomes obvious when one considers the problem of meeting our nation's increasing multilingual commitments to international business, industrial, and governmental affairs around the globe.

When the problem is solved at the junior high school level or earlier—and it begins to seem possible to do so by combining today's audio-lingual approach with the analytical techniques used originally by the structural linguist to describe and codify the unwritten tongues of "primitive" peoples—the school and college curricula in foreign languages will undergo still another revolution.

References

1 Supported under the authority of the *National Defense Education Act of 1958,* Title VI—Language Development, Section 602, Research and Studies.
2 *National Defense Education Act of 1958,* Title III—Financial Assistance for Strengthening Science, Mathematics, and Modern Foreign Language Instruction.
3 Supported, in part, under the authority of the *National Defense Education Act of 1958,* Title VII—Research and Experimentation in More Effective Utilization of Television, Radio, Motion Pictures, and Related Media for Educational Purposes.
4 Supported in part under the authority of the *National Defense Education Act of 1958,* Title VII.
5 Wilder Penfield, "The Learning of Languages," in Wilder Penfield and Lamar Roberts, *Speech and Brain Mechanisms,* Princeton University Press, Princeton, N.J., 1959, chap. 11, Epilogue, pp. 235–257.
6 John B. Carroll, "Use of the Modern Language Aptitude Test in Secondary Schools," in Edith M. Huddlestone (ed.), *Sixteenth Yearbook of the National*

Council on Measurements Used in Education, New York: the Council, 1959, pp. 155-159.
7 Ralph Garry and Edna Mauriello, Summary of Research on Parlons Français, First Year Program, Massachusetts Council for Public Schools—Modern Language Project, Boston, 1960. (Mimeographed.)

7 ❦ CURRICULUM IMPROVEMENT IN THE CLASSICS: PROGRESS IN TEACHING—MOTIVES OF LEARNING
Carolyn E. Bock* Montclair State Teachers College

Latin was first taught in this country as one of the original compulsory subjects, offered with Greek and some four or five other subjects in the boys' academy, the female seminary, and the college or university. With the decline of Greek it became the prestige subject in the private, parochial, and public high school; the only foreign language in the small high school; and the foreign language with the longest sequence of study in the large high school. Usually begun in the ninth grade—occasionally in the seventh or eighth—it was continued through the twelfth, and often pursued further in the liberal arts program of the college.

American education, reflecting European emphasis on excellence, depended on the classics to provide the kind of intellectual, literary, and cultural supports that characterized the Western tradition. The rigorous attention given to, and the thorough memorization of, grammatical forms and rules was believed to be good mental discipline. The struggle to build Caesar's bridge fortified this belief. A natural interest in rhetoric and oratory made Cicero the ideal model. Both his immortal phrases and his style rang through the Friday afternoon elocution exercises, school debates, and weekly editorials. And Vergil was the dessert: the heroic, the adventurous, the romantic, the mythical, and the mystical. Meter and rhyme—"This is the forest primeval . . ."— the *Iliad*, the *Odyssey*, figures of speech, Dante, Milton, the Trojan War cycle, the Dido-Aeneas theme in literary masterpieces, all were interwoven in the study of this poetic genius.

The Latin class, a bona fide Latin class, was language- and literature-centered. Grade school readers had exposed the pupil to classical mythology. The English class had parsed and analyzed, and so equipped the pupil with the terminology associated with the teacher's and the text's explanation of grammar. Ancient history grounded the student in the facts of the Greco-Roman world. Classes or subject-matter areas rather naturally and unconsciously, if not unintentionally, reinforced each other so that there was a unity or body of common knowledge which was in the student's possession. Respect for authority and obedience to command went unchallenged. And so Latin was learned—and learned well, whether or not for the right reasons

* Carolyn E. Bock is Professor of Latin, Classics Department, Montclair State Teachers College, Montclair, New Jersey.

57 | Curriculum improvement in the classics: progress in teaching

or in the right ways; and the old-fashioned, deductive, grammar-and-translation method represents the kind of training poured on us by some of the great and memorable among the schoolmasters. The question always has been, "Did Latin make them good?", "Did they make Latin good?", or is it a combination of the goodness and strength of the personality and the strength and timeliness of the language that makes the Latin class something special, whether the best or the worst, in the school?

The introduction of psychology raised some questions about learning, questioned transfer of training, and led to much exploration and examination. The Classical Investigation of 1924[1], based on findings from extensive and extensively circulated questionnaires, established a revised set of objectives for the study of Latin, listing "the ability to read and understand Latin" as the major aim. This led to a reordering of materials, the writing and selecting of connected passages in lieu of the isolated word, phrase, and sentence formerly used in the pre-Caesar sections of the texts. Additional attention to English derivatives, and information about Roman life and history were deemed desirable inclusions. This change in goals led to controlled experimentation and testing. The Wrightstone evaluation of the mid-thirties established the superiority of the "new learning," and the new texts appeared in the early forties. The new format illustrated a new approach analogous to the "new psychology"—the inductive, functional reading method. Some teachers still have not recognized or accepted it, even though the text they use, in its presentation of new material and concepts in context, is a perfect example of the procedure.

Education for all American youth, life adjustment, vicarious experience, cocurricular activities, were slogans in the wake of the burgeoning curriculum expanded to accommodate those affected by the increase in the compulsory attendance age law. The widely construed interpretation and application of Dewey's philosophy spelled a progressivism that shook the heretofore single-purpose, college-bound high school curriculum, even though only a small percentage of its graduates went to college.

Encouragement to sample a wide variety of courses forced choices and cut down on the number of long-sequence courses a pupil might pursue. Only three units of English and United States history were required for graduation among the accumulated units. Latin III and IV declined, were combined, and even disappeared in many schools. Many teachers of Latin I and II, in order to gain and hold students, resorted to the bread and circus fare of the day, popularizing the subject to the point that the teaching was more "about Latin" than it was Latin. The extremes of the teaching spectrum were represented in Latin classes—the unrelated, meaningless rote learning on the one hand, and the soap carving, doll dressing, Roman banqueting on the other. It became even more important for the pupil not going to college to take Latin in order that the avenue to the world of thought might be opened to him. A shorter workweek and more leisure time made it imperative for him to develop tastes that would be sustaining when his formal schooling stopped. The Latin class and club, with all the opportunities for projects it

---

[1] Advisory Committee of the American Classical League, *The Classical Investigation*, Part I, "General Report," Princeton University Press, Princeton, N.J., 1924. (The investigation was supported by a grant from the Carnegie Corporation.)

presents, gave the handy as well as the heady a chance. Presented as a social study with all kinds of correlation between the past and the present, the Latin class became a valuable, and sometimes even successful way, to reach and interest the mediocre and the poor pupil. The teacher argued, and the pupil often proved, that the Latin class had plenty in its integrated program to contribute to "Johnny-the-average" growing into John Q. (average) Citizen.

Many teachers, cognizant of the changing complexion of the general public and of education, utilized their picture-loaded texts, the omnipresence of the classical allusion, and the ready reference to the past, and streamlined their class activities so as to hold the line along with all the innovation. The alert teacher thought of and planned Latin I as an exploratory course open to all, Latin I-II as a terminal course for the non-college-bound, and the I-IV sequence for the college and college classics-bound.

When Latin ceased to be a compulsory subject, when the number of years required for college entrance, for graduation, or for professional preparation was reduced or removed, its future was no longer guaranteed. Its survival became largely dependent upon the resources of the teachers of Latin. It had the enamored and the disenchanted among its alumni. It had the indifference of those who had bypassed its study, and the veto of those who had succeeded without it. And yet its resilience was remarkable. Temporarily interrupted, displaced, discontinued, instruction in Latin, one of the oldest of the disciplines, nevertheless represents an unbroken continuum. If we can explain this tenacity perhaps we can understand its motivation.

Whatever rationale underlies, for the parents, the children, or the school administration, the scheduling of Latin—whether it be all the well-known arguments, specious or genuine, whether it be status or value—the scholar-teacher knows that the assumptions and the claims must be separated from the myth of the mouth and translated into reality. The supporting public need not be disillusioned in its former assertions, but it must come to count on more that is reliable and essential. For example, "I never knew any English grammar until I studied Latin," is commonly heard testimony. The usual assumption is that English grammar is based on Latin grammar, which the Latinists pointed out early as untrue. There are similarities in the structure of the two languages, but the significant factor for understanding English is the difference—the contrast—in the two languages. It is the emphasis on and illustration of these differences that facilitates comprehension. Similarly, the Latin teacher bemoans the fact that a class knows no English grammar, which she must teach before she can do anything with Latin. This is beside the point. *Learning* is the result of observation of the language's *own* pattern. *Understanding* is the result of observation of operational patterns of languages, the philosophy and psychology behind their structure.

The rise of linguistics as a "new science" has done much to clear up the confusion, to point out the fallacy in much of language learning, and to surrender language to a more accurate description. Latin has been submitted to a complete linguistic analysis which led to a new methodology known as the linguistic or structural approach. The Carnegie Corporation underwrote the experimental work begun by Waldo Sweet at the William Penn Charter

School in Philadelphia by subsidizing the preparation of experimental materials along linguistic principles by a small group of teachers under Professor Sweet's direction at summer workshops at the University of Michigan. This involved the use of *sententiae* as pattern practices, employing a tape recorder for class use. This project dates back to the early 1950s. Mimeographed materials were used and evaluated in pilot schools, revised in succeeding years; readings were developed, and printed texts and commercial tapes marketed. Summer schools and workshops, demonstration classes, and progress reports in the classical journals exposed a number of teachers to the new method. It represented a radical departure from the grammar or reading methods, but, according to its advocates, realized the objectives of both much more quickly and expediently and, more importantly, *in the language,* meaning a model thought to be far superior to that of the "made" or "canned" Latin previously used. To traditionalists, it seemed to deal indiscriminately with big segments of the language: nouns of different declensions, and verbs of different tenses and conjugations, all at the same time in the same framework. Actually, it represented the "normal" as found in Latin literature. By repetition, overlearning, and multiple practice the pattern was fixed, and a class was working with the language in the language. Sufficient examples allowed summaries and conclusions to be drawn from usage. This involved the student all the more in the learning and gave him surer grasp and possession. The installation of the language laboratory increased and enhanced the pattern practice procedure. By the time the laboratory had spread, Sweet's Latin materials were already on tape. Again, through workshops, conferences, and demonstrations, teachers were encouraged to design tapes to accompany the texts they were using in order to provide extra drill on the difficult material. This suggestion has gained a wider following and is the natural bridge from the old to the new. The recently produced DeWitt-Forbes (University of Minnesota) tapes made to accompany *Using Latin*[2], a widely used text, provides another sample for the teacher in creating her own materials.

Programmed instruction provides another boost to the audio-lingual method. Language learning adapts well to this kind of massive drill, which will be a great boon in illustrating structure and fixing forms as it stamps in the correct response to the stimulus. Professor Sweet is also pioneering in this area, testing his first materials with an eighth-grade group in the Latin Workshop at the University of Michigan in the summer of 1962.

The net result of this early and advanced experimentation with structural linguistics as applied to Latin has been twofold: first, to point up the need for a sound linguistic grounding, implying formal course work in linguistics for Latin teachers; and second, to provide an awareness of timesaving devices for the student in acquiring linguistic proficiency, and of timemaking devices for the teacher in cultivating the intellectual and aesthetic in the student. Time and thoroughness are valuable assets, carrying a high premium in the race for students' talents.

The new approach has proved sufficiently successful with limited numbers

[2] John Gummere, and Annabel Horn, *Using Latin,* Scott, Foresman and Company, Chicago, 1961.

to merit widespread adoption and become part of the "new learning" represented by the new mathematics and science programs. With further subvention for the purpose of developing and circulating additional materials, of training teachers, of providing model teaching stations, for demonstration classes, supervision of instruction, team teaching, and evaluation, widespread reform could be effected which would make language learning more meaningful and serviceable.

Language, flexible and open-ended as it is, nevertheless has a form and structure, demands precision and accuracy in its use, exacts choices and requires discrimination, can be simple and direct or subtle and sophisticated, express or imply meaning, and have varied meanings in varied contexts. The way of the word and the idea of the idiom can be the key to the mind-set, explaining how people think and act. Skill and care in communication is of the utmost importance. Latin, a language stopped in time, provides the perfect model for study, unchanging but displaying change in its development as the language of a vigorous people—a live language in contrast to an artificial or synthetic language which never represented the thought process of an active people. Exempt from being contemporary, spoken, and constantly changing, Latin is present in the vocabulary of the Romance languages, English, and in neologisms. Being a "dead" language, and ideal for comparison and contrast, for observation and conclusion, it becomes the most vital language for scientific analysis and study in the present-day world. This permanently arrested state of the subject allows the scholar-teacher to mine its literature as a creative outlet for the needs and enrichment of students and society. The Latin class can and should be a natural laboratory for interdisciplinary learning as well as a resource for instilling ethics and aesthetics.

If tape recorders, language laboratories, and programmed instruction are revamping the linguistic experiences of Latin classes, the historic-cultural literary emphases have been sparked by required programs in general education in colleges, the Great Books in adult education, and the explosion of classics in paperback translations, not to mention *Winnie the Pooh* and *Ferdinand the Bull* in Latin translation, or Moses Hadas' *Florilegium* of Latin authors with Latin and English on facing pages. The use, and often the abuse, of the classical theme and motif by the lay world of entertainment and advertisement invite all to "drink from Pirene's spring" or "mount Pegasus to Parnassus." It is interesting to note that when quality is available to quantity, a stiffening and upgrading is in order to maintain standards and extend the stretch. The original must be known to understand on what the popular is based. It is interesting also that European—roughly translated "Russian"—excellence has challenged us; and when we think, talk, plan, and write about the gifted, the superior, and the talented, the "solid subjects" which dominated the original curriculum are in great demand, and the demand for great revision to guarantee more, sooner, and better is the charge placed upon these subjects.

Gains in language mastery are more easily achieved and measured than are the developing of attitudes, strengthening of ideals, assessing of values, and facing of reality which the study of literature may promote. Honors classes and the advanced placement program have been attempts to realize some of these intangibles and inexplicables that are the spirit and substance of humane learning.

How can teachers of the classics lead students to the thresholds of their own minds, kindle their imagination, fire their curiosity, generate creativity, help them to develop an intellectual and emotional independence? How can the teacher help the student develop a consciousness of style of the literary masters, realize the nobility and force, the pithiness and pungency, the poetry and pageantry of a passage? How can the student, reading the essayist, the orator, the journalist, the historian, the dramatist, the satirist, the writer of epic, ode, and elegy, become one with the reformer of 60 B.C. and the 1960s, feel the pressures and the problems, and share the fears and dreams of the creative spirit as it reflects its day and is a reflection of its times? Can the great ideas and examples to be found in the classics liberate man, help to create the positive man, the man of heroic proportions and potential, with a vision of greatness? Can study of the original in depth enable the student to piece together the history and tradition of a people that shows him how functional a nation was in having its public and private life serve its purpose and achieve its aim?

This direct, intertemporal communication has the advantage of a dispassionate, objective viewing of problems that are much the same in all ages. It enables the student to see how "facts" are established and gives a set of time-tested standards to use as a gauge in measuring the significance of the present. We have the whole Roman fabric to study, the opportunity of seeing one nation *in toto* or *in situ* which allows one to study the progression of the pattern as a nation evolves its culture. The student pondering the question of how the Roman figure emerged and developed the characteristics so conspicuously identified as Roman qualities, is easily directed in his thinking to the rise of his own nation, the meaning of Americana, and the image created and developing in the world's mind of American power and influence. This juxtaposition of civilizations should create in the student an awareness of and sensitivity to his role as a citizen of the world.

As the founding fathers of our country studied the organization of the Greek city-state and Roman law, and read the Greek and Roman historians and orators, so the leaders of the new colonies of Africa and Asia are adopting the Western way, assimilating Western culture. The Greco-Roman tradition meets itself in the enduring monuments to its early civilization on these frontiers. This penetration and wider spread of Western thought and action demands that we master its tenets in order to understand the East and Africa as their ways fuse with those of the West.

The thoughtful reading of the original that produces the kind of analysis and synthesis that makes the past eminently present and the future less fearsome suggests the socialized recitation that fosters discussion, debate, and leads to individualized and personalized reading and writing which may result in a seminar type report, a theme, a comprehensive study, an original project. It permits independent study on a self-imposed and regulated basis stimulated by the excitement of the ideas found in the text.

The motives for learning, whatever they may be—self-recognition, self-realization, the broadening of sympathies, cultural orientation, the deepening of perception, a greater acuteness of observation, additional training in problem solving, the attraction of the unknown or the unfamiliar, the gaining of a point of reference, the serious study of language and literature, or preparation for a career—any or all can be attained if the teacher is sufficiently flexible, has and can use materials, and can communicate with the class. Experience with the language must be extended long enough and high enough to coincide with the maturity of the student. Teaching of ability to control vocabulary and the elements of language should be relegated to the seventh and eighth grades. Reading materials connected with a theme, e.g., "Rome and Italy," would give geographic and archaeological orientation; this would be followed by such a theme as "Roman life and institutions," providing sociological orientation through selected readings from Latin authors in the ninth grade. Readings at the next level would be concentrated on the Romans, the heroes, their portraits and images. The curriculum of the senior high school years would include a year of prose featuring the period of the republic and its historic-economic rise and fall; this would be followed by a year of poetry, with emphasis on a carefully ordered structure and art form, and by a final year of logic and philosophy.

It is this kind of ambitious program that students living in an explosion-of-knowledge age deserve, and the 25 per cent of all students currently enrolled in foreign languages in the public high schools of the United States who are studying Latin—still the first language to be studied in this country—need to have the advantage and support of the newest thinking and planning. Every link in the academic chain must be strong to produce a genuinely intellectual élite and a generally intelligent citizenry.

A classics progress report

1. The Carnegie Corporation of New York has made a grant to Prof. Waldo Sweet of the William Penn Charter School to develop linguistic materials in summer workshops at the University of Michigan, and grants-in-aid to a select number of Latin teachers to develop and use materials in and from the workshops of 1952 and 1953.

2. A Committee on Educational Training and Trends of the American Philological Association was appointed, and surveys made and published in classical journals. There has been nationwide publicity on the value of Latin III-IV, in an effort to close the gap between Latin II in the tenth grade and college Latin and to guarantee a continuum of study for future teachers.

3. A Joint Committee of American Classical Organizations has been formed, and two subcommittees named, (1) Recruitment and Preparation of Latin Teachers, and (2) The Latin Curriculum. Extensive work has been carried on by numerous committees, the results of which, circulated and publicized, has led to the establishment of state studies, and of state- and organization-sponsored scholarships for high school students planning to continue the study of Latin in college, for teachers to travel and study in summer programs, and for work conferences.

4. The American Council of Learned Societies sponsored a monograph, *Latin in the Curriculum.*

5. The American Council of Learned Societies underwrote twenty scholarships for a Latin workshop featuring the linguistic approach, at the University of Wisconsin, for the summer of 1960.

6. The University of Michigan sponsored an advanced placement seminar in connection with its Advanced Placement Institute in the summer of 1960.

7. The Fulbright Commission awards twenty summer grants to the American Academy in Rome.

8. The American Council of Learned Societies subsidized the Workshop in Programmed Learning at the University of Michigan during the summer of 1962.

9. Educational Services, Inc., and the American Council of Learned Societies sponsored a Conference on the Humanities and the Social Sciences at Endicott House, MIT, during the summer of 1962.

10. The American Classical League and the regional Classical Associations, together with state and city organizations interested in promoting the classics, carry on projects, studies, and research within their limited framework.

Classics recommendations

The following suggestions and recommendations are put forth as offering possibilities for bringing about improvement in the teaching of classics:

1. The preparation of a course sequence and syllabuses for Latin, grades 7–12, with model lessons, units, tests, and sample tapes, pattern practices, and programmed learning materials, as a suggested Latin curriculum which teachers may follow or adapt.

2. Preparation of bibliographies, pamphlets, monographs, packets, slide tape lectures, and kits of artifacts for professional enrichment of Latin teachers and classes.

3. Installation of a Greek and Latin materials center for distribution of materials suggested in 1 and 2, above, and continuous development of new materials.

4. Installation of a national and state consultation service to establish liaison and improve articulation between the various levels of instruction: junior high, senior high, college, graduate, and professional schools, through intervisitations, demonstration and supervision, newsletters, and conferences.

5. Extension of scholarship assistance for recruiting, training, and retraining of teachers through (1) apprenticeships, (2) institutes, (3) in-service seminars, (4) summer seminars and workshops, and (5) study-travel programs abroad at Classical sites.

6. Establishment of a summer school program for high school students in Advanced Latin and Greek.

Establishment of a summer program for high school students in archaeology in cooperation with the Extra-Mural Program in Archaeology of the University of Birmingham, England.

7. Establishment of an inter-disciplinary council: mathematics, science, English, foreign languages, social sciences, fine arts, and psychology to feed ideas for and report programs, projects, research to the teaching profession

and the lay public; to develop team teaching approaches to learning and educational problems.

8. Establishment of an intereducation council with representatives from school administration, guidance, curriculum, supervision, PTA, school boards, citizens commissions, and education study groups of organizations (e.g., American Association of University Women, League of Women Voters, etc.) as an interaction group interested in experimentation, interpretation, and evaluation of learning in subject-matter areas.

9. Establishment of an educational resources council: libraries, museums, businesses, and industries to develop and make available speakers, displays, field trips, traveling exhibits, inexpensive reproductions and replicas, and special services to the classroom teacher.

10. A cross-fertilization of the interest groups represented in 7, 8, and 9 through an annual forum, digest, or whatever medium that could produce representation and coverage at the local, state, regional, and national levels: a built-in sounding and resounding board for curriculum experimentation and educational progress.

References*

1 American Philological Association, Committee of Educational Training and Trends, *Teaching Latin and Greek: New Approaches.*
2 H. O. Ault, "The Oral-Aural Approach to Caesar," *Classical Journal,* May, 1948.
3 D. Desberg, "Structural Linguistics and High School Language Teaching," *Classical Outlook,* November, 1959.
4 M. Fowler, "The Historical-Comparative Method," *Classical Journal,* March, 1957.
5 C. C. Fries, "Structural Linguistics and Language Teaching," *Classical Journal,* March, 1957.
6 John Gummere, "Latin Grammar in Proper Perspective," *Classical Journal,* October, 1949.
7 E. Huzar, "Structural Linguistics and Latin," *Classical Journal,* March, 1957.
8 Incorporated Association of Assistant Masters in Secondary Schools, *The Teaching of Classics,* Cambridge University Press, London, 1961.
9 Van Johnson, "Latin Is More than Linguistics," *Classical Journal,* vol. 53, 1957.
10 T. P. Klammer, "The Comprehensive Approach," *Classical Journal,* May, 1959.
11 R. Lado, *Linguistics across Culture; Applied Linguistics for Language Teachers,* The University of Michigan Press, Ann Arbor, Mich., 1957.
12 H. L. Levy, "Disciplina Mores Facit," *Classical Journal,* vol. 55, 1959.
13 Departments of Foreign Languages, University of Michigan, "Programmed Learning in Latin," *The Foreign Language Courier,* no. 27, June, 1961.
14 University of Michigan, *Tentative Advanced Placement Program in Latin,* Advanced Placement Latin Institute and Seminar, 1960.
15 *Working Reports of the Northeast Conference on the Teaching of Foreign*

* The list represents a selection of titles, mainly from periodicals, which reflect the new thinking about the linguistic approach to the teaching of Latin, which has attracted a limited amount of attention and support from the foundations. References to the literary and cultural objectives of the study and teaching of the classics are conspicuously missing from this list.

Languages, 1955, 1956, 1957, 1958, 1959, 1960, 1962. (Available from Service Bureau of American Classical League, Miami University, Oxford, Ohio.)
16 L. R. Palmer, *The Latin Language,* Faber & Faber, Ltd., London, 1954.
17 J. F. Reilly, "Latin Language Laboratories," *Classical Outlook,* May, 1959.
18 G. Seligson, "General Meaning and Its Place in Syntax," *Classical Outlook,* November, 1959.
19 W. E. Sweet, "The Carrot on the Stick," *Language Learning,* vol. 9, 1959.
20 W. E. Sweet, "Latin without a Dictionary," *Classical Outlook,* December, 1950.
21 W. E. Sweet, *Latin: A Structural Approach,* The University of Michigan Press, Ann Arbor, Mich., 1957.
22 W. E. Sweet, *Latin Workshop Experimental Materials, Book I,* The University of Michigan Press, Ann Arbor, Mich., 1953.
23 W. E. Sweet, *Latin Workshop Experimental Materials, Book II,* rev. ed., The University of Michigan Press, Ann Arbor, Mich., 1957.
24 W. E. Sweet, *Vergil's Aeneid: A Structural Approach,* vol. 1, The University of Michigan Press, Ann Arbor, Mich., 1960.
25 W. E. Sweet, *Clozes and Vocabulary Exercises for Books I–II of the Aeneid,* The University of Michigan Press, Ann Arbor, Mich., 1961.
26 M. H. Wampler, "The Old and the New," *Classical Outlook,* January, 1960.
27 R. L. Ward, "Evidence for the Pronunciation of Latin," *Classical World,* vol. 55, March and May, 1962.
28 "Classics in American Secondary Schools: A Survey," *Classical World,* vol. 55, April and May, 1962.

8 ❀ WANTED: BREAKTHROUGH FOR BETTER SOCIAL STUDIES INSTRUCTION
John H. Haefner* *State University of Iowa*

There is certainly no need to remind you that the events of October 4, 1957, had profound and far-reaching effects on superintendents, schools, teachers, curricula, and every other aspect of American public education. To be sure, a great deal of interest was exhibited in what the schools were doing throughout the late 1940s and the early 1950s. But the criticism, the charges, the condemnation of our educational system reached a new crescendo as Sputnik orbited the earth. It is not really surprising that we Americans made the schools the scapegoats when confronted with a situation in which we had lost face and prestige. For, historically, education has always been America's panacea.

It is not my intention to review this criticism of the schools. There were charges and countercharges; there was name-calling and backbiting. But there was also honest and sympathetic concern for the jobs the schools were doing and had to do. Out of all this controversy there gradually emerged a common denominator: thoughtful Americans who cared were concerned with excellence in our schools.

* John H. Haefner is Professor of Social Studies Education at the State University of Iowa.

But what does excellence in education mean? And how can excellence in education be achieved? There seem to be as many answers to these questions as there are people who speak or write about them.

The August 28, 1961, issue of *U.S. News and World Report* records one such answer from an impressive source. That issue contains a report of an interview with Sterling M. McMurrin, U.S. Commissioner of Education, entitled "The Real Weakness in American Schools." It is not entirely fair to take a single question and answer out of the context of the complete interview, but the nubbin of the recorded conversation is contained in the following:

Q. *Are you saying that the quality of teachers is the basic weakness in our schools?*

A. *I think it is most important—the kind of person we get for teaching, and the kind of education he has, is the No. 1 problem in American education.* [p. 58]

What Mr. McMurrin said, I think is true—but only half true. He was looking at only one face of the coin of excellence in education.

It is the purpose of this National Conference on Curriculum Experimentation, as I understand it, to examine various facets of the problem of making good American schools even better. There will be reports of progress already being made, summaries of promising projects under way, and proposals for action leading to better school practices and better education for American boys and girls. Our central concern is with a more excellent total curriculum—in physics, mathematics, earth science, biological science, modern languages, classics, as well as with the social studies and humanities.

What of the social studies and social studies instruction? Unfortunately—at least from my confined point of view—the present climate of opinion is not one of great friendliness to the humanities and social sciences. In part, this unfriendliness and unconcern appears to be a manifestation of the tremendous lag between our knowledge of physical science and technology and our somewhat terrifying lack of knowledge of the social and behavioral sciences and humanities. This factor impresses me so strongly because it has immense implications for any thinking we do about the curriculum. None of the basic problems confronting us today, at least none that I can think of, are soluble solely through the application of science and technology. The population explosion and the problem of nuclear disarmament are only two illustrations. The means for limiting the birth rate are relatively well known, but the human factor restricts the application of the known means for solving the problem. By the same token, it is *not* the lack of scientific know-how which is preventing nuclear disarmament, but rather the human equation. Indeed, there are times when it appears almost to be true that as technology advances, man's inability to live with man increases in equal or even greater proportion. Perhaps this has always been the world's number one problem, but today it is the key to survival. Perhaps it is only natural, as we face up to the overpowering problems of the present, that we should place our emphasis and pin our hopes on the development of the cumulative areas of knowledge—notably the sciences and mathematics—rather than on the noncumulative areas of history, literature, the arts, and the social sciences.

But what is expedient is not always wise or judicious. It seems neither wise nor judicious that in the area of social studies instruction there simply are no plans or projects, that I am aware of, which are comparable to those in physics, chemistry, mathematics, biology, or foreign languages. At the very best, I can only point to the Joint Project of the American Council of Learned Societies and the National Council for the Social Studies (5). In this instance, scholars from the various disciplines have drafted preliminary working papers outlining the minimum essentials of the content of their fields which need to be taught. Knowledgeable educators have formulated the purposes and objectives of social studies instruction in American public schools. Here, for the moment, the project rests, primarily because the financial support necessary to push beyond this modest beginning has not, as yet, been forthcoming.

To be sure, individual schools and school systems across the country are engaged in curriculum revision and various experiments, some of them exciting and imaginative (1, 2). But these are sometimes sporadic, often isolated, and cannot, I think, provide the all-out thrust needed for a breakthrough to nationwide excellence in social studies instruction.

The time has come, I believe, when those of us concerned with excellence in American schools need to unite our efforts and work for the establishment of a nongovernmental national commission for curriculum research and development. For the past two years, following a conference held at the Center for Advanced Study in the Behavioral Sciences in 1959 (3), Professor Paul Hanna of Stanford has, with great vigor, competency, and cogency, carried his plea for such a commission to the nation via professional journals and the public platform. You are all familiar, I am sure, with his argument and his plan. I propose that this conference focus a portion of its discussion time on this problem and seek ways for getting action on it under way. Although he was referring to a different matter, the need for common action has never been expressed more succinctly than when Benjamin Franklin remarked, nearly two centuries ago: "We must all hang together in this thing, or we shall hang separately."

But what, specifically, could be done to improve the social studies curriculum and social studies instruction? Where, for example, might the social studies division of the proposed national commission for curriculum research and development start its task?

The problems involved in the rehabilitation of social studies instruction are varied and complex, and a mere enumeration of them would be dull and unproductive. I have therefore sought for the smallest number of changes which hold promise of starting us on our way to revitalized social studies instruction. I fear that these are not new, nor startling, nor dramatic. Others before me have advocated them. My comments are really those of an old worker in the vineyard, distilling his thoughts concerning what is desirable, needed, and feasible if a breakthrough in social education is to occur.

Task number one, it appears to me, is to take an inventory of the manpower available for more effective curricular revision and teaching, and to relocate these teachers where they belong—in the social studies classroom. To many of you representing different areas of the curriculum, this suggestion must sound at least slightly absurd. My contention is that there are more reasonably well-trained social studies teachers available than we think, but that many of them are assigned to classes outside their field of interest and competency. Conversely, I believe that no other area of the curriculum is so cursed with the problem of classes taught by teachers who are ill-prepared and largely disinterested in the academic area in which they are teaching. This problem is certainly not confined to the social studies, but it appears to be more virulent and deleterious there than anywhere else.

In a study of our graduates who entered teaching, we found that only 30 per cent of the social studies majors were assigned classes exclusively in their major field. Five per cent taught *entirely outside* both their major and minor fields, and ten per cent taught only in their minor and in outside fields. This study did not reveal the number of social studies classes being taught by teachers for whom the social sciences were at best a minor, and at worst, an outside field. Another and more recent study, however, revealed that approximately one-fourth of the economics classes offered in Iowa high schools were being taught by teachers who had had no college course of any kind in economics.

I am sure that there are places, perhaps a good many of them, where this situation is not as serious as it is in my own state. But I think it would be fallacious to assume that Iowa alone has the problem. Nationwide, it is sufficiently serious, I believe, so that we must start from the premise that genuine curriculum revision in social studies cannot and will not occur until there is a better allocation of the trained manpower already available and at work in the schools. It is a truism that a teacher will teach best that which he knows and loves best. It is also true that a teacher is most unlikely to demonstrate any initiative in curricular revision and experimentation in a field in which he has not been trained and for which he feels little, if any, scholarly affection.

This problem is far from insoluble. There is action which can be taken. Studies can be made to determine its real status and extent. A valuable by-product would be the identification of teachers adequately prepared, and interested in developing and teaching classes for the academically able. A campaign can be directed at superintendents and principals to improve their teacher assignment practices. Ways can be devised for working with associations of school board members, with school boards directly, and with other interested lay groups in finding ways and means by which a given school can be easily and regularly evaluated on the quality of teacher assignment. Accrediting agencies such as the North Central Association can be urged to pay closer attention to this problem. It is not enough that accrediting agencies verify the technical qualifications of teachers to teach the courses they have been assigned to teach. The problem cannot be solved merely by increasing the requirements for a teaching minor. We must take the next and more difficult step of inquiring whether or not teachers are properly assigned to classes for which they are best suited both in interest and preparation.

I have chosen this matter of teacher assignment as task number one because a solution for it must be found before we can hope for much progress on task number two.

The second prerequisite for progress in the social studies is that we must find a valid *cohesive principle* for our instruction. At the turn of the century we sought this by creating courses which we called "the new history" and "the new civics." We have sought it since in new forms of curricular organization—common learning, general education, fusion, integration, core curriculum, and social living. We have sought it through new methods of organizing and presenting subject matter materials: the "source method" the topical method, the unit method, the problem-solving approach. While most, or all, of these have contributed in greater or lesser degree to better instruction, none has provided the cohesive principle for social studies instruction which now appears imperative.

For purposes of discussion, I propose that the cohesive principle we seek is this: that, through the content of the social sciences, we attempt to develop in all boys and girls, to the limit of their individual capacities, those intellectual skills and abilities which are requisite to carrying on reflective thought and which underlie informed action.

This idea is certainly not original with me, nor are these abilities the exclusive domain of the social studies. Our failure lies in the fact that we have not viewed these abilities as the primary purpose of social studies instruction, but have contented ourselves with formulating objectives so vague, so fuzzy, and so ethereal that they are of little use in shaping instruction or helping to determine what shall be taught. In this unifying principle, with this focus on the development of the abilities needed for reflective thinking, we would have at hand a tool for setting goals of instruction which are significant, vital, and achievable.

There are several reasons why I believe this cohesive principle will make for progress toward a better social studies curriculum and better instruction. In the first place, it promises the greatest possible contribution to the individual in the unstable and unpredictable world in which he must live in the second half of the twentieth century. Nowhere has this point been made more persuasively than in the significant volume entitled *Taxonomy of Educational Objectives,* edited by Benjamin S. Bloom (4):

Whatever the case in the past, it is very clear that in the middle of the 20th century we find ourselves in a rapidly changing and unpredictable culture. It seems almost impossible to foresee the particular ways in which it will change in the near future or the particular problems which will be be paramount in five or ten years. Under these conditions, much emphasis must be placed in the schools on the development of generalized ways of attacking problems and on knowledge which can be applied to a wide range of new situations. That is, we have the task of preparing individuals for problems that cannot be foreseen in advance, and about all that can be done under such conditions is to help the student acquire generalized intellectual abilities and skills which will serve him well in many new situations. This places faith in the intellectual virtues as providing some form of stability for the individual who must find or make some order in his world. [p. 40]

In the second place, this focus places the mastery of facts and the command of substantive knowledge in the social sciences in their proper context. These intellectual abilities can be developed only through substantive content materials and learning experiences. Most, if not all, of these skills are intimately involved in the methods of inquiry employed by social scientists. A major limitation of present instruction lies in the fact that insufficient effort has been made to give students an understanding of how the social science scholar works. Perhaps most important, the worth and significance of the substantive content can be demonstrated to students through their improved mastery of these intellectual abilities. Perhaps no aspect has frustrated teachers more than the fact that so many of their students have failed to see any real point to history and the social studies, and consequently have remained disinterested and apathetic. The possibility of demonstrating to students their growth in concrete, highly specific, and immensely useful abilities should improve motivation for learning in a way which present courses do not.

In the third place, I think that when we begin to experiment with the development of specific skills of reflective thought as the focus of the curriculum, we are likely to find that success will not be dependent on a single educational philosophy, a singular approach to curricular organization, or a single pedagogical method or device. I feel confident that we shall find that this focus will succeed and can be utilized in curricula organized on the basis of separate subject-matter courses as well as in core curriculum classes. While there is some inconclusive evidence that the problem-solving approach to organizing learning materials facilitates the development of these abilities, there is also every reason to believe that they can be developed by means of other approaches. Our lack of reliable data in this matter underscores the need for large-scale research and experimentation.

In the fourth place, enough spade work has already been done to give some assurance that we are not looking down an empty hole. Probably no single individual has been more influential in pointing the way than Prof. Ralph Tyler, Executive Director of the Center for Advanced Study in the Behavioral Sciences at Stanford. *The Taxonomy of Educational Objectives,* though not completed, provides an immensely useful tool for further experimentation and research. Studies at various institutions throughout the country, as well as experiments by individual classroom teachers, are beginning to turn up important pieces of information. At least tentatively, it seems fair to conclude that intellectual abilities related to reflective thought can be identified with considerable specificity, that they can be taught and they can be learned, that most of them can be measured, that significantly better results are obtained when the development of them becomes the *focus* of instruction rather than a hoped-for by-product, that the development of these abilities need not entail a sacrifice of subject-matter mastery, and that these abilities are not limited to the intellectually superior even though the degree and sophistication of mastery varies widely. With these findings as a base, what is needed now is a full-power thrust to extend and refine our research and to make possible widespread experimentation and dissemination of the findings.

Finally, the cohesive principle of concentrating on the development of definable intellectual abilities provides the most promising criterion for one of the most difficult problems confronting curriculum revision in the social studies, namely the matter of omission and selection. The crucial questions are "What must be taught?" and "What must, perforce, be omitted?" To date we have no common standard to which both scholars and educators can adhere. Much of the most virulent and debilitating controversy of the past decade, I believe, has had its origin in this fact. It is my conviction that such a yardstick is now at hand.

It is not at all difficult to suggest some courses of action which could be started, once the organization and the means are provided. Here are only six possibilities:

1. *The Taxonomy of Educational Objectives* should be further refined and completed.

2. The personnel of the social sciences and the behavioral disciplines should be mobilized to concentrate on the problem of identifying the abilities particularly germane to their areas of concentration and to provide content materials and organization which will implement these abilities.

3. We need to draft a competent body of scholars, curriculum specialists, and teachers to produce learning materials which focus on these abilities.

4. We need to borrow the most successful of the techniques already developed in the fields of physics and biology to provide in-service opportunities, so that teachers can become familiar with these new materials and their use.

5. Active cooperation should be undertaken with the leading publishing companies, to encourage them to engage in producing more creative and experimental textual materials.

6. We require a clearing house to coordinate and encourage research dealing with various facets of this problem, and most particularly, perhaps, with the matter of retention and application.

There is no doubt in my mind that, once we were started, there would be no want of meaningful projects which might—and should—be undertaken.

In this paper I have besought your attention to three matters which I consider crucial. Perhaps it would be more accurate to say I have made three pleas. They are, first, that we unite professionally for purposes of curricular revision, to make certain that balanced attention is paid to all aspects of the curriculum. At this moment, the establishment of a nongovernmental national commission for curriculum research seems the most feasible solution.

Second, so far as the social studies are concerned, we need a manpower inventory, and we need to reallocate our teaching resources.

Finally, we need, urgently, to find a cohesive principle for the social studies—an overriding objective to which both scholars and teachers can adhere. We need to deprive ourselves of the luxury of formulating our aims in terms which are so ethereal as to be ludicrous and so vague that they can neither guide instruction nor be measured.

However much you may take exception to my proposals and my logic, in whole or in part, on one matter I am confident that we are not at odds: Curricular revision and experimentation is urgent, and it is already later than we think.

In spring, 1963, the U.S. Office of Education initiated Project Social Studies. The following grants were made in 1963 under this program:

Carnegie Institute of Technology: A high school social studies curriculum for able students. Duration: 4 years, 7 months. Federal costs: $250,000. Director: Edwin Senton.

University of Minnesota: Preparation and evaluation of social studies curriculum guides and materials for grades K-14. Duration 4 years, 2 months. Federal costs: $221,150. Director: Edith West.

Syracuse University: Identification of major social science concepts and their utilization in instructional materials. Duration: 5 years. Federal costs: $249,555. Director: Roy A. Price.

Harvard University: A law and social science curriculum based on the analysis of public issues. Duration: 5 years. Federal costs: $250,450. Director: Donald Oliver.

References

1 Harold M. Long, Program for Improving the Teaching of World Affairs, Glens Falls High School, Glens Falls, New York.
2 H. David Van Dyck, "Improving the Teaching of World Affairs," *New York State Education,* June, 1959.
3 Ralph W. Tyler, "A Conference Report," *The Clearing House, a Journal for Modern Junior and Senior High Schools,* vol. 34, no. 3, pp. 141–148, November, 1959. Report of the Conference on Policies and Strategy for Strengthening the Curriculum of the American Public Schools, (reprinted in part as Supplement 6, this volume).
4 B. S. Bloom, (ed.), *Taxonomy of Educational Objectives,* David McKay Co., Inc., New York, 1956.
5 Merrill F. Hartshorn, Joint Project for the National Council for the Social Studies and the American Council of Learned Societies, National Council for the Social Studies, Washington, D.C.

9 ❈ THE NEW MATHEMATICS PROGRAMS*
Edwin Moise** *Harvard University*

One of the handicaps of school mathematics in our generation has been the

* Reprinted from *The School Review,* vol. 70, no. 1, pp. 82–101, The University of Chicago Press, Chicago, Spring, 1962, with permission.
** Edwin Moise is the James Bryant Conant Professor of Education and Mathematics at Harvard University.

gulf between the professional mathematicians and the schools. Another has been a general lack of sympathy for mathematics in the popular culture. Not long ago, and perhaps even now, there were some circles in which mathematics was regarded as an activity which might be all right for certain eccentric and spiritless adults, but which surely ought not to be inflicted on helpless children.

In the last few years, for reasons that are not entirely clear, both of these tendencies have been reversed; and one result of the changes has been a remarkable development of new programs. Most of these have been developed by collaborations between professional mathematicians and professional school teachers; and they have gotten—from schools, teachers, and students—a more favorable reception than most of us dared to hope for.

In this article, I shall try to explain the spirit and the meaning of these developments, as I understand them. For two reasons, I ask the reader's patience.

First, of all the sciences, mathematics is notoriously the least intelligible to non-specialists. Nevertheless, it would make no sense at all to try to discuss changes in curriculum and methodology without giving concrete mathematical illustrations of what these changes mean.

Second, the sheer volume of new programs and experimental text materials is by now overwhelming. The publications of the School Mathematics Study Group (SMSG) now fill over three linear feet on a bookshelf high enough to hold them in a vertical position; the productions of the University of Illinois Committee on School Mathematics (UICSM) are quantitatively less, but still impressive; and if we add those of the Maryland group, the Ball State group, and others, it is plain that a full critical survey of this literature would require a book rather than an article. The most that I shall try to do here is to describe the leading features of the programs that seem to me to be the most important and to explain the ideas that underlie them.

In 1955 the College Entrance Examination Board set up a Commission on Mathematics to study the problem of the curriculum in Grades 9 through 12 and recommend reforms. It may seem a little strange for such an initiative to be taken by an organization whose primary function is to design and administer examinations. But in its context, this initiative was natural. Any agency that writes examinations influences the curriculum, whether it wants to or not; and the board was quite rightly afraid that it was freezing the mathematics curriculum at a time when changes were needed. It therefore sought the advice of the mathematical world. In fact, the commission was rather large and rather broadly representative, both of the universities and of the schools.

The commission's report appeared in 1958. The basic thesis of the report was that high-school courses needed to be recast to bring them into harmony with the methods and spirit of modern mathematics. This idea is fundamental in all the new programs. Later, we shall examine how the idea applies to the presentation of particular topics. We should, however, understand at the outset what it does not mean: it does not mean that recently discovered theorems should be taught early and often. In fact, the program recommended by the commission did not include, in Grades 9 through 11, a single topic that was not well understood in the year 1800. (It is true that the idea of a set, or collection of objects, was to be presented in the ninth grade; but this idea is not new, in mathematics or even in common speech.) As far as I know, none of the new programs in the United States includes such topics before the twelfth grade. This does not convict anyone of being unmodern. The point, rather, is that mathematics, uniquely among the sciences, does not fall into fundamental errors; much of the best mathematics that we have has been with us for a long time; and we should not be surprised if rather old material turns out to be adequate and suitable for the first three years of high school.

On the other hand, mathematics is constantly being reformulated; its language and its conceptual apparatus change faster and faster as time goes on; some ideas and methods lapse into relative insignificance, while others move into central roles. For example, the value of Horner's method (for the numerical solution of algebraic equations) has by now sunk to absolute zero; everything that can be done with it can be done better without it. Meanwhile, the idea of a set, which was hardly made explicit by the mathematicians of Horner's generation, has become part of the basic apparatus, even at the most elementary level.

The commission's purely curricular recommendations are far easier to summarize. Following is an outline of their outline:

Ninth grade. An introduction to algebra, as far as quadratic equations with real roots. Novelties: the idea of a set (at the start of the course); a proof that 2 has no rational square root; descriptive statistics (optional); numerical trigonometry of the right triangle (optional).

Tenth grade. Introduction to geometry, including plane and solid synthetic geometry and a short introduction to coordinate geometry. Coordinate systems are introduced somewhat after the middle of the introduction to plane synthetic geometry; and the unit on solid geometry appears at the end.

Eleventh grade. This is a course in algebra, analytic geometry, and trigonometry. The main topics are basic properties of the real number system; linear functions; radicals; quadratic functions; quadratic equations, in the general case, allowing complex roots; systems of two or three linear equations in two or three unknowns; exponents and logarithms; arithmetic and geometric series, including infinite geometric series; subfields of the real and complex number systems; plane vectors; coordinate trigonometry, using vectors; trigonometric formulas, including addition formulas and the laws of sines and cosines; complex numbers in polar form.

Twelfth grade, first semester. This was to be a course in "elementary functions." Main topics: sets and combinations; permutations; mathematical induction; functions and relations; polynomial functions; solution of polynomial equations; exponential and logarithmic functions; trigonometric functions; the inverse sine and tangent.

For the second semester of the twelfth grade, the commission proposed two possible courses: introductory probability with statistical applications or an introduction to modern algebra. For the first of these courses, the commission published a book, entitled *Introductory Probability and Statistical Inference* (1). As a text, this book is very original and is remarkable in many ways. The technical mathematical apparatus is held to a minimum, as it would have to be at this level. But the probabilistic and statistical concepts are presented in a quite modern and rather abstract form. A television course of this type taught by Frederick Mosteller in the spring of 1961 on "Continental Classroom" was very well received. A new textbook to accompany the course has been written by Mosteller, Rourke, and Thomas (2).

The proposed course[1] in modern algebra dealt with groups, rings and fields, including permutation groups. It presents a treatment of the real number system considered as an ordered field in which every bounded set has a least upper bound.

The differences between this scheme and the old curriculum are rather striking. Solid geometry, which commonly has a semester to itself in the twelfth grade, now appears merely as a unit at the end of the tenth grade. Trigonometry has disappeared as a separate course. Algebra appears as a branch of mathematics, dealing with the properties of various number systems, rather than a collection of manipulative tricks. There is a similar reform in the treatment of trigonometry, stressing the kind of trigonometry that is going to get used in later studies and omitting the long and almost useless calculations that used to appear as the grand climax of the twelfth-grade trigonometry course. In the same spirit, the twelfth-grade course includes material on the functions that are going to be studied in calculus.

A student who finishes the first three and a half years of this program is amply prepared to start his college work with analytic geometry and calculus. In fact, many schools teach calculus in the twelfth grade; and the experience of the last few years shows that this is quite workable, if qualified teachers are available. But the *if* is important. High-school calculus courses have become status symbols, pursued, in some cases, without proper regard to staff resources. It is fortunate that the commission avoided accelerating the latter trend by recommending calculus in twelfth grade as an immediate national objective.

The commission's program is radical in some ways and conservative in others. Probably the most imaginative of the commission's contributions was the twelfth-grade probability course, and the least imaginative was the tenth-grade course, which was formed by fitting together portions of existing conventional programs, with innovations and improvements merely in matters of detail. Many people, including the author, dissent from a number of the commission's judgments, both philosophical and curricular. But there would be small profit in discussing these dissents here. The commission was not writing, or trying to write, a bible. They asked that their program be regarded as a "point of departure." Thus, their report is the sort of document which, if successful, is superseded by events; and one measure of the commission's success is the fact that their report has been superseded in this way.

We have already pointed out that the commission's policy on twelfth-grade calculus was a response to practical considerations governing the near future. The same considerations applied, in less simple ways, to their program as a whole. Their program was designed to be feasible in this decade;

[1] As far as I know, this course has never been written up.

and it was supposed to require only the sort of additional teacher-training which in practice is available. Fortunately, such additional training is now available on a fairly large scale, in summer institutes and academic-year institutes sponsored by the National Science Foundation. The importance of these institutes can hardly be overestimated. Without them, the sort of reforms that we have been discussing could proceed only at a small fraction of their present pace.

Even this advantage, however, would not have been enough. In practice, high-school courses—and for that matter, most college courses—are taught out of books; and the commission's ideas were not carried out, even approximately, in the textbooks that were available. It is even doubtful whether the feasibility of a really new program can be judged until books have been written for it. It is well known that almost any course works well in the classroom if it is taught by its inventors or by a few of their highly trained converts. This principle helps to account for the fact that so many enthusiastic innovators have fired shots heard round the immediate vicinity. To get a valid test of feasibility, you must turn over the program to teachers who are a fair sample of the people who would be teaching it if it were adopted on the scale for which it is intended. For these reasons—either of which would have been compelling—the natural next step was the production of experimental textbooks.

The School Mathematics Study Group started its work at Yale University in the summer of 1958, under a grant from the National Science Foundation. The director is E. G. Begle, formerly of Yale and now at Stanford University. At the start, the total writing team included some forty people, about half being from the schools and the other half from the universities. This arrangement reflected a policy that has been fundamental in the School Mathematics Study Group ever since: all its work has been carried out in collaboration between mathematicians and experienced classroom teachers; and this policy is now formally stated in its bylaws.

The exact relation between the School Mathematics Study Group and the commission is not easy to determine. It was agreed, at the first writing session at Yale, that the commission's program would form a provisional outline. The immediate purpose of this arrangement was to permit a division-of-labor scheme, with one writing group for each of the four high-school grades. But surely this scheme would not have been used if the group as a whole had not been in general sympathy with the commission's program. Within the limits of its assigned grade, each writing team made its own policies. (There was, of course, enough consultation between the teams to avoid serious duplications and incongruities.) The members of each group, moreover, were not selected for their adherence to particular viewpoints. At the outset, disagreements were extensive, and the discussions were vigorous and prolonged. As a member of the tenth-grade team, I can testify that the 1958 session was educational in a number of ways; everybody in the room was teaching everybody else, by the Socratic method; and this process took so long that after four weeks we had arrived only at a course outline and a few pages of sample text. It seems, in retrospect, that one of the main results of our first session was a common understanding that formed the basis of the rest of our work.

In the summer of 1959 all four of the groups met again at the University of Colorado, with many recruits, and finished four textbooks. Each of these was tried out at about seventy experimental centers throughout the country. Consultants were available to help the teachers, but the teachers had no special training to prepare them for the job (except, of course, those few who had participated in the writing project). In fact, they had not even seen the books until the week before the opening of school. On the basis of these reports, all the books were revised at a writing session at Stanford in the summer of 1960 and were put on the market for use in the academic year 1960–61.

The response of the schools was favorable beyond all expectations. At first, about fifty thousand copies were ordered from the printer; after a few weeks, the order was doubled; and a few weeks later it was plain that this was still not enough. In 1961–62, the total circulation of these books approximately tripled. This was especially significant in the light of the fact that none of them had been adopted in any state. Thus every SMSG book that was ordered for school use had to be paid for in some awkward fashion.

In addition to its high-school work, the SMSG has also produced books for use in the elementary schools. The problems involved here are rather peculiar. Just as a student who can ever learn calculus can learn it in the twelfth grade, so a student who can ever learn algebra can learn it in the eighth grade or the seventh. But in most schools, it is not practical simply to move high-school courses downward. Few teachers are trained to handle them. Moreover, a large proportion of elementary-school pupils are headed for courses in "general mathematics" rather than ninth-grade algebra courses; and such students need frequent fresh starts. For these reasons, much of the new elementary-school writing is in the form of short units, largely independent of one another. The need for new programs in the seventh and eighth grades is especially acute. By this time, an able student has learned all the arithmetic that he needs to know; and marking time for two years is not only wasteful but demoralizing. It is a sad fact that most of the mathematics that gets taught at this level is disliked for the excellent reason that it deserves to be disliked.

Some of the most novel and most interesting of the new text materials are designed for use in the early grades. I mention these briefly, because I am not qualified to discuss them fully. It is obvious, however, even from a distance, that young children can learn much more and much better mathematics than is ordinarily taught to them. The possibilities shown by some of the recent experimental teaching in the early grades are a great challenge both to course design and to teacher education.

In addition to publishing textbooks for students, the SMSG has published a rather large amount of material for the use of teachers. The manuals accompanying the textbooks go much further than is customary in discussing the mathematical backgrounds of courses. Some of them include short essays on various related topics. The SMSG has published a series of separate books, including several new ones, some reprints, and one translation from the Russian. It has also promoted the preparation of a series of mathematical monographs intended for independent reading by superior high-school students. Recently it has begun a study of the possibilities of programmed instruction in its own courses.

All this work has been remarkable, not merely for its quality and its variety, but for the speed with which it has been carried out. The starting point, we recall, was June of 1958.

The SMSG is now beginning a different sort of work. Its "crash program" is finished; and it is expected that its high-school books will be withdrawn from circulation in another two or three years, when similar books become available through commercial publishers. From now on, the main job of the SMSG will be long-range experimentation with courses and programs that are not necessarily suitable for wide use in the near future.

In the discussion of federal aid to schools, warnings have been given about undesirable side effects, notably the possibility of federal interference with the traditional state and local control. In the case of the SMSG, this danger seems remote: its work has consisted in the development of programs that various school systems can adopt if they want to. The influence of the organization has of course been great, but it has worked by example and by positive contributions rather than by any attempt to exercise authority. It would be easy to name individual authors who have exerted a similar influence on the teaching of college calculus by making the sort of positive contributions that the SMSG has made.

Obviously the volume and speed of the SMSG's work have been in some ways wasteful. One wag has suggested that its whole style of operation is based on a misinterpretation of a "word problem" in algebra: "If one man can do a job in three years, how many men does it take to do the same job in half an hour?" It would be fairer, however, to say that the style of the SMSG's work has been based on the idea that the teaching of school mathematics is so large and expensive an enterprise that if you save even a single year in making an improvement, you have justified a large budget.

The shift in choice and order of topics is by no means the most important aspect of the new programs; it is merely the easiest to explain. To see the sort of issue that is involved in the reform of ninth-grade algebra, let us start with a simple example.

Most teachers of college Freshmen fight an annual war against the supposed algebraic identity

$$\sqrt{x^2} = x.$$

Annually, thousands of students arrive on college campuses with the firm conviction that this formula is a universal law of nature. They have seen it as a displayed formula in textbooks. Some books enclose it in boxes. And sometimes it appears in color.

In fact, the formula is about as valid as the statement that on a checkerboard all the squares are red. We recall that if y is positive, then $\sqrt{y}$ denotes the positive number whose square is y. Thus $\sqrt{4} = 2$, $\sqrt{64} = 8$, and so on. If we want to describe the negative number whose square is y, we write $-\sqrt{y}$. Thus every positive number y has two square roots: $\sqrt{y}$ (which is positive) and $-\sqrt{y}$ (which is the corresponding negative number). Of course, $\sqrt{0} = 0$.

79 | *The new mathematics programs*

Thus, if you substitute 2 for x, in the above displayed formula, you get
$$\sqrt{2^2} = 2,$$
which means that
$$\sqrt{4} = 2.$$
This statement is true. But if you substitute -2 for x, in the supposed universal law, you get
$$\sqrt{(-2)^2} = -2,$$
which means that
$$\sqrt{4} = -2$$
or
$$2 = -2,$$
which is surely false. In fact, the formula
$$\sqrt{x^2} = x$$
is right about half of the time: it is true when x is positive or zero, and false when x is negative. Hence our analogy of the all-red checkerboard. The correct formula is
$$\sqrt{x^2} = |x|.$$
Here $|x|$ is defined by two conditions:
If x is positive, then $|x|$ is x.
If x is negative, then $|x|$ is the corresponding positive number. (Thus $|2| = 2$ and $|-2| = 2$.)

If this seems an overabstract fine point, the reader should bear in mind that it is never practical—for mathematicians, physicists, engineers, or anybody else—to get the wrong answer. Some years ago, there was a sad case in which an engineer's Master's degree was delayed for a year because he was unable to get his experiments to agree with his theoretical predictions. The trouble with his "theory" was that he thought that the formula
$$\sqrt{1 - \sin^2 x} = \cos x$$
was a trigonometric identity. This is merely an elaboration of the error that we have just been discussing: the correct formula is
$$\sqrt{1 - \sin^2 x} = |\cos x|.$$

It may seem a simple matter to correct such errors. But to many of us who have struggled with them, such trifles as this seem like the tip of a dragon's tail, sticking up out of the sand: they are small symptoms of a large problem. When I have pointed out to college Freshmen that the supposed identity $\sqrt{x^2} = x$ is false for $x = -2$, repeatedly I have gotten the impression that the students felt that they were being tricked. They seemed to think that I had changed the subject from algebra to arithmetic; arithmetic deals with particular numbers (like 2 and -2), while algebra deals with "general num-

Current problems in various fields | 80

bers" like x, y, and so on. Perhaps the equation $\sqrt{x^2} = x$ fails for certain particular numbers, such as -2 and -3, but it holds for "general numbers," such as x and y.

Now these ideas are, in a literal sense, nonsense. There is no such thing as a general number; and the idea suggested by the phrase is incapable of rehabilitation. Expressions such as

$$\sqrt{x^2} = x$$

or

$$x^2 + 5x + 6 = 0$$

are not statements about general numbers. In fact, they are not statements at all. To get statements, you must substitute numbers for x. An expression of this kind is called an *open sentence*. In an open sentence, the letter x merely marks the spot where a number is to be inserted. Some numbers, when substituted for x, may give true statements; others may give false statements. The set of all numbers which give true statements is called the *solution set* of the open sentence. For example, the solution of the open sentence

$$\sqrt{x^2} = x$$

is the set of all non-negative numbers; and the solution of the open sentence
$$x^2 + 5x + 6 = 0$$
is the set whose only members are -2 and -3.

If you think of algebra in these terms, then you see that algebra is the study of numbers; it is not the art of manipulating letters like x, y, and z. The pursuit of this idea to its logical and pedagogic conclusions is (in my opinion) the main basis of the revolution that is now being carried out in the teaching of algebra by the SMSG, the UICSM, and others.

It should be understood that the issue involved here is not one of logical rigor in the sense that mathematicians attach to the term. The question is one of intuitive understanding versus mystical illusions and gross misconceptions. The most radical response to the problem that I know of is that of the UICSM; and the UICSM is firmly committed to the doctrine that in mathematics teaching, logic is not enough.

Far from relying on logic alone, the UICSM takes the position that mathematical knowledge need not always be verbalized at all and that at some stages the student learns better if he is not asked either to produce or to read verbalizations. If this seems odd, let us recall that in the first year of its life, a baby learns to interpret, three dimensionally, the two-dimensional images received by the retina. Thus, a one-year-old understands, in an important sense, the laws of perspective. This is probably the most striking example of the efficiency of non-verbal learning. And it does not stop with childhood. Adults have an understanding of human nature; but few of us can formulate, explicitly, a single valid principle of behavioral psychology.

It may well be that this principle has been overstressed by UICSM. But the stress laid on it serves, at least, to exonerate UICSM of naïve reliance on abstract preachments. One striking illustration of the UICSM's approach is the treatment given to multiplication in the general case, where each factor may be positive, negative, or zero. The problem is to explain why the product of two negative numbers is positive. From the standpoint of purely deductive mathematics, the problem is trivial: in one style of treatment, the statement is part of the definition of the product, so that no question of fact appears to be involved at all; and in another style of treatment, the statement appears as a very easy theorem. The UICSM, however, has set itself the task of furnishing an intuitive foundation for statements of this sort by supplying concrete interpretations for them. The concrete interpretation furnished for multiplication in the general case is rather complicated. It involves a tank of water; a pump, which can pump water either into or out of the tank; a movie camera; and a projector, in which the developed film can be run off either forward or backward. Max Beberman, the founder and the leading spirit of UICSM, is fond of telling about this device. It is obvious that he feels proud of it and considers it important. Some critics of the UICSM program have said that it stresses the deductive aspect of mathematics at the expense of everything else. These critics have quite misunderstood the situation. No doubt the program has its faults, but this does not happen to be one of them.

I have stressed that the issues discussed so far are independent of the question of deduction and logical rigor. If this is plain, I may now add that all the new programs in algebra stress the deductive structure far more than the conventional ones do. (Indeed, it is rather hard to see how they could stress it any less.) Usually, there is a fair amount of intuitive material, discussion of special cases, "discovery exercises," and so on. But at some point the basic laws governing numbers are made explicit, and later statements are based on them, in somewhat the style that is familiar in geometry.

The reasons for this are by no means so simple as one might suppose; they have little or nothing to do with the sort of logical conscience that tells a mathematical research worker that he must not use other people's theorems until he has read and understood their proofs. One of the ideas underlying the new deductive treatments of algebra is that a subject is easier to learn and to remember if it is presented in such a way as to make plain the coherence which the subject really has. When we prove some algebraic theorems on the basis of others, one of our purposes is to exhibit the coherence of the subject by explaining how the theorems of algebra are related to one another. Thus rational thinking is, among other things, a mnemonic device. To serve this purpose, the deductive method does not need to be used consistently or compulsively. Even an occasional contribution to coherence may be useful.

Moreover, if we want to convey to the student that the theorems of algebra are statements of fact (about the real number system) then we need to make some visible attempt to ascertain whether they are true; and we should, at least some of the time, refer to them on the occasions when they are needed to justify our algebraic operations. If we do neither of these things, the sense of *reality* may easily be lost, and the student may get the idea that writing

$$\frac{1}{a+b} = \frac{1}{a} + \frac{1}{b}$$

is merely an offense against convention, rather than an offense against the truth. Here again it should be emphasized that the use of the deductive method is not governed by an all-or-none principle; the contribution of deduction to the sense of reality in algebra can be made piecemeal, and commonly is.[2]

While the objectives of the SMSG and UICSM ninth-grade courses are similar, the methods used are different. Much of the terminology and notation in the UICSM course is novel, and the pedagogy is of a special type. (The teachers' manual is about as long as the book; and there is, essentially, only one way to teach the course.) For this reason, the program has a practical disadvantage independent of its essential merits: it is far less flexible and calls for much more special preparation on the part of the teacher.

In geometry, other issues are involved. To understand the history of the teaching of geometry, we must begin with the history of geometry itself. Nearly all elementary books are modelled on Euclid's *Elements* or on adaptations of the *Elements* (notably the famous textbook of Legendre). In the context of modern mathematics, Euclid's book is very peculiar indeed. It is impossible to do justice to this topic in a general article. For a fuller account of the matter, see the section on geometry in a book soon to be published by the SMSG (3). Here we merely cite two facts, which may suggest the sort of thing that is going on. First, in Euclid, there is no such thing as the length of a segment. Second, in Euclid, there is not even such a thing as the ratio of the lengths of two segments.

Instead of these ideas, Euclid used the idea of *same-length* (or "equality") between segments, and the idea of a four-term proportionality of the form
$$AB : CD :: EF : GH.$$
This has a meaning; it says that "AB is to CD as EF is to GH." Thus we have the idea of *same-ratio*, but not the idea of ratio: in Euclid, the expression $AB : CD$ has no meaning at all if it stands alone.

The root of these delicacies and oddities was the fact that lengths and ratios are real numbers, and Euclid did not profess to know anything about the algebra of the real numbers. Later, of course, the real number system came to play a central role. Algebra is now commonly taught before geometry. And algebra appears, as it should appear, in geometry courses. Segments are labelled with numbers, in figures, to indicate their lengths; and proportionality is treated by equations between fractions, with real numbers in the numerators and denominators. As far as I know, there is only one high school in the country (the Priory School at Portsmouth) where students are taught the Euclidean theory of proportionality. Nevertheless, nearly all the existing textbooks state Euclid's postulates and describe, in some fashion, Euclid's conceptual apparatus. These Greek vestiges are hardly more functional than the Roman togas that are sometimes worn at meetings of high-school Latin clubs.

The first policy decision of the SMSG geometry group was that Euclid's postulates should be replaced by metric postulates, describing the connections between geometry and algebra. Under such a scheme, the postulates describe the mathematical system which in fact is going to be studied and suggest the methods which in fact are going to be used.

[2] This paragraph, and the one preceding it, were added by Professor Moise for this volume—Editor.

(The reader is reminded that as a member of the SMSG geometry team, I am not a neutral on this subject. You may attribute to me special prejudice, special knowledge, or both, according to your taste and mood.)

This scheme in elementary geometry was first proposed by the late G. D. Birkhoff, of Harvard, and was used in a textbook written by him and Ralph Beatley, over twenty years ago (4). Aside from its basic advantage of directness and candor, the book vastly simplifies the logic of the subject. A logically accurate treatment, in the Euclidean spirit, is so complicated that people seldom even try to present it in the tenth grade. (The only plausible recent attempt is in the book of Brumfiel, Eicholz, and Shanks (5); it uses a metric treatment of proportionality.) In the Birkhoff scheme you do not start from scratch; you need deal only with the transition from algebra to geometry. This head start vastly reduces the number of pedagogic compromises that you need to make with the logic of the subject, to get a course that moves at a proper speed and is intelligible to the student.

The reader is warned that this topic is—or recently was—highly controversial. I am not qualified to summarize the opposing views, because I have not been able to understand them. Meanwhile, once the SMSG had written a book on metric geometry, the idea spread with rapidity. The UICSM, which had tried three other schemes during the preceding few years, and professed dissatisfaction with all three, is now trying the metric scheme. Presumably because the tenth is the most controversial of the high-school grades, the SMSG set up, last year, a new writing group to produce an alternative geometry book. The new book includes important innovations but retains the metric scheme.

It remains to discuss the pedagogic ideas behind the first (and presumably the second) SMSG geometry book. In connection with algebra, we have mentioned disagreements on the extent to which the learning process should be verbalized. It is clear, however, that the ability to verbalize must be, at some point, an objective in itself. The alternative is mathematical illiteracy. Here by a mathematical illiterate we mean a person who can neither read mathematics nor write it. The phenomenon is not rare: a very large number of mathematics students make no real attempt to read their textbooks; they rely on classroom discussions to prepare them to do homework, and beg for assurances that on written examinations they "will not be held responsible for the theory."

To avoid this sort of thing is no easy job. The mathematical theory must be simple enough that an explicit formulation of it is intelligible to an immature student. (This was one reason for the choice of the metric theory.) The verbalizations must be introduced by intuitive discussions that indicate what they are driving at. (In fact, the process of transition from intuitive ideas to exact formulations is one of the things we need to teach.) The formulations must be valid. (All too often, authors write definitions so loosely and inaccurately that students learn by experience not to waste attention on them.) Finally, the verbalizations must be put to work; if they are not used, they are not learned and are not worth learning. For example, it is useless to say, as Euclid says, that "a line is length without breadth." At no point are we going to infer anything about lines from this supposed definition. In fact, the only real purpose of Euclid's first page of definitions is to suggest—falsely, of course—that all the terms used in geometry are defined.

Obviously the present article is not a contribution to scientific literature. It is, rather, an attempt to describe an enterprise; and any valid description of the enterprise in question must be full of the sort of subjective judgments that we have been discussing. The point is that the design of new mathematics programs has not been guided by scientific research in any commonly understood sense of the term. The only science involved has been mathematics itself, and pedagogy has appeared as a practical art, learned by experience. A study is now being made of the operation of the SMSG programs, from the viewpoint of cognitive psychology. During the first year in which they were tried, standard achievement tests were given before and after. These have not been published. Roughly speaking, they indicated that the SMSG students did approximately as well, on tests based on traditional courses, as they would have done if they had taken the traditional courses. Valuation by traditional tests is the handicap that new programs are expected to accept and overcome; and if the shift in objectives and emphasis is great—as it was in these cases—the handicap is correspondingly large.

All the new programs are in process of growth, and most bibliographic references would soon be out of date. It seems better, therefore, to refer the reader to sources of current information on the publications of the SMSG and the UICSM. The UICSM textbooks are published by the University of Illinois Press, Urbana, Illinois. Those of the SMSG are published by the Yale University Press, New Haven, Connecticut. Lists of current SMSG books are given in its *Newsletter*; requests for this should be addressed to SMSG, Stanford University, Stanford, California. We have already mentioned the forthcoming book of the SMSG (3). The best source on the spirit of the UICSM program is Max Beberman's Inglis Lecture at Harvard (6).

The task of surveying this literature, and judging its merits, involves a number of hazards, some of which may not be obvious. Some of these hazards are as follows:

Innovations in the treatment of mathematics, or in the language used to explain it, are usually confusing to a reader who is accustomed to something else. From this it does not follow that the innovations are harder for the student; for the student, both the subject matter and the language would be new in any case.

Much of the current theorizing on mathematical pedagogy is intellectually subtle and may often seem obscure. It does not follow that the resulting textbooks are equally subtle or equally obscure to the student. The whole purpose of hard thinking about pedagogy is to make the student's work simpler and easier, and this purpose is often achieved.

The new books seldom explain the reasons behind the methods that they use. (Such explanations belong in the teachers' manuals. To put them into the text usually represents a lapse from intellectual discipline.) Often the reasons are far from obvious. For these reasons, many passages in the new books, considered in isolation, may seem at first to be actually silly. Sometimes, no doubt, they are; to err is human. But most of the time, they are not.

The new books try very hard to convey mathematical concepts. From this it should not be inferred that they are addressed solely to the superior student. In fact, nearly all of them are intended for the same students who now study the corresponding conventional courses. There is even some fragmentary evidence which suggests that the advantages of the new courses are greater for mediocre students than for brilliant ones. If this turns out to be true, we should not be surprised. It is the mediocre students who need the most help in grasping concepts; the brilliant students are more likely to figure things out for themselves.

A brief and casual inspection of the new books may convey the impression that they neglect the traditional material, including the material useful in science, and replace it by "modern" mathematics which is of interest only to research mathematicians. This is not true. Some of the changes are curricular, but most of them are merely changes in style of treatment. All the new programs lead to analytic geometry and calculus, in the usual four years. At the laboratory school at the University of Illinois, the students begin algebra in the eighth grade. With this head start, they take a twelfth-grade course that covers more than half of the calculus textbook now being used at Massachusetts Institute of Technology.

These possibilities for misunderstanding are due basically to the fact that the ideas underlying the new programs are not intellectually trivial. They are the results of long, hard work, at both mathematics and teaching. I cannot believe that anybody has found the final answer to any of our problems; I cannot even believe that such final answers exist. But the progress made in the past few years forms the basis of a long overdue revolution in mathematical education, and I am convinced that even better work is soon to come.

References

1 Commission on Mathematics, College Entrance Examination Board, *Introductory Probability and Statistical Inference,* College Entrance Examination Board, New York, 1959. (Generally known as the Gray Book.)
2 Frederick Mosteller, Robert E. K. Rourke, and George B. Thomas, Jr., *Probability: A First Course,* Addison-Wesley Publishing Company, Inc., Reading, Mass., 1961.
3 This book will probably be published by the School Mathematics Study Group soon. In the meantime, we refer the reader to the excellent book by Moise, *Elementary Geometry from the Advanced Standpoint,* Addison-Wesley Publishing Company, Inc., Reading, Mass., 1963. [Added Ed.]
4 G. D. Birkhoff and Ralph Beatley, *Basic Geometry,* Chelsea Publishing Company, New York, 1958.
5 Charles F. Brumfiel, Robert E. Eicholz, and Merrill E. Shanks, *Geometry,* Addison-Wesley Publishing Company, Inc., Reading, Mass., 1960.
6 Max Beberman, *An Emerging Program of Secondary School Mathematics,* Harvard University Press, Cambridge, Mass., 1958.

Supplementary references

1 G. A. W. Boehm, *The New World of Math,* The Dial Press, Inc., New York, 1959.
2 C. F. Brumfiel, R. E. Eicholz, and M. E. Shanks, *Introduction to Mathematics,* Addison-Wesley Publishing Company, Inc., Reading, Mass., 1961.

3 C. F. Brumfiel, R. E. Eicholtz, and M. E. Shanks, *Algebra I*, Addison-Wesley Publishing Co., Inc., Reading, Mass., 1961.
4 V. Bush, *Science, the Endless Frontier,* Washington, D.C., 1945. (Report to the President.)
5 Commission on Mathematics, College Entrance Examination Board, *Program for College Preparatory Mathematics,* College Entrance Examination Board, Princeton, N.J., 1959. (Report and Appendixes.)
6 Commission on Mathematics, College Entrance Examination Board, *Introductory Probability and Statistical Inference,* rev. preliminary ed., and *Teachers' Notes and Answer Guide,* College Entrance Examination Board, Princeton, N.J., 1958.
7 R. B. Davis, *Madison Project,* Syracuse University, Syracuse, N.Y.
8 A. H. Dupree, *Science in the Federal Government,* The Belknap Press, Harvard University Press, Cambridge, Mass., 1957.
9 Educational Research Council of Greater Cleveland. Director, Dr. G. H. Baird.
10 M. Kline, *Mathematics in Western Culture,* Oxford University Press, London, 1953.
11 M. Kline, *Mathematics and the Physical World,* Ambassador Books, Ltd., Toronto, 1960.
12 W. H. Meyer, "Report of the Committee on High School Mathematics Courses," *California Schools,* September, 1960, pp. 384–397.
13 Organization for European Economic Cooperation, *New Thinking in School Mathematics,* O.E.E.C. Mission, Publications Office, Washington, D.C., 1961.
14 H. A. Rademacher and O. Toeplitz, *The Enjoyment of Mathematics,* Princeton University Press, Princeton, N.J., 1957.
15 P. C. Rosenbloom, "A Leap Ahead in School Mathematics," in *Proceedings of Symposium on Elementary School Science and Mathematics,* Oklahoma, Frontiers of Science Foundation, 1959.
16 P. C. Rosenbloom, "What Is Coming in the Elementary Mathematics Curriculum," *Educational Leadership,* November, 1960, pp. 96–100.
17 School Mathematics Study Group. Executive Director, Prof. E. G. Begle, Stanford University, Calif.
18 *Science Education News,* American Association for the Advancement of Science, Washington, D.C.
19 *Science Education News,* December, 1960 and 1962, American Association for the Advancement of Science, Washington, D.C.
20 *Studies in Mathematics Education,* Scott, Foresman and Company, Chicago, 1960.
21 J. R. Steelman, *Science and Public Policy,* Washington, D.C., 1947. (Report to the President.)
22 P. Suppes, *Sets and Numbers,* Books 1A, 1C, 2A, and *Teacher's Manuals,* Stanford University Press, Stanford, Calif., 1961.
23 P. Suppes and S. A. Hill, *Mathematical Logic for the Schools,* Book 1, Stanford University Press, Stanford, Calif., 1961.
24 University of Illinois Arithmetic Project. Director, Prof. D. A. Page, University of Illinois, Urbana, Ill.
25 University of Illinois Committee on School Mathematics. Director, Prof. M. Beberman, University of Illinois, Urbana, Ill.
26 University of Maryland Mathematics Project. Director, Prof. J. R. Mayor, University of Maryland, College Park, Md.
27 *Guidelines for Preparation Programs of Teachers of Secondary School Science and Mathematics,* NASDTEC-AAAS Studies, 1515 Massachusetts Ave., N.W., Washington, D.C.

10 ❧ CURRENT PROGRESS IN ENGLISH
Harold B. Allen* *University of Minnesota*

We have been brought together by what is by no means a new problem. Ever since man became man he must have had to deal with the problem of selecting from the accumulated wisdom of the tribe that which could appropriately be passed on, at appropriate times, to the children as they themselves grew to manhood. The Australian bushman, still in his stone age, teaches his son how to catch insects and desert rodents for food before he teaches him how to make and throw a boomerang. The Sioux Indian taught his son how to hunt the prairie dog and the rabbit before allowing him to venture on the dangerous hunt for the buffalo.

In my own field, language and literature, the problem is also an old one. The ancient Greeks found that they had to choose what they felt the child could learn, and to order that content in some kind of sequence. The two influential grammars of the Middle Ages, those of Donatus and Priscian, presented systematically a description of the Latin language, but one book was only a selection of the known facts and was studied on the school level before the student went on to the second in his higher education.

True, little was known about child psychology or the psychology of learning. Often the selections were simply selections from adult materials—no more. There was no adaptation for the growing mind, no re-presentation to accord with the changing interests of the adolescent. *The Babee's Book* and *Abecedarium* of the Middle Ages now seem to be funny—if we forget how tedious they must have seemed to the children. The stuffiness and pedantry of the eighteenth century grammars, to say nothing of their lack of realism, did much to establish the tradition that grammar is a horrible subject; and the platitudinous moralizing of the McGuffey readers was almost equally efficacious in keeping alive the image of the school of tortures to which the reluctant schoolboy crept with shining morning-face.

Unhappily, human inertia, the apparently normal tendency to keep on doing what has been done, compounded the situation by retaining materials and methods long after newer materials and better methods were known. I found *The Saber-tooth Curriculum* a very funny book, until it struck me that Professor Benjamin was talking about English as well as about the caveman's course of study. He was talking about the teaching of *Silas Marner* in ninth-grade English; he was talking about grimly teaching the chronological sequence of literature from Beowulf to Hardy; he was talking about solemnly presenting to our students such unprovable and nonoperational definitions as "A sentence is an expression of a complete thought" and "A noun is the name of a person, place, thing, or action"; he was talking about insistence upon memorizing such terms as *synecdoche* and *hendiadys* and *anacoluthon* instead of learning to write by writing.

Yet, having said that, I shall now say the opposite: What has dominantly

* Harold B. Allen is Professor of English at the University of Minnesota and in 1961 was President of the National Council of Teachers of English.

characterized the English-teaching profession in this country in recent years is not this massive inertia but, rather, a mounting and insistent demand for change—for improvement in content, in methods, and in the preparation of the teachers.

These teachers are pretty important people in American education. There are more teachers of English than of any other subject in the United States. But it is not just numbers that make them important. They are important because of what they teach—the language and its literature. I grant that other teachers are important—even a teacher of driver training is important when he teaches children to control their reactions so that they can drive without mowing down pedestrians. I grant that science teachers are important —science has produced not only the hydrogen bomb (which can destroy the Twin Cities within the next few minutes) but also the Salk vaccine (which saves the lives for the bombs to kill).

But teachers of English, I would insist, are important because they deal with what—to ignore possible theological questions—distinguishes man from other animals: language and the creative imagination that produces his literature.

With keen awareness of this importance—an awareness both humble and self-conscious—leaders among English teachers have for many years sought to better the course of study in our schools. Confronted after the First World War with the tremendous surge of pupils from homes with few books and nonstandard English, they have tried valiantly to help these students gain control of standard English and acquire some appreciation of the good things written in it.

When Professor Rosenbloom first asked me to appear on this program, he suggested that I talk about the "grass-roots" curriculum movement in English. I would not wish to overemphasize that aspect, yet the expression is a good one. For most of the inspired effort of this past generation of English teachers has been precisely that. On local and national levels, this effort has arisen from among teachers themselves. No dramatic orbiting of a sputnik sparked its rise; no official directive from a minister of education compelled its appearance. It has indeed been a voluntary and dedicated grass-roots movement.

Much, though not all, of this striving toward better courses of study in English has been within the professional organization of English teachers themselves—the National Council of Teachers of English (NCTE). Now with nearly seventy thousand members and subscribers it is by far the largest independent subject-matter teachers' organization in the world. It will be fifty years old on December 2, 1961. Within this half-century, the first major step toward study and improvement came with the volume, *The Experience Curriculum*, edited in the mid-thirties by W. Wilbur Hatfield, then secretary of the council. This book set forth the principles of curricular revision by which the course of study could be better adapted to the lives and needs of contemporary American boys and girls. It had a profound effect upon curriculum making during the next decade and more.

But the socioeconomic changes of the depression and of the Second World War, a changing educational philosophy, and advances both in literary criticism and in the study of the English language, all compelled further and more comprehensive curricular study. Accordingly, in 1945, the National Council appointed a major subsidiary group, the Commission on the English Curriculum, charged with producing both a descriptive and a creative study of the English program in American schools and colleges. Three volumes of its five-volume series have now appeared: the first, in 1952, a general introduction; the second, in 1954, dealing with the elementary school; and the third, in 1956, dealing with the secondary school. Volume 4, delayed by the death and replacement of its editor, will deal with the college curriculum when it is published in the summer of 1962. Volume 5 will treat the training of the English teacher; its manuscript deadline is today, and it should be published in the spring of 1962.

I venture to assert that no single influence has been greater upon the teaching of English than has the published material in the curriculum series of the council. The first three volumes have been used as textbooks in teacher preparation and as guides in the work of scores of groups preparing courses of study. Already the value of this commission is seen to be so great that plans are now being made to replace it, when its responsibility is discharged in 1962, with a permanent curriculum commission with rotating membership.

In the meantime, the NCTE is carrying on numerous activities more or less directly related to curriculum study and experimentation. Before the annual convention in Philadelphia in November, 1961, a special preconvention study group of about forty teachers will concentrate for three days on the topic of the articulated program in the schools. Also at the convention will be a display of curriculum guides from all over the country, a display arranged by the committee to revise curriculum bulletins. Each guide on display will have been reviewed by three members of the committee. The Committee on High School–College Articulation is currently preparing a report on 110 statements from as many colleges telling how students should be prepared for college entrance. This report is valuable especially to schools with many college-bound students, many of whom in the past have been misled by what colleges actually do require as preparation in composition and literature.

I should not of course omit the convention itself, when each year many discussions and speeches deal with both general and specific matters of curriculum. Since most of the several thousand persons in attendance are themselves representatives of smaller groups, they serve as agents by which information and points of view are disseminated for productive further activity upon local and state levels. In 1957, for example, papers upon structural linguistics at the national meeting in Minneapolis, together with a classroom demonstration in our University High School, led to such intensive curricular activity in central California that that region now leads the country in the extent of its adoption of the new materials and approach. And the California group is only one of the 150 local and regional affiliates of the national council.

Indeed, what many of these affiliates are doing in curriculum is amazing. I will comment upon only three or four, but I assure you that these are by no means unusual; they are typical.

Vivid in my remembrance is the group I met with for two days in the summer of 1961 near Little Rock. These members of the Arkansas Council of Teachers of English worked for two years with the state department of education to prepare a new state curriculum in English. In the summer of 1961 the working group, at their own expense, met to put the material into final shape for submission and publication.

The South Dakota State Council, another NCTE affiliate, is likewise preparing a complete curriculum guide in English. This was the first time the South Dakota department invited such cooperation from outside the state educational office.

These two state councils of Arkansas and South Dakota thus joined those of Alabama, Oklahoma, Wisconsin, Nebraska, and New York in producing, for state departments, major curricular guides with NCTE affiliate sponsorship. The curricular guide produced in New York has had an interesting sequel. The state commissioner of education issued a directive requiring all New York colleges preparing teachers to include in their offerings by 1963 certain work in literature, criticism, and linguistics so that future teachers will be adequately trained to work with the new curriculum. The new Minnesota council, in the spring of 1961, passed resolutions that it is hoped will eventually lead to similar action here.

Preparing such guides is not the only curriculum-related activity of affiliates. The English Association of Ohio has just embarked upon a detailed study of current practices with respect to the effect of standardized English examinations upon the curriculum. I need not detail the important implications that the findings of this study will have, implications that in such a relatively amorphous subject field as English may be of much greater import than in a more rigidly structured field such as mathematics or chemistry.

More specialized studies are also going on. The Hutchinson, Kansas, council, for example, is preparing a detailed guide to the teaching of written composition. In some communities, the English teachers who are members of the state affiliate but do not have a local group are nevertheless exerting pioneering leadership. In the summer of 1960, for instance, a committee of teachers spent two months in the small city of Bend, Oregon, in a thoroughgoing reconstruction of the English course of study for the local schools. In Brentwood, New York, there has been an extremely important, and so far unique, carefully controlled experimental two-year testing of two parallel curriculums in English-language teaching—one group of pupils using the modern structural approach. This project, involving the close supervision and teamwork of several testing experts from New York City, was supported by a research grant from the New York State Department of Education.

In 1958 a summer planning curriculum workshop for the fields of literature, grammar, and composition was held in Westport, Connecticut. Westport English teachers spent the summer preparing the new guides. Especially in the area of language did revolutionary results develop. The committee resolved to make a complete experimental adoption of the structural approach based upon modern descriptive linguistics. This drastic step was seen to require in-service training, so during the following winter an in-service seminar was conducted for ten weeks for senior and junior high teachers, with some administrators, and even a PTA member present for flavor. It was the director of this course, Miss V. Louise Higgins, who therefore was chosen by the NCTE as the leader for the preconvention study group in linguistics in Chicago in 1960. The new Westport curriculum is now in operation.

More comprehensive and thoroughgoing, quite likely to make a deeper nationwide impact, is the already famous Portland, Oregon, curriculum survey. Not precisely a grass-roots project, since it was requested by the Portland board of education and financed by the Ford Foundation, it was nevertheless operated by working teachers brought in to make the study and to combine with local teachers in preparing the subsequent full curriculum. Three national council leaders, Professors Gorrell and Laird of the University of Nevada, and Professor Roberts of San José State College, made the original investigation. This summer of 1961, with the job of finishing the curriculum, the group met for a two-month arduous final task. Roberts, out of the country at the time, was replaced by W. Nelson Francis of Franklin and Marshall College, now the first director of the national council's Commission on the English Language. By insisting upon the language as content in the secondary curriculum and by demanding sound linguistic information as the basis for a sound sequence in expository composition, the group evolved a curriculum which has attracted nationwide attention and is likely to have dynamic effects upon curricular developments.

Another major project, with probably still more far-reaching results, began in September, 1961. With the financial backing of the College Entrance Examination Board, and under the general direction of the board's Commission on English, there was held at the University of Michigan a curriculum-planning institute. Sixty persons, representing twenty selected universities, met in three groups of twenty each to explore trends and needs and prepare sample syllabuses in the field of literature, composition, and language. In the summer of 1962 each of these twenty universities will hold a similar institute, with its own three representatives directing corresponding groups of outstanding secondary school teachers in the study and application of these developed curricular guides. Although the College Entrance Examination Board incurred some adverse criticism because it thus assumed a function quite different from that which it has previously exercised—it could have underwritten the project and had it administered by a teachers' organization—the enterprise itself is without doubt one of admirable promise. An informal preliminary report of the initial training institute was very favorable and gave clear indication that certain fears of authoritarian adoption of an arbitrary sequence were groundless.

If now I have almost overwhelmed and perhaps bored you with specifics in this presentation of grass-roots activity in English curricular study and creation, I confess having done this deliberately. I have sought to make quite clear that the leaders in the English-teaching profession are well aware of the needs and of desirable courses of action. When it is possible and practicable, they act to meet these needs.

All this action I have indicated to you, and much more, has originated almost entirely because of certain pressures in the three principal areas of English teaching: literature, language, and composition. I should like to point out briefly some of the principal pressures.

In the field of literature, one very strong drive has been away from the traditional historical and biographical approach to literature, with its preoccupation with the social context and biographical data, to an approach which, beginning perhaps with so-called topical units appropriate to the junior high school, moves to the thematic units more suitable to the senior high years. Such a theme as "The meaning of justice," as treated by poets and playwrights and novelists over the years, requires deeper study by the student and compels his attention to the meaning of the literature itself. He must read the literature, not what is said about the literature. The NCTE Committee on the Academically Talented recently referred, for instance, to a thematic unit on "the problem of evil," in which admittedly fairly mature students read and discussed with care and insight the related treatments found in Conrad's *Heart of Darkness*, the Old Testament Book of Jonah, Marlowe's *Doctor Faustus*, O'Neill's *The Emperor Jones*, and Henry James's *The Turn of the Screw*.

The field of literature is experiencing pressure, also, with respect to a desirable sequence and balance of materials through the junior and senior high schools. How much from each of the various types of literature should be included? How much attention should be given to material from the various literary periods? How much attention relatively belongs to American literature and how much to British literature? Although these particular issues are perhaps perennial and are usually related to certain assumptions to be accepted without proof, nevertheless they involve a large area of teaching which is susceptible to reasonable experimentation and testing. This is the area to which various groups have already addressed themselves.

But the really dynamic pressure for revolutionary change has come in the field of English language study and teaching. Since about 1930 a basic reorientation in the discipline of linguistics has increasingly presented both facts and concepts to powerfully challenge the validity of the time-honored corpus of grammatical statements in the curriculum we inherited. And even this new description of English, based upon its observable and objectively determined structural characteristics, is now being complemented by an extremely promising new way of looking at the language. Without discarding the analytic approach of the structuralist, the teacher who keeps up with the swiftly moving currents of discovery in linguistics may now want to adopt the principles of what is called generative or transformational grammar to help the student to create his own effective sentences instead of simply breaking down what someone else wrote.

These new linguistic ideas have gripped the minds of English teachers as no other dynamism in the field has done. Nearly all of the curriculum projects I earlier specified were engaged in applying linguistics to the teaching of English—most notably those in Westport, Connecticut, and in Portland, Oregon. The NCTE conventions of 1960 and 1961 are conspicuously concerned with this impact of linguistics upon our thinking and our teaching. In 1961 articles on linguistics have been prominent in two-thirds of the affiliate publications in the country. Half of the summer cosponsored workshops dealt specifically with linguistic applications in the classroom. The council has appointed a new major permanent commission which is to be concerned with teaching of the language in schools and colleges.

But pressures related to the ancient field of composition have also appeared. An article in *Look* magazine, "Why Johnny Can't Write," based upon data largely supplied from our 1960 study, presents facts about the poor state of composition teaching. This situation for some time has deeply concerned the leaders in the profession. They have sought to emphasize more and more the need for rigorous training in expository writing and for close attention to logical organization and structural support. At the same time, teachers have more and more rebelled against the impossible imposition of a load of weekly compositions from upwards of 180 to 200 students. But curricular revision to include adequate time for correcting compositions can occur only when teaching load is reduced. At the Minneapolis convention in 1957, the NCTE recognized this in a resolution calling for a maximum of 100 students and four classes per teacher, a resolution soon echoed by President Conant of Harvard in the well-known report upon the secondary schools.

Yet just what is most effectively done by the teacher and student to produce better writing was still a matter of opinion and empirical observation. That is why, in the winter of 1961, the NCTE authorized a special committee to determine the state of knowledge about the teaching of composition. This committee engaged in an exhaustive study to determine what really valid research there is and what it has revealed, and its report should help channel future research so as to produce better curricular planning in composition.

But in our multiplex educational picture, with local and state authorities overlapping and sometimes conflicting, with uneven financial support in different sections, the best that can be done to improve the curriculum on local or even state levels will never be quite adequate to the need. In January, 1961, the NCTE published its comprehensive book-length study, *The National Interest and the Teaching of English,* a report of a 1960 survey made to provide data for the Congress in revising the National Defense Education Act of 1958. Just as the curriculum development in the foreign language and mathematics and science programs had been invigorated, if, indeed, not actually created in some places, by the massive support of the act and of the National Science Foundation, so we hoped that the present Congress would amend the act by including English within the provisions of Titles III, IV, and VI. All members of the Congress received this study. When I testified for the council, I received very favorable reactions from both Senate and House committees. But, as you know too well, extraneous issues led to the defeat of these administration-sponsored House and Senate bills and even to the defeat of the proposal for a one-year extension so that revision might occur in 1962. The present two-year extension without change will, however, simply postpone the issue. The NCTE is determined to make an even stronger fight before the next Congress.

In the meantime, the NCTE's Commission on the Profession is completing detailed plans for a series of summer institutes to upgrade the teachers of English methods in colleges of education and teachers' colleges; foundation support will be sought for this project, through which the next generation of teachers will be better equipped to work with new curricular developments. We hope to see foundation support also for other projects, particularly those designed to upgrade present teachers. Our survey indicated that about one-half of the high school teachers of English in the United States do not have a major in English in their college background. These people need help.

Most encouraging, at the moment, is the rapidly maturing plan of Dr. Sterling McMurrin, U.S. Commissioner of Education, to apply U.S. Office of Education funds toward the realization of what has been called "Project English." This project purposes to encourage research and experimentation. It calls for the establishment of three demonstration centers at three different universities, each center to try out new curricular materials. The project will also entail the holding of conferences and seminars throughout the country. The NCTE will be ready to cooperate to the fullest in this broadly conceived enterprise.

Indeed, English teachers everywhere, and the National Council of Teachers of English as their representative, will constantly be alert to improve their teaching and their courses of study. When time and money can be provided, they will be ready to undertake the job even more intensively and extensively than they have so far been able to do on a voluntary or locally supported basis. For the improvement of the English curriculum *is* in the national interest.

(*Author's Note.*) Events anticipated in the foregoing paper have occurred, or not occurred, as follows: The NCTE curriculum series has been further delayed, so that Volume 5 is now scheduled for publication in November, 1963, and Volume 4 in the spring of 1964. The College Entrance Examination Board summer institutes were held successfully in 1962, so successfully that twenty-two universities decided to support similar institutes in the summer of 1963. The NCTE committee on the state of knowledge about the teaching of composition received a Federal grant, through the fiscal agency of the University of Iowa, and consequently was able to carry on a much more extensive investigation. The results are to be made available in November, 1963. Revision of the National Defense Education Act has not yet included specific reference to English, but independent support from the U.S. Office of Education has already greatly stimulated research and materials preparation in the English field. Through Project English eight curriculum development centers have been established, each for a five-year period with a grant of about a quarter of a million dollars. Seven of these are at the following universities and colleges: Hunter, Northwestern, Nebraska, Carnegie Institute of Technology, Oregon, Minnesota, and Florida State. One is in Madison, Wisconsin, with the grant to the state department of education to be administered through the University of Wisconsin. In addition, the U.S. Office of Education has tremendously expanded its concern with the field of English through smaller grants for specific research projects.

11 ❀ A POSSIBLE APPROACH TO HIGH SCHOOL CHEMISTRY ❀ Laurence E. Strong* *Earlham College*

Chemistry is one of several sciences offered by high schools to the typical American high school student. Whether or not the student elects to study

* Laurence E. Strong is Professor of Chemistry at Earlham College, Richmond, Indiana, and Director of the Chemical Bond Approach Project, supported by the National Science Foundation.

this particular subject is a matter decided sometimes by accident and sometimes by careful choice. For many students who do chose chemistry, this will prove to be the only physical science they study. For them, this will be the only systematic introduction to modern ideas about atoms, molecules, energy, structure, and the possibilities of applying quantitative reasoning to physical systems. This means that a course in chemistry can play a significant role in the intellectual development of the student.

The Chemical Bond Approach Project is exploring some of the possibilities for a stimulating presentation of the intellectual problems in the field of chemistry. During the past 2½ years, a group of high school and college chemistry teachers have been developing and testing materials and classroom strategies to see what is useful.

Basic to the new course is the attempt to organize the study around a central theme. The idea of chemical bonds has been chosen as a suitable theme. This is, in brief, the idea that materials are made up of atoms held together by forces or bonds. Many of the properties of materials are best understood by reference to the bonds imagined to be present. A chemical reaction is then viewed as a process in which bonds initially present are broken and new bonds are formed.

Experimental investigation of chemical reactions reveals a number of puzzling problems. Chief among these is the mysterious way in which the properties of a system change whenever a chemical change occurs. Many of the properties characteristic of the initial system change markedly during the reaction. Thus the volume of the system may shrink sharply as an accompaniment to chemical change, even though no material leaves the system. Again, the color of the system may change, so that there appears to be no reasonable connection between initial color and final color.

The chemical bond approach course attempts to get the student to see the intellectual problem involved in the fact that the properties of chemical reaction products cannot be simply related to the properties of the initial reagents, and then to explore how ideas about bonds can suggest understanding. Such a procedure involves imagination, logic, and experimentation. The course suggests the procedure, in an early experiment, in the form of an analogy. This is commonly called the "black box." The point is made that chemicals are to be treated as if they are black boxes.

For the actual black box experiment, the student is given a sealed box which contains some loose object. By shaking, rolling, and twisting the box, he obtains a number of observations. To "explain" his observations, the student is asked to imagine an object whose behavior ought logically to produce the same results as those observed. Of course, the student is told not to open the box in order to gain additional data, although his teacher may subsequently show him what is inside. There is no way to open real chemicals and see atoms and molecules, except by imagination and logic.

Laboratory

To proceed in the study of chemical change at first hand, the student finds it necessary to acquire data. Laboratory activity is, therefore, an important part of the course. Two principles underlie the design of useful student laboratory experiments. First, each experiment should pose a problem for the student to solve with a minimum of formal direction. Second, the various experiments should be connected with the text and with each other.

If we are to pose a problem for the student to solve, this means that some situation, similar to that being studied in class, but sufficiently different that its answer is not immediately apparent to the student, must be found. He obtains a solution by collecting laboratory data and analyzing it in terms of the logic of the course. In general, more emphasis is placed on the student's reasoned argument than on the precision of a particular piece of numerical data.

For example, early in the course the student is asked to take two solutions at the same temperature and mix them. He then determines the change in temperature. The problem he is asked to solve is, "What will be the magnitude of the temperature change if double the volume of each solution is taken?" In this particular experiment, the student can actually get an experimental answer to compare with his reasoned answer. Such an experiment as this has been found most useful as a basis for discussing the difference between heat and temperature.

The interconnection of experiments, or *vertical development*, is exhibited by several sequences. Thus a number of experiments are concerned with the use of the idea of energy in studying chemical change. The development moves from the simple question of the effect of volume on heat of mixing to a final experiment on the heat which is transferred during the formation of a compound from its elements.

Throughout the course, frequent reference is made to the various ways which scientists have found useful for organizing information. To develop classification schemes which aid understanding, resort is had to "mental models."

Mental Models

At first sight, one can only conclude that chemistry consists of a great mass of unrelated data. A glance at any handbook of data certainly must so impress the uninitiated. Can one possibly, for instance, relate the silvery color of sodium metal to the colorlessness of a sodium chloride crystal?

To provide a logical pattern for the events in the laboratory, the chemist resorts to theory. Without theory there is little in the way of logic to guide one through the maze. For the student, the difficulty is that theory arises in the imagination rather than in the critical examination of evidence alone. But it is precisely when imaginative theory and factual evidence are united that the modern intellectual dimensions of chemistry begin to be apparent.

In the chemical bond approach course we attempt to confront the student, in a number of ways, with the implications of logical arguments based on theory. A major part of this is done through the discussion of "mental models." These are introduced as logical devices based on a set of convenient assumptions. Particular attention is given to three such models: structure, kinetic theory, and energy.

Actually, the name of the project, Chemical Bond Approach Project, is intended to emphasize the role given to bonds between atoms. Several approaches are used with the student. Underlying all of them is the general proposition that chemicals can be regarded as structures, so that chemical change is thought of in terms of structural change. An initial introduction to such thinking arises in the discussion of allotropic forms of carbon and of sulfur, since in each of these cases there are differences in properties without differences in composition.

Examination of the properties of a variety of substances suggests three major groups. These are identified with covalent, metallic, and ionic bonds. Major attention is given to electrostatic properties of matter and to the development of electronic structures.

Structural models for atoms, molecules, and crystals are developed in two somewhat different ways. First, electrons are considered as represented by spherical clouds of negative charge and referred to as charge clouds. Under the action of electrostatic forces, these charge clouds arrange themselves into patterns which conform to the geometric properties of a system of spheres pulled tightly together. Our experience with students indicates that this presentation and the use of geometrical analogies is quite satisfactory.

Such a charge-cloud model does not, in its present development, deal adequately with energy relations. For this reason, a more conventional electron orbital model is introduced and developed to show, at least qualitatively, energy relationships. It falls down, however, in the description of geometrical properties. The orbital model and the charge-cloud model are brought nearer together by the introduction of a hybridized orbital model.

In a discussion of the two structure models, students get some idea of the successes and limitations of each. It is one of our aims to have students realize that it is not proper to ask which is the right model. Rather, we judge the models on the basis of their logical effectiveness for a particular problem. This is presumably the way which modern scientific discussion proceeds.

Evaluation

Classroom trials of the materials developed are used for evaluation and as a basis for revision. We are trying out text materials, laboratory experiments, lecture demonstrations, teachers' guides, supplementary readings, and examinations.

It appears that the teachers in the program tend to change their classroom behavior to a less authoritarian one. Independent thinking on the part of the student is encouraged and a good deal of student initiative is developed in the laboratory. Particular emphasis is placed on close correlation of laboratory and classroom work by the development of experimental problems which require for their solution both data and theory.

A major feature of the course is the presentation of the subject in the form of a rather tightly organized discussion. The organization has, however, developed as a consequence of the discipline itself, rather than for some reason more or less external to the subject.

At this stage in our development, the only other comparable course is that devised by the Physical Science Study Committee in physics. It is most intriguing that examination results in the two courses are quite parallel, yet different from customary experience. Briefly stated, a set of achievement examinations, to be administered at stated intervals in the course, has been prepared. These are multiple choice examinations, and the questions are based on situations presented to the student as new problems for him to study.

When the student scores are correlated with aptitude scores obtained by examinations administered by the Educational Testing Service, remarkably low correlations are found. Early in the course, correlation values of about .6 are obtained, but on successive examinations these decline steadily to values below .4. Analyses are still incomplete, but they suggest that the low correlations are primarily the reflection of the unusually high performance obtained from a fair proportion of the low-ability students. To explore the implications of these findings is certainly desirable, and further work is under way.

Conclusion

The Chemical Bond Approach Project is well along in the development and trial of a possibly new approach for the introduction of students to chemistry. Its goal is the development of a course which integrates laboratory data and conceptual schemes. To achieve this integration, the logical structure and methods of chemistry itself are used, rather than some external appeal to utilitarian or other values claimed for the subject. Much of the course is centered on the idea of chemical bonds or structure as a major intellectual tool for the discussion of chemical systems.

Classroom trials over a period of more than two years indicate that much of the course is meaningful to students. It is our experience that many of the teachers involved also find it possible to reduce their insistence on authoritarian pronouncements. With this change, there is a decreased emphasis on rote learning and an increased emphasis on experimental inquiry and logical argument.

Since the project was designed to try out some new possibilities for the presentation of a subject, it will leave at least one major question unanswered. This has to do with what a particular science teacher decides to teach. Presumably, developments in course content, such as the chemical bond approach, offer additional possibilities for classroom presentations and widen the field of choice for the teacher. Through his own efforts, or through his profession, he needs to develop criteria for making an effective choice.

12 ❦ THE CHEMICAL EDUCATION MATERIAL STUDY
Paul R. O'Connor[*] *University of Minnesota*

The Chemical Education Material Study, or CHEMStudy, is an approach to high school chemistry that is primarily oriented around a laboratory or experimental approach. The title on the syllabus for this course states, suc-

[*] Paul R. O'Connor is Associate Chairman of the Chemistry Department at the University of Minnesota.

cinctly, this view: "Chemistry, an Experimental Science." The basic philosophy that has directed the development of this program includes asking a student to accept a minimum of information on faith; laboratory experiments to precede topics in the class discussions whenever possible; and a gradual growth of principles which are subjected to quantitative examination.

The CHEMStudy was developed during the summer of 1960 through the cooperative efforts of college and high school teachers, under a grant from the National Science Foundation. In 1961, at two summer institutes, approximately one hundred more high school teachers became thoroughly grounded in this new program. There were seven high school teachers from the Twin Cities area who accompanied me to Harvey Mudd College for one of these institutes. I am very pleased to tell you that the excitement and enthusiasm we all felt continue in their high school classes.

Perhaps the best way for you to appreciate the nature of the program is through a discussion of the laboratory program and the syllabus that accompanies it. Within the first two weeks a student is introduced to the entire philosophy of the CHEMStudy.

What is the nature of scientific study?
What is the nature of chemistry?
We shall try to find the answers in this course, not through words alone, but through experience.

This is the opening paragraph in the syllabus, and the student starts the course in the laboratory. From his first experiment, to record all his observations of a burning candle, through the fifth experiment, to measure the heat of combustion of wax and the heat of fusion of wax, the student has been led through the basic activities of science:

to accumulate information through observation
to organize this information and to seek regularities in it
to wonder why regularities exist
to communicate the findings to others

From observations and qualitative measurements on a system, he has moved to organization of his information and quantitative experiments.

Let me give one other example of how the learning process is developed in the CHEMStudy. Oxidation is one of the more difficult topics encountered in a beginning chemistry course, and is formally encountered in Chapter 12 of the syllabus. However, let us see the ways in which the student begins to encounter this type of reaction early in his laboratory work. Experiment 6 involves the reduction of silver ion by metallic copper, but the immediate purpose of the experiment is the concept of the mole in chemistry. In experiment 14, the reaction between oxalate and permanganate ions is studied, although no use of the words *oxidation* or *reduction* is made at this time. The idea of the rate of reaction between these ions is developed in the discussion periods, and the concept of catalysis is encountered. Experiments 16 and 17 are quantitative measurements of the rates of some oxidation-reduction.

Current problems in various fields | 100

It is not until experiments 24 and 25 that the emphasis shifts specifically to the topic of oxidation-reduction (the teacher can and should refer back to the earlier experiments), and the words are used for the first time. These are quantitative experiments. Later, in the study of iodine chemistry, the principles of oxidation-reduction are encountered in the laboratory. Although the emphasis here is on the preparation and reactions of some compounds of iodine, the chemistry is almost entirely made up of oxidation or reduction reactions.

Other areas have been treated in the same fashion as in the difficult topic of oxidation-reduction. (An outline of the syllabus and the laboratory manual are included at the end of this report so that you may see the organization and suggested time schedule for the course.) As he does during the first five experiments and the first two weeks of the program, a student moves from qualitative observations in the laboratory to a discussion which attempts to correlate this information, and finally to quantitative experiments which test the principles and models which are set up. This is of course the essence of science and of what a scientist does.

Syllabus

Part I. Observation and interpretation

Chapter 1. Chemistry: An Experimental Science (2 weeks, experiments 1–5)

Part II. An overview of chemistry (7 weeks, experiments 6–13)

Chapters 2. Scientific Models and Atomic Theory
3. Atoms Combined in Substances
4. The Gas Phase: Kinetic Theory
5. Liquids and Solids
6. Chemistry and the Periodic Table
   Supplementary reading: Geochemistry
7. Energy

Part III. Chemical reactions and principles (11 weeks, experiments 14–25)

Chapters 8. Rates of Chemical Reactions
9. Equilibrium in Chemical Systems
10. Ionic Solutions
11. Acids and Bases
12. Oxidation-Reduction
13. Stoichiometry

Part IV. Atomic structure, chemical bonds (6 weeks, experiments 26–31)

Chapters 14. Believing in Atoms
15. Electrons and the Periodic Table
16. Molecules in the Gas Phase
17. Bonding in Liquids and Solids

Part V. Descriptive chemistry (8 weeks, experiments 32–41)

Chapters 18. Carbon Chemistry
         19. The Halogens
         20. The Third Row of the Periodic Table
         21. The Second Column of the Periodic Table
         22. The Transition Elements
         23. Biochemistry

Laboratory manual

Experiment 1. Scientific Observation
         2. Observing Regularities
         3. The Melting Point of a Pure Substance
         4. Chemistry of a Candle
         5. Heat Effects
         6. Reaction of Metallic Copper with a Solution of Silver Nitrate
         7. The Empirical Formula of a Compound
         8. The Formula of a Hydrate
         9. Mass Relationships in a Chemical Reaction
         10. Comparing the Weights of Gases
         11. The Relation between Weight and Volume of Hydrogen
         12. Some Aspects of Solubility
         13. Reactions between Ions in Solution
         14. A Study of Reactions
         15. The Heat of Reaction
         16. Reaction Rates I
         17. Reaction Rates II
         18. LeChatelier's Principle Applied to Some Reversible Chemical Reactions
         19. Chemical Equilibrium
         20. The Heats of Some Acid-Base Reactions
         21. Indicators; Ionization Constants
         22. A Quantitative Titration
         23. An Introduction to Oxidation-Reduction
         24. Electrochemical Cells
         25. Ionic Reactions
         26. The Relation between Moles of Electrons and Moles of Copper in Electrolysis
         27. Construction of Some Molecular Models
         28. The Packing of Atoms or Ions in Crystals
         29. Some Properties of a Pair of Cis-Trans Isomers
         30. A Qualitative Analysis Scheme Using Reagents Labeled A, B, and C
         31. A Qualitative Analysis Scheme for Various Anions of Sulfur
         32. Some Reactions of Hydrocarbons and of Alcohols
         33. The Preparation of Some Derivatives of Organic Acids
         34. The Electrolysis of Iodine
         35. Some Chemistry of Iodine

36. Some Chemistry of the Elements of Row 3 of the Periodic Table
37. The Separation of Some Transition Metals with an Ion-exchange Resin
38. The Corrosion of Iron
39. Preparation of a Complex Salt and of a Double Salt
40. Preparation of Potassium Dichromate
41. Preparation of Chrome Alum

13 ❀ THE MUSIC EDUCATION CURRICULUM RECENT DEVELOPMENTS AND EXPERIMENTATION
Marguerite V. Hood* *University of Michigan*

Most areas of the curriculum today have that atmosphere of excitement and unrest which permeates a period of change. In the field of music there seems to be, under the surface, something like a volcanic bubbling which erupts from time to time in response to certain pressures, and which constantly threatens a really big explosion. The recent changes which have occurred have altered the outline of the music curriculum appreciably, and the volcano is still boiling and forecasting more eruptions.

Every school curriculum has its own history of ups and downs and shifts in emphasis. These have resulted from changes in educational philosophy and from developments in our country and in the world. The periods that have occurred in the history of the music program are directly influencing today's curriculum, so it is important to review them here briefly. In this case, as the words above the national archives building in Washington say, "What is Past is Prologue."

Music came into the American public schools as a direct outgrowth of the activities of the old-time singing schools. Singing, as a group activity, very early became an accepted part of what was considered a good elementary school curriculum. The first regularly organized program of music throughout a school system which is on general record was begun in Boston in the 1830s, under Lowell Mason's supervision. During the years which followed, in addition to the elementary school singing instruction, the secondary schools sometimes included the activity of choral singing in the program. In a very few cases there were also instrumental groups and even classes in music theory and history. The latter subject, of course, was usually taught entirely from a book, since phonograph records were not yet available and live concerts were few and far between.

This type of school music curriculum remained fairly constant for many years. It developed, and it was implemented increasingly by the publication of textbook materials, but it was not changed appreciably until well into the

* Marguerite V. Hood is Professor of Music Education at the University of Michigan.

first decades of the twentieth century. The growing acceptance of music in the schools during these years was probably fostered to a considerable degree by the musical interests of immigrants from European countries. It seems also to have been influenced by the desires of our westward moving pioneers to carry with them as much as possible of both their European and their Eastern seaboard cultural traditions.

The first big changes in the music program came during the period just before and within the 1920s—a time of change in many areas of life, and especially in education. Almost concurrently, two apparently unrelated happenings had a resounding joint impact on music in this country. Progressive education proponents started talking about the child-centered school, calling for increased emphasis on the importance of the individual in education and stressing the necessity for flexibility in the curriculum in order to serve individual needs. And, at about the same time, the musical instrument manufacturers of the country, with an apparent vision of things to come, began to provide an adequate supply of instruments designed in price and type to meet the needs of young players. Playing an instrument was recognized and widely heralded as an ideal means of taking care of some individual differences. To complete the picture, only the coming of the music contest, especially in the field of band, was needed. The school instrumental program had arrived.

Many other developments of this period influenced the music curriculum. The junior high school came into being, and with it came growing attention to some special music teaching problems, such as the changing voice and the general music class. Administrators began to schedule music classes during the school day rather than before and after school, as had been usual heretofore. An increasing demand for school music teachers led to the development of courses for the training of specialists in the field. Here the United States broke away from the European tradition of confining such work to the conservatories and began to provide training for music educators also in the colleges and universities.

Although it is dangerous to assign dates to movements which are as ponderous as most of those in curriculum development, it would seem that the depression-ridden period of the 1930s left some very distinctive marks on the music curriculum. Verbal expression of a professional philosophy became more common, and "Music for every child—every child for music" became the motto of the music teachers. These were days of shortages of funds, however, and some communities considered music a frill which might well be eliminated from the curriculum. One of the changes that often resulted in the elementary school music curriculum, when the time allotted to the music teacher was cut, was a lessening of emphasis on music reading activities. The newly-popular concentration on integration or correlation of music with an academic subject, usually social studies, sometimes became a substitute for the more strictly disciplined music reading activity. The shortage of funds may also have helped to promote a relatively new plan for group instruction for beginners in applied music: piano, violin, clarinet, etc., in place of private lessons. Today this is recognized as a standard, efficient way of teaching. The music appreciation, history, and theory classes in secondary schools were often discontinued during this period in favor of more and larger performing groups. Great festivals of bands, orchestras and choirs were the order of the day.

Each historical period, unless subjected to special outside pressures, produces its own normal developments in the music curriculum, most of which grow out of and supplement earlier programs. But few periods in life are allowed a so-called "normal" development. The 1940s, for example, brought some curriculum changes which could normally have been expected, and some others which resulted from the war. New applications of emerging educational philosophies, which had earlier had only a nominal impact on music, suddenly became household words in the profession, and new ideas flourished. The belief in the importance of self-expression in helping a child learn was implemented by an emphasis on what was familiarly called *creative activity* through singing, playing instruments, dancing, creating tunes, etc. Rhythmic activity became a highly-respected part of the music curriculum. The movement of the human body in time to the rhythmic beat of music was recognized as valuable not only for free self-expression, but also as a means for laying a foundation for basic musical skills. "Learn to do by doing" was a popular motto, and one of the ways the idea was put into action in music was through the use of instruments in the classroom—rhythm, melody, and harmony instruments, which provided the child with a variety of independent learning experiences. The latter type of activity led directly to some of today's most interesting curriculum experimentation. Folk music had been growing in popularity for years in our country, but it is probable that the influence of the war and our interest in trying to understand people on both sides of the conflict greatly enhanced this popularity. The study of indigenous cultures became important, and folk music became an essential part of the music literature used in the schools.

A shortage of music teachers during the war threw an increasingly heavy load of responsibility for teaching music on the elementary classroom teacher. One approach to the problem, which represented an extreme view of the self-contained classroom philosophy, was the idea that, though the elementary teacher had little or no musical background herself, she would, because she was with the children constantly, understand them better and therefore do a better job of teaching music than the specialist. This idea still continues to create problems, and it has had a profound influence on the elementary school music curriculum. In schools where special music teachers provide enough assistance to the classroom teacher to insure for the children a good continuous, well-balanced music curriculum, the idea works. But when unskilled classroom teachers are thrown almost entirely on their own resources, the result is that boys and girls have little or no musical experience of either immediate or lasting value. However, the situation has inspired some excellent experimentation to improve the music instruction given to the classroom teacher in college. As yet not enough attention has been given to research into how to assist the elementary teacher through in-service education—to the problem of what kind of help she needs, how much of it, and how often.

The current period has brought changes in the musical life of these United States which have continually and powerfully influenced the music curriculum. The concert world, after years of very gradual growth, has suddenly experienced a tremendous expansion. Fine professional concerts are heard live in every part of the country. A survey shows that there are over twelve hundred symphony orchestras, most of them civic groups which include both amateurs and professionals. The orchestra boom has revealed a shortage of string players, and now the schools and colleges are not only promoting string classes, but also developing activities to encourage continued participation—festivals, youth orchestras, small ensembles, etc. Thousands follow the activities of the marching bands at football games every fall. Composers today are experimenting with new idioms, and the public, while not necessarily liking the results, is more interested in listening than ever before. Opera groups throughout the land play to audiences which a generation ago would have had neither an understanding or an interest in opera. There is a new emphasis on scholarly research activities, as contrasted with concentration on performance or relatively elementary music history and theory, in the college and university music departments. These, and other changes like them, are bringing important new areas into the present music curriculum at every school level.

One of the most interesting points of focus in the music curriculum today is the study of music as an academic subject, both for members of school performing groups and for consumers or listeners. For example, the Music Educators National Conference, a professional organization of about forty thousand teachers, will hold a biennial convention in Chicago in the spring of 1962. President Allen P. Britton planned the general sessions of that meeting around the overall subject, "The study of music: an academic discipline." There will be four general sessions: "Music, an academic discipline," "The creation of music," "The value of music," "The study of music through performance."

The humanities courses being taught today in many colleges and in an increasing number of high schools often illustrate an academic approach to music as it is related to various other areas. At Edsel Ford High School in Dearborn, Michigan, music teachers have been cooperating with teachers of art and English in a humanities course. The expressed aim of the course is to develop appreciation and enjoyment of the cultural richness of all these areas. In a similar high school humanities course, offered at the campus training school at the State University of New York College for Teachers at Albany, masterpieces of music, literature, painting, sculpture, and architecture are utilized as materials for instruction. The aims of this course are to develop not only wider artistic horizons, but also awareness of the interrelationships between any one of the arts and any or all the others.

In the highly specialized professional field of music, the Juilliard School of Music inaugurated several years ago an experimental curriculum for teaching the literature and materials of music in a large block instead of in many different courses in music history, form, harmony, counterpoint, literature, etc., as is common in most music departments. The emphasis is placed on the oneness of music as a complete discipline, with the music of a period seen always in the light of the social, political, and cultural climate of that period. This course has become one of the most famous in the musical world.

All through the years, music instruction in the schools has continually adjusted and readjusted its emphases to meet new needs and fulfill special objectives which were timely. But always there have been some specific aims which were constant and basic. One such aim was to raise the standard of public taste. In November, 1958, in a bulletin on the American Secondary Schools, the American Council of Learned Societies published a report of a music panel on the secondary school music curriculum (11). One of the recommendations of this group was for a course which they called "consumer music education," and of which they said, in part, "Such a course should be humanistic in its approach, relating music to other subjects in the curriculum and other aspects of our culture. . . . Its objective would be the development of musical taste and positive attitudes toward music." Again and again, the development of good taste is a stated objective of this type of course in music. It seems to be a general hope of the profession.

But there is more to developing good taste than just aiming for it. In the Gilbert and Sullivan opera, *Patience*, someone says, "You can't get high aesthetic tastes like trousers, ready-made." People do not even agree as to what good taste is. In his book, *The Tastemakers* (7), Russell Lynes says of taste, "Unless I completely misunderstand the real reasons for having taste, they are to increase one's faculties for enjoyment. Taste in itself is nothing. It is only what taste leads to that makes any difference in our lives."

One of the big problems in music teaching today is to find out *how* to go about developing taste. Can a course in music appreciation or history or theory or any related subject develop good taste in music? Does it result from learning about the structure of music, or about the composer's purpose, or the historical period to which the music belongs?

Kate Hevner Mueller, in reporting in the *Journal of Research in Music Education* on "Studies in Music Appreciation," (8) says, "The training of our audiences is as important as the training of performers and composers if music is to flourish in our society. . . . Music appreciation must be taught not only widely but well, and must include any material, any approach, which enlivens the music for the listener. . . ."

If we are to hope to help in some way to improve the public taste through our teaching of music, we need to have more research than has thus far been done to answer some of our many questions. John H. Mueller in his article, "Music and Education: A Sociological Approach," in *Basic Concepts in Music Education* (9), says of taste: "Fundamentally musical tastes are only very deeply ingrained habits of thought, supported by ethnocentric rationalizations"; further, "These tastes are formed just as other forms of social behavior are set up." They are influenced, he says, by many factors, including social heritage or tradition, biological limiting factors, technological factors such as technical inventions and developments, and factors connected with social relationships. As to the latter, existing courses which include study of music theory and history, together with the variety of music experiences, direct and indirect, which a school student has today, must certainly have some impact on his musical taste—at least that type of taste which results from group or social approval.

Dean Marten ten Hoor, in "The Role of Culture in Music" (12), described the importance of social approval to taste in very clear terms: "We cannot . . . easily dismiss the composite opinion of a great many people, either of a geographical area, of a nation, or of a substantial time period.

For it is by this composite opinion that taste is formed. . . . There is a kind of . . . order of acceptance here: first by the individual innovator, then by the professional group, and finally by the general public, or at least part of it." Informal observation of the development of taste in the student consumer of music seems to indicate that general public approval is his first aim. The student usually wants to feel the backing of some of his peers as he forms his opinions regarding music. After some experience and knowledge have been acquired, his independence develops and his attitude often becomes one of more professional, critical evaluation.

A second and very interesting current subject—in this case a specific project—of great importance to the American school music curriculum is the Ford Foundation Composers' Program.[1] This program sends selected promising young composers into a group of the nation's schools on one-year grants as composers-in-residence. It is part of the Ford Foundation program in the humanities and the arts. The grant to each young composer is commensurate with the annual salary scale of the school, plus a modest addition to help meet expenses connected with the program, such as the preparation of parts for performance. The composer has the opportunity to become well acquainted with the musical needs, abilities, and limitations of school singers and players of all ages, and to experiment in writing music for them. He also has the golden opportunity of hearing his music performed and being able to revise and rewrite it if he wishes. New, original music of excellent quality for use in the schools is being produced as a result of this program. Also, the pupils, teachers, and the entire community gain a first-hand opportunity to get an understanding of music in the contemporary idiom. Horizons are definitely expanding—or perhaps it would be more correct to say that tastes are becoming broader, more discerning, and more sophisticated.

In the spring of 1961 at a regional Music Educators National Conference meeting in Asheville, North Carolina, a stunning program of high school band, orchestra, and choir music composed by these grantees in a variety of schools was performed by student groups. The experiment, which began in 1958, has been so successful that in 1961 the Ford Foundation appointed a young composer as a field representative to observe school music programs in all parts of the United States. This representative was one of those who received a grant the first year of the project, and his new activity was planned as a source of information for the committees charged with assigning grants for 1962–1963.

A rather unique development in the field of music instruction is the work started by the German composer Carl Orff. Orff is probably the favorite living German composer, at least of the average music lover of that country. In the United States there is an unfortunate lack of contact between school musicians and most American composers. Breaking down that barrier is one

[1] In January, 1963, it was announced that the Ford Foundation will support ($1,380,000) a six-year project designed to emphasize the creative aspects of music in the public schools. The project is entitled "Contemporary Music Project for Creativity in Music Education" and is under the direction of the Music Educators National Conference. One part of the new project is the continuation of the Young Composers Project described above. Many other areas have been added, including the study of creativity in music and the development of the creative talents of school children (see *Music Educators Journal*, vol. 49, no. 4, February–March 1963, p. 37).

of the aims of the Ford Foundation project. But in Europe no such barrier exists, and it seems perfectly natural to find a leading composer developing new plans and materials for teaching music to children.

Orff started his *Musik für Kinder* experiments (10) in the 1930s, after years of dissatisfaction with the methods and materials being used in teaching children. He based his system on the belief that the learning processes of small children follow the same pattern as the learning processes of the race. Primitive man has used free bodily movement in dance and also simple rhythmic drum patterns, and so Orff began with drums suited to the children's physical size and skill, combining bodily movements with the beat of the drum. He also added rhythmic chants, synchronizing the spoken rhythm with the other movements.

Next came melodic experimentation. Many primitive peoples' first musical utterances employ only one or two pitches, and perhaps finally progress to the use of the five-tone scale. Using this same sequence, Orff started the musical experiences planned for little folks by writing songs with only two or three notes and, at the most, five notes from the pentatonic scale. He expanded the melodic vocabulary to include other steps only after the children had had a great deal of experience with the very simple melodies. He also believed that boys and girls would best develop musical ears and a real understanding of intervals if each of them had a simple melodic instrument to play. In order to assure absolute accuracy of pitch, he laid down strict requirements for the making of new schoolroom instruments, most of which look like marimbas or xylophones. The bars can be removed from each instrument, and the children can learn to play only one or two notes at a time as they sing, gradually adding bars as their melodic vocabulary increases.

Space does not permit description of the variety of activities Carl Orff introduced with his materials, but it is rich and fascinating. Because he did the original experimentation so long ago, probably no one is more surprised than he that so many European schools are now trying his ideas, and that a considerable number of American music teachers are now showing an interest in them.

Another subject of current interest in the realm of curriculum development is that of individual differences in education and the importance of training each child to the limits of his capacity, be he gifted, average, or handicapped. In music education as elsewhere, this subject is extremely important. One of the best recent publications of the Music Educators National Conference is a book entitled *Music for the Academically Talented Student* (5), done jointly with the NEA Project on the Academically Talented Student, with the aid of a grant from the Carnegie Corporation of New York.

In these days of intensified academic activity for gifted youngsters, we in music are gravely concerned about two phases of this subject. First, there is the problem of the instruction of the child who is gifted in music and will probably become a specialist in some musical field: how to identify him; how to educate him. Second, there is the problem of the function of music in the life of the academically talented student—the one who is spending long hours of concentration in one or several academic disciplines and who has increasing need for the kind of relief from tension which music may be able to give him. Our problem concerning him is this: How can we see to it that this student has the opportunity right now to continue some musical activity if he enjoys it, along with his load of academic work?

Such students need time for sufficient activity not only to give them relaxation and satisfaction now, but also to provide for the growth in musical skill and intelligence necessary to insure continuing satisfaction. I am not sure how many string quartets and informal musical groups are currently active among the faculty members of medical schools in such universities as Michigan or Minnesota, but there are usually several in any such professional (and many business) establishments everywhere. Gifted boys and girls should have stimulating opportunities to perform, if they are performers. And whether they are both performers and listeners or just listeners *to* music, they should have opportunities at their own intellectual levels to build a growing knowledge and understanding of music itself from a variety of viewpoints: its history, form, periods, styles; its scientific and mathematical bases; its relationships to other areas, etc. Such experiences will lead not only to increased enjoyment but also to the formation of intelligent, discriminating taste. The subject of the book *Music for the Academically Talented Student* (5) is the planning of a curriculum for these students as well as scheduling, implementing, and enriching it. Russia has many special music schools to which very young musically gifted children are sent for continued intensive training. The fact that we have a different approach to educational problems in our country does not absolve us from the responsibility for providing excellent training for gifted children.

Several practical approaches to the problem of the musically gifted youngster are being tried in our country. Probably the best known project is the National Music Camp at Interlochen, Michigan. For over thirty years it has provided summer instruction and inspiration for young people who are musically gifted, as well as for those who will be amateurs and music lovers though not professionals. In 1962, to further serve the needs of the musically gifted group, the Interlochen Arts Academy, a year-round school, was opened.

A careful study of curriculum development and experimentation in the areas of the exceptional or handicapped child cannot be made here. There are two possible relationships of music teaching to this special area:

1. How to teach music to the exceptional child so that he enjoys it and learns to use it to his own satisfaction so far as his capabilities allow.
2. How to use music to overcome or alleviate the existing handicap.

There are experiments in almost every division of both these categories—with problems of mental handicap, speech handicap, post-polio physical therapy, hearing and sight handicaps, etc. One reason it is difficult to report on this area is that many of the projects are being carried on by dedicated teachers who have not the time, the money, or the skill in research to keep a complete record of their work. Their projects are labors of love, designed to meet the needs of certain individuals and situations. There is, of course, considerable scientific and medical research of a highly technical nature being done, but a great deal of study which might influence the regular music curriculum is still of the informal, unrecorded type.

Investigations in the field of folk music form another large segment of research which is influencing the music curriculum. It would be difficult to list here (even if one knew all of them) the many projects which have been undertaken. An interesting project was the Pittsburgh public schools program, in which children were encouraged to sing to teachers any folk songs they had learned from members of their families, adding, if possible, the geographical source of each song. A great wealth of music and of information was collected by the teachers involved in the program. Such a project, if carried through to completion, would be of interest also to social scientists and to collectors of folk songs.

It should be mentioned that the type of folk song used in the schools and included in the school song books has changed greatly in the last twenty years. Previously, the song literature usually included in the curriculum was made up almost entirely of a few familiar British, Western European, or American pioneer songs. Now our children are enjoying folk music of many types, some of it strange to our ears because it may be based on unfamiliar scales. This change has probably resulted from the great increase in the amount of international cultural exchange which is presently taking place. It may also have been influenced by the fact that many of these songs which might be difficult for the average teacher to teach are now available on records for classroom use.

Of course there is a great deal of experimental activity related to the employment of electronic devices in the teaching of music, since many of these devices—the phonograph, tape recorder, radio, TV, and even teaching machines—lend themselves very naturally to such use. The National Educational Television and Radio Center (familiarly known as NET) has as one of its purposes the evaluation of educational TV programs in all subject areas. A recent research project accomplished with the assistance of a NET grant, was in investigation of a large sampling of educational TV music programs—ways of using them, and their acceptance by and values for different types of groups and individuals. Many of these programs are now available on film and have become an important part of the body of materials used in the music curriculum.

Closed-circuit TV is the subject of considerable experiment in the field of music teaching. Further, the airplane hovering over northern Indiana, sending out the Ford Foundation's Midwest Program on Airborne Television, has music programs at two school levels as part of its curriculum. And radio, sometimes said to be dead and gone, is having a surprising revival in school music circles. From our own University of Michigan campus a school music broadcast is heard by about seventy-five thousand children weekly. There are many such radio programs throughout the country. These programs enrich the regular school music curriculum in some classrooms; in many, they provide the sole source of instruction.

The emphasis on performance in the music curriculum of the average American high school has been receiving a steadily increasing amount of criticism. The American Council of Learned Societies report mentioned earlier (11) included a statement regarding specific weaknesses in the present high school program, emphasizing the fact that in many schools the music curriculum is limited to the activities of performing organizations, thus automatically shutting off nonperformers from musical contacts while in school. Further, the report seriously questioned the present strong emphasis on marching band activity and on competitive festivals, and suggested that there is need for better use of rehearsal time, with more stress on developing musical skills, on the understanding of musical style, and on the historical and literary significance of music. So far, not many results of this line of thinking are obvious, but the critical voices do seem to be growing louder.

And so, the examples of curriculum criticism, development, change, and experimentation in music form a long and constantly growing list. Studies (some informal, others scientific) are in progress on various phases of the teacher education program in music, including in-service teaching; on the evaluation of teaching materials and tools; on the evaluation of students and courses; on the ways of teaching creative composition for children; on team teaching in music classes; on teaching note reading; on teaching music skills, such as piano playing, to adults; on refining a college music entrance examination to make it valid for prognostication of success or failure of a student; on the use of time in instrumental class teaching; etc.

We in music education need other studies, some of which seem too expensive to undertake at present. We need, for example, more research in the academic areas of music instruction. It would be valuable to have experimentation on certain kinds of administrative procedures in music education. Interpretation of the music program and its objectives to the public and to the rest of the teaching profession needs serious study. The best use of units on science in the elementary general music class is an area which is in need of attention. And so it goes, on and on. The possibilities seem almost endless. Meanwhile, probably what the rank and file of the profession need most of all is to get acquainted with what has already been learned through research and to find out how best to use the results. And the curriculum in the field of music continues that volcanic bubbling and erupting which gives evidence of life and vitality—and music programs in the schools continue to grow, change, develop, and flourish.

Selected references

1 Allen P. Britton, "Music in Early American Public Education: A Historical Critique," in *Basic Concepts in Music Education*, Fifty-seventh Yearbook of the National Society for the Study of Education, distributed by The University of Chicago Press, Chicago, 1958, part I, chap. 8, pp. 195–211.
2 Allen P. Britton, "The Singing School Movement in the United States," *Report of the Eighth Congress, New York 1961, International Musicological Society*, Bärenreiter-Verlag, Kassel, 1961, vol. I, pp. 89–99.
3 Dolores D. Dudley, *Singing, Listening, Doing: Music for You*, Midwest Program on Airborne Television Instruction, Lafayette, Ind., Resource Series, no. 4, 1960.
4 "Ford Foundation Composers' Project in Music Education," *Music Educators Journal*, vol. 45, p. 39, February–March, 1959.

5 William C. Hartshorn, *Music for the Academically Talented Student in the Secondary School*, National Education Association and Music Educators National Conference, Washington, D.C., 1960.
6 *The Juilliard Report on Teaching the Literature and Materials of Music*, W. W. Norton & Company, Inc., New York, 1953.
7 Russell Lynes, *The Tastemakers*, Harper and Row, Publishers, Incorporated, New York, 1954.
8 Kate Hevner Mueller, "Studies in Music Appreciation," *Journal of Research in Music Education*, vol. 4, Music Educators National Conference, Washington, D.C., Spring, 1960.
9 John H. Mueller, "Music and Education: A Sociological Approach," in *Basic Concepts in Music Education*, Fifty-seventh Yearbook of the National Society for the Study of Education, distributed by The University of Chicago Press, Chicago, 1958, part I, chap. 4, pp. 88–122.
10 Carl Orff and Gunhild Keetman, *Orff-Schulwerk: Musik für Kinder*, B. Schott's Sohne, Mainz, 1950–1953, 5 vols. (Also Associated Music Publishers, New York.)
11 *Secondary School Problems*, American Council of Learned Societies, New York, 1958. (Reprinted from the American Council of Learned Society *Newsletter*, vol. 9, no. 9, vol. 10, no. 9.)
12 Marten ten Hoor, *The Role of Music in Culture*, University of Michigan Official Publication, School of Music Studies, no. 4, The University of Michigan Press, Ann Arbor, Mich., 1961.
13 Roy York, Jr., "Humanities in the High School," *Music Educators Journal*, vol. 45, pp. 44–48, February–March, 1959.

14 CURRICULUM EXPERIMENTATION IN ART EDUCATION AS SEEN THROUGH RECENT RESEARCH Kenneth R. Beittel*
Pennsylvania State University

Research, in the modern sense in which the word is used in the behavioral sciences, is a relatively recent innovation in art education. Its growth appears to an outsider to be spontaneous rather than planned or programmatic (1). The early research contributions to art education were made by related disciplines—notably by psychology (2), and the art education profession itself has up to now been largely inimical or indifferent to research. At present, the opinion of the rank and file is changing, probably under the impact of research into general creativity in psychology, science, and education, and under the impact of a productive empirical research orientation in art education itself at a few university centers. The artist's distrust of verbal and quantitative attacks on the visual and qualitative core of his craft are doubtlessly destined to persist, but the excitement proper to research activity itself and its unmistakable connection with curriculum experimentation are hard to ignore.

* Kenneth R. Beittel is Professor of Art Education at Pennsylvania State University.

It is also true, historically, that some of the giants of art education, and a certain type of romance, are gone. With the departure of trust in a kind of Hegelian universal reason integrated through one man's brain, theory and methods tend to become dogmatic or technical. One man's brain usually greatly oversimplifies the dynamics and complexities of things, arriving at the detail through fugue-like constructions of what were originally improvised motifs. These tend to become reified and dogmatic as they are invested with power and prestige, especially for other minds uninclined to think or experiment for themselves.

At the same time, our ideals are more or less delineated. They need, however, more than courageous restatement, for they are apt to atrophy if they cannot meet the challenge of changing conditions and opportunities. The younger contingent of our profession is beginning to see that in research, theory and methods are given "a local habitation and a name."

There has been a general philosophy of art education extending, in theory but not practice, from preschool to old age. Its central tenet is that art, *as art,* is educative, therapeutic, ameliorative, and integrative for all people. At the elementary level, such an image finds support by teachers, administrators, and a growing number of parents. The same cannot be said for adolescent, postadolescent, and adult levels.

Basic to the acceptance of art at the elementary level, however, are the same beliefs that make art valuable at any level, namely, (1) the development and refinement of sensory experiences, (2) the development of creativity, (3) personal adjustment, and (4) the development of appreciation, of open aesthetic attitudes, and of confidence and competency in matters of aesthetic judgment.

I played a tape for my graduate class in the history and philosophy of art education in the summer of 1961. It was recorded from a summarizing lecture by the late Viktor Lowenfeld to his class in the art of the elementary school child. Lowenfeld was saying that the great need of our time is sensitivity, and that the greatest need is to be sensitive to one's own needs. I take this to mean the need for our own creativity, expression, and aesthetic involvement—needs which, to paraphrase Kierkegaard's formulation for despair (3), are greatest when we are not even aware of them. And, to borrow a construction from Buber (4), it is one of the prime roles of education to keep the pain of the lack of this need alive.

The centering of a productive orientation and of the creative process in art education encourages curriculum experimentation. Much of such experimentation, however, lives and dies with its originators. Much of it, also, takes place in sensitive interaction between individual teacher and individual student. Only larger cooperative ventures, such as the Bauhaus movement after World War I in Germany or the Owatonna art project here in Minnesota, get to be recorded. Experimental research is beginning to fill this need.

Another hopeful sign is seen in the idea which is abroad that all may participate in the visual arts, no matter what their preexisting talents or skills. In a large general education course called "the arts," which I taught and coordinated as part of a team, including a music man and a theater arts man, and about which I will have more to say later, it was found that over 80 per cent of the 329 students chose to work in graphic or three-dimensional media when they were asked to do an independent creative project. Almost two-thirds also elected visual arts studios for a four-week studio session planned as an integral part of the course. Apparently ideas nurtured during the days of the progressive movement, and lately in the elementary schools, have helped to remove much of the fear that people still show when they are expected to participate in creative origination as opposed to performance in music, theater, or the literary arts.

One other fact should be mentioned at this point. In many schools art is elective after the eighth or ninth grades. Committees such as that sponsored by the American Council of Learned Societies, by the National Art Education Association (which, by the way, appointed a National Commission on Art Education in 1961 to summarize, consolidate, and project forward the position of art education in modern times), and by various governors' commissions on education, are pointing out the great need for courses for all secondary and college students. Most of the art education profession and many school administrations are not presently oriented in this direction, so that this statement of needed curriculum revision and experimentation will catch many unprepared. Furthermore, there is only a little in the way of empirical research to guide us.

I wish to develop, in the rest of this paper, what is known. The recommendations of the American Council of Learned Societies panel on secondary school curriculum problems (5) on art were broad. They bear repeating:

1. That the basic approach should be creative through work in the studio or workshop, during which the student becomes personally involved. Since this part of art teaching is necessarily planned for the individual, it is altogether unadaptable to any textbook approach.

2. That historical matter must be incorporated to develop the student's awareness of his inheritance in this field. Instead of teaching survey courses in art history, an attempt should be made to involve the student in a meaningful consideration of art as it represents various epochs and cultures and as it might affect his own creativity. Films, slides, books, exhibits, and all other useful devices should accompany this part of the original works of art. The practice of art, seeing good examples of it, and reading and hearing about them, would develop the framework for critical judgment on the part of the student.

I am going to group my statements under three large headings which I am calling (1) the aesthetic-forming or studio participation dimension, (2) the evaluative-appreciative or judgmental dimension, and (3) the general creativity dimension.

1. The aesthetic-forming or studio participation dimension

I use the phrase "aesthetic-forming orientation" because there is no strong English equivalent to the German verb signifying "to make or form a gestalt." This is precisely my meaning. Part of the magic of visual art resides in its process-centered thinking and in its unitary, gestalt-bound product. Both require the participation of the student, if he is truly to understand the nature of art—that is, the student must create in a medium and must evaluate art objects. Philosophers like Dewey, Whitehead, Buber, and Langer have pointed this out. Buber states that the communicative content of a work of art is locked in its gestalt and that it cannot be abstracted from it. Langer refers to the arts as presentational and nondiscursive. There is a proper mystical dimension to the arts which cannot be wished away by the most rigorous thinker. Even Whitehead was forced to conclude that what is needed in life as well as in art is the immediate apprehension of a variety of vivid values with a minimum of eviscerating analysis. Charles W. Morris (6) defines this domain as the "appraisive valuative universe of discourse." Jungian theory has it that artistic creativity involves transfer of content from the realm of "intuitive perception" to the realm of "sense perception," whereas scientific creativity involves transfer from the realm of "feeling judgment" to the realm of "thinking judgment."

Just what is known about studio participation and what methods of instruction and curriculum organization are most effective? A recently concluded study on "The Effect of a 'Depth' vs. a 'Breadth' Method of Art Instruction at the Ninth Grade Level" (7), conducted by the Art Education Department of the Pennsylvania State University in collaboration with the school system of a middle-sized Pennsylvania city, gives some guidance along curricular lines. In this study, two methods of studio participation were compared with a normal control studio. A *depth* teaching program may be defined as one which allows a sustained concentration in one area of study. There may be variety within this area, but the different activities are such that they permit an easy transition from one problem to another. This approach stimulates both sequential and cumulative learning. A *breadth* teaching program is one in which a variety of well-chosen subjects and activities are dispersed in such a way as to accommodate differences in the interests and experience of pupils. A strong supporting argument for such a program is that it maintains the pupil's interests while providing a survey type of introduction to many media. The breadth approach is most widely accepted in junior high schools.

The study was conducted over the 1960–1961 school year. All instruction was handled by one highly experienced art teacher not trained at the Pennsylvania State University. Three comparable groups of students were designated as depth, breadth, and control sections. An extensive battery of pre- and post-tests was administered, and art works from the beginning and end of the year were collected and judged. The teacher was accustomed to what might be termed an unenriched breadth approach. The experimental breadth group was given enrichment in terms of materials, visual aids, and curriculum planning.

Findings demonstrated a noticeable retrogression, on virtually all the criterion measures of the test batteries, except in the depth group, which won the day by not becoming worse, by most measures. This in itself is a kind of commentary on what may be taking place at this level in school. There was a marked decline, in both the control and breadth groups, in ideational self-determination and divergent thinking, in openness to new perceptual experiences, and in the level of their art work as well. There was a noticeable relationship between spontaneity of the student's working methods and improvement in his achievement.

In short, this study showed that the less popular method, the depth method, produced the greatest gain in individual student progress over a one-year period. Students preferred the breadth approach, but learned less from it. Another recent study by Lienard (8), whose subjects were of the same age level, indicates that dissatisfaction, and not satisfaction, is related to progress in art. Our study showed that where a drive for depth and involvement is made possible through sustained work in a limited area of activity (in this case, painting), it is possible to hold and perhaps develop a positive, aesthetic, self-determining orientation. Only when there is a series of works, so that progress can be discerned and evaluation can take place, is it likely that an entire group of students will grow—not only in their creativity in art, but perhaps also as creative individuals, as indicated by their divergent thinking and openness to new experiences.

Since mention has been made of the spontaneity of the working method, I would like to develop this concept briefly. Burkhart (9) has described two methods of working and perceiving in art, the spontaneous and the deliberate. This suggests the existence of creative and perhaps less creative styles which are reflections of strong differences in personality structure. Spontaneous highs differ from deliberate highs in a number of ways other than their art. The former describe themselves as feeling "distinctive, self-confident, involved, uninhibited, loose, and versatile" during the creative process; the deliberate subjects feel "clever, conservative, moderate, practical, fussy, and organized." The spontaneous students see more movement in unstructured stimuli, they are more open perceptually, they are more complex persons, they score higher on aestheticism and theoretical interest in art, they are less authoritarian, and they tend to come from permissive or mother-dominated homes. At the same time, when aesthetic quality is judged in products, spontaneous and deliberate students may do equally well. It should be noted that in our present culture there tend to be proportionately more spontaneous high aesthetic achievers at upper levels (graduate majors) and fewer in the lower and general (non-major) student groups. The ratio may vary from one in twenty to eight in twenty.

It has already been indicated that spontaneity in method, or intuitive, process-bound thinking is related to progress in art. A second methods study was conducted by the speaker (10) with general (non-major), inexperienced college students in an introductory pottery studio class in which throwing on the potter's wheel was emphasized. Students were preclassified, by means of a questionnaire, as preferring spontaneous or deliberate working methods, and were randomly assigned, from a group of over one hundred volunteers (mostly freshmen), to four groups of eight students each. Two were called holistic and two were called analytical. Each group of eight included four deliberate and four spontaneous students. It will be noted that a depth approach was used in both methods—analytical and holistic—in preference to a survey approach. It has been the speaker's practice to define the realities of instruction in terms of the realities of the craft or art. Calvin Taylor recently reported to us at the Pennsylvania State University on the plan to place high school students directly into laboratories in colleges and universities in order that they may learn the rules of the right "ball game." This is an instance of the reality dimension as it appears in science. I am convinced that the same is true in art.

The analytical is a step-by-step method, with goals and objectives clearly delineated. It is a more verbal, didactic method. The holistic method presents the working process as a whole, without benefit of analyzing procedures in detail. I understand there is a method in dramatics and in creative dance termed "total gesture" which would be comparable. This method is less verbal, more dependent on "feel" and on an intuition of what is right during the process. In the arts, much is made of self-discovery and self-developed theory and method; thus the holistic method has a certain tradition and value attached to it. The academic tradition, on the other hand, is more verbal and analytical. In the study mentioned, the students worked eight sessions of two hours each. Four of these were led by a team of two instructors, four were proctored without instruction. A proctored practice period followed each instruction period the next day. The best materials and equipment were used. Pre-wedged balls of clay of uniform size and consistency were prepared. Students made and saved as many pots as they wished, and each pot kept was coded as to session, group, and individual for later expert judgments. One of the nonstatistical findings of this study was the great achievement possible to non-art college freshmen over a short period. Their motivational level put to shame many of the art majors. Of course, we gave them an unusual amount of attention. On the statistical side, the analytical methods always proved superior to the holistic, and the spontaneous group always learned more than the deliberate, regardless of method.

A side issue has to do with methods experimentation. I favor the holistic philosophy and do not intend to conclude, as a result of this brief experiment, that it is always less effective with beginning non-art students. It may well represent a missing creative dimension to our educational system. Second, I felt previously that methods and personalities went together. In this study I felt the actuality of retreating to my office and changing methods between groups. The situational realities made both approaches very credible to me.

A third methods experiment had to do with the general education arts class which covers art, music, and theater, and utilized team teaching, studio participation, and independent work. As I mentioned earlier, this class had an enrollment of 329 in 1960 and in many administrative aspects was a mess. Yet it represents the challenge of art education at the college and university level, when such education is thought of in terms of all students and the desirability of their learning through art. In administering the studio assignments of this large group of students, I was dependent on the good graces of instructors and graduate assistants who volunteered to hold studios in their specialties over a four-week period. As an escape valve, I scheduled the large auditorium, in which the entire group ordinarily met, for a drawing studio. About 90 students participated in this. I was aided by three graduate students in art education. The study I wish to speak of here might be termed "the instructional value of forced holistic visual experience."

For this study, use was made of the Eidophor, the trade name of a closed-circuit television apparatus which projects a televised image on a large 24-foot screen. The image originates from a studio in another building. It was not known what effect stimulus materials from a flat screen would have on art production. The device described, however, had in its favor, in addition to its size, the fact that several cameras could be kept continually in motion, projecting a still life, for instance, in such a way that the objects were seen selectively and as constantly changing. A double image, or even the superimposition of two entirely different still life arrangements, could be managed. Pace and concentration could be manipulated. In one instance, even performance aspects were brought in by the superimposition of an artist's hand "thinking" on the subject, having the artist paint in white on black paper as he received the monitor image, and then having his drawing picked up by another camera and superimposed on the subject matter for an instant only. In this instance, it was important *not* to suggest how to draw the subject, but rather to suggest *attitudes* toward performance—that is, freedom, confidence, probing for essentials, etc. Support for this approach may be found from art psychologists such as Arnheim (11), who believes art to be a joint phenomenon of perceiving and performing aspects, or more recently from McFee (12), who outlines what she calls a "perception-delineation theory."

An analysis of Eidophor versus independent or outside drawings revealed two interesting findings. The deliberate students, high and low, profited greatly from the Eidophor treatment. The low students, both deliberate and spontaneous, also gained greatly. Perhaps this was because these students were forced away from overly preconceived or subjective approaches or away from a low motivational level. Only the "spontaneous highs," who still did the best work, did worse on the Eidophor treatment. In almost all instances their independent work was superior. Apparently the more advanced spontaneous students need other, probably more individualized, forms of instruction and possibly more self-evaluative kinds of experiences relating to their self-initiated art activities. These more gifted students may have also reacted negatively to the large group setting. This one group may thus pose a separate curricular problem.

Further study of creative personality characteristics and of general creativity tests of this studio sample indicated a lack of relationship between art, personality, and general creativity dimensions. Such a gap, as will be reported later, seems to be partially bridged by higher, more select samples, contrary to my expectations. The best students, also, when asked to do a completely independent creative project and keep a creative process journal, often turned in tight work because they felt colleges required this kind of thing. One particularly creative girl whom I interviewed told me, when I asked her whether she had thought of going into the arts or art education, that she had not because she knew she would have to take drawing studios and that she was too much of a nonconformist to draw as someone told her to.

One further comment before going on. As the depth-breadth study, the Eidophor study and the pottery studies demonstrate, the move to bring art to all as a part of secondary and post-secondary general education will require new methods and new administrative organizational approaches. The traditional studio and artistic medium categories may have to be extended if they are to be adequate for new conditions and new environments for creative action and expression. At the same time, there is a reality dimension and a balancing that comes from the discipline and expressive potential which is the artistic medium itself, even as traditionally defined. But large classes, more independent study, and other changes are before us.

2. The evaluative-appreciative or judgmental dimension

The problems of art appreciation relate directly to the study of the art judgment task. The judgmental problem is also the key to research in art education and to teaching art, since the teacher must make value judgments of his student's work.

A judgment may be viewed simply as an answer to a question. The questions of importance in art education are: "What is quality?" and "What is creative?" These are essentially unanswerable questions which must be kept open-ended. In the arts, a divergent and relative, as opposed to a factual and absolute, viewpoint seems to be required. Thus, the criterion problem, and the need to risk judgment upon it sooner or later, is what makes research potentially "interesting" in art education. It essentially puts us on the hot plate, since a judge can be neither right nor wrong. Relativized, as are all judges of things creative or aesthetic, the aesthetician squirms—understandably, for he knows that there are values which seem to count over others. In facing the art object, the content of which can be experienced but not otherwise communicated, the judge actually faces himself. He must struggle for some image of excellence. The questions he is trying to answer are: What is art? What is man? What is quality in action? What is to be?

As the relativized nature of the judgmental problem becomes clearer, we can begin to ask more varied exploratory questions about it with newer research techniques. Thus, in a given judgment task, we have studied, structurally, relationships between verbal rating scales, between art objects, and between the personality characteristics of clusters of judges. Each perspective seems to yield its own insights.

In a recent study (13) we selected twenty representative art products, produced under a common motivational topic by Pennsylvania State and Ohio State University undergraduate and graduate art and art education majors. The judges studied were seventeen experienced teachers and graduate art education students. They rated each of the twenty works by means of twelve bipolar seven-point semantic scales such as are used by Osgood and his collaborators in their book, *The Measurement of Meaning* (14). The criteria used were representative of several factorial dimensions found repeatedly in Osgood's work. We first factor-analyzed the drawings themselves. There were five clear factors: (1) art quality (good-bad), (2) masculinity-femininity, (3) spontaneity-deliberateness, (4) feeling for nature, (5) complexity-simplicity. The strong factors here appear to be the first, the product-evaluative, and the third, the process judgment.

Second, we factor-analyzed the twelve bipolar semantic scales. There were three clear factors. The first, and by far the strongest, might be called the "product evaluative dimension." The scale "good-bad" in this factor is the key one, and it might be called an "absolute product evaluative criterion." It is behind every judgment of art quality. The other evaluative criteria in this factor might be called "relative product evaluative criteria." They may be associated with art quality in some instances; in others, not. It is apparent, for example, that if the scale "sophisticated-naïve" is used, a picture might be designated "sophisticated" but judged either "good" or "bad," depending upon other considerations.

Relative product evaluation criteria under Factor 1 are:

1. Controlled-accidental
2. Complex-simple
3. Serious-humorous
4. Mature-youthful
5. Full-empty
6. Interesting-boring
7. Vibrant-still
8. Sophisticated-naïve

The second factor might be called a *process judgment factor,* and is represented by the following scales:

1. Intuitive-rational
2. Informal-formal
3. Accidental-controlled (splits its loading between this and the evaluative factor)

The third factor is a descriptive, nonevaluative, nonprocess criterion on femininity-masculinity.

As a third analysis, the judges themselves were sorted into clusters. Two common factors and several lesser specific factors emerged. The first factor contained what might be called the *deliberate judges,* who are apparently in the majority even among graduate students and teachers. The second factor contained the *spontaneous* or *process-evaluative* judges.

For personal descriptions of these judges, we resorted to an experimental creative personality inventory[1] made up of 23 sub-scales (15). For each of these scales we had a predicted scoring direction for the creative personality —many of these directions coming from previous research. The process-evaluative judges were superior to the deliberate judges on fifteen of the twenty-three scales, and there were no differences on the others. In brief, the process-evaluative judges were more individualistic, casual, flexible (on three different flexibility scales), bohemian, spontaneous, creatively oriented, intuitive, percept-bound, self-involved, abstract and poetic, value-determined, and nonauthoritarian. Still more briefly, the process-evaluative judges might be called spontaneous-abstract-nonauthoritarian; the deliberate judges might be termed deliberate, concrete, and authoritarian. There were ten clearly deliberate judges and seven clearly spontaneous ones. The spontaneous judges favored the use of these rating polarities: good, full, vibrant, and mature (from the product evaluative dimension); and intuitive, informal, and accidental (from the process dimension). The deliberate judges favored

[1] There have been two versions of this inventory, developed by Beittel and Burgart, called the BBC1-X1 and the BBC1-X2. The latter is the second version of the descriptive creative personality inventory and is made up of 233 items, seventy-three of which are word pairs. The latter, and one of the sentence-type scales, were originated by Beittel and Burgart. In all, twenty-three scales are derivable, nine of these from the work of the above researchers, the other fourteen from the work of Gough (16), Bales and Couch (17), Cattell (18), and Schaie (19). All of the scales have been subjected to item analyses. Six factor scores have also been developed from a series of factor analyses of a graduate art population, an undergraduate art population, and a general undergraduate population.

the opposite: bad, empty, still, youthful, and rational, formal, and controlled. It is little wonder that Picasso has said in effect: "You think you're judging my painting, but it's judging you."

One further comment. Both groups of judges are reliable on the product evaluative dimension—but the deliberate judges are internally more reliable because they make fewer relative distinctions. It's all a matter of "good-bad." But the deliberate judges seem unable to make process distinctions. For them, intuitive, informal, and accidental are uncorrelated, usually negatively correlated, whereas the opposite is true for the process-evaluative judges. In sixteen out of seventeen cases, the behavior of the judges in using the two criteria—intuitive-rational and formal-informal—would place them in their proper cluster. The creative personality rating and the process-evaluative rating correlated .73. Inter-judge reliability becomes a different thing, therefore, when both types of evaluations—product and process—are taken into account.

There is evidence, however, that deliberate judges can learn to use process criteria. It is important that they do so, for these are necessary in the areas of art appreciation, teaching, and research. Apparently special judgmental and evaluative training is needed, since all the judges studied were experienced art teachers. Since signs of spontaneity of process appear to be related to the ability to progress in one's art achievement, the importance of this training is quite clear.

Several other developments provoke thought about the evaluative-appreciative dimension. One of the few attempts in recent years to study experimentally the changes in art judgment resulting from courses in art appreciation was carried out by Heller (20). He first constructed a test of art judgment validated against judgments of art experts and degrees of training. (By the way, it now appears that this is not sufficient validation.) This he used as a pre- and post-test for about 700 students, half of whom were taught one semester by the traditional historical approach rooted in the problems of the artist and his materials (verbally and pictorially presented). The other half were presented, the following semester, with a more "dynamic" approach based upon the present scene and the problems of students. Heller concluded that art judgment could be measured, that it could be changed by instruction, and that the "dynamic" method showed a significant advantage.

A study by Horn (21) reported that knowledge and understanding of art principles in the abstract were not significantly related to the application of the same principles in the various areas of design. She further reported very limited transfer from abstract to concrete forms.

These studies argue for the student's undergoing himself the evaluative and forming aspects of the arts. To my knowledge, there has been no rigorous study of the effect of involved discussion groups in changing taste. I refer here to the type of program sponsored by the Fund for Adult Education and utilized in Continuing Liberal Education, college extension divisions, alumni institutes, and community centers. From earlier studies of my own (22), I feel that good discussion groups can effect changes in attitudes and in taste.

Lastly, I would like to point out the possibilities of nonverbal evaluative training. One of our students recently completing his doctorate, William

Stewart (23), has worked in this direction. He took five stimulus pictures about which he had already learned a great deal through his doctoral research. Through verbal ratings, he knew how art and non-art college students tended to apperceive the five pictures—whether personally, extrinsically, intrinsically, aesthetically, or spontaneously. He then used the complete method of triad differences as developed in psychophysics. This requires presenting the five pictures in thirty different triads. The judge merely indicates which of a pair of pictures a third picture resembles more. Development of this type of evaluation appears to be most hopeful.

We used a variation of this method in judging the effect of a free and rigid drawing influence on the drawings of a cow made by people of all ages, five to ninety. Kenneth Gogel (24), one of our doctoral students, submitted a broad population to two treatment influences of how to draw a cow. There were many drawings of cows, preceding and following the treatment days. The problem was how to plot what happened in the series. Verbal checklists proved cumbersome and inadequate. Finally, we hit on the system of superimposing two pre-treatment cows on each other, similarly two treatment cows, and also two post-treatment cows. In this way, a judge could be presented by the three superimpositions and make a judgment on which two were more alike, which two more different. Thus, by a simple means, influence or its lack could be established.

Influence on one's drawing style and concepts appears to be a much subtler thing than allowed for by most theorists. The work of one third-grader touchingly showed this. She began with a naïve drawing of a cow, obviously her own representation. Exposed to the rigid example of how to draw a cow, step by step, she took over many of the influences. Then these influences began to break down and she wavered between her own version and the how-to-draw-it version. Finally, she drew a corral, and in it she placed two cows—one the influenced cow, one more like her earlier, idiosyncratic version.

3. The general creativity dimension

The notion that art affects one's creativity is a key one in art education. What evidence is there that art education changes a man? What effect do art experiences, or better, an aesthetic-forming orientation, have on general and applied creativity (applied in extra-art activities)? We have evidence of only an oblique kind—namely, through the correlates of art experience or quality of achievement. Let me review some of the recent findings.

Meinz (25) recently set out to determine whether general creativity, as it has been defined and measured by other researchers, could be enhanced through a method of teaching art which had as its major aim the promotion of creativity. In this case, two areas, industrial arts and art education, both of which were taught to elementary education majors, were studied. On the basis of significant gains in scores, Meinz concluded that the art education creative approach significantly affected general creativity scores. She also reported greater self-involvement, greater aesthetic perception, and greater creative independence.

Burkhart (26) recently completed a study which has implications for parallel structure of creativity in different settings. He studied creativity in art and in student teaching in two independent populations. Using a battery of personality and creativity measures, he defined four personality factors relating to both criterion areas. The criterion for creativity in teaching (in areas other than art education) was a count of divergent versus factual questions asked by the teachers, and a count of relative versus absolute evaluations made by the teachers, within a specified time period. The criterion in art was a judgment of art products of each student on the basis of spontaneity of working process and on the level of quality within working method.

Burkhart found four creative personality factors of importance: (1) spontaneous abstract orientation, (2) divergent power, (3) ideational and perceptual openness, and (4) social self-determination. The teaching criterion involved only the first two of these, while the art criterion involved all four. The highest loading of the criterion for teaching fell under divergent power, whereas for art it fell under the spontaneous abstract orientation (where the teacher criterion had a secondary loading). Using six predictors, Burkhart was able to predict the creativity criterion in art with a multiple correlation of .80. What appears to be functioning, in the measures used, was the difference between divergent and relative values as opposed to factual and absolute values. Relative evaluation and divergent questioning requires an alive and interacting teacher and student, and a view of learning as a process phenomenon advancing along nonauthoritarian, open, ideational pathways.

One of the tests developed and used by Burkhart may illustrate what is involved. In this test, one is asked to ask as many questions about a given object as possible in a brief period of time. He is cautioned to ask questions which do not have "yes" or "no" answers, and to seek questions leading to a variety of replies.

Suppose that a student is writing on the topic "piccolo." Factual questions concerning the piccolo would be: "What does a piccolo look like?" or "How is a piccolo made?" Common divergent questions are: "How do you feel when playing a piccolo?" and "What could be used in place of a piccolo?" But much more potent and exciting divergent questions are possible: "How would you convey what a piccolo means to you without describing or drawing a piccolo?" or "Can you imagine a person who means 'piccolo' to you?" or "What might a piccolo mean from the point of view of a fruit salad?" (This last question is supposed to cause a little eyebrow lifting.)

Such approaches help the student to think or perceive in a new way, which is certainly a prime function of teaching. It will soon be seen that to teach in divergent terms means to evaluate products in relative terms. It is our feeling that a type of relative evaluation, comparing one's own works done at various times, is a hopeful direction. The teacher shares his own views concerning student progress, also in relative terms, concerning the evidence before him. In this way, creative learning is a self-propagating, interactional affair, occurring, it has been said (27), in an environment containing high dither and high security.

If I seem to be spending time delineating predictors of criteria of creativity, it is because of the clear linkage between their isolation and valid curriculum experimentation. On the basis of present information, I am inclined to change a previous feeling of mine that prediction of creative performance is most difficult for select groups. We have concluded a study of fifty graduate students in art education, as a part of a study on Interdisciplinary Aspects of Creativity under an NSF grant (28). In this study, which we have cross-validated, we set up seven criterion measures, performance tasks, or products of one type or another, as targets for a carefully selected set of predictors. Among the latter were self-ratings, descriptive personality scales, word pairs, evaluative and judgmental tasks, a divergent question test, and several others. We began with 116 separate scores, but many of these were variations and combinations of each other. We reduced these to twenty-four predictors, then dropped some and tried a second time with twenty-three, and finally ended up with twelve strong predictors. Seventy-nine per cent of the intercorrelations of these predictors and the seven criterion measures were significant. The average multiple correlation of the seven criterion measures was .81.

Seven out of the twelve predictors are termed "hierarchies." To us this means a super-scale made up of one's behavior on several scales which are related through theory and meaning. The hierarchical scale is really a combination of signs. As in a true scale, each score or position means only one pattern of responses. To illustrate: in the items of one of the tests which Burkhart and I originated for this study, five words instead of a pair, are presented to the subject. The subject is asked to choose, from each five, the two which are most attractive to him. Each of the five words in each item stands for a dimension termed (1) abstract, (2) process, (3) impulsivity, (4) theory, and (5) nonconventionality. By analyzing his choices, item by item, we learn the relative value the subject places on each of these dimensions. A hierarchy might be formed by favoring any combination of these and by establishing cutoff points on the favored dimensions. Thus the *abstraction hierarchy* favors, in this order, (1) abstract versus concrete, (2) process versus static orientation, (3) impulsive versus nonimpulsive, and (4) nonconventional versus conventional. A "16" type, we know, is above the cutoff point on each of these. A "7," similarly, is up only on the abstract dimension, while a "2" is only nonconventional, etc.

We are finding such systems, as opposed to single scales, useful as predictors. Our first love affair with computers is over, and we find this kind of pre-thinking invaluable before the computer is used.

Space does not allow great detail here, but the twelve useful predictors in this graduate art education group are: (1) an art self-rating hierarchy; (2) a hierarchy from an inventory measuring complexity, aestheticism, theoretical interest, and nonauthoritarianism; (3) an abstract thinking hierarchy from the five-words-per-item test mentioned above; (4) a score on the number of divergent questions asked on a word question test; (5) a single score on the complexity dimension alone; (6) an abstract orientation hierarchy made up of scales from four different sources (personality and otherwise); (7) a spontaneity hierarchy from scales originated by Beittel and Burgart in the personality inventory described above (BBC1-X2); (8) a separate word-pair test of flexibility, originated by us also; (9) total scores (subtracting difference scores—e.g., concrete from abstract—on the five-words-per-item test); (10) a nonauthoritarian hierarchy (from three separate scales); (11) a score representing the ratio of divergent to factual questions on the word-question test; and (12) what we called the "spontaneous abstract creative personality hierarchy" (a kind of "daddy" hierarchy merging the two major areas of spontaneity and abstract thinking).

In brief, self-rating as a creative artist in comparison with one's peers, ideational and social self-determination, abstract thinking, divergent power, spontaneity, and nonauthoritarianism account for about 66 per cent of the variance of our criterion measures.

In concluding, I would like to point out that one of the criterion measures was two independent art works done away from the school setting; another product was made at a testing session; and a fourth was a test requiring fifteen thumbnail sketches on the basis of five stimulus line arrangements. Judgments of these four performances determined the aesthetic quality and the spontaneity while working (as rated from the product). Judgments of spontaneity (process judgments) appear to be somewhat more easily predicted (.84 average correlation) than those of quality (.78 average correlation).

On the basis of the present findings, it appears essential to develop in art teachers those attributes which might lead them to teach creatively: aesthetic quality, spontaneity, and self-confidence in their art; and divergent and abstract power in the world of ideas. Either one, without the other, appears to be insufficient.

Summary

One of our able doctoral students this summer did a paper on what would be known about art education if we knew only the research in art education. This raises a question about what is known about curriculum experimentation from a research viewpoint only, and from the viewpoint of research that I know best.

I have tried to point out the state of research and experimentation in art education as I know them from current research. Under the aesthetic-forming or studio category I have discussed the probable superiority of depth over breadth approaches, both in art achievement and in areas of divergent ideational orientation and perceptual openness. Spontaneity was seen to be the necessary ingredient for aesthetic growth. Both analytical and holistic working methods were described in a second experiment, which showed that the former method is better for both spontaneous and deliberate workers, and that the spontaneous workers always surpass the deliberate, regardless of method. Another study, in which a specialized television device (the Eidophor) and a similar, but much larger group were used, showed the positive effect of forced holistic methods on the deliberate and less able students. Spontaneous high students did better in independent work.

Under the evaluative-appreciative or judgmental dimension, mention was made of a study of object, criteria, and judge personality dimensions of the art judgment task. The latter was emphasized, along with the importance of developing process-evaluative as well as product-evaluative abilities in judges who appear to be spontaneous, abstract, and nonauthoritarian. Two experimental studies were briefly mentioned, one showing that art judgment could be changed by dynamic methods, the other that verbally presented and abstract art principles were not transferred to various areas of design or to concrete forms. The hopefulness of purely nonverbal evaluative tasks was then discussed.

Finally, under the general creativity dimension, one experiment demonstrated that an art education creative approach significantly affected general creativity scores, as opposed to a differing orientation where this did not happen. Then a study was reported which demonstrated a certain parallel structure between predictors and two distinctly different criterion measures, one in teaching, the other in art. The importance of divergent and relative-evaluative as opposed to factual and absolute-evaluative orientations in teaching, was brought out in this study. Lastly, twelve strong predictors or art performance criteria for a population of art teachers (who were also graduate students) were outlined. It was concluded that art teachers needed aesthetic quality, spontaneity, and self-confidence in their art, and divergent and abstract power in the world of ideas.

Finally, it may be said that the study of predictors, of the criterion problem in both product and process, of methods, and of the evaluative-judgmental domain, places art education in a position where it is now uniquely ready to engage in curriculum experimentation both in order to meet the challenges and problems of the present educational scene and also in order to test empirically the meaning of its theoretical and philosophical foundations, which stress aesthetic sensitivity and creativity as a part of the education of all.

References

1 Frank R. Hartman, "The Future of Research in Art Education," *Studies in Art Education*, vol. 3, no. 1, Fall, 1961.
2 Kenneth R. Beittel, "Art," in Chester W. Harris (ed.), *Encyclopedia of Educational Research*, The Macmillan Company, New York, 1960, pp. 77–87.
3 Soren Kierkegaard, *The Sickness unto Death*, Anchor Books, Doubleday & Company, Inc., Garden City, N.Y., 1954.
4 Martin Buber, *Between Man and Man*, The Macmillan Company, New York, 1948.
5 "Secondary School Curriculum Problems," American Council of Learned Societies *Newsletter*, vol. 9, no. 9, and vol. 10, no. 9, 1958, 1959.
6 Charles W. Morris, *Signs, Language, and Behavior*, Prentice-Hall, Inc., Englewood Cliffs, N.J., 1946.
7 Edward L. Mattil, Robert C. Burkhart, Kenneth R. Beittel, and Herbert J. Burgart, "The Effect of a 'Depth' vs. a 'Breadth' Method of Art Instruction at the Ninth Grade Level," *Studies in Art Education*, vol. 3, no. 1, Fall, 1961.
8 M. Lienard, "What is the Relationship of Children's Satisfaction with Their Art Products to Improvement in Art?" *Studies in Art Education*, vol. 3, no. 3, Fall, 1961.
9 Robert C. Burkhart, "The Creativity-Personality Continuum Based on Spontaneity and Deliberateness in Art," *Studies in Art Education*, vol. 2, no. 1, pp. 43–65, Fall, 1960.
10 Kenneth R. Beittel, "The Effects of Analytical vs. Holistic Methods of Instruction on the Potter's Wheel with Inexperienced General College Undergraduates." (Study supported by a grant from the College of Education, The Pennsylvania State University, 1961 and aided by Herbert J. Burgart, graduate research assistant in art education.)

11 Rudolph Arnheim, *Art and Visual Perception,* University of California Press, Berkeley, Calif., 1954.
12 June Mc Fee, *Preparation for Art,* Wadsworth Publishing Co., Inc., San Francisco, Calif., 1961.
13 Kenneth R. Beittel, "Factor Analyses of Three Dimensions of the Art Judgment Complex: Criteria, Art Objects, and Judges." (Presented Oct. 28, 1961, at Wayne State University, Detroit, Mich., Annual Meeting of the American Society for Aesthetics.)
14 Osgood, Suci and Tannenbaum, *The Measurement of Meaning,* The University of Illinois Press, Urbana, Ill., 1957.
15 Kenneth R. Beittel and Herbert J. Burgart, "Factor Analyses of an Experimental Creative Personality Inventory—the BBC1," unpublished report, Pennsylvania State University, Department of Art Education, 1961.
16 Harrison G. Gough, *The California Psychological Inventory,* Consulting Psychologists Press, Inc., Palo Alto, Calif., 1957.
17 Robert F. Bales, and Arthur S. Couch, *The Value Profile: A Factor Analytic Study of Value Statements,* Harvard University, Cambridge, Mass. (Mimeographed.)
18 Raymond B. Cattell et al., *The Sixteen Personality Factor Questionnaire,* Institute for Personality and Ability Testing, Champaign, Ill.
19 K. Warner Schaie, *Test of Behavioral Rigidity,* Consulting Psychologists Press, Palo Alto, Calif., 1960.
20 Julius Heller, "Changes in Art Judgment Resulting from Courses in Art Appreciation," doctoral thesis. University of Southern California, 1948.
21 Marilyn J. Horn, "The Ability of College Students to Apply Art Principles in Concrete and Abstract Situations and Its Relation to Art Interest," doctoral thesis, Cornell University, 1953.
22 Kenneth R. Beittel, "Experimental Studies of the Aesthetic Attitudes of College Students," *Research in Art Education,* Seventh Yearbook, National Art Education Association, 1956. pp. 47–61.
23 William Ross Stewart, "The Interaction of Certain Variables in the Apperception of Painting," doctoral thesis, Pennsylvania State University, 1961.
24 Kenneth Gogel, "Effects of Spontaneous and Deliberate Drawing Examples and Instructions on Drawings of a Cow in a Barnyard," doctoral dissertation in progress, Pennsylvania State University, 1961.
25 Algalee Pool Meinz, "General Creativity of Elementary Education Majors as Influenced by Courses in Industrial Arts and Art Education," doctoral thesis, Pennsylvania State University, 1960.
26 Robert C. Burkhart, "The Interrelationship of Separate Criteria for Creativity in Art and Student Teaching to Four Personality Factors," *Studies in Art Education,* vol. 3, no. 1, Fall, 1961.
27 "Creativity," *Carnegie Corporation of New York Quarterly,* vol. 9, no. 3, July, 1961.
28 Kenneth R. Beittel, "Interdisciplinary Study of Creativity," Pennsylvania State University. (Supported by a one-year grant, National Science Foundation, 1961–1962.)

15 ❀ THE THRESHOLD OF A REVOLUTION IN BIOLOGICAL EDUCATION *
Arnold B. Grobman** *University of Colorado*

Introduction

The modern world makes increasingly complex demands on its citizens and requires greater adaptability on their part. This adaptability must include an analytical ability of high order and an awareness and an understanding of how knowledge is obtained, for the fact of rapid change in our world is about all we can safely promise our young people. President Julius Stratton, of M.I.T., has put it this way, "The world into which we were born is gone; we have little or no idea of the world into which our children may grow to maturity. It is this rate of change, even more than the change itself, that I see as the dominant fact of our time."

The youngsters attending our primary and secondary schools today will be the leaders of the 21st century. They are beginning their schooling in an age during which our real knowledge seems to be doubling every 10 years, and they can well anticipate an acceleration of this rate of change.

These considerations have important implications for education in the biological sciences. An education based on facts alone is not sufficient. Many of the facts of yesterday are not the facts of today. An education based primarily on concepts and principles is not enough. Not only do our ideas evolve with increasing knowledge, but principles that are taught as "facts"— or as nonsense syllables—have an educational value that is virtually nil. An education based solely on classical case histories is less than sufficient. While a knowledge of evolution, of spontaneous generation, of the germ theory of disease, of the alternations of generations, of ecological succession, is valuable to the student, as a citizen he will face decisions about radiation, fluoridation, conservation policies, population control, medical care for the aged, and other problems unknown to his teachers. An education based only on logical manipulations will not do. To reach intelligent decisions, the student must have or be able to find the appropriate information required as a basis for reasoned conclusions and must know how to use it.

This is not so much a question of preparing tomorrow's scientists but providing the necessary degree of scientific literacy for all future citizens. Whitehead put it very succinctly 35 years ago by saying:

> When one considers in its length and in its breadth the importance of this question of the education of a nation's youth, the broken lives, the defeated hopes, the national failures, which result from the frivolous inertia with which it is treated, it is difficult to restrain within oneself a savage rage. In

---

* Reprinted from *The Journal of Medical Education*, vol. 36, no. 10, pp. 1253–1265, October, 1961, with permission. The footnote material and the last paragraph were added by the author for this volume—Editor.

** Arnold Grobman is Director, Biological Sciences Curriculum Study, at the University of Colorado.

the conditions of modern life the rule is absolute, the race which does not value trained intelligence is doomed. Not all your heroism, not all your social charm, not all your wit, not all your victories on land or at sea, can move back the finger of fate. Today we maintain ourselves. Tomorrow science will have moved forward yet one more step, and there will be no appeal from the judgment which will then be pronounced on the uneducated.[1]

It is, perhaps, fitting for readers of the *Journal*, to note that the 50th anniversary of the Flexner report finds a very serious—and very promising—revolution occurring in high school science. The present revolution is broader in scope and involves many more people—both at the teaching and learning ends of the spectrum—than that of 1910. Also, it involves a younger age group, and this may well increase the effectiveness of its impact.

There are now several major course content improvement groups, financed by the National Science Foundation, that are focusing on secondary school science and mathematics. The Physical Sciences Study Committee at the Massachusetts Institute of Technology, which began work in 1956, was the first to receive substantial support. Others include the School Mathematics Study Group at Yale University; the Chemical Bond Approach at Reed and Earlham Colleges; the Chemical Education Material Study at Harvey Mudd College and the University of California; and the Biological Sciences Curriculum Study of the American Institute of Biological Sciences.

Of the national science curricular groups, the Biological Sciences Curriculum Study is in the most critical position in terms of broad scientific education for future citizens, since the majority of high school students take biology as their only senior high school science course. A majority of students entering high school do not go on to college. High school biology is, therefore, the last science course taken by most of our students.

Discussions leading to a systematic effort to improve biological education at all levels were initiated in 1955 by the American Institute of Biological Sciences (AIBS), a professional society representing about 85,000 biologists. In January, 1959, the AIBS received a small initial grant from the National Science Foundation to organize the Biological Sciences Curriculum Study (BSCS); this and subsequent grants to date total $2,000,000. The original grant proposal to the NSF outlined the function of the BSCS with the following words, "to evaluate the content of present biology course offerings, to determine what biological knowledge can and should be learned at each school level, and to recommend how this latter goal can best be achieved." Headquarters for the AIBS Study were established at the University of Colorado in Boulder.

Early decisions of the BSCS

For a variety of practical reasons, the first focus of the BSCS has been upon the secondary school level. In discussing this first phase of the study, Dr. Bentley Glass of the Johns Hopkins University, who is chairman of the study, has used these words:

[1] Alfred North Whitehead, *The Aims of Education,* The Macmillan Company, New York, 1929.

The problem is this: In many high schools today biology consists primarily of either hygiene or animal biology, presented in terms of invertebrate and vertebrate anatomy. Often, the emphasis is on memorization of long lists of scientific names. And even more often, biology is presented as a crystallized science—one in which all the answers are known.

As the BSCS works on the high school biology program, we hope that biology—and indeed all science—will be presented as an unending search for meaning, rather than as a body of dogma or as a series of taxonomic exercises. It is not our purpose to establish a standard or definitive body of knowledge. On the contrary, our main objective is to lead each student to conceive of biology as a science, and of the process of science as a reliable method of gaining objective knowledge.

To a very great extent the key to this understanding lies in meaningful laboratory and field study which incorporates honest investigation of real scientific problems. However, today, what commonly passes for "lab" is often routine cookbook-type exercises or a mere naming of structures on drawings and answering of questions by looking them up in a textbook.

The man and woman of tomorrow will live in a scientific world which they must understand and adjust to. In fact, the survival of democracy in this country will probably be dependent on the citizen's ability to foster scientific advancement.

This will necessitate, first, a respect for an understanding of scientific method; second, an understanding of the very real distinction between pure science and the "research and development" activities that now receive most of our Federal support to science; and, third, a recognition of the dependence of the latter on the former.

The aim of the BSCS is to place biological knowledge in its fullest modern perspective. If we are successful, students of the new biology should acquire not only an intellectual and esthetic appreciation for the complexities of living things and their interrelationships in nature, but also for the ways in which new knowledge is gained and tested, old errors eliminated, and an ever closer approximation to truth attained.[2]

According to Dr. John Moore (Chairman of the BSCS Committee on the Content of the Curriculum), of Columbia University, a biology course for the secondary school student should provide him with "an understanding of: his own place in the scheme of nature, namely that he is a living organism and has much in common with all living organisms; the diversity of life and of the interrelations of all creatures; what man presently knows and believes regarding basic biological problems of evolution, development, and inheritance; the biological basis of many of the problems and procedures in medicine, public health, agriculture, and conservation; and examples of the historical development of the concepts of biology to show that these are dependent on the contemporary techniques, technology, and the nature of society." It should also provide him with "an appreciation of the beauty, drama, and tragedy of the living world."

The general policy of the BSCS is determined by a Steering Committee composed of 27 members (nine of whom are replaced annually) currently

[2] Bentley Glass, BSCS Annual Report, *BSCS Newsletter*, no. 6, December, 1960.

representing the following categories: professors of biology, high school biology teachers, science supervisors, science educators, medical and agricultural educators, and university and school administrators. The Chairman is Dr. Bentley Glass of Johns Hopkins University. At the present time the largest single group on the Steering Committee consists of professional biologists, since it is felt that the design of new curricula in biology should depend heavily upon those who have an intensive knowledge of the various facets of the field. Men working on the frontiers of the science have such a knowledge. A greater proportion of in-service secondary school biology teachers has been recruited as the study became more deeply involved in the production and implementation of curricular materials.

An early decision facing the Steering Committee was the grade level for which BSCS materials should be designed. A few schools currently offer a biology course in the ninth grade, but there are serious disadvantages in recommending that this be practiced widely. One reason is that the greater maturity of students in higher grades should afford them a better opportunity to assimilate a conceptual biological course of the BSCS type, especially if some effective instruction in the physical sciences precedes the biology course. Another reason is that the ninth grade, in many school systems, is located in the junior high school. It is often the case that the junior high school teacher is less well prepared in biology than his senior high school colleague, and, with very few exceptions, the laboratory facilities in the junior high school building are even less satisfactory than those in the senior high school building.

A small group of schools has a pattern in which for some students the first course in biology is taken in the eleventh or twelfth grade. At this level, the greater maturity of the students could be advantageous. Perhaps more important is the opportunity (not always grasped) for them to have had courses in both physics and chemistry, prior to biology, so that at least the molecular aspects of such a biology course could be presented at a higher level.

In most schools (about 80 per cent), the biology course is offered at the tenth grade level. Since the majority of high school students now take only one science course, most students would not take biology if a different science were standard for the tenth grade.

Thus, the question before the BSCS resolved itself into whether it was better to design a general education course in biology for the large majority of high school students or whether it was better to design a more sophisticated course for a small number of select students.

The decision of the Steering Committee was to give priority to the preparation of materials for a first course in biology for the tenth grade level where there is a potential of reaching 1,750,000 students annually. (A second course, for eleventh and twelfth grades, would be considered later.)

Since a majority of these tenth grade students do not go on to college, the tenth grade biology course is the last chance in the classroom to prepare such students (who will comprise over one-half of our adult population) for the rapid changes in scientific knowledge and concepts they will face during their lifetimes—to teach them how to handle and evaluate new scientific knowledge as it becomes available. At best this is a difficult task; but the difficulty is compounded by the fact that a realistic general biology program, suitable for wide use in American schools today, must take into account a wider range of student ability, interest, and potential than is present in other high school science courses. It must be a course that most tenth grade students can handle and, at the same time, prove challenging to the above-average student. These are some of the factors that were considered as the BSCS began preparation of new materials for a first general biology course.

This position led to a second important decision reached by the Steering Committee. Philosophically, the Committee felt it undesirable for the BSCS to design a single approach to the study of biology for tenth grade students. This decision was unrelated to the question of a national curriculum in the coercive sense, since, eventually, BSCS materials will be on the open market to be utilized, modified, or discarded by the schools in open and free competition with other existing materials. Even so, it was considered desirable to introduce the greatest possible flexibility in the BSCS materials themselves, since biology is a diffuse field (as contrasted with the relative linearity of mathematics, chemistry, and physics) and a variety of good and interesting approaches is possible. It was felt, also, that the special background of the teacher and his local situation could be more advantageously used if multiple approaches were available.

The three versions of BSCS high school biology

One of the early suggestions was that the BSCS prepare a series of fresh and modern pamphlets on a wide array of biological topics so that the teacher could, by judicious selection, design his own course with them. The practicalities of the actual classroom situation in America, however, negate the pamphlet series as a primary method of producing usable school materials. The facts are that most teachers have to meet five or more classes a day for 5 days a week, in addition to the extra curricular assignments, and the grading of the papers of upwards of 150 students, many of whom are not specifically interested in their studies. Also, there is a large number of high school biology teachers with deficient training in the field, who have come into their positions through an indirect pathway (home economics, physical education) or by default. (Principal to newly appointed Social Studies teacher: "Our enrollment in biology is larger this year than anticipated so I'd like you to teach two classes of biology.") These considerations led to the decision that most teachers, because of conditions beyond their control require some kind of a "package" presentation and could not make effective use of a pamphlet series as the basis for building their courses.

The net result of such discussion was the decision to prepare three different verions of a first course in biology for typical students in American secondary schools.

To accomplish this a Writing Conference was held at the University of Colorado during the summer of 1960. Here 69 writers—high school biology teachers and collegiate research biologists—prepared materials for three preliminary experimental versions of new basic courses. Each of these would utilize a different approach. The teams prepared texts, laboratory manuals, teachers' commentaries and guides, and brief techniques films.

The Blue Version (supervisor: Dr. Ingrith Deyrup, Barnard College[3]) develops the fundamental biological concepts with stress on the ideas and experimental approach of physiology and biochemistry. It begins with the basis of life in the properties and organization of matter. It then moves to the activities of these organizations as seen in the capture and use of energy, then to the organ level, and finally to the level of the whole organism and of populations. Genetics is couched in terms of the conservation and modification of molecular organization from generation to generation; evolution is the basis for long-term changes in the development of diversity among living organisms. The treatment of certain open-ended biological problems which face man as a citizen of a socially organized community concludes the text presentation.

The Yellow Version (supervisor: Dr. John Moore, Columbia University) begins with the whole organism, and man as exemplar of the animal, from a functional point of view. The traditional major functions are treated system by system, rarely going below the organ level. Next is a similar treatment for the green plant, with more detail and a variety of examples. Concepts of evolution and adaptation are emphasized in the various examples. Then the student is confronted with the fundamental chemistry and dynamics of the living cell, including the detail of chemical action necessary to a genuine understanding of "being alive" and involving DNA, RNA, and ATP. The remaining chapters concern microbiology, diversity in the plant and animal kingdoms, genetics, reproduction and development, and evolution.

The Green Version (supervisor: Dr. Marston Bates, University of Michigan[4]) takes the individual organism as the primary unit of study. It is concerned with how individuals are organized into populations, species, and communities, and with what organisms do and how they do it. It starts with cycles of energy and materials in the biosphere, then turns to such structural units as individuals, populations, and communities. Following the taxonomic diversity of animals, plants, and micro-organisms, it deals with ecological diversity on land, in fresh water, in the seas; with geographical diversity among the continents and oceans; and then with the history of life and the problem of evolution. The student studies the cellular structures of organisms; genetics; the physiology and development of plants and animals; animal behavior; the relations of the parts to the functioning of the whole organism; and the human animal in the perspective of his biological setting.

All three of these new programs share several common aims: to make clear to the student the nature of scientific inquiry, the intellectual history of biological concepts, genetic continuity, homeostasis, complementarity of structure and function, diversity, and other similar important concepts. In addition, each program is infused with such ideas as the quantitative approach, incertitude, aesthetics, limits of knowledge, speculation, temporal parameters, dynamic systems, and multiple variables.

In all three of the versions, the laboratory takes a more important place than is found in most current biology courses, and the emphasis is quite different. In these versions, the laboratory program (which was under the

---

[3] With Dr. Claude A. Welch, Michigan State University.
[4] With Mr. C. Haven Kolb, Overlea Senior High School, Baltimore.

supervision of Dr. Glass) reflects both the investigatory as well as the illustrative function of laboratory work. The students not only examine materials, but they conduct experiments and investigate real open-ended problems.

Testing of the new materials

The three versions of the BSCS high school biology courses were tested in a systematic program during the 1960–61 school year. To accomplish this, a series of fifteen Testing Centers had been organized throughout the country. Each Testing Center consisted of six to nine biology teachers, within a commuting area, who were using the new material with their classes. One of these teachers was designated Center Leader and was responsible for Center management. Each Center was assigned a university research biologist as a Consultant to advise on biological content of the program. In addition, one biology teacher in each of thirteen Independent Test Schools used the new materials.

All Test Center Leaders and Consultants and all teachers involved in the Independent Test Schools were participants in the BSCS Summer Writing Conference. In addition, all the teachers and Consultants participating in the BSCS Testing Program attended a 6-day Briefing Session in Boulder, Colorado, before school opened to discuss the purposes of the new materials and to prepare for using them in their classes. Thus, a total of 118 teachers, with their 14,000 pupils, used the new materials in a wide variety of classroom situations during the 1960–61 school year. The participating schools included private and public, parochial and non-sectarian, urban and rural, large and small, and senior and junior high schools.

Systematic feedback on the experiences of the participating teachers with these new BSCS experimental materials was obtained throughout the year in several ways:

1. Each Testing Center conducted a weekly 3-hour meeting at which the teachers discussed their experiences with BSCS materials during the previous week and their plans for the coming week's work. Reports on these meetings were sent regularly to the BSCS headquarters office.

2. BSCS staff members visited each participating school during the school year to discuss the program with principals, supervisors, teachers, and students.

3. In cooperation with the Educational Testing Service, several objective tests were given throughout the year to all students using the new materials, to determine the extent to which students were learning the information and ideas that the writers consider important.

A second Writing Conference followed in Boulder during the summer of 1961 where the experimental materials were completely rewritten, based upon the feedback that had been obtained. The BSCS is now organizing a more comprehensive evaluation program, involving about 350 teachers and 36,000 students, for the 1961–62 school year. In the summer of 1962 a Third Writing Conference will rewrite the materials to produce a final series of manuscripts. These materials—which by then will have been tested in real classroom situations with about 50,000 students and 400 teachers and will have undergone two major revisions by large and representative teams of outstanding research biologists and secondary school biology teachers—will then be available as model courses. It is hoped that there will be widespread adoption of these courses designed by the BSCS. It is also hoped that independent authors will use our materials as a point of departure to design their own courses and that such courses will also have extensive use.

A tremendous amount of work has already gone into the design of secondary school biology curricula at state and local levels. Much of it is good, sound and solid. What is the justification, then, for this new effort by the BSCS, and what advantages over existing biology curricula might accrue from the study? If there is a single important way in which the BSCS differs in its approach from these many independent studies made over the years by high school faculty members and state and urban education department staffs, it is that the BSCS involves the active participation of a large number of professional biologists who know the life sciences intimately through first-hand investigations. These biologists bring to the new biology curricula an extensive store of modern knowledge, overview, and perspective that is available nowhere else in our society. The unique aspect of the BSCS is that it brings to a cooperative team the special competencies of the biological scholars in our universities and the teachers in our high schools.

The present generation of scientists is beginning to cooperate extensively with teachers and educators in a way that had been customary in the 1800's. There is an unprecedented activity developing today on college and university campuses where scientists are helping to design new courses and bring recent advances into the classroom. Examples include NSF summer and academic year institute programs and the teacher education and professional standards meetings. Biologists are participating fully in such activities. However, although extremely valuable, summer and academic year institutes cannot by themselves introduce large-scale coordinated curricular revision.

School administrators should begin to inquire whether the new programs are suitable and whether the recommended curricula are superior to those now being offered in our high schools. Only after affirmative judgments are reached would it be timely to become concerned with details of implementation on a local level.

We confidently anticipate that students and teachers who participate in BSCS courses will experience the excitement and thrill of the scientific revolution that is reshaping our modern society. Besides enjoying the satisfaction that comes with acquiring solid knowledge in the life sciences, we hope that students will be able to distinguish between science and superstition and, as citizens, that they will be prepared to deal intelligently with the thousands of problems in which scientific attitudes are appropriate.

The laboratory blocks

Even in schools where good biological laboratory facilities exist, their tremendous educational potential is not always realized. Too often laboratory exercises are sterile routine affairs giving little insight into the ways in which scientists think and work, the processes by which knowledge is uncovered, and the reasons for precise measurements and controlled experiments. Our laboratory program is attempting to rectify this situation. In addition, the BSCS Committee on Laboratory Innovations, under the chairmanship of Dr. Addison E. Lee, of the University of Texas, is designing a new kind of laboratory experience—a block approach—to supplement the BSCS general biology course materials. These blocks comprise an enrichment program designed to reach beyond the extensive laboratory experiences already built into the three versions.

In practice, a teacher would select one block, from among several available, for use during a particular school year. Each laboratory block requires 6 weeks of intensive work. For these 6 weeks, all class activities—whether discussion, laboratory work, reading, or field work—center on a single area of biology. The students progress from simple to more sophisticated experiments and gain an experience in depth in the problem area. Because of the time that will be spent working on a single problem area, and the increasing complexity of the experiments, it is hoped that the student will be able to derive a sense of the processes of science and the nature of scientific inquiry and discovery, and that he will learn why science requires precise measurements, accurate observations, and conciseness and clarity in communication. He should obtain an understanding of teamwork in the laboratory, the importance of experimental controls, and how hypotheses are developed and tested. He should come to recognize good investigatory precedures and be better prepared to bring a scientific attitude to those problems he will face as an adult that are susceptible to such analyses. The seven laboratory blocks now completed are: *Plant Growth and Development; Microbes, Their Growth, Nutrition and Interaction; Animal Growth and Development; Interdependence of Structure and Function; Regulation in Plants by Hormones; Animal Behavior;* and *The Ecology of Land Plants and Animals.*

These blocks were tested during the 1960–61 school year. Eight of the BSCS Testing Centers and four of the Independent Test Schools each utilized one block in conjunction with their BSCS courses. It is planned to design about five more blocks in the immediate future. During the 1961–62 school year, four schools will be experimenting with a second level high school course based upon a series of blocks. In addition to their intrinsic value, the blocks provide for increased flexibility in the BSCS program for secondary school biology.

The gifted student

Although the major efforts of the BSCS have been directed toward a new general biology program suitable for virtually all high school students, the special needs of the student talented in science have not been neglected. The Committee on the Gifted Student—under the Chairmanship of Dr. Paul Brandwein of Harcourt, Brace, and World—has been exploring the needs of teachers in their work with the science-prone student and has prepared an experimental volume which is designed to meet some of these needs. *Biological Investigations for Secondary School Students* is intended to be shared by teacher and student and includes 100 research prospectuses suitable for out-of-class investigations by the more able science student. The volume begins with a discussion intended to orient the student in the selection and use of a research prospectus. To obtain these prospectuses, the Gifted Student Committee invited biologists throughout the country to contribute suitable research projects for which the results are currently not available in the literature. Of more than 500 prospectuses contributed, 100 were selected and edited for inclusion in this first experimental volume. This book is being made available to teachers in the BSCS Testing Program and to other interested persons, for use on an experimental basis before additional volumes of prospectuses are prepared.

Teacher preparation

Of prime importance in any teaching activity is the teacher. A highly qualified and representative group has been recruited to serve as a Committee on Teacher Preparation. Dr. Joseph J. Schwab, University of Chicago, is its chairman.

The members of this Committee are well aware that the high school teacher, who needs to be a generalist and an interpreter of science, is usually taught biology by men who are specialists and investigators. It is obviously important that the high school teacher understand the ways in which biologists accumulate the knowledge of their science. Teachers should be appreciative and informed concerning the nature of the scientific enterprise. Unfortunately, this experience is typically gained only at the post-graduate level in a research program. Provision is not normally made for such training at lower levels of instruction. Until recently, few specific recommendations for alleviating this condition have been made. Most suggestions for teacher training in biology have been based on surveys of existing practices with the result that there are few real innovations in teacher education. Some courses that satisfy certification requirements are too frequently of little benefit to pre- or in-service teachers, and often desirable courses are not recommended. Example: although courses for teachers on the history and philosophy of science would appear to be potentially valuable in improving the climate of high school science courses, they are not required for certification in any state.

Much of the criticism levied against the teaching of science today is related to the difficulty of encompassing the entire range of subject matter included in the field of biology. Redesign of existing in-service and pre-service courses is certainly part of the answer. Perhaps even more important, however, scientists must learn how to communicate their findings to teachers in understandable language and to make their ideas available through less technical publications than are now available. To help satisfy this need the BSCS is planning the production of an extensive pamphlet series. We hope to prepare a series of pamphlets, on a periodic basis, that collectively will comprise a specific reference library for secondary school teachers of biology.

The pamphlet series will probably consist of 32-page pamphlets issued monthly during the school year. Each is to be written by a specialist in an area of his interest and meaningfully illustrated. Where necessary, the manuscripts will be rewritten by competent science writers so that the finished pamphlets will be interesting and informative to an average high school teacher as well as scientifically accurate and up-to-date. Early topics under preparation include animal orientation, biological clocks, and oceanography. It is hoped that the series will be comprehensive enough to form a background library for those teachers with incomplete training and will be representative enough to provide for an updating of all teachers. In addition to use by teachers for their own self-improvement, the series might provide a few especially competent and ambitious teachers the opportunity to design their own courses based on this periodical material. The series should also be useful as collateral reading for college and medical students.

As one phase of the Teacher Preparation program, during the summer of 1960, the BSCS produced three short biological techniques films. The aim of this series is to present, in compact visual form, practical information about modern biological techniques with which many teachers have not had firsthand experience. The three films so far produced deal with techniques in bacteriology, Drosophila genetics, and removal of frog pituitary. These three succinct 16-mm. sound and color films total 10 minutes of running time. Preparation of additional films is underway.

In preparation for the secondary school projects of the BSCS, Dr. Paul DeH. Hurd of Stanford University made an exhaustive historical study of high school biological education in the United States. His study examines the recommendations of national committees appointed since 1890 that have considered the problem of science education with special reference to the secondary schools. It also reviews research studies in science education, analyzes books on the teaching of biology, and summarizes the problems, issues and trends in the teaching of secondary school biology. Dr. Hurd's report is now available as the first number of the *BSCS Bulletin* series.

International cooperation

Educators from outside the United States have shown great interest in BSCS activities. Inquiries concerning use of BSCS materials have been received from 41 foreign countries. Overseas visitors at the BSCS office in Boulder have included scientists and educators from India, Ceylon, Great Britain, Switzerland, Holland, and Nigeria. Because of this widespread interest by foreign educators, a Committee on International Cooperation—with the late Dr. James G. Dickson of the University of Wisconsin as Chairman—was established in 1960.

At the Seventh National Conference of the U.S. National Commission for UNESCO in Denver, September 29–October 2, 1959, the possibility of coordinating efforts of biologists of the Americas in improving biological education was discussed at some length. The Latin American biologists present expressed interest in cooperating with the BSCS in the preparation of general biology courses for use in Latin America. Following this, the Rockefeller Foundation made a grant of $1,898 to the AIBS to support the expenses of two biologists—Dr. Humberto Gómez of the Universidad del Valle, Cali, Colombia, and Dr. José Herrera, Universidad de Chile, Santiago, Chile—to meet with the BSCS Steering Committee at a planning session in New Orleans in January, 1960.

Although the BSCS was established to produce course materials for use in the United States, the Study would be pleased to have the results of its work used elsewhere in the advancement of biological education. However, the *BSCS High School Biology* was designed for students in the United States; before use in any other country, the materials should be specifically adapted for that country by its resident biologists and educators. Climatic, ecological, and other differences must be taken into account. For example, discussions of familiar plants of commercial importance in the United States might cite corn and wheat, while in India the examples would more properly be rice and millet. Also, many plants and animals referred to in the present materials as examples of diversity are not familiar to residents outside the North Temperate Zone of the Western Hemisphere. Among the other topics that obviously need modification in overseas versions of BSCS materials are: conservation, agriculture, sanitation, medicine, hygiene and other applications of biological knowledge.

The BSCS began to cooperate with representative foreign teams during the summer of 1961 in making such adaptations. Teams of biologists from Argentina, Brazil, Colombia, Nigeria and Thailand worked with the BSCS in Boulder in adapting the materials for use in their own countries. This pilot international program was supported jointly by The Rockefeller Foundation and The National Science Foundation.

Future programs and problems

Among the future programs for the improvement of biological education currently planned by the BSCS are recommendations for a second course in high school biology and a cooperative arrangement with other scientists in a study of elementary and junior high school science. A college committee has been established with Dr. Herman Speith, Chancellor of the Riverside Campus of the University of California, as chairman. It has just completed a feasibility study on introductory college biology courses and the matter is now under review by the AIBS.

Perhaps a word should be said about some of the broad implications of the present program. Many high school teachers are now giving good courses in biology. There is no reason why they should feel any pressures for change, real or imagined, when final recommendations are made by the BSCS. There is at the present time perhaps too much of a trend to change simply for the sake of change itself without a full evaluation of the programs concerned. The BSCS materials will be on the open market and can be utilized or not as seems best locally. There is no desire on the part of the AIBS or the BSCS to promote a national curriculum. It is hoped that the biology courses that are finally developed by the BSCS will be adopted completely on their merits. The eventual success of the program does seem assured because of the quality of the members of the working committees and the rare enthusiasm with which they are working.

The solution of important problems in science education will require the attention of many experts and scholars both from within and without the BSCS. Major changes in science education will depend upon the cooperative activities of the various curriculum studies, both current and planned, as well as upon teachers, educators, parents, scientists, and administrators. Small groups, such as the BSCS, can wield great influence and can sometimes trigger widespread demands for reform. However, the implementation of details for a new school curriculum, for improved professional preparation of teachers, and for the development of community support for the physical improvement of schools, requires an uncommon degree of mutual understanding and cooperation by diverse groups interested in better science education.

There are a number of important problems which must be, but have not yet been, investigated by the BSCS. Two of these are (*a*) the proper interrelations of biology with the other succeeding or preceding science courses given at the intermediate and secondary school levels and (*b*) grade level placement and development of biological concepts from kindergarten through grade 12. Related questions that must be considered by the various BSCS committees and other interested persons are: How can scientists representing all fields of biology best contribute to the development of an improved elementary school program in science? Is the current general pattern of a year of biology, chemistry, and physics in the senior high school satisfactory? Should there be a year of life sciences in junior high school?

The efficiency of education, in terms of human learning, is an extremely important area in a rapidly advancing technological society. There is a fair amount of dependable information available on education that has not been widely utilized by those involved with instruction. Much of this information relates to the psychology of human learning and is of potential importance in curricular design. However, much additional research of an investigative nature must be brought to bear on many educational problems. One of the more important of these is the nature of human learning. Psychologists concerned with this field should be encouraged to conduct appropriate research structured so that their conclusions can be advantageously incorporated in the development of new courses of study. Cooperative activities among these investigators and the various curricular studies is highly desirable. Some efforts along these lines are being initiated at the present time.

Much work needs to be done in the area of educational media, because these are the vehicles of instruction. It is interesting that reliance on traditional and unproved educational methodology is slowly being broken down. In cooperation with other specialists, biologists must try to determine how lasting are behavioral changes in student attitudes when different media are exploited in biological science education. How effective are such changes, if any? The present trend to automation through such devices as TV, films, and teaching machines will certainly cause us to look more closely at the total role of the individual instructor in the biology classroom.

We need to know more about the educational values of departmentalized successive courses (biology, chemistry, physics) versus an integrated science sequence of similar time duration. We need to probe deeper for better methods of preparing teachers, and the BSCS is conducting a modest inquiry along these lines. We need to translate into daily practice such difficult but promising ideas referred to by educators as readiness, motivation, whole child, and others.

In the education column of *The New York Times,* Fred Hechinger had this to say of the Biological Sciences Curriculum Study: "Aside from its significance for the teaching of biology, the study highlights a new trend of school reform in America; it removes the barriers of isolationism among different levels, and, perhaps more important, among teachers, professors, and researchers. At the same time it aims at planning the curriculum, not as a series of 1-year blocks but as a body of knowledge. And it looks on the student's progress, not as a process of registration in separate courses but as a mountain path toward greater understanding for all and toward a summit for some."[5]

The next half-dozen years should be exciting ones in American higher education. During this period medical schools should begin to receive a trickle of students who, during high school, were exposed to the new mathematics, the new chemistry, the new physics, and the new biology, and who were fortunate enough to attend colleges ready to receive them. These new programs may well contribute to an expansion of the reservoir of research-minded scientists. More important, perhaps, among people generally they may improve the understanding of the function of basic research in our modern society. It is probably not too extravagant to anticipate that the medical care of our people will be directly benefited by the impact of these new programs both on our future physicians and the general public they serve.

Since this manuscript was prepared in 1961, the programs of the BSCS have moved ahead rapidly. After extensive testing of the BSCS Biology materials during 1961–62 and again in 1962–63, revised editions of *BSCS High School Biology* materials scheduled for commercial release in September, 1963, include: the Blue, Yellow and Green Versions of *BSCS High School Biology* (texts, lab manuals, tests and teacher's guides), four laboratory blocks, gifted student materials, and the *Teacher's Handbook*. The BSCS Pamphlet Series was initiated commercially in September, 1962, with pamphlets to be issued monthly during the school year for an initial three-year period. *BSCS Bulletin No. 2*, about working with the creative science student, has been issued, and *Bulletin No. 3*, concerning administrative arrangements for BSCS Biology, is in press. Experimental editions of a second high school biology course and of several units of a first course for the unsuccessful learner will be available through the BSCS in fall 1963. BSCS *Special Publications No. 1* and *No. 2*, on preparation of teachers for BSCS Biology, reflect the recommendations of participants in a series of conferences of collegiate and public school personnel concerned with preparation of biology teachers, as well as the experience of the BSCS in its own teacher preparation activities. Additional overseas countries are interested in adaptation of BSCS materials, and a Philippine adaptation is currently in progress. It is suggested that persons who wish to obtain continuing information on the BSCS program write to the BSCS, University of Colorado, Boulder, Colorado, and request the BSCS *Newsletter*.

[5] *The New York Times*, September 25, 1960.

16 ❀ CURRICULUM EXPERIMENTATION PROBLEMS IN THE EARTH SCIENCES
Robert C. Stephenson* American Geological Institute

The historical background

The years since 1956 have brought a renaissance of earth science as an important facet of the secondary school science curriculum, one which is moving ahead at an amazing pace. At the turn of the century, courses in the natural sciences, including geology and astronomy, were not uncommon in our schools. As the sciences of chemistry, physics, and biology developed, courses in these sciences displaced the natural sciences. Earth science was relegated to the level of a unit in the general science course, which in many schools was accorded second-class status among course offerings. Most college students who were products of this era were not fortunate enough to have been introduced to the most rudimentary concepts of the science of the atmosphere, the hydrosphere, and the lithosphere. Many of these students completed their studies and have taken their places as the intelligentsia of our society with only a folklore level of knowledge about the earth, its oceans, and its atmosphere.

With the post-World War II blossoming of science and technology, the challenge to improve our elementary and secondary school educational efforts, particularly in science, began to take shape. Within the past five years, the PSSC, the Biological Sciences Curriculum Study, and the Chemical Bond Approach have stimulated educators, teachers, and even scientists to devote unprecedented efforts to the upgrading of secondary science programs in our schools across the nation, and the tapering off of these efforts is not yet in sight.

The newfound aura of respect and esteem for science rapidly reached down into the elementary grades, with the result that the general science normally taught at the junior high school under the old pattern was no longer adequate to hold the interest of the growing numbers of science-inclined students whose general science training started at the elementary level.

As the traditional chemistry, physics, and biology courses in our high schools have been reorganized and revitalized, and the teaching of scientific subject matter has been introduced at earlier levels in our elementary schools, a breach has developed in school science programs. More general science is not the solution to this problem, for various reasons. To bridge this gap, new courses have been introduced essentially at the eighth- and ninth-grade levels. Here is the spot in which the earth science course, long absent as a significant part of school science programs, is making its appearance. Earth science courses are being developed and adopted by state, regional, and local school systems across the country at an explosive rate.

In the early '50s, and before the advent of the National Science Foundation support of major course improvement efforts in the sciences, New York State experimented with an earth science course as the bridge between ele-

* Robert C. Stephenson is Executive Director of the American Geological Institute, Washington, D.C.

mentary school general science and high school chemistry, physics, and biology. The experiment was successful, and earth science found its place as a ninth-grade course for the better students who are science-inclined. The course met with enthusiasm and has expanded as rapidly as qualified teachers can be found to teach it. Other states studied the New York State developments, and the pace of the nationwide movement toward the introduction of earth science changed from a walk to a gallop in 1959 when Pennsylvania adopted its course in earth and space science, built around an outline contained in a teaching guide prepared by a group of Pennsylvania earth scientists.

In a recent survey by the School Division of the McGraw-Hill Book Company, it was found that at least twenty-four states offer, or are contemplating offering, earth science courses, for the most part at the ninth-grade level. About one-third of the states reported having developed a course of study.

These historical highlights which have been reviewed are essential to the understanding of problems relating to experimental efforts in earth science education.

The problems

1. Why is earth science important?
2. At what grade level should earth science logically be introduced?
3. Should a specific course of study be developed?
4. What are the problems of teacher training?
5. Are adequate teaching resources available?
6. To whom can we turn for assistance?

1. Why is earth science important?

Science is a means to an end. Chemistry, physics, and biology are important in the education of people who are to wear the tag "educated people" not merely for the sake of collecting and storing information but as an aid to them in discharging their responsibilities to society. Pursuit of these sciences by scientists is directed toward creating a better life. The same is the case with the earth sciences. Most of us—and our children's children—appear destined to live out our lives on the planet Earth, and as we look ahead, we can see the ever-mounting problems which are due to a rapidly expanding population and a world-wide rise in standards of living, and to the growing competition for the renewable and nonrenewable resources of the world. Some problems of the past, such as the adequacy of resources of fossil fuels, can conceivably become relatively inconsequential in the future, as a result of advances in science and technology. However, it seems entirely illogical and unlikely that new resource problems will not emerge. As long as we are primarily earth-bound, it is essential that we know all we can about our environment and how we can best utilize the resources of this environment. In its most refined form, earth science must apply the maximum of basic mathematics, physics, chemistry, biology, and engineering toward these ends. Earth science is an excellent medium in which to demonstrate the interdependence of all fields of science. The lithosphere, hydrosphere, and atmosphere are in reality a giant laboratory in which we can apply the physical and biological sciences to the task of purposeful advance. In the long run, scientists may be required to readjust some of their current objectives, which are in certain instances rather exotic, in favor of basic, fundamental pursuit of the stark problems related to population survival. Not only must scientists be aware of such possible eventualities, but all educated people must have the background to envision the far-reaching implications of such problems.

Certainly the student who has moved to the college level without some comprehension of the science of the earth as a discrete and unique body of knowledge is ill-equipped to make the most of additional academic training which will presuppose such background.

2. At what grade level should earth science logically be introduced?

The first elementary concepts of earth science can be taught early in the elementary grades as children are introduced to some of the whys and wherefores of the world around them. On the other hand, truly effective understanding of the underlying scientific phenomena in the earth sciences requires an adequate background in mathematics, physics, chemistry, and biology which is not normally acquired by the student prior to his advanced high school science courses.

As a compromise—and a very logical compromise—earth science can be introduced between the general, superficial science of the elementary grades and the more exacting high school science courses in physics, chemistry, and biology. In the area of geology, for example, the study of the formation of bauxite or hematite deposits affords an excellent opportunity to draw attention to the importance of chemical reactions in nature; the study of earthquakes, to the importance of basic phenomena of physics. In other words, earth science—if skillfully presented—can serve as a catalyst to the imaginative young mind and can stimulate interest in a more meaningful approach to subsequent courses in chemistry and physics. This approach is not without pitfalls—many laws of science and engineering are based on the reactions of homogeneous bodies under homogeneous conditions. In meteorology, oceanography, and geology, the inhomogeneities of materials and forces often so obscure phenomena observed in nature that even the most capable scientists find these problems perplexing, if not completely baffling.

Despite arguments which might be advanced to the contrary, it appears that an organized body of scientific knowledge—earth science—can be effectively presented at the eighth- or ninth-grade level and that it can serve as an effective springboard to high school physics, chemistry, and biology.

3. Should a specific course of study be developed?

With the rapidly developing nationwide trend to institute an earth science course at the ninth-grade level, to replace the traditional but outmoded general science course, there appears to be an urgent need for a single, recommended course of study in the earth sciences. The course must in reality be built from the ground up, since in contrast to biology, chemistry, and physics there are no existing courses to be overhauled. The New York and Pennsylvania state efforts offer some guidelines. To start with, the concepts and balance of subject matter should be established. Then, within this basic framework, various experimental approaches to presentation should be tried.

4. What are the problems of teacher training?

The problems of training teachers to teach earth science are formidable. The earth science teacher who is truly well prepared must have adequate college training in basic mathematics, physics, and chemistry, on which must be superimposed courses in astronomy, geology, and meteorology. Such a course of study, when the required education courses are added, leaves little, if any, room for the necessary enrichment courses in the humanities. Obviously, schools educating earth science teachers must develop special courses of study which will coordinate and integrate the needed earth science subject matter. Such efforts will require a new and higher order of cooperation between educators and scientists and also between the scientists of the various earth science specialties.

Currently, earth science courses are being developed and adopted at a much faster rate than qualified teachers can be found or developed to teach them. Few teachers' colleges offer specific, well-rounded programs of training which are adequate. There have been a growing number of earth science summer institutes, many of which are well-organized and staffed, and capable of doing a good job. Other earth science institutes are being offered by schools which appear to lack the necessary faculty background, depth, and balance to do an effective job.

Teacher training is hampered by the fact that all the elements of earth science are rarely integrated into a single department. This is particularly so in the larger universities and colleges. In some instances there are as many as four departments dealing with various facets of the earth sciences. The fragmentation of the various specialties of the earth sciences for purposes of graduate training and research may be justified, but it certainly inhibits science teacher training.

5. Are adequate teaching resources available?

There are abundant teaching resources in the earth sciences. These resources are as yet inadequately catalogued; moreover, the adequacy of the subject content and its suitability as a teaching tool have not been adequately evaluated. Unfortunately, a large amount of available resource material is scientifically unsound. Poor resources in the hands of poorly trained teachers obviously cannot be expected to produce good results.

The American Geological Institute and the American Meteorological Society have, over the years, carried on modest education programs, significant portions of which have been financed through their own limited resources. Currently the meteorologists, astronomers, and geologists are planning or have in preparation various kinds of resource materials such as sourcebooks (1), monographs, films, and other materials. Some of these materials are already available. The International Geophysical Year generated a substantial amount of educational material, but a large part of this deals with the hardware and glamour of the projects involved rather than with the basic fundamental phenomena of earth science.

To date, in the earth sciences, there has been no intensive course improvement effort such as that of the PSSC and the Biological Science Curriculum Study. What is now needed in the earth sciences is a massive, across-the-board inventory, a cataloging and evaluation of existing teaching resources, and the generation of new, well-conceived courses, resource materials, and teacher training programs. This effort must involve the coordinated and integrated efforts of the various scientific groups in the earth sciences.

6. To whom can we turn for assistance in meeting earth science education problems?[1]

The efforts of individual scientists in the various areas of the earth sciences must be harnessed and coordinated with the work of qualified teachers and educators, if the problems of developing courses, resources, and teacher training are to be met.

The assembling of scientists to work on education problems encompassing all of earth science is in itself a formidable task. Unlike chemistry, physics, and biology, earth science cannot draw on the experience and assistance of a host of seasoned high school teachers, for this reservoir of experienced personnel is relatively very limited.

A logical and possible way to bring the necessary scientific talent to bear on earth science education problems would be to organize the working forces of scientists into three parallel units: *lithosphere, hydrosphere,* and *atmosphere,* with ample overall provisions for the interchange and coordination of views. This would permit a most logical attack on course and teaching resource development in earth science. A central body, representing all three areas, could provide the necessary coordination and integration of effort and could attack the difficult, overriding problems of teacher training.

Conclusions

There is evidence that earth science has a definite place in elementary and secondary school science teaching. A specific earth science course is rapidly being introduced, for the most part at the ninth-grade level, in many school systems. The introduction of these courses is posing serious problems with regard to subject matter, teaching resources, and teacher training. There is a need for a massive effort to attack these problems. The efforts of the most competent scientists available in the various areas of the earth sciences must be coordinated with the efforts of teachers and educators if these problems are to be successfully solved.

Reference

1 Robert L. Heller (ed.), *Geology and Earth Sciences Sourcebook for Elementary and Secondary Science Teachers,* Holt, Rinehart and Winston, Inc.,

[1] Since this was written the Earth Sciences Project (ESP) and the GEO Study Projects, to develop courses for junior high school and college, respectively, have been started.—Editor.

New York, 1962. This sourcebook was developed through an eight-week writing conference of geological scientists and school science teachers during the summer of 1959 at the University of Minnesota, Duluth (Duluth conference), under the auspices of the Teaching Resource Development Program of the American Geological Institute, conducted with the aid of a grant from the National Science Foundation.

EXPERIMENTATION AND EVALUATION

part iv

In my paper I describe the Minnesota National Laboratory, in which an attempt has been made to do in education what has been done for agriculture through the agricultural experiment station. I also survey briefly the scientific and social problems which arise in curriculum experimentation.

Dr. Sitgreaves discusses some of the serious technical problems of curriculum experimentation. Her paper underlines the importance of involving a professional statistician from the beginning, in the planning of educational experiments.

Dr. Barnes tells of the problems which an experimenter creates for the school administrators. When one disturbs a system one must be aware of the strains and stresses involved and be sensitive to possible reactions.

17 ❈ THE MINNESOTA NATIONAL LABORATORY
Paul C. Rosenbloom* *University of Minnesota*

I. The creation of an institution

The Minnesota National Laboratory is the closest analog, so far as I know, to the agricultural experiment stations. Its organization and its activities to date are described in Supplement 9 of this volume. We have been struggling to create in Minnesota a new type of institution to serve national purposes, both directly and as a model for what can be done elsewhere.

This agency is part of the state department of education, the central administrative department for the public schools and junior colleges in the state. We are located, then, in the heart of the state educational system, where data are gathered from all the schools, from which curriculum guides and consultants are sent, where teachers are certified, and where teacher education programs are accredited. We are where we can communicate easily with schoolmen all over the state. Also, because of our close association with policy makers in the state educational system, we are in a position to influence decisions affecting the entire state.

Yet it should be clear that the Minnesota National Laboratory is an agency for scientific research, with no enforcement or regulatory functions. We do not recommend materials for adoption. We merely carry out experiments. Schoolmen may make their own decisions on the basis of our findings. Colleges may participate voluntarily in the teacher education programs we

---

* Paul C. Rosenbloom is Professor of Mathematics in the Institute of Technology, University of Minnesota, and Director, Mathematics Section, Minnesota National Laboratory.

set up, but we have no authority to establish requirements for preservice education of teachers.

We have a small central staff which is financed by the state, but our work is supported mainly by contracts with outside agencies. About half of our work has been financed through contracts with the School Mathematics Study Group. The rest has been supported through contracts with the National Science Foundation and the U.S. Office of Education, granted, in the usual way, in open competition on the basis of the merits of our proposals.

For this reason, most of our work has been on projects of direct national significance, such as the evaluation of new curricular materials, the investigation of the relation between characteristics of teachers and what their students learn, the development of correspondence courses for gifted students, the production of films for in-service education, and the preparation of new materials for the primary grades.

Other work which we have done is indirectly of national significance, in that it shows what can be done when one views an entire state as a natural political unit. An example is our program of summer workshops for teachers, in which we reeducated more than 10 per cent of the Minnesota mathematics teachers in nineteen of the colleges in the state in one summer. Another is a project, about to be launched, to make certain courses available for the preservice education of mathematics teachers at every college in the state.

In 1961 the Minnesota legislature authorized us to appoint directors for any subject matter, to establish in any other field programs similar to what we have been doing in mathematics. We are prepared to cooperate with curriculum projects in such fields as biology, English, and foreign languages in carrying out experiments for the field testing and evaluation of new curricular materials. We can provide the administrative and statistical services required for such experimentation. Our policy in selecting a director of a program would be that he must command the respect of the scholars and the educators in his field and be qualified for a joint appointment, in the corresponding department, with the University of Minnesota.

We hope that our venture in Minnesota can serve as a model for such centers for research and development in education as have been proposed by the Advisory Board on Education of the National Academy of Sciences and in the *Improvement of Educational Quality Act of 1962* now before Congress.

II. The scientific problems of curriculum experimentation

Since I entered the field of educational research in 1958 after some twenty years of experience as a research mathematician, I have constantly been shocked at the state of the art. During my first few years, my major contributions rested not so much on my competence as a mathematician as on my general background as a professional scientist, educated to formulate problems sharply and to identify the observations and comparisons which must be made. More recently I have been impressed by the problems arising in experimentation in all branches of the curriculum which call for the attention of a professional research mathematician.

Experimentation and evaluation

Surprisingly enough, I have found that experienced experimental scientists in other fields often do not appreciate the scientific problems which arise in educational experimentation. This may be due in part to a lack of respect for the caliber of educational research as it has usually been performed in the past. We may hope that the improvement stimulated by the Cooperative Research Branch of the U.S. Office of Education alters the situation within a few years.

The analogy between the Minnesota National Laboratory and the agricultural experiment stations is not accidental. We are both dealing with variables whose values, at least in part, are determined by chance factors—the aptitude of a randomly selected student, the ability of a randomly selected teacher, the effect of the school and community environment, soil fertility, weather, the yield of crops, the milk productivity of offspring, etc. The effects of this random variation are great in relation to the effects we are trying to observe. We must replicate our experiments on a fairly large scale. We must analyze our data statistically in order to separate out the effects due to our new treatments from those ascribable to chance.

The major difference is that we must get the voluntary cooperation of people—teachers, administrators, and parents—in carrying out our experiments, whereas the agricultural experimenter does not need the consent of corn plants or pigs to obtain their cooperation.

In evaluating a new curriculum, the first step is to define the objective clearly. The aim of the School Mathematics Study Group (SMSG) was to develop a course which could be taught by teachers with at most a summer of in-service education, or with the help of consultant service during the first year of experience with the new course. The course prepared by the Illinois Committee on School Mathematics and the physics course produced by the Physical Science Study Committee (PSSC) were both intended for teachers who were specially trained to teach the new curriculum. The SMSG course was aimed at all students below grade 9, whereas the PSSC course was aimed at the self-selected group who choose physics in the eleventh or twelfth grades.

The SMSG tried to introduce new ideas, and, at the same time, to teach the conventional skills at least as well as they are taught in the conventional courses. The PSSC considered that the content of the conventional course was largely irrelevant to its goals.

Professor Sitgreaves discusses in considerable detail some of the statistical problems which arise. The importance of sound design is illustrated by one of the worst scandals in American education. The conventional grade placement of topics in arithmetic in grades 1–8 is based on the study conducted by the so-called Committee of Seven in 1927. This "research" was statistically incompetent, and was completely exploded by Brownell and others about thirty years ago. Yet until very recently there was no series of arithmetic texts available which deviated seriously from the recommendations of this study.

Let me mention briefly some difficulties connected with commonly used experimental designs. It is often suggested that one choose pairs of "matched" teachers, and assign the new course to one teacher in each pair and the conventional course to the other. This type of design is a relic of the days of hand computation, when it was very laborious to calculate even a correlation coefficient. Furthermore, there are no known predictors of teacher effectiveness which can be used as a basis for matching. I don't know of any information about a teacher which you can get from a transcript or an application form, including course grades or supervisors' ratings, which has any significant correlation with what the students learn.

Another design which has been used by reputable investigators is to choose at random from a certain population of teachers two groups, one to teach the new course and the other to teach the conventional. According to our experimental data, the differences in teacher ability are much greater than the differences in achievement attributable to the curriculum. To detect reliably the differences ascribable to the curriculum by this method, one would need a much larger sample of teachers than has been used in any curriculum experiment of this type of which I am aware.

In his paper, Cronbach has discussed the "race horse" type of experiment, in which one has each teacher teach the courses under comparison to two classes. Care must be taken to randomize the assignment of students to the two sections. Public relations must be handled tactfully to gain acceptance for this, as was the case with the oral vaccine tests. If, for example, parental consent is a condition, then an unknown bias is introduced. With each teacher there is a little self-contained experiment, with the factor of teacher ability equalized between the two courses.

This design, while sounder than the other two, leads to difficulties of its own. First, the comparison is valid only with respect to objectives common to the two courses. It makes no sense to find out whether students in the SMSG eighth-grade course learn probability better than those in the conventional course, since probability is not part of the content of the conventional course. A course which is supposed to teach students to speak French cannot be compared, with respect to this outcome, to a course which concentrates entirely on reading.

Second, when preliminary in-service education is required of the teachers before they are assigned to the experimental course, as in the cases of the Illinois mathematics program and the PSSC physics course, the effects of the in-service education are confounded with those attributable to the different courses. It is frequently suggested that with suitable preparation in subject matter, and perhaps also in pedagogy, the teacher would do an adequate job with any textbook, and that the preparation of new courses is largely superfluous. Our experience in mathematics is that teaching one of the new courses is, itself, an excellent form of in-service education. Until now no one has carried out a satisfactory experiment to separate out this halo effect on the alternative courses. The five-state project which our laboratory has started is designed to do just this.

Third, one must take into account both the positive and the negative effects of experience. Our results indicate that during the first year of teaching a new course, the teacher is usually learning it himself, and tends to dwell on the aspects which are new or difficult for him. One rarely gets a balanced allocation of time and emphasis before the second year. On the other hand, both teachers and students are usually better motivated in an experimental situation. Almost every educational innovation constitutes an improvement when it is first introduced, but the improvement often disappears when the innovation stagnates into a routine.

Fourth, this type of design is not well adapted to the elementary school with the self-contained classroom. The best approach I know of for this problem is to have one teacher present, in alternate years, the two courses being compared. To do this, and also have sufficient replication, one must be able to control the school conditions for at least four years.

In some experiments, only the experimental course is taught, and comparisons are made with the "national norms," or standard achievement tests. This is usually nonsense. First, national norms may not be valid for a particular state, school system, or school. Minnesota norms run consistently higher than the publishers' national norms. The average IQ of the student bodies in various Minneapolis schools alone varies from about 95 to 114. We have made analyses of the populations on which some of the standard tests were normed, and we found that the population distribution was often unrepresentative, both geographically and with respect to community size. There is virtually no information available on the distribution of the intelligence, aptitude, or achievement a year before in the population on which the tests were normed. One also wonders what, for example, eleventh-grade norms mean, when one doesn't know what proportion of the norming population was taking college preparatory mathematics, what proportion was taking general or shop mathematics, and what proportion had dropped mathematics altogether. Usually no information exists on the relation between any pre-tests for aptitude or achievement and the results attained with the conventional curriculum on standard achievement tests the following spring or fall.

A statistical analysis is based on a mathematical model, that is, certain assumptions about what the relevant variables are and what relations exist among them. Usually, analyses of educational experiments are made by cookbook applications of formulas in textbooks, without any attempt to test whether the model on which they are based fits the facts, without any statement of the assumptions, even without any awareness of what assumptions are being made. The statistical problems of design and analysis are far from routine, and less than a dozen American colleges of education have an "educational statistician" who would qualify for an appointment in a statistics department.

No matter how nice a design you have on paper, the experiment is meaningless unless you measure the right things. We come, then, to the problem of what variables should be observed and what instruments—tests and the like—should be used to observe them.

The first step is to define the objectives of the course precisely, and in terms of observable behavior. Test constructors know very well how to get at relatively easy objectives such as the ability to solve a quadratic equation, the knowledge of the date of the Civil War, or the ability to translate a French sentence. A few test constructors know how to get at more subtle objectives such as ability to make a scientific inference. I don't know of any existing instrument which tests adequately the ability to make a proof, the ability to form a hypothesis, the skills of critical thinking, the appreciation of literature or of French culture.

These are often-stated objectives of the conventional curriculum, and usually of the proposals for reform as well. You are paying only lip service to an objective unless you test to find out whether you have achieved it. If no existing instrument measures what you want to observe, then you must make the construction of new instruments part of the curriculum experiment.

None of the standard achievement tests in school mathematics does a satisfactory job of testing anything more than rote mastery of mechanical skills. One widely-used test labeled "arithmetical concepts" turns out to be largely a vocabulary test. No one has done for school mathematics the kind of penetrating analysis that Ralph Tyler did for college biology about thirty years ago. I suspect that the situation is not much better in other fields than it is in mathematics.

While the existing state of the art of testing is bad enough in the field of measurement of cognitive processes, it is even worse in the affective domain, in the observation of interests, attitudes, values, and appreciations. Several scales for measuring attitudes toward mathematics have been constructed, but, so far as I know, none of them has been validated against any observation of behavior.

A good start has been made in the cognitive domain, the objectives which deal with recall or recognition of knowledge, and with intellectual skills and abilities, in a report issued by a group of college examiners (1). Unfortunately this group has not published their promised second volume on the affective domain. An indication both of the scientific problems in the measurement of attitudes and of the quality of the work really competent people can do is provided by the work of Stouffer and his associates (2). The use of any test assumes certain relations between the student's responses and the quantity you are trying to measure. The statistical problems which arise are extensively analyzed by Sitgreaves, Solomon, and others in a recent study (3).

The objectives of a course usually consist of several incommensurable components. The new developments in the foreign language curriculum are aimed at teaching skills in speaking, listening, reading, and writing, some understanding of linguistics, some transfer to the understanding of English syntax, and an appreciation of a foreign culture. One must be prepared, when comparing two courses, to find that one meets some objectives better and that the second achieves other objectives better. What weights one chooses to assign to the several objectives is a matter of value judgment, not a scientific problem.

A recurring problem is that of correcting for the intelligence or aptitude of the students. This must be done with caution. Existing intelligence tests measure only six factors of intelligence, while at least fifty have been identified by such investigators as Guilford and Vernon. Existing aptitude tests are hardly distinguishable from achievement tests.

Clearly, in curriculum experimentation one must make, at present, some practical compromise between using the existing instruments, with all their limitations, and doing everything over again from scratch. Where such a

Experimentation and evaluation | 154

compromise is made, one must temper statistical inference with due caution as one interprets the results of curriculum experiments. You cannot compare a text which gives a correct presentation of algebra with one full of serious mathematical errors, solely on the basis of the student's ability to solve quadratic equations by rote.

III. The social problems of curriculum experimentation

Obviously, the proper execution of curriculum experiments calls for a variety of talents which are not found in any one person. One needs experts in content, pedagogy, statistics, psychology, and administration. People of the required level of competence usually already have very good jobs and are already heavily committed to other work. Rarely is even the combination of talents needed located at a single university. The work is much more strenuous than that of most academic positions, and it requires a fairly continuous effort over a period of several years. It cannot be done by occasional consultant service.

To carry out the task one must create an organization with sufficient stability to attract good people, and positions which have career possibilities. The organization must be created where it can execute its tasks. It must also have enough backing from the professional communities concerned to make these positions attractive to people of the caliber required.

Research of this kind is expensive. The results are only as reliable as the data. The data must be gathered through the cooperation of many people. This demands extra time and effort of them, but there is evidence to show that the quality of the data is improved enormously when one pays people for their extra work. This must, therefore, be taken into account in the planning of experiments. As far as I know, tax money is the only source available to finance work of this type adequately.

One faces the same types of time problems as one does in agricultural experiments. It takes a year to find out how much students learn in a year. The significant outcomes of a science curriculum project for grades K-9 may not be observable until high school graduation, and so an adequate evaluation may take some fifteen years.

When in-service education is essential to the experiment, one must have both the authority and the resources to arrange for the necessary program. A very promising project at one university is running into trouble because the administration has not been able to get its elementary and secondary education departments to cooperate in preparing the specially trained teachers called for in the plan.

Since one must obtain the voluntary cooperation of many people—teachers, administrators, parents, and public officials—to do many things, often without a full appreciation of why these actions are necessary in a scientific investigation, one must pay some attention to public relations. Such people must have enough confidence in the leadership of the experiment to do what is asked of them even when they do not really understand why. Until 1955, my main work was mathematical research and teaching at the graduate level. To do what had to be done in the Laboratory, I have had to do everything from teaching kindergarten to lobbying with the state legislature.

IV. The need for centers

The kind of research needed for proper evaluation of curricula cannot be done under the usual conditions. Educational research now consists largely of doctoral dissertations written by people for whom the research is the end of their scholarly career rather than the beginning. They are usually past the optimum age of creativity, as judged by estimates from other fields. Their academic background in subject matter, statistics, and psychology rarely goes beyond the undergraduate level. They rarely command the resources in manpower and money for serious educational experimentation. And they must usually limit themselves to problems which can be finished in a year or so, often to be done as a spare-time activity while holding down a full-time job of teaching or administration.

The Cooperative Research Branch of the U.S. Office of Education is changing this picture slowly. The Course Content Improvement Section of the National Science Foundation is now also supporting certain types of research in curriculum evaluation.

While these agencies have contributed mightily to the improvement of educational research, and have, generally, been administered wisely and effectively, they suffer from certain limitations imposed from above or outside. They have marked out certain lines of jurisdiction, concerning what they can support and whom they can deal with, which sometimes makes it necessary to split an investigation artificially into pieces in order to fit the policies of the supporting agencies. They have both, probably with proper caution, expected much more detailed descriptions of research plans and methods than is usual in the administration of the support of scientific research by the National Science Foundation itself, or by the Office of Naval Research, for example. Since, in serious research, one may very well come up with new ideas in the course of the investigation, it is difficult to plan in such detail too far in advance. If one wishes to make arrangements for the assignment of teachers and students in September, one must notify the school administrators by the preceding February, before they begin work on the fall schedule. This means that decisions on the scale of the project and the budget must be made by the preceding winter. These decisions may depend precariously on both evaluation panels and Congressional appropriations, but, unfortunately, the flow of ideas is not regulated by fiscal years.

The only way that I can see to accomplish the necessary tasks is to follow the model of the agricultural experiment stations. We must establish research centers with the necessary stability, and the necessary resources of both staff and budget to carry out a continuous research program. The time of the research personnel must not be largely devoted, as at present, to the task of securing funds for further operation. The creation of such centers must be a social decision, since the support of this work will inevitably come from public funds. We need, then, to make a decision on public policy.

When we spend billions of dollars of public funds annually on education, can we afford *not* to spend a reasonable proportion of this money on the improvement of the quality of education? We spend annually more than two hundred and fifty million dollars on school textbooks alone. Can we afford *not* to invest adequately in a minimum of quality control, the evaluation of the effectiveness of these books?

The Advisory Board on Education of the National Academy of Sciences has proposed the establishment of an organization for research in education which would accomplish many of the purposes which we have discussed. To a large extent, the program of centers for educational research and development incorporated in the *Improvement of Educational Quality Act of 1962*, submitted by the President to Congress on February 6, 1962, would enable us to do what is needed.

In order to bring about the decision on public policy which is necessary, we shall have to do a much better job than we have done so far of educating educators, scholars, statesmen, and the general public.

References

1 B. S. Bloom (ed.), *Taxonomy of Educational Objectives*, David McKay Company, Inc., New York, 1956.
2 S. A. Stouffer et al., *Studies in Social Psychology in World War II*, Vol. IV, *Measurement and Prediction*, Princeton University Press, Princeton, N.J., 1950.
3 H. Solomon (ed.), *Studies in Item Analysis and Prediction*, Stanford University Press, Stanford, Calif., 1961.

18 ❊ STATISTICAL PROBLEMS IN CURRICULUM EXPERIMENTATION AND EVALUATION
Rosedith Sitgreaves* Columbia University

The term *statistical problems* is used here not in the narrow sense of problems requiring the use of particular statistical techniques, but more generally to refer to problems that arise in the course of a statistical investigation. We may consider that a statistical investigation, as opposed to other kinds of investigations to obtain knowledge, is concerned with obtaining knowledge from quantitative data. In curriculum experimentation, the aim of any program is generally to consider methods for deepening and extending the learning experiences of the individual. To the extent that these programs are to be evaluated quantitatively, they become statistical investigations.

In planning any statistical investigation, we must usually answer questions of the following sort:

1. What categories of individuals (or elements) do we want to obtain knowledge about? In statistical terms, what are the populations of interest?

2. How are these individuals (or elements) to be identified? What groups can actually be studied?

* Rosedith Sitgreaves is Associate Professor of Education, Teachers College, Columbia University.

3. What attributes of the individuals (or elements) do we want to study? That is, what are the variables of interest? Frequently, we are interested not only in attributes at a single point in time, but also in the manner in which they change or develop over time, particularly when some specified treatment or condition is introduced during the time period under study.

4. How are these attributes to be measured? How are changes over time to be evaluated quantitatively? What are the variables we actually observe? How are they related to the latent variables of interest?

5. How many individuals can be studied? Is this the totality of individuals of interest to the experimenter or does it represent only some fraction of that group, i.e., a sample? If the experiment is carried on with samples, how are the samples to be chosen? More than this, how is the experiment to be designed?

6. Once the experiment is in progress and data are collected, how are these data to be summarized numerically? What kind of descriptive statistics are needed? What is the meaning of the descriptive statistics for the group or groups that have been studied?

7. If we have been studying samples from the classes of interest, how do we generalize from the data for the samples to the totality of individuals of interest? What techniques of statistical inference do we need? How are these generalizations to be interpreted?

These questions are phrased here in general terms as they arise in any statistical investigation. Let us consider now the form they take in some types of curriculum experimentation.

In the discussion we will speak of three types of curriculum experimentation which may be briefly and somewhat glibly described as follows: (1) the introduction of new courses, (2) the introduction of new content for standard courses, and (3) the introduction of new teaching programs for standard courses. The glibness becomes apparent when we try to classify some particular examples according to these types. Does the teaching of sets and variables to first graders constitute a new course, or is it rather new content in the teaching of first-grade arithmetic? Can the development and use of new texts in a general biology course in high school be considered as the introduction of new content for a standard course, or is it rather a new program for standard content? We understand that, in many practical instances, the three types given are not clearly differentiable; still they are useful as a basis for discussion.

Let us consider now, in relation to these types of curriculum experimentation, the questions that were formulated earlier. The first two questions concern the definition and identification of the groups which are of interest to the experimenter. Generally, in all types of curriculum experimentation these groups can be defined verbally with relative ease. We talk about new programs for first graders, for academically talented fifth graders, or for college-bound high school students. The groups are identified by their definitions. In other cases, for example in the case of academically talented fifth graders or students with reading difficulties, some criteria must be set up in terms of which the individuals of interest are to be identified. These criteria are frequently based either on the results of objective tests, on

Experimentation and evaluation | 158

subjective ratings of teachers, or on some combination of the two. In any particular case, the criteria adopted for identification need careful examination if we are to be sure that the individuals being identified are the individuals of primary interest.

Questions 3 and 4 concern the definition and measurement of the variables of interest to the experimenter. These variables, in many curriculum experiments, fall naturally into two categories. One category represents what might be termed "background variables"—age, sex, IQ level, socioeconomic status, etc.; the other category includes variables of a more dynamic character, associated with the learning process.

The background variables studied in any experiment are selected usually because they seem pertinent to the investigation. By this we mean that the experimenter may be interested in seeing whether the learning process under study is different for boys and girls, say, or for children of different IQ levels. In general, these variables need to be selected thoughtfully and should not be included indiscriminately. For some background variables, such as age and sex, the question of measurement or of categorization is easily solved. For other variables, such as IQ and socioeconomic status, suitable measuring instruments must be found.

The problems of measuring dynamic variables which are associated with the learning process and of evaluating changes in an individual over time are generally much more difficult. In many areas of learning, pencil and paper tests which are useful for measurement purposes have been, or can be, developed. In some learning situations, however, for example, in learning to speak a foreign language, ratings of performance are needed. When ratings are given by teachers or others, care should be taken to develop objective criteria on which the ratings can be based. In the discussion, we will use the term *test* to include any suitable evaluative procedure.

Consider now a curriculum experiment in which a new course has been introduced for the first time. Tests which measure the progress of individuals taking the course are needed, and these tests must be suitable not only to the material in the course but also to the individuals being tested. Tests prepared for other learning situations, or for other groups, may not prove particularly useful in evaluating the progress of the experimental group except when it is desired to compare the performance of the experimental group with that of other groups. For example, in teaching logic to academically talented fifth graders, it would seem desirable to develop some tests particularly for fifth graders. On the other hand, if the fifth-grade course material is comparable to material in a course currently being taught to college freshmen, it may also be of interest to compare the performance of the two groups on the same test.

The early stages of developing a new course are frequently evolutionary. Tests are needed, during the initial presentation of a course, to determine whether the individuals taking the course are able to learn the skills and concepts which are introduced. These tests are also useful in giving some notion of the relative difficulty of various aspects of the material. On the basis of the test results, the course material may be substantially altered or revised, leading in turn to changes or revisions in the tests.

If the curriculum experiment has involved the introduction of new material into a standard course, new tests need to be developed for the new material. If the new material is supplementary to the material ordinarily included in the course, standard tests can also be given to determine the possible effect of the additional new material on the learning of the standard content. If the experiment involves a new teaching program for a standard course, then presumably standard tests which have already been developed can be used to evaluate progress under the new program.

So far we have talked of test scores as indicators of the level of development of learning. In a number of instances we may be interested not only in the actual level of learning at the end of a given period of time, but also in the development or change in the individual's level since the beginning of the course. In such cases, a series of comparable tests are usually given during the course, the first test providing a base line for the individual.

We have assumed here that tests can be or have been developed to measure those variables in the learning process which are of interest to the experimenter. This is not an assumption to be made lightly. In many instances, however, if the goals of a particular program have been clearly and precisely formulated, and the material for the course has been prepared with these goals in mind, it is possible, with the help of both testing experts and subject matter specialists, to develop suitable evaluative procedures.

We come now to 5, the questions concerned with experimental design. Perhaps the biggest statistical problem in curriculum experimentation is the formulation of and adherence to a good experimental design. A good design for a particular problem must of necessity be developed in terms of the requirements of the problem and the resources available, but a few general remarks can be made.

Except, perhaps, where the curriculum investigation is an evaluation of current practices in a particular school district, curriculum studies and, in particular, curriculum experiments are based on samples of individuals. The term *sample* is used here in the sense that the results attained with the group under study are to be generalized to other groups, the studied group constituting a sample of the totality of individuals about whom the experimenter would like to draw conclusions.

In curriculum experimentation, the sampling process is frequently two-dimensional, and time constitutes one of the dimensions. For example, suppose all first graders in the United States participated in a particular new program for 1961–1962, and the results of this experience are used in planning the program for first graders in 1962–1963. The group studied in 1960–1961 is thus a sample of first graders on which generalizations to other (later) first graders are based. While this sampling dimension does not usually present any particular problems in experimental design, it will come up again later when we discuss problems of generalization.

The second dimension in the sampling process is the one with which we are usually more directly concerned, namely, the selection of groups of individuals for study from the totality of potential subjects available. There are usually two stages in this selection process. The first stage involves the determination of a number of potential groups for study who are judged to be representative of the groups of interest. The groups so determined

Experimentation and evaluation | 160

constitute a judgment, or purposive sample, from the groups of interest. The second stage involves the actual selection of subjects for study from designated groups. Usually some element of randomness is introduced at this stage.

In much of curriculum experimentation, as in other scientific research, we are interested in making comparisons among groups. This may be less in evidence in the development of a completely new course where the experimental process is evolutionary and the primary purpose is exploratory. Even here it may be desirable to make comparisons of groups in terms of background variables such as sex and IQ. In many cases of curriculum experimentation, however, the matter of primary interest is the comparison of experimental and control groups. In evaluating the effectiveness of a particular experimental program by comparing the results with experimental and control groups, it is vitally important to be certain that any observed differences are due essentially to the difference between the experimental and control programs, and not to other factors which may affect the learning process. In planning these experiments, every effort should be made to ensure that, except for the particular experimental variables under study, all the groups in the experiment are as comparable as possible with respect to other pertinent factors. This can be achieved partly by the precise definition of the criteria by which the groups of interest are identified. In addition, if there are large numbers of individuals available for study, it may be possible to set up classes which are matched on some of the pertinent background variables. Thus, it may be possible to schedule classes for the different experimental conditions at the same time of day.

It is obviously impossible, however, to match all the pertinent variables. For example, an extremely important factor in any classroom situation is the teacher. While general criteria for teachers in the experiment can and should be set up, experience has shown that teaching effectiveness within a program tends to vary, and that the same teacher may not be equally effective in two different classroom situations. In designing the experiment it is important, therefore, to introduce the two Rs of experimentation: randomness and replication. Randomization should be used wherever possible, so that the effects of the uncontrolled variables tend to balance out in the long run. Thus, if classes within a particular school district are to be set up to participate in an experiment, it may be possible to form the classes by randomly selecting students from the available supply, to assign teachers to the classes in a random way, and to use randomization in determining the particular program to be followed in each class. Replications of the experiment should be carried through to obtain some measures of the variation in the results which are introduced by some of the uncontrolled variables. Thus, replications of the same program in different classes within the same school should enable one to measure the variation in results attributable to the difference between teachers. Replication of the program in different schools within the same area should lead to a measure of interschool variability.

A number of experimental problems are not statistical problems *per se*, but are of statistical importance because of the manner in which they affect the data. One such is the problem of carrying through an experiment according to the specifications set up at the time the experiment is designed and initiated. It cannot be emphasized too strongly that, unless the final results are to be viewed as exploratory, programs in experimental and control classes should not be changed in the course of the experiment. This means that it is desirable to make preliminary investigations and a number of pilot studies to make sure that the proposed experiment is workable. The teachers in the experiment need a thorough orientation not only in the purposes and methods of the study but in the need for adhering to the program as planned. It is important also that evaluation tests given during the course of the experiment be administered in a uniform way in all the cooperating classes.

Another problem that frequently arises is the problem of the attrition of subjects. Since most curriculum experiments require a period of time such as a semester or a school year before they are completed, and human beings are very mobile, it is quite likely that not all individuals in the experiment at the beginning will continue until the end. If such attrition occurs, then presumably we would want to investigate some of the pertinent characteristics of the individuals who have left, in order to make sure that there are no differences in the individuals leaving the experimental and control groups which may affect the results. Notice that a common factor throughout the various problems is the need for comparability of control and experimental groups on all factors except the particular programs under investigation.

Once the data have been collected, the questions of 6 and 7, concerning suitable description and analysis, arise. The methods of descriptive statistics are useful in summarizing the observed data numerically. Test scores for a particular group can be tallied in a frequency distribution, and the distribution characterized by a suitable measure of central tendency and a measure of dispersion. Two distributions can be compared by comparing corresponding descriptive constants such as the values of the mean or standard deviation computed for them. If the evaluation measure used is a standard test for which norms have been developed, the results for the groups under study can be compared with the norms.

After the results for the studied groups have been characterized numerically, statements concerning the applicability of the observed results to other groups are usually desired. The techniques of statistical inference make it possible to evaluate the degree of stability of the observed results which can be expected when the experiment is replicated. The term frequently used in this connection is that of examining the statistical significance of the results. It should be emphasized that *statistical significance* does not imply meaningfulness from the content point of view, but refers only to the statistical evaluation of the expected stability of the observed results. We may suppose that in some cases a difference in the means of test scores for an experimental and control group may be statistically significant, i.e., stable, but at the same time so small numerically that it would not justify the cost of installing the new program in the entire school system.

A final caution might be mentioned in connection with the matter of generalization. Statistical methods are useful in making generalizations to other *comparable* groups. Groups within a school district are presumably comparable from year to year; thus, with suitable statistical evaluation, the results obtained in a current year in a particular school district should be useful in making decisions for the following year. In generalizing to other school districts, judgment must be exercised to make sure that the school districts actually studied are similar with respect to various relevant variables.

19 ❊ THE PRACTICAL PROBLEMS OF PARTICIPATING IN EXPERIMENTAL PROJECTS
Melvin W. Barnes   *Superintendent of Schools*
Portland, Oregon

My assignment deals with the problems that are experienced when public schools participate in curriculum experiments. To find what everyday practitioners in school administration have to say on this topic, I asked a number of my professional colleagues about it. The questions that I asked included the following:

1. What are the headaches connected with participation in experimental projects?
2. What community relationships are involved and how do you handle them?
3. How are school board relationships affected?
4. What kinds of projects can best be conducted by a school system?
5. What kinds of programs are best done by, or in cooperation with, outsiders?
6. How do you manage and coordinate varied experiments?
7. How do you use the findings that research projects yield?
8. Have you any hints as to how to approach school administrators with proposals for research?

First among the major barriers that school administrators say they encounter in the conduct of experimentation are vested interests, preconceived ideas, and the established ways of doing things—the inertia that resides in people. For example, if you propose a study that cuts across all of the curriculum, the subject-matter specialists are likely to become disturbed. On the other hand, if you attempt to change the curriculum by revising content, subject by subject, you create anxiety in the people who oppose this approach to curriculum change. Thus teachers who have learned to teach ninth-grade English and social studies as a fused course, when asked to teach the subjects separately, are reluctant to leave their established ways of working.

A second problem that school administrators encounter is that of coordinating talent, particularly when they use consultants. They run into difficulty in getting teachers and professors to work effectively together.

Consultants need time to adjust to a school staff. Some say this may take as long as two or three years. Teachers, of course, have to learn how to work with consultants. It is interesting to note that in many of the current ventures to update the teaching of such subjects as chemistry, physics, mathematics, and English, the teachers and professors have had, initially, quite wrong perceptions of each other. In the course of the first year's association, the professors see the teachers as ignorant of subject matter. Accordingly, they feel that their first task is to teach them subject matter. The second year, the professors discover what a complex task the management of a school classroom is, and they are surprised that teachers are able to bring off the job as well as they do. Continued contact results in better understanding for both.

One barrier to participation in experimentation that is often mentioned lies in the nature of the proposals that are submitted. School administrators feel that they are sometimes asked to conduct experiments that are designed to prove what is already assumed; that is, some research sets out to support a point of view rather than to find the truth.

The demands of controlled experimentation may be irksome to practitioners in public schools. As experimentation proceeds, conditions may change and new hunches arise which sometimes make it seem advisable to shift the direction of the project or to make adjustments in it. School administrators like the freedom and flexibility to make such changes, although it is obvious that the necessity for controlled conditions might be thus overlooked.

Administrators say that experimentation puts a heavy burden on certain members of the staff. Conducting an experiment inevitably means that some people will do a good deal of extra work. Frequently it is said that planning time is too short. For example, one group of schoolmen said that the plan they devised for conducting some research was a "two-weeks wonder" into which "they had thrown everything, including the kitchen sink." The lack of adequate research design is often cited as a serious weakness in experimental projects.

One of the major difficulties is the lack of trained personnel. It is difficult to get people to conduct experimentation on a short-term basis. Dr. Roy Hall, who was head of research in the U.S. Office of Education, indicated that the lack of leadership for research projects was a major barrier to progress. Dr. Sam Lambert, research director for the NEA, says that money is more easily obtained than trained personnel. If a school system brings in additional leadership and pays the new staff higher salaries than the going scale, morale is injured. Although the problem of finding adequate personnel to handle research projects is difficult to solve, school administrators suggest that the best person is usually somebody already on the scene. An insider has a head start because he knows the staff and is able to adapt to his new assignment better than an outsider who must first become acquainted with the staff and the situation.

Budgets, of course, are a problem. Experiments take money. No matter how much money is provided in the original grant, there is seldom enough to handle the whole job and the local district has to use its own funds. Small school districts, of course, have very little budgetary leeway. Large districts are not unlimited. It is not characteristic of school systems to set aside very much money for curriculum research. This is a major weakness in planning and budget making. One school administrator said, of an experimental project that he had conducted, that one of the heaviest expenses was publishing the final report, which ran to thirteen volumes—an unexpected expense.

Community relationships

The schools belong to the people. Schools are under local control, so community relationships are important in anything undertaken by the schools. School administrators report, however, that the danger of friction in community relationships resulting from experimental projects is overestimated. In several situations reported, community acceptance was said to be one of the easiest conditions to meet. One gets the impression that today most people are interested in finding better ways to teach. And a school system that is engaged in experimentation is given credit for trying. Newspapers usually give good coverage to experimental projects. They like to present the local school district as being progressive and, of course, reports of their experiments and projects are grist for the newspaperman's mill.

There is, of course, the problem of maintaining balance within a school system. If there is a project for gifted students, citizens may wonder what is happening to the average students. Thus, it is necessary to reassure the board and the community that a well-proportioned school program is being maintained. Because teachers and other school employees are a main avenue of public relations, it is very important that the staff have general understanding of the projects. Teachers talk in the grocery store, on the street, in church and civic groups, and they, of course, are expected to know about new curriculum experiments. Parents sometimes wonder why a new project, which sounds like an improvement, can be conducted in only two or three schools. They commonly ask, "If it is good, why not give it to all children?"

Relationships with the board

If a board of education properly understands a project at the time that it approves it, no difficulty should arise in board relationships. It is important, of course, to keep the board informed. Board members usually get favorable publicity from an experimental project. They like to think of their school district as progressive, and so are interested in favorable comments about what they are doing. One thing is rather noticeable. School board members are becoming increasingly sophisticated. State school board associations are becoming more effective and aggressive. Many of them now employ competent executive secretaries. The national school boards meeting is a forum where all sorts of school issues and questions are discussed. Thus there is an increasing tendency for boards to initiate experimentation and change. It is possible, of course, for a board, carried away with the possibilities of a particular plan, to impose on the school staff the task of managing a project that the board really initiated. Such instances suggest the importance of forward-looking professional leadership that is able to seize the initiative in planning projects.

165 | *The practical problems of participating in experimental projects*

What kinds of programs are best initiated by schools?

School administrators think they do best with curriculum development projects—the kind that we call "action research" or experimental teaching programs—efforts of the sort designed to find more successful ways of teaching. Moreover, a school district ought to undertake only something that it really wants to do. For example, if one is conducting a study of "underachievers" in a school system, it would be wise to initiate the study in a school where the faculty is already showing special interest in this kind of thing. And, of course, a school district ought not to undertake something it is not willing to carry through. Unless it commits itself to mobilize personnel and resources in order to conduct the study, the study ought not to be attempted at all.

It has been mentioned by both researchers and school administrators that much of what is being done in schools today does not deserve the term "research." Many thesis projects, which are a major source of research in our profession, are hardly genuine research. Some school administrators distinguish between data gatherers and genuine researchers.

Where does outside help come in?

There are some kinds of experimentation that require the prestige of national leadership. In many instances, as everybody knows, national groups have initiated and paid the costs of experimentation. One example is the National Science Foundation, and the many institutes that it has conducted. Others are the various efforts in mathematics, physics, biology, chemistry, and English. If a project in a particular school district has the stamp of approval of a recognized national group, such backing generally guarantees local acceptance of it.

School people recognize, in connection with experimentation, that under many circumstances the schools are not legally free to delegate their responsibility for children. Thus, because of the schools' responsibility, it is not permissible for them to provide a group of children for outside researchers to handle as they please.

How do you manage and coordinate projects?

Many a school district today has more projects on the fire than it can handle. There are serious difficulties in keeping track of a number of experiments in ways that guarantee effective use of results. Proven techniques fall into disuse, better ways of teaching are known but neglected. It is easier to initiate a project than to utilize the conclusions. School administrators say that even if adequate evaluation is provided, it is not a simple matter to incorporate new features into established practice. Many times we have found improved methods but have not used them because they did not fit the habitual routine. The findings of the Eight-Year Study were a high-water mark in curriculum advance, but it is safe to say that in many of the high schools that participated in that study one could find today only the vestigial remains of what was going on there twenty-five years ago.

What are the best ways to approach school administrators?

To this question some of my colleagues gave some tongue-in-cheek answers, so do not take these replies too seriously. They said, "The first thing the administrator wants to know, when he is approached on the matter of engaging in an experiment, is how much money he is going to get." Another question he will ask is, "How much good publicity will it gain for us?" And third, "Are there any strings attached?" These remarks are included simply for what they may be worth.

In order to find out how school administrators appear to one on the other side of the fence, I asked the representatives of research agencies who have been administering foundation grants what kinds of response they get from school administrators when they invite their participation in experimentation.

They said that one of the first things school administrators will say is, "It's going to cost us too much." "There'll be expense in it, and we're not prepared to spend our money for such a purpose." They are not willing to supply money for research. A second comment was, "Research demands change, and school administrators fear change." Change makes people uncomfortable. It is easier to stay with what you have. A third reaction was that school administrators don't understand research and what it is, therefore they do not value it. A fourth statement they made is that one of the serious problems has to do with the scarcity of research people, the problem of getting trained personnel to design and conduct research. These persons, representing foundations and research organizations, said also that after the results are in and administrators are confronted with the findings, they tend to shy away from the task of incorporating the results into their everyday practice.

This leads to the conclusion that the real problem is how to institute change. Somebody said that changing the curriculum was like moving a cemetery. How do you motivate a faculty? Or a school system? New ideas are plants of tender growth, and there are many techniques for killing new ideas. There is a lag of years in putting into practice what we know to be good. We know better but do worse. Perhaps we need to teach teachers to apply research. Maybe we should do our best to grow a generation of teachers who are research-minded, because it is necessary for teachers to teach experimentally if they are to make use of the research available to them.

THE ROLE OF
PROFESSIONAL SOCIETIES

part V

In order to keep the conference program within manageable dimensions, we were forced to work with the "holding companies" which pull together the activities of many more specialized societies.

Dr. Page describes the variegated activities of the American Association for the Advancement of Science and its affiliates.

Dr. Turner does the same for the American Council of Learned Societies and its affiliates in the social sciences and the humanities.

Dean Cook tells of the work of the American Educational Research Association.

Dr. Van Til emphasizes the importance of working with the "middlemen" in his organization to get improved curricula actually used in the schools.

Dr. Pomeroy deals with the problem of preparing teachers to teach the new developments in the curriculum.

20 ❁ THE CHANGING ART OF SCIENCE TEACHING
Thornton Page* Wesleyan University

The goal of science teaching is twofold: first, it must produce well-trained scientists to carry on scientific research and the multitudinous applications so necessary in our society today. Second (and this is of growing concern to both educators and scientists), science teaching must acquaint the general public with what the scientist is after, with what he has to offer, and with what he cannot provide.

It is in this second respect that the art of science teaching has changed markedly in the past decade, and it may be that science and mathematics will soon be recognized for what they are—part of the humanities, to be taught as some of the most fascinating intellectual and creative achievements of man. This second goal involves reforms in both school curricula and the training of teachers of science.

It would be like beating a dead horse to criticize science teaching of the 1930–1940 era, were it not for the fact that many of our present scientists and teachers had their training then and continue now to present science as they learned it then—a body of facts and conclusions. By contrast, it is

* Thornton Page is Professor of Astronomy at Wesleyan University, and Chairman of the American Association for the Advancement of Science Cooperative Committee on the Teaching of Science and Mathematics.

the thesis of most of the serious thinkers in science and education today that the simple results of science are of passing interest only; many of these results are modified over a period of a few decades, and popular interest shifts among them in even shorter time-spans. The shift of interest to nuclear physics and to space technology in recent years bears witness to this view.

Far more significant than the conclusions, I believe, are the methods of science and the spirit of discovery that have caused increasingly frequent changes in concepts and modes of exploration. As in most fields of learning, true understanding of the facts themselves comes only from an appreciation of various interpretations—of the many concepts that have been tried, some of which have been rejected. No one can be sure that the earth moves round the sun until he has examined the Ptolemaic hypothesis that it is fixed in the center of the universe and found the defects in that view.

In any case, the subject matter of science is far more interesting to the student when it is unfolded in the manner of a continuing investigation rather than a set piece. No one would deny that a student must learn that the earth goes round the sun; but if it is simply presented as a fact to be memorized it loses its appeal as a discovery—as a scientific advance. Moreover, the most appealing topics in science are those being subjected to active research; the conclusions are far from certain. If these tentative conclusions were presented as true, we would be in danger of teaching wrong facts. Most textbooks, for example, present a story of the earth's origin that has been proven false.

The present problem in science teaching in the United States is this: How can we shift the emphasis of a million teachers of science from the mere facts and the often outdated conclusions of science to something more enlightening? Until recently, the attitude of the scientific societies was primarily to insist on more thorough subject-matter training of teachers. On this basis the National Science Foundation has supported fellowships, summer institutes, and academic-year institutes for teachers. I do not question the essential value of these programs, but it may be fairly said that they have not fully solved the problem of improving science teaching in high school and the lower grades. In fact, the emphasis on subject-matter teaching may have simply provided teachers with more facts and conclusions that students can be required to memorize. The result, as implied above, is to make science courses less attractive and to widen the chasm between the sciences and the other humanities.

One of the early indications of this unhappy state of affairs was exposed by the American Association for the Advancement of Science (AAAS) Cooperative Committee for the Teaching of Science and Mathematics. This committee, first formed in 1941 by the biologists, chemists, mathematicians, and physicists, was expanded in 1944 to represent over fifteen national scientific societies and teachers' associations. It was and is concerned with teacher certification and training, teacher recognition, teaching aids of all sorts, curriculum improvement, and so on, mainly at the high school and college levels. The early studies I refer to showed that the proportion of college students majoring in the sciences and mathematics is on the decline in the United States. In fact, not to dramatize the finding unduly, the

The role of professional societies

United States was surpassed by the Soviet Union several years ago in annual output of trained scientists and engineers.

It is difficult to believe these statistics—or to understand their cause in our culture, dependent as it is on science and technology. The best interpretation our committee can find is that poor teaching of science and mathematics, probably well before high school, tends to convince many students (for one reason or another) that they "can't do science," or that they have "nonmathematical minds." In my opinion, this also accounts for the "C. P. Snow syndrome"—the growing isolation of science from the other humanities, the "two cultures." Speculating a bit further, I suspect that the decline of science teaching in the United States may have come about through the greatly enhanced demand for scientists in government and industry—a demand that has drawn many competent scientists out of teaching.

The AAAS cooperative committee has done a great deal to bring these matters to the attention of the professional scientists, and I believe that all of the national scientific societies now have committees or larger groups working on the improvement of teaching, in practice and as a profession. In my own professional society, the American Astronomical Society, the Committee on Education in Astronomy is encouraging curriculum improvements, teaching aids, and a kind of public relations campaign to make astronomy more attractive as a career. We estimate that we need to double our output of trained astronomers to meet the demand over the next ten years.

To return to the AAAS cooperative committee, which best represents the combined attitude of the national scientific societies: one of the committee's major achievements was its "Report on Teacher Certification" (1). A subcommittee chaired by Prof. Alfred B. Garrett of Ohio State University, and including representatives of five sciences and mathematics, developed a set of college course curricula in biology, chemistry, physics, general science, and mathematics which were recommended as norms on which state certification requirements can be based. The totals, up to ninty-five semester hours, are high. This is because the subcommittee felt that a teacher should be well enough grounded in undergraduate work to qualify for study for an advanced degree; teachers in training should not be segregated, during undergraduate years, from students preparing for research careers.

The difficulty, of course, is that a number of education courses are also required for certification, and that most colleges and universities add further requirements—general courses, foreign languages, etc. The total can add up to an impossible load for four undergraduate years. For this reason, it was recommended that high school science teachers should spend five years in training—an ideal that admittedly may be difficult to achieve.

The National Association of State Directors of Teacher Education and Certification, in cooperation with AAAS, expanded on these matters in a pamphlet, *Guidelines for Preparation of Teachers of Secondary School Science and Mathematics* (2), that is focused on approved college programs for the training and certification of teachers. Numbers of semester hours in each area are not specified, but the need for a fifth year is again recognized. A good deal more thought is needed in devising practical curricula for teacher preparation.

The programs of high school curriculum reform that offer the greatest promise have been those supported by the National Science Foundation, with the encouragement of the professional scientific societies—in physics (PSSC), biology (Biological Sciences Curriculum Study), mathematics (The School Mathematics Study Group), and chemistry (The Chemical Bonds Approach Project and CHEMStudy). All these programs are coordinated efforts, involving the writing of new textbooks, teaching guides, laboratory manuals, and so forth; the training of high school teachers; and the support of high schools instituting the change. In each case, the revised curriculum has been tested in representative high schools and modified as a result of this trial. Colleges are already feeling some of the results; freshmen with the PSSC training have a more mature view of physics than in the past. In many ways these new high school science curricula have provided the enlightenment we so badly need.

However, students can, and do, elect to avoid science in high school because of prejudices formed and poor training received in their earlier years. With this in mind, the AAAS organized in 1960 a series of conferences on the teaching of science from kindergarten to the ninth grade. A proposal has been made to the National Science Foundation for support of an extended effort to improve elementary science teaching.[1]

The problem is a good deal more difficult than the improvement of the high school curriculum; there are a few thousand high school teachers of science but there are nearly a million elementary teachers conducting classes in science, most of them ill-prepared in the subject. It is patently impracticable to train these teachers in special institute programs; moreover, the variation in local conditions (rural versus urban, large school versus small, etc.) probably rules out a single "best" curriculum. Educational psychology is far more important in the early school years, and it is doubtful that anyone knows at what level it is best to introduce abstraction, or how the native curiosity of children can best be guided into study of natural phenomena.

Many of the university scientists who served on the AAAS steering committee concerned with elementary science teaching agree that the greatest promise lies in developing several improved curricula, writing textbooks, teacher guides, tests, and preparing other aids to teachers, trying out these materials in a broad sample of elementary schools, and then making them available to teachers. If this very considerable effort is supported fully by the scientists and educational psychologists, there is hope that we can correct the present deficiencies of elementary science teaching in the United States. Among other things, this may be expected to encourage more students to take up science as a career, and to reverse the trend separating the two cultures.

References

[1] American Association for the Advancement of Science Cooperative Committee on the Teaching of Science and Mathematics, "Preparation of High School Science Teachers," *Science,* vol. 131, no. 3406, pp. 1024–1029, Apr. 8, 1960.

[1] For recent developments see *Science Education News,* December, 1962, published by AAAS.—Editor.

2 *Guidelines for Preparation Programs of Teachers of Secondary School Science and Mathematics,* NASDTEC-AAAS Studies, 1515 Massachusetts Ave., N.W., Washington, D.C.

3 American Association for the Advancement of Science, "Science Teaching in Elementary and Junior Schools," *Science,* vol. 133, no. 3469, pp. 2019–2024, June 23, 1961.

21 ❃ THE ROLE OF THE AMERICAN COUNCIL OF LEARNED SOCIETIES IN SECONDARY EDUCATION
Gordon B. Turner* American Council of Learned Societies

Curriculum development is the core of any program designed to raise educational standards, but it is only one of a series of steps that must be taken if secondary education in this country is to achieve the level of excellence expected of it. A good many steps must precede and follow the work of curriculum development if the latter is to be effectively planned and brought to fruition in the classroom. Before there can be an intelligent revision of the curriculum, there must be a marshalling of the forces for change, a marshalling of funds to underwrite the task, and a marshalling of talents to get the job done. And, of course, subsequent to the actual development of new or revised courses, there must be preparation of materials, preparation of teachers, and preparation of school officials in order to induce them to experiment with and ultimately adopt the new curriculum.

If scholars are to play an effective part in this process, and it is the assumption of this conference that they should, then it is desirable and perhaps even essential for the professional societies to be involved in almost every step along the way. Since, in a very real sense, however, each of these stages is dependent upon the other, and frequently they must be carried on simultaneously, it is not entirely feasible to single out curriculum experimentation and discuss only this part of the role of professional societies in secondary education.

Moreover, the size and complexity of the task—indeed, the very nature of the task and the means of accomplishing it—vary tremendously from field to field and even from subject to subject. It is therefore no simple matter to discuss the role of the American Council of Learned Societies (ACLS) in curriculum development, as this paper is supposed to do.

The ACLS is a federation of thirty learned societies, of which perhaps half are concerned with fields that are relevant to secondary education. They normally work on a highly theoretical level and are therefore unfamiliar with the technical aspects of secondary education. Moreover, these societies are for the most part without funds of their own, and a few of them have

* Gordon B. Turner is Vice President of the American Council of Learned Societies, New York City.

not even begun to take an active interest in secondary education. It is evident, then, that one of the most important parts of the council's work is to encourage its constituent societies and a variety of other organizations and institutions to provide the substantive and financial underpinnings for the revision of secondary education. Beyond this, there are severe limitations upon what the council can do, for its staff is small, and, unless it is to expand to the point where the tail begins to wag the dog, it cannot become involved in operational matters. In a sense, therefore, the council's major role is exhortation and initiation.

In order to clarify this point for those of you who are not familiar with the American Council of Learned Societies, let me explain more fully what the council is, what it conceives its function to be, and the means available to it, before taking up the specific subject with which the conference is concerned.

The purpose of the council is to advance humanistic studies in all fields of learning, including the humanities *per se* and the humanistic aspects of the social sciences, and to maintain and strengthen relations among the national societies devoted to such studies. For a number of years the council confined itself almost exclusively to humanistic research and scholarship, and did not consider the problems of secondary education as within its purview. More recently, however, it has taken a different view, and, while the promotion of scholarship and research necessarily continues to occupy the major portion of its funds and energies, it believes that, as the only national organization representing the humanities in this country, it should now look upon the humanities in a broader sense, as encompassing not only scholarship but education. Nevertheless, the core of the council's work consists of the promotion of scholarly research through assistance to individual scholars in the form of grants and fellowships, through committees appointed to develop and supervise effective long-range plans related to scholarly needs in the humanities, and through the support of small conferences which bring scholars together to discuss problems of mutual interest.

It would be irrelevant to the concerns of this conference to catalog all the activities in which the ACLS is engaged beyond this core program as a result of its new attitude about the humanities and humanistic scholarship, so let me make my point simply by saying that only about 5 per cent of the energies and funds of the council are devoted to secondary education. This is not, let me assure you, an accurate reflection of our assessment of the importance of secondary education or of the desirability of having scholars take an active part in it, but it is an accurate statement of the facts of our financial life. The ACLS is dependent for its existence and for the support of its programs principally upon the philanthropic foundations, supplemented occasionally by government contracts for specific purposes, and the fact is that had we been successful in all of our efforts to raise funds last year (a feat that one may hope for but seldom expects to achieve), the percentage of 1961's budget devoted to secondary and higher education, including curriculum development, would have been enormously increased. Moreover, it should be made clear that the ACLS and a number of its constituent societies have made vigorous efforts to convince the Federal government of the need for programs and appropriations in aid of secondary education in the humanities and the social studies, again, as you know, without success. I cite these facts not to catalog disappointments, nor to offer a counsel of despair, nor to draw invidious comparisons between support for the humanities and other divisions of learning. Nor do I mean to imply that the foundations are uninterested in education, for they have poured millions of dollars into it over the last few years.

My reasons for discussing the financial situation are twofold: first, to set forth certain factors that limit the role of the council in secondary education, and, second, to indicate that the attempt to raise funds must continue to be one of the most important features of that role. And I might add that there is reason for some optimism in the long run.

If the Council has certain limitations in this area, however, it also has some unique abilities. Through its position as a federation of learned societies concerned with the humanities and the social sciences, and as the national representative of the humanities, the ACLS is in close touch with humanists and social scientists all over the country, not only indirectly through the medium of its constituent societies, but directly as individuals who serve upon its numerous committees and who act as its associates on the nation's campuses. Given this source of latent talent for improving secondary education, and the Council's "new look" with respect to the humanities, it was natural that we should be led to relate the two, for secondary education will never reach the high plateau of quality the country needs unless scholars who are specialists in the subject matter of the schools take an active part in the whole process of revision.

There is no need to refer here to the regrettable gap that developed over the years between the scholars and the professional educators, other than to say that we can no longer afford the luxury of feuding and that any conflicts that exist between the needs of mass education and the traditional aims of higher education must be squarely faced. The scholars, in other words, must once again become actively engaged in education at all levels, and this means they must be concerned with curriculum development not only in the schools but in the institutions of higher education where the next generation of teachers will be trained.

A number of years ago this conviction on the part of the council led it to appoint a Committee on the Secondary Schools composed of members representing the teachers, the scholars, the administrators of the colleges and the schools, the learned societies, the departments of public instruction, and the field of teacher education. One of the first steps this committee took was to call a conference of teachers from the universities and the schools to advise the council on matters pertaining to secondary school curricula in the humanities and the social studies. In this and a subsequent conference, teachers of English, foreign languages, social studies, art, music, and the classics, met in subject-matter panels to discuss a variety of problems dealing with curriculum development and teacher education, and to determine whether effective methods could be devised to introduce the findings of recent research into the curriculum. The report (1) of these panels contains numerous recommendations which have stimulated a variety of activities both within the ACLS and its constituent societies.

I want to concentrate on two programs, both of which had their origins in these panels, which seem to me to illustrate particularly well the council's role in secondary education, because collectively they involve almost the whole range of things that I have been saying must be accomplished if secondary education is to meet the challenge that confronts it. The first is a program of summer institutes in the humanities, and the second is in the field of social studies.

In determining what contributions it could make in the area of secondary education, the council did not want to duplicate other efforts already under way, and it therefore sought ways in which it could use its unique ability to bring the talents of university people to bear on the problems that existed. It also realized that if it were to concentrate its efforts too narrowly on a single line of attack it would not be discharging its full responsibility, for the basic problems of secondary education are so varied in nature that they must be attacked on a broad front.

The ACLS program of summer institutes was designed with these considerations in mind. It is intended not only to meet a specific need in the high schools, but to have a bearing upon three basic problems that exist in secondary education today. These may be classified as: (1) teacher education, (2) curriculum development, and (3) recruitment of superior students to the teaching profession. For long-range improvement of the secondary schools, the quality of teacher education must, of course, be raised at the undergraduate level, but for immediate improvement the ACLS believes that summer institutes for humanities teachers are needed to raise the educational level of current high school teachers. For purposes of curriculum development, the ACLS has asked that, whenever feasible, each of its institutes design a demonstration course complete with syllabus, reading materials, and bibliography, and to work out with the participating teachers the best pedagogical methods of introducing the new course. Finally, it was assumed that the problems of recruitment would automatically be alleviated to a considerable degree if, as hoped, the institutes' participants returned to their classrooms with renewed enthusiasm and morale and with courses that would in turn excite their students.

You may wonder about my emphasis on the council's institute program when the National Science Foundation has scheduled hundreds of institutes and has the funds available for thousands of science and mathematics teachers to attend them. The fact is that there is no program on a comparable scale in the humanities except for the National Defense Education Act institutes in modern foreign languages, and I believe that the ACLS program, both because it has been small and because it has been experimental in nature, has some lessons that may be useful to discuss here.

The goals of these institutes are, I suppose, similar to those supported by the NSF: (1) to revitalize the high school teacher's interest in his subject by introducing him to new materials and placing him abreast of new scholarly developments in his field, (2) to advance his competence and to stimulate habits of reflective thinking in order to raise the level of his instruction, and (3) to provide him with the tools and techniques necessary to introduce his new knowledge and insights into his classroom teaching. But here, I suspect, the similarities end between the NSF institutes and ours, since our objective has been to experiment with pilot institutes until large-scale funds become available. We were encouraged to do this in 1959 by the Secretary of Health, Education, and Welfare, when he informed us that he intended to throw the full weight of his department behind a move to include summer institutes in the humanities in the provisions of the National Defense Education Act when it came up for renewal. In an effort to demonstrate to the Congress the scholarly community's interest in such institutes, and to work out practices and procedures which would enable a future governmental program to get into high gear rapidly and effectively, we therefore drew up certain policies and procedures to serve as guidelines for the directors of the institutes we intended to support. These may be summarized as follows:

1. Whenever possible, try to include a number of curriculum supervisors and principals either as participants or as part-time observers, on the theory that it does little good for a teacher to attend an institute unless the educational attitudes and sympathies of his administrative officers permit him to put his experience into practice, and, indeed, the result might merely be to create frustration.

2. For the same reasons, clusters of teachers should be drawn to the institute from the same high school or district, because a group will be more effective than a single individual in subsequently introducing into the school system the ideas and techniques acquired during the summer.

3. In selecting participants, explain the program to the principals, interview the teachers nominated by the principals, and select only those whom the interviews have disclosed will be most likely to benefit.

4. The program of the institute should try not only to provide instruction and demand work that will in themselves advance the intellectual dimensions and power of the teacher and give him graduate credit for purposes of promotion, but it should require readings, assignments, and activities apposite to the teachers' own situations in classrooms.

5. Institute directors are expected to arrange a follow-up program during the succeeding school year in order to reinforce the knowledge and stimulation acquired during the summer, to ascertain whether the teachers are translating their experiences into practical results in their classes, and finally to determine the strengths and weaknesses of the institute's "demonstration" lectures.

The ACLS has now supported institutes in English, Latin, history, art, and music. In almost every case the host institution has demonstrated its belief in the value of the program by sharing with us the costs involved, and the faculty members have spent weeks designing new courses specifically for the high school level and specifically geared to the needs of the teachers. In the case of one of the history institutes, the demonstration course now published by the American Historical Association's Service Center for Teachers of History (Publication no. 31, 1960), is available to teachers. In another case, all of the institute's participants enrolled in a follow-up seminar for twelve Saturdays during the subsequent school year in order to discuss the practical application of methods of teaching their subject, and to prepare and tests assignments, teaching plans, syllabi, and other materials. The institute instructor who conducted this course also made one or more visits to each school during the fall semester in order to observe the teachers at work, to consult with them about their programs, and to explain to school administrators the aims and methods of the institute program. A unique feature of another institute was the commitment made by school superintendents to allocate funds for the purchase of desired equipment, with the result that the teachers have been able to purchase books, films, and tape recorders for use in their classrooms and laboratories.

During the summer of 1961 I had the privilege of visiting some of these institutes, attending the classes, and talking freely with the staff and participants. The main impression gained from this experience is that the program is having a considerably greater impact and wider significance than we had realized. Written reports cannot convey the electric atmosphere that pervades these institutes, nor do they indicate the new respect and rapport that is developing between the school teachers and the scholars. Furthermore, only personal conversations with a wide variety of people on the spot can reveal the extent to which both administrative and teaching staffs of the participating schools and universities welcome these as unequalled opportunities to raise the level of secondary education.

As I have said, one unplanned result of the institute program is the new relationship that is developing between the teaching faculties of the schools and the universities. This is admittedly still a fledgling development, but it gives evidence that the program can be an important means of fulfilling what the ACLS views as its primary role in the area of secondary education; namely, to promote an interest on the part of scholars in educational matters at all levels, and especially to bring about a rapprochement between subject-matter specialists and professional educators.

The high school teachers participating in these institutes have found their instructors to have not only great depth of knowledge but also the ability to make their subjects come alive. The participants discovered, in other words, that specialization and research do not necessarily make pedants of scholars, but in fact give them the insights essential for proper presentation of their subjects. The implications of this for teacher education are simply enormous, for if a large number of educators can be similarly convinced that knowledge of subject matter is of first importance to successful teaching, they will find ways to give greater emphasis to this facet of teacher education.

The instructors, for their part, were extremely impressed by the participants' eagerness to learn and willingness to work. The fact that the teachers were buying large numbers of books with their own money for use by their colleagues, their students, and themselves, combined with the fact that on all occasions, formal and informal, they displayed an active interest in their subject, did a great deal to convince the instructors that they were dealing with a devoted group of people who need and want help.

A second important result of these institutes is the extent to which they raise the confidence and morale of the teachers involved. This comes in part, of course, from learning more about their subjects, and is an inevitable byproduct of any good course of instruction. But these institutes have some rather unique inspirational features. In the first place, the very fact that there is an organization sufficiently interested in secondary school teachers of humanistic subjects to support ventures of this kind affords a tremendous psychological boost. It is doubtful whether many people fully realize the adverse effect that the National Science Foundation program, weighted as it is in favor of the sciences, has had upon this group of teachers. One has only to visit a few of these institutes to see the dissatisfaction and even bitterness they feel at this neglect, and the rise in esprit which the ACLS institutes are producing.

It is not simply that the American Council of Learned Societies has given them scholarships, however; it is the fact that the ACLS, the university administrators, and the faculties have given concrete evidence of their interest by investing heavily in time, funds, and energy in order to provide them with this opportunity to become better teachers. By quickening their minds and enlarging the scope of their knowledge, the institutes have given them the means, the motivation, and the self-assurance to become vastly improved teachers.

Finally, let me briefly sketch the main outlines of what the ACLS is doing in the area of social studies. The need for major revision of the social studies in the schools requires no argument. The present curriculum does not reflect the content of the underlying academic fields, because it hasn't been substantially reviewed or revised on a national basis for over forty years. Suffice it to say that both the National Council for the Social Studies and the American Council of Learned Societies, working independently, became convinced of the urgent need for revision, and have now joined forces to see what can be done.

After some initial exploration, it was generally agreed that, before any intelligent revision of the social studies can be achieved, substantial agreement must be reached between the scholars and the secondary school people on just what the objectives of the social studies should be. Any other course would only lead to patchwork solutions. To this end, the ACLS decided to ask one scholar from each of the disciplines and areas concerned in the social studies to prepare a statement on the content objectives of the social studies from the point of view of his particular field of scholarship. On the basis of recommendations from the learned societies we then commissioned nine scholars with distinguished reputations in their fields and with some experience in secondary education. In their papers they are dealing primarily with the content or scope of the social studies program, identifying the major concepts of thought and the main topics in the broad fields of knowledge which, in their opinion, should have been studied by the end of high school. The purpose is not to devise specific courses of study, but to set forth curricular goals which can be utilized later as bases for framing sound programs of study. At the same time, the National Council for the Social Studies appointed a group that has drafted a single statement of general objectives, without specific reference to content, which reflects the thinking of the secondary schools.

Six of the scholars' papers have already been subjected to searching scrutiny by a group of social studies teachers and social scientists, and the papers will be revised in light of the comments made about them. All will be subjected to similar scrutiny at the annual meeting of the National Council for the Social Studies in November, 1961, and it is expected that they will then be revised, edited, and published with an introductory chapter setting forth the common themes emerging from the ten papers (published in 1962 by Harcourt, Brace & World, Inc., New York, under the title *The Social Studies and the Social Sciences*, G. B. Turner, editor).

This, of course, is only the first step in the long process of curriculum revision. It is obvious that there is nowhere near enough time in the social studies programs of the schools to introduce anthropology, economics, geography, history, political science, psychology, sociology, Asian studies, and Russian studies—certainly not enough time to present what each of these specialists have suggested as ideal. A good deal of selecting and meshing, therefore, will have to be done. Decisions will have to be made about which subjects should have separate courses, which may be merged into other courses without diluting them so much as to render them valueless, and whether, for example, it would be feasible and useful to frame a single course in the behavioral sciences, including appropriate branches of anthropology, sociology, and psychology. It is questions of this kind that make curriculum development in the social studies a peculiarly difficult problem—one, in other words, that is not present in the revision of curricula that are concerned with only single discipline. This factor lends strength to the case for the establishment of some kind of a national commission of experts including scholars and teachers to weld the organization of the curriculum into a sensible form, or, in other words, to present a reasonably detailed outline, or alternative outlines, of what a model social studies curriculum should include and in what sequence.

The objective of such an effort would not be to establish a rigid curriculum pattern—this could not succeed in any case, given the controversiality of the subject matter of most of the social studies and the autonomy of the state and local school systems—but it would present useful guidelines for curriculum makers. I need not spell out in detail the steps that would have to follow the preparation of such a curriculum guide: the actual development of courses and materials, experimentation, evaluation, teacher training, and all the rest. Let me merely say that the ACLS and the National Council for the Social Studies have given a good deal of thought to these questions, and that the attempt to raise funds to initiate a program of revision is already under way.

Reference

1 American Council of Learned Societies Committee on the Secondary Schools, "Reports of Secondary School Curriculum Problems," *ACLS Newsletter*, vol. 9, November, 1958, and vol. 10, November, 1959.

22 ❧ THE ROLE OF THE ASSOCIATION FOR SUPERVISION AND CURRICULUM DEVELOPMENT IN CURRICULUM EXPERIMENTATION
William Van Til* New York University

The Association for Supervision and Curriculum Development is a department of the giant National Education Association. The National Education Association, or the NEA as it is commonly referred to in these days of dependence upon initials, is the national organization of the educational profession in the United States of America. It aspires to a membership of "a million or more by '64." As part of its pattern of operations, the NEA depends upon departments which serve specific groups of educators. For instance, the National Council for the Social Studies is the department of the National Education Association which enrolls teachers of the social studies: history, geography, civics, economics, and sociology. Similarly, the Association for Supervision and Curriculum Development, familiarly abbreviated to ASCD, is the department of the NEA which enrolls those whose primary responsibility in the American school program lies in the fields of supervision and curriculum development.

The titles of supervisors and curriculum workers in the American school program are diverse. Individuals may be called supervisor, coordinator, consultant, or helping teacher, as they carry out supervisory activities. Similarly, those who work with curriculum development may be called curriculum director, director of instruction, assistant superintendent in charge of instruction, etc. We are far from any standardization of terminology with respect to posts in supervision and curriculum development. Possibly, however, we might communicate to specialists in other disciplines the proper roles of supervisors and curriculum workers by describing these workers, however labeled, as usually second in command in the public school hierarchy. First in command, naturally, is the school superintendent. In effect, the supervisor or curriculum worker is the person to whom the superintendent turns for advice on matters of instruction. Instruction, after all, can be only one aspect of the superintendent's multiple responsibilities, which include building programs, community relations, administration of personnel, and other problems, almost *ad infinitum*. In turn, all employed personnel turn to local boards of education for policy-making in accordance with the American tradition.

There are approximately eight thousand members of the Association for Supervision and Curriculum Development. The overwhelming majority are actively associated with public schools in curricular and supervisory work. A minority are employed in private and parochial school systems in the same roles. Another minority is made up of college professors, again of various titles and specializations, but each deeply concerned with matters of supervision and curriculum development.

* William Van Til was President of the Association for Supervision and Curriculum Development, 1961–1962, and is Chairman of the Department of Secondary Education, New York University.

The activities of the Association for Supervision and Curriculum Development are multiple. For instance, as with many organizations, publications are prepared by the group. The organization issues yearbooks, such as: *Research for Curriculum Improvement* (1957), *A Look at Continuity in the School Program* (1958), *Learning and the Teacher* (1959), *Leadership for Improving Instruction* (1960), *Balance in the Curriculum* (1961). The association publishes a magazine, *Educational Leadership,* whose themes for 1961–1962 were, for example: Who Plans the Curriculum?, The Supervisor at Work, What is Teaching?, Science in the School, Language Arts in the School, Mathematics in the School, Arts in the School, and Cultural Understanding in a World Community. Varied booklets are issued, and some typical titles are: *What Does Research Say About Arithmetic?, Foreign Language Teaching in Elementary Schools, The Self-Contained Classroom, Discipline for Today's Children and Youth, Extending the School Year, The High School We Need, The Junior High School We Need.*

Like most organizations, the Association for Supervision and Curriculum Development holds meetings, notably an annual conference, the location of which shifts in turn from the East Coast, to the Middle West, the Far West, the Middle West, and then back to the East again. At Chicago, in 1961, the theme was curriculum frontiers of the 1960s. In Las Vegas, in 1962, the theme was coordinating educational resources.

An unusual feature of conferences of the Association for Supervision and Curriculum Development is the wide participation of the membership. ASCD members do not simply listen to a few talented speakers. While key speakers are part of the program, the heart of the conference is in small group meetings of approximately twenty-five persons who meet for several extended sessions on topics of concern to supervisors and curriculum workers. There are sustained hours within an ASCD conference during which the conference participants share their ideas in scores of small groups while no other conference activity takes place. Such sessions grow out of a deep conviction of the importance of participation and identification in achieving curriculum change.

In addition to annual conferences, the ASCD sponsors occasional meetings, such as the research institutes which have been held across the country, for the purpose of sharing the research insights of specialists in disciplines and communicating skills to those interested in initiating and conducting cooperative curriculum research.

Last, but far from least, are the activities carried on by the twenty-one current committees and commissions of the organization which are responsible for the business, organization, and operation of the ASCD, and which explore current problems in their areas of responsibility, facilitate the exchange of information, and recommend association action. The activities of these twenty-one active groups, which meet for a minimum of a day at the annual conference and which often hold sessions of all members or some members of the committees and commissions between conferences, are coordinated by the board of directors, the executive committee, and a Washington staff housed in the NEA building. Characteristic commissions include those dealing with programs on particular levels: elementary curriculum, secondary curriculum, and teacher education. Other commissions deal with major human problems of our times: international understanding, intergroup education, economic competence. Some deal with tasks and ways of organization: research, preparation of instructional leaders, core curriculum, and evaluation.

What is the role of the Association for Supervision and Curriculum Development in curriculum experimentation, the theme of this conference? While no official statement of policy has ever been judged necessary, it is safe to say that the membership essentially conceives the role of the organization and its members as twofold. The association serves as encourager of experimentation, facilitator of local, state, and national curriculum programs, translator of outstanding ideas and insights, and disseminator of the winnowed best. A second role of the association (more especially, one played by individual members because of the nature of their work) might well be described as the role of gatekeeper. By gatekeeper, I mean to imply that the membership of the organization occupies strategic places in American education. Through these positions which they hold they influence curriculum decisions made on the local level.

It should be clear that supervisors and curriculum workers, of whatever title, do not have exclusive control of the gates in school systems. They share their responsibility with many others, including the basic policy setters—boards of education; the top administrators—the superintendents; the creators of materials—including textbook authors and audio-visual workers; and the vast corps of people who are in daily charge of the learning experiences of children and youth—the teachers. Nor should we imply that the gatekeepers have complete control over the gates. Indeed, in curriculum work, even as at sporting events, there may well be successful gate-crashers! Yet persisting in their responsibilities year by year, as projects, programs, new textbooks and subsidies come and go, are the specialists in supervision and curriculum development in schools and school systems across the nation.

Let us consider each of these roles in turn. The first role was described essentially as encouragement, facilitation, translation, and dissemination of curriculum experimentation. Naturally, the organization plays its role in this respect through publications, meetings, and commissions. As one illustration, the ASCD in recent years has encouraged experimentation through a monthly column and an annual issue of its journal. Its 1957 Yearbook, *Research for Curriculum Improvement*, was prepared and published well before the first sputnik which focused national attention on the school curriculum. (In these days of curriculum Johnny-come-latelies, one had best define the dates of curriculum emphases, even as politicians date support for their candidate as prior to or subsequent to the national convention—an important distinction!) Essentially, the magazine issues and the yearbook were milestones in the continuing effort by the ASCD to acquaint members with research which resulted in curriculum improvement, to help foster research programs, to help the researcher understand his interpersonal relationships, and to bring about the desired culmination of the conduct of research in the school setting.

Characteristically, in the role of disseminator, the ASCD has published such issues of *Educational Leadership* as the December, 1959, issue: *Projects*

That Will Influence Instruction. For this issue, Elbert P. Little wrote "PSSC: A Physics Program"; Max Beberman wrote "Improving High School Mathematics Teaching"; M. L. Keedy wrote "Mathematics in Junior High School"; Arnold B. Grobman wrote "Life Sciences in American Schools"; James R. Powers and Simone Oudot wrote "Parlons français"; and Eugene E. Slaughter wrote "Improving English Teaching."

All conferences of the ASCD contribute to fostering curriculum experimentation. At the 1962 Conference, area meetings were held on broad fields such as science and mathematics, communications (including language arts and foreign languages), self and society, social studies, physical fitness, and the arts. Each area meeting was initiated by an educator whose role was essentially that of a middleman between the specialist in subject disciplines and the generalist in professional education. For instance, new science and mathematics horizons were explored by specialists in science education and mathematics education.

At the second in the series of area meetings, reports of curriculum experimentation, such as The School Mathematics Study Group, the Youth Physical Fitness Program, and the National Task Force in Economic Education, were heard. In the third sessions there were reports of local curriculum development experimentation, new patterns of organizations, teaching innovations and new instructional materials. In a final summary session, coordinators of these area meetings talked about relationships among the fields of study in the curriculum. Each series of presentations in area meetings was commented upon by a continuing panel which included specialists in the learning process, in the society in which we live, in philosophy of education, and also grass roots practitioners of supervision and curriculum development.

Perhaps the most notable role of the ASCD in encouraging current curriculum experimentation, as contrasted to its role as disseminator, is represented by the research institutes. The Association for Supervision and Curriculum Development has faith in research carried on by the personnel of local school systems, particularly when they are aided by varied specialists. The first two research institutes focused on helping those who attended to initiate and conduct cooperative curriculum research. This emphasis was never abandoned, but by the time of the third institute, consultants also participated, in order to review research findings about human learning. Thus, the third and succeeding institutes combined assistance to the participants who learned about research techniques with the building of a body of knowledge about the learning process.

The purposes of a characteristic Association for Supervision and Curriculum Development Research Institute include (1) to translate research findings in the behavioral sciences into educational practices; (2) to stimulate curriculum research and field study in school situations; and (3) to expand the participants' knowledge of curriculum research design by having them participate in the designing of research. In addition, there have been specific purposes, such as the 1960 attempt to identify areas for research and for field study concerning human variability and learning. This emphasis eventuated in the pamphlet, *Human Variability and Learning.* The Association for Supervision and Curriculum Development was one of the first organizations to use an interdisciplinary approach in such institutes. The institutes have included teams from school systems rather than single individuals, and this procedure has been continued in order that a greater impact be made when the participants return home.

In these days of giant foundation grants, it is interesting to know that the Association for Supervision and Curriculum Development has financed the institutes simply by requiring that each participant pay his own expenses plus a $40 registration fee. The institutes were jointly sponsored and staffed by the National Institute of Mental Health.

To an audience dedicated to curriculum experimentation in varied subject disciplines, an audience proceeding on highly varied assumptions and characterized by differing approaches to curriculum change, the second role of the Association for Supervision and Curriculum and its members may be of highest interest. To understand the gatekeeper role, one must understand the functions of instructional leaders. Gordon N. Mackenzie of Teachers College, Columbia University, Chairman of the ASCD Commission on Instructional Leaders, defined these functions well in *Educational Leadership,* March, 1961. He said that supervisors and curriculum workers characteristically carried on at least the following seven major groups of activities:

1. Clarification of goals
2. Development of work structure
3. Assistance to individuals
4. Providing resources
5. Communication among staff
6. Coordination of effort
7. Work with lay citizens

On the local level, the typical ASCD member serves as a strategic advisor to people who ask advice on inclusion of new proposals, often national in origin and scope, and now potential for use here at home in "Crossroads, U.S.A." For instance, while experimentation is going on through foundations or studies in the varied disciplines, and sometimes after the completion of such experimentation, schoolmen often turn to supervisors and curriculum workers for aid in making decisions about its utilization. Sometimes those who ask for aid are superintendents in high places; often those seeking advice and various aids are teachers in the classroom.

Thus the supervisor and curriculum worker are called upon to examine all new proposals with care. For instance, the characteristic supervisor or curriculum director examines newly proposed emphases in the light of his own conception of a proper philosophy of education for American schools. He examines the new proposal in the light of the social realities, the urgent social demands of our times. He studies the new proposal in terms of what he knows about the learner, the learning process, and the needs of children and youth.

As he scrutinizes new proposals, the curriculum worker, or the supervisor, is quite aware of an old axiom of his profession, that nobody loves a supervisor or a curriculum worker. Even when the supervisor or curriculum worker is on the side of the enthusiast for some aspect of the school program, he is not on his side to the extent the specialist judges necessary. Always the supervisor and curriculum director must be followers of Plato, striving for the legendary golden mean, attempting to achieve balance.

Sometimes the supervisor and curriculum worker even seem to the dedicated specialist to violate common sense. Perhaps they have learned this from the scientists who tell us that obviously solid matter is not, as common sense describes, actually solid and substantial, but really is a mass of jostling, interacting particles. Admittedly, from a common sense point of view, this is an outrageous concept.

For instance, a contemporary supervisor or curriculum worker may not be willing to accept supposedly homogeneous grouping into the bright, the average, and the dull, which common sense endorses as self-evident. Instead, the supervisor and curriculum worker may be heard asking, "What does research say?" Incidentally, so far, research reports indicate that there is no evidence that ability grouping, of itself, leads to improved mastery of subject matter. Studies of grouping show that the dull group more often benefits than the bright on whose behalf many grouping approaches are currently being instituted. The supervisor and curriculum worker may be found, too, checking proposals for grouping against the philosophical, social, and psychological foundations upon which he depends for decision making. He may emerge, for instance, with reservations as to the long-range societal effects of today's demands by upper-middle-class intellectuals, who thoroughly repudiate racial segregation, that segregation by intellect be substituted. The supervisor and curriculum worker may even conclude that less able students may need exactly the reverse of intellectual segregation in order to reach their potentiality in the kind of American society in which we live.

There appears to be one subject of outstanding priority for those who have independently developed varied projects in the disciplines and those who represent professional organizations in education. That priority must be assigned to the development of mutual understanding between the educators, whose responsibility it is to live and work daily with the school program, and the specialists who know well the knowledge and concepts associated with a separate discipline. We are all now familiar with the split which exists between the scientist and the humanist, of which C. P. Snow writes persuasively in *Two Cultures and the Scientific Revolution*. But we may be less familiar, or perhaps less concerned, about the equally wide gap between the specialist in various disciplines and the educator who fosters the broad instructional program of the schools. At the very least, we need to talk to each other. Perhaps at most, we need to work together toward greater coordination of educational resources. Coordination of educational resources, however, should not be mistaken for a national curriculum—standardized, orthodox, identical in all places; a consummation, in my opinion, devoutly *not* to be wished.

As a step toward mutual understanding, we need humility and a degree of respect for each other rather than the arrogance and disrespect which too often has characterized relationships among professionals who happen to have differing specializations. We need to be mutually involved in the developing projects, rather than to call upon professional bodies to endorse projects after the fact and despite their lack of real participation in decision-making.

We need close examination of the highly varied assumptions as to how curriculum change comes about—assumptions which have been accepted, sometimes without sufficient examination, by specialists in disciplines who find themselves newly engaged in secondary curriculum work. For instance, participants at this National Conference on Curriculum Experimentation have reported assumptions about techniques for curricular change which range from the preparation of a single textbook for a physics course, through the preparation of three possible books for biology courses, and through identification of concepts in economics for stress in varied economics and history programs. Some proposals have involved many teachers; others have involved few. Some proposals have used the insights of professional educators; others have bypassed professional educators other than classroom teachers. Proposals for the dissemination of new programs have ranged from the use of established local and state procedures to the advocacy of national establishment of a curriculum for the schools.

As part of genuine coordination, we need recognition among supervisors and curriculum directors that specialists can up-date knowledge and contribute insights as to concepts. Conversely, we need recognition by specialists in disciplines that there exist men and women in American education with experience and insight into the difficult business of curriculum change. These include schoolmen who have learned through experience that effective curriculum change does not come about through edict or by publication of materials alone, as the conventional wisdom of "common sense" too often tends to assume.

23 ❊ THE ROLE OF THE AMERICAN EDUCATIONAL RESEARCH ASSOCIATION IN CURRICULUM EXPERIMENTATION AND IMPROVEMENT
Walter W. Cook* University of Minnesota

The first national organization in the area of educational research was the National Association of Directors of Educational Research, organized in 1915.

By then, three movements in education leading to the development of educational research were under way—the testing movement, the school adjustment movement, and the school survey movement.

Although the measurement of school achievement can be traced back many centuries, the testing movement is commonly dated from the work of Thorndike and his students. Stone, in 1908, and Courtis, in 1909, published tests to measure achievement in elementary arithmetic. Thorndike's handwriting

* Walter W. Cook is Dean of the College of Education at the University of Minnesota.

scale appeared in 1910; the next year Ayres published a scale in which the samples of handwriting were arranged in order of increasing legibility as determined by the rate at which they could be read. The Hillegas composition scale in 1912 followed the Thorndike quality-scale pattern. In 1913, Buckingham published a spelling scale in which the words were arranged in order of increasing difficulty. The criterion of difficulty was used by Woody in building an arithmetic scale, and by Tribue in constructing a language scale, both published in 1916.

The school adjustment movement had its origin in the studies of retardation by Thorndike and Ayres. In the early 1900s, beginning with age-grade studies, and running its course—through the various "patented" plans for promotion, classification, and homogeneous grouping, to child guidance clinics, diagnostic and remedial teaching—this movement has been a potent factor in the promotion of educational research.

The school survey movement is considered to have begun with the Pittsburgh survey of 1907. Rapid growth of industrial centers, and the consequent increase of school enrollment, threw into the laps of relatively untrained superintendents administrative problems with which they were unable to cope—problems related to the school plant, school finance, keeping track of pupils, teacher personnel, and the curriculum. Some superintendents required expert advice and assistance. The rapidly developing colleges of education in universities were able to furnish specialists, industry had already set the example of efficiency experts, and the school survey movement was the result.

Although the first school survey was the Pittsburgh survey of 1907, it was not until the survey of the New York City schools in 1911 and 1912 that achievement tests were used. In 1911, Courtis had reported the results of his tests in the fundamentals of arithmetic conducted in the Detroit schools. The report attracted so much attention that Courtis was asked to participate in the New York survey and administer his test to 30,000 pupils. The report of the use of tests in this survey stimulated much interest among superintendents, who were eager to compare the achievement of their pupils with that of pupils in other schools. Courtis stressed the advantage of norms or standards, and offered to cooperate with schools which wished to administer his test. As a result of this movement, bureaus were established in a number of universities and state colleges to cooperate with schoolmen in their testing programs. The first bureau of educational research was established at the University of Oklahoma in 1913, and this was followed by a bureau at Indiana University in 1914, at Kansas State Normal School in 1914, at Iowa State University in 1914, at the University of Minnesota in 1915, and at the Wisconsin State Department of Public Instruction in 1916. It was the directors of these bureaus and the builders of these standardized tests who joined to form the National Association of Directors of Educational Research in 1915.

In 1930, this organization became the American Educational Research Association (AERA) and a department of the National Education Association. The purposes of the organization are to advance the status of educational research through improving research design and statistical analysis of data, to keep the members aware of the research and development that is taking place in different areas of the country, to encourage and promote a sound application of research findings, and to make research results available to teachers and superintendents. Membership is restricted to those with an active interest in, and the ability to contribute constructively to, educational research. Active members must possess not less than a Master's degree.

The AERA first published the *Review of Educational Research,* a summary of current research in education, in 1931. The five to seven numbers issued each year treat a cycle of recurring topics, summarizing briefly the research findings and listing extensive bibliographies. A given topic usually reoccurs every third year. Examples are: higher education, methodology of educational research, language arts, fine arts, natural sciences, social sciences, mathematics, curriculum, the psychology of learning, mental hygiene, personality, and so on.

The AERA also publishes, in cooperation with the NEA department of classroom teachers, a series of popular treatments of research entitled *What Research Says to the Teacher.* Each issue deals with important topics of interest to elementary or secondary classroom teachers. It is prepared by an outstanding specialist and presents the gist of educational research in clear language on a topic related to classroom problems such as the teaching of reading, arithmetic, spelling, handwriting, high school mathematics, and high school science; juvenile delinquency; audio-visual instruction; and the gifted child in the elementary school. There are now twenty-eight bulletins in this series.

The AERA also publishes the *Encyclopedia of Educational Research,* which is available from The Macmillan Company. This encyclopedia covers all areas of educational research. It was first published in 1941, with revised editions in 1950 and again in 1960.

The AERA is planning a series of handbooks in research organized around important areas of education. The first, *A Handbook of Research on Teaching,* was published by Rand, McNally & Company in February, 1963.

The AERA holds an annual convention in February, lasting usually four days, each day being given over to a number of sectional meetings at which members report and discuss recent research studies and methods. Joint meetings are also held with other educational organizations reporting research of interest to these organizations.

The AERA does not attempt to direct educational research into particular channels, nor has it been successful in financing research. It is an organization to encourage research, to improve research, to keep its members aware of what is going on in educational research, and to make research results available to school people.

Since its beginning, educational research has been under severe handicaps; until the last five years there has been no systematic financing of educational research. No foundation has dedicated funds to this enterprise. Occasionally the foundations were willing to finance a research project, but frequently the money went to an effective promoter rather than to an effective research worker and the publicity was related to the granting of the research fund rather than to the results of the research. There has been no attempt to find competent research specialists in education and to subsidize them as such. Most research in education has been done by men on their own time and with their own funds. A large proportion of it is of the Master's-thesis and Ph.D.-dissertation type; a few professors have been able to organize the research of their students around a central topic.

Another handicap to educational research arises out of its application. If it were possible to put the results of educational research into a pill, a hypodermic needle, a machine, or any other device for making its application relatively foolproof, its influence on instruction would be much greater. Typically, the results of educational research must be applied by someone who understands human behavior and the proper application of research discoveries to the changing of human behavior. Misapplication is frequent. Even when research findings are built into textbooks, the textbooks are improperly used. Perhaps some day we shall have foolproof learning machines, but I am skeptical.

When we were asked to consider "the role of the American Education Research Association in curriculum experimentation and development" it occurred to me that we should probably give some consideration to what we mean by curriculum. There are several definitions. The usual ones are: (1) the aggregate of courses of study given in a school, college, or university; or (2) a particular course of study in a school, such as the curriculum in nursing, medicine, pharmacy, law, etc. Sometimes we speak of the curriculum in arithmetic, or of the reading curriculum. Over the past thirty years many educators specializing in curriculum have tended to define the curriculum broadly as consisting of all the experiences that a student has under the guidance and direction of the school. Recognizing the wide range of individual and trait differences in a class, differences in interests and social background, these educators differentiate between the resource curriculum, which consists of all the activities, reading materials, laboratory experiments, problems, etc., which might be of value to the development of certain pupils, and the actual curriculum of the individual pupil. That is, in order to avoid attempting to teach all the children the same things in the same way at the same time, they have a variety of approaches to topics or themes or units which enable them to individualize instruction and meet the needs of different children.

There is hardly any research in education which does not have implications for the curriculum when it is thus broadly conceived. In addition to the study of the skills, attitudes, abilities, and understandings which are inherent in a given discipline, we must concern ourselves with research in the area of human needs—that is, in the development of interests in the light of individual differences and trait differences in all areas—child growth and development, learning, motivation, and social classes and their characteristics. The curriculum of the school is related to every aspect of the development, status, and future of a culture, as well as to the social and biological characteristics of the species we attempt to humanize.

Curriculum research before 1930 was simple and direct and could be labelled as such. Learning was largely verbal; textbooks were extremely difficult; the amount of material to be learned was enormous. Over half the pupils in the seventh grade were overage and had been failed at least once. Spelling books contained lists of words such as *mordacity, taciturnity, perspicacity, oleaginous,* and *vertiginous,* and an eighth grader was required to compute both square and cube root.

Following the lead of such utilitarians as John Stuart Mill and Herbert Spencer, the research workers applied various criteria in determining what knowledge is most worth teaching.

First in importance was the frequency of use in adult life. This criterion was applied in Thorndike's list of 10,000 words most commonly used in reading, Ernest Horn's 10,000 words most commonly used in writing, Wilson's arithmetic processes most commonly used by adults, Earl Rugg's most frequently referred to (in journals and newspapers) countries, cities, rivers, mountains, island groups, statesmen, military leaders, and so forth, Harold Rugg's most frequently used generalizations by frontier thinkers in the social sciences. Frequency of use in child life at different ages and grade levels was also studied, and served as a basis for determining at which grade level materials should be taught. The criterion of quality was applied in the selection of materials to be studied. Rugg's basic generalizations were based on the analysis of the books of twenty frontier thinkers in the social studies; word counts were made of material in the *Encyclopaedia Britannica* as well as in the more sophisticated journals; the writing vocabularies of men of superior literary ability, rather than those of the common man, were studied.

Frequency of use was analyzed by geographic areas, by vocational areas, and by time periods in history, the assumption being that the knowledge, skills, and abilities found useful over the longest period of time, in the largest number of geographic areas, and in the various vocations were more valuable than those of more specialized usage. These studies are still valuable in building the curriculum of today. Not that instruction is organized around these itemized, piecemeal goals, learned in sequence once and for all time outside of their functional setting; rather, the information is used in tests and evaluation instruments to determine the needs of individual pupils.

The development of educational measurement, and with it, of norms for different ages and grades, made educators more conscious of the wide range of ability in classes, and the necessity of adapting the curriculum to different levels of ability.

Before 1930, every conceivable mechanical method of adapting instruction to the ability of the child had been tried. Acceleration and retardation through annual promotion, semi-annual promotion, quarterly promotion, subject promotion, and special promotion—all were tried. Other remedies involved the attempt to hold grade levels constant by increasing the amount of instruction for slow pupils. Assistant teachers were hired for the slow pupils; summer schools were set up for failing pupils. In other schools, the course of study and grade standards were held constant, but the time required to complete the elementary school was set at six years for the bright, seven for the average, and eight for the slow learners. Still another remedy was to limit the time spent in the school to eight years, but to present a differentiated curriculum for slow-, medium-, and fast-learning pupils. All of these remedies ignored trait differences or the variability of the average pupil.

Most of these practices only confirmed the old adage that "a little learning is a dangerous thing." Certainly, a little knowledge of individual differences has led to foolish conclusions. For example, in the middle twenties a committee was set up to regrade arithmetic, the Committee of Seven. This committee set about to grade arithmetic in such a way that 80 per cent of the pupils would be succesful with 80 per cent of the content at a given grade level. As the result of this research, third-grade material was put into the fourth grade, fourth-grade into the fifth grade, and so on. It seemed obvious to me that anyone with above-average ability in mathematics would be completely bored with the study of arithmetic, and instead of being challenged would simply learn to dislike it. But the textbooks were changed, and it is only within recent years that any hope of challenging potential mathematicians at the elementary school level became possible. From 1930 to 1950 the research which had perhaps the greatest impact on the curriculum of the common school, dealt with methods, personality, and the social characteristics of teachers and the school population.

The Eight-Year Study of the Progressive Education Association compared success in college of students who had graduated from traditional high schools with those graduating from the more liberalized, experimental high schools. Dr. Ralph Tyler directed the evaluation of this study.

Wrightstone made several similar studies of elementary schools. He studied the schools in six metropolitan communities, some of which were characteristically traditional in their curriculum programs, and some of which had experimental programs. Matched pairs of pupils were used in a six-year experiment, and a raw comparison of the outcome favored the new or experimental groups in all cases. The differences were most significant with regard to such outcomes as desirable social relationships, appreciation of worthwhile activities, and critical thinking.

Certain studies revealing the educational significance of the social caste structure of our society are already accepted as classic. Of particular significance to the curriculum are the researches of Lloyd Warner and his group. Davis's study of *Social Class Influences upon Learning* had a strong impact on the thinking of curriculum consultants and teachers. Another study, *Father of the Man*, by Davis and Havighurst, and also *Elmtown's Youth*, by August Hollingshead, helped to place many curriculum problems in a new context.

Research in classroom group atmosphere, and the social dynamics of the classroom by Lewin and Lippitt, White, Bradford, Polansky, Thelen, Rosen, and others reveals a neglected aspect of the problem of effective classroom group procedures. Other areas of research that were important during this period were studies of needs, both biological and psychological, felt and unfelt, individual differences, trait differences, and child growth and development.

To my thinking, the most promising and satisfying single contribution that has been made to curriculum development in the past several years is Jerome S. Bruner's little book, *The Process of Education*, published by Harvard University Press (1960). It is a report of the Woods Hole Conference, which was composed of the specialists in the various academic areas now working to improve the curriculum, and educational psychologists. Although the ideas are not new, they are well selected and effectively presented. I believe it is the outline of a sound intellectual basis for curriculum development.

Curriculum is too important to be left to haphazard development—even by experts. We need a national curriculum commission, with adequate Federal financing, operating constantly to develop curriculum materials for all areas—not as a prescribed curriculum but as resource materials, in order that teachers may select that which they find most effective in meeting the needs of widely different pupils.

24 ❁ THE AMERICAN ASSOCIATION OF COLLEGES FOR TEACHER EDUCATION—A COLLEGE-WIDE APPROACH TO IMPROVED CURRICULUM
Edward C. Pomeroy* American Association of Colleges for Teacher Education

Change has become commonplace in our society. Since World War II, the world has been going through a series of revolutions that have deeply affected every aspect of our lives. We have been experiencing a social revolution that has changed our living habits, our traditional actions, and our standards. A political revolution has brought new freedoms, accompanied by new responsibilities, to millions of people throughout the world. An economic revolution has opened up new production capabilities and greatly increased needs for materials and services. Undergirding and providing a framework for the aforementioned changes has been a vast scientific revolution starting with the discovery of atomic energy and opening up vast new areas for research throughout this world and into space. As J. Robert Oppenheimer has stated:[1]

In an important sense, this world of ours is a new world. . . . One thing that is new is the prevalence of newness, the changing scale and scope of change itself, so that the world alters as we walk in it, so the years of a man's life measure not some small growth or rearrangement or moderation of what he learned in childhood, but a great upheaval. . .

These facts are not new to leaders of American higher education and those concerned with the education of teachers. However, as we consider curriculum change and experimentation, we must consider the social, economic, and political setting in which our institutions exist and for which colleges and universities attempt to educate their students. Any consideration of the curriculum in American schools must, of course, consider the education of

* Edward C. Pomeroy is Executive Secretary, American Association of Colleges for Teacher Education, Washington, D.C.
[1] J. Robert Oppenheimer, "Prospects in the Arts and Sciences," *The New York Times,* Dec. 27, 1954.

the teachers, who will be instrumental to a great degree in developing the curriculum and in working with it. Because of the centrality of teachers to the matter of curriculum improvement, the colleges and universities which comprise the American Association of Colleges for Teacher Education (AACTE) are pleased to be represented in these important discussions.

The AACTE is a national, voluntary association, currently made up of 609 leading colleges and universities which prepare teachers. Institutions that are members of the association are to be found in every state of the union. They include all types of higher education institutions, both publicly and privately supported, and ranging from the very small to the very large. They share a common interest, namely, a continuing search for improved programs of teacher education.

The strength of the association's program for the improvement of teacher education is based upon its voluntary nature and on the contributed services of educational leaders in the member institutions. By means of a series of appointed and elected committees, of annual conferences, workshops, and regional meetings, by publications and clearinghouse activities, the AACTE has, over the years, made an important contribution to the strengthening of formal teacher-education programs in the United States.

In the carrying out of its program, the association has worked closely with other organizations and agencies on the national and state levels. The AACTE was proud to be associated with the National Commission on Teacher Education and Professional Standards in cosponsoring the three national conferences, in 1958, 1959, and 1960, which have been instrumental in bringing about a more unified approach to the education of teachers in this country. For many years the AACTE and the national commission have worked together to improve teacher education. Formal relationships with the Council of Chief State School Officers has proved to be valuable to the colleges and universities preparing teachers, and, hopefully, to the improvement of state standards governing teacher education. From time to time, the association has proved the appropriate organization to represent colleges and universities in cooperative action with many educational organizations and agencies which represent special subject-matter fields and interests, in what have proven to be important cooperative study projects. In short, the American Association of Colleges for Teacher Education, representing most of the leading teacher-education institutions in the country, is a voluntary action group, working on behalf of institutions of higher education in our common task of preparing better teachers for the schools of our country. The association is geared to change, and a study of developments in teacher education in the United States will reveal that it has been actively pressing for higher standards and for improved curricular offerings to prospective teachers.

As we work together in this National Conference on Curriculum Experimentation, it becomes clear that the basic theme of AACTE—namely, improved programs of teacher education—implies changing the curriculum, not only in higher education institutions, but also in the elementary and secondary schools. Let us turn our attention to how the preparatory institutions can cooperate in curriculum experimentation and change.

The curriculum at all levels of education—elementary, secondary, and higher—are closely interrelated. A change cannot be made in the content of secondary school chemistry, for example, without affecting the preparatory programs for teachers of these subjects in higher education or without involving modifications in the elementary program to be sure that a proper foundation is laid for the secondary school subject. Because the teacher, either at the elementary and secondary school level, is affected by these changes, so must the college and university where the teacher is prepared be alert to new developments, new concepts, and new methods. Many people and many organizations and educational societies are involved in our common task of revamping our educational programs and standards in the light of new knowledge, new needs, and new opportunities.

One of the basic concepts that has received renewed support in recent years is that the education of teachers is a college-wide responsibility and not merely the concern of the school or department of education. Because of its institution-wide membership, the AACTE has a unique opportunity to encourage the participation and support of all aspects of institutional life in improved teacher education. Traditionally, the official representative of the college or university to the association has been an administrative officer, or at least one who has primary responsibility for organizing and conducting the teacher-education program. These contacts with college and university administrators have been most useful to the association and to teacher education in that they have provided a direct line of encouragement and understanding to campus leaders of teacher education. The importance of these relationships to curriculum changes should not be underestimated. How much easier it is to bring about a change in course offering or curriculum pattern when the modifications have the endorsement of the institutional leadership!

In this connection, it is important to note not only the line of communication with administrators of teacher-education institutions but also to consider the responsibilities which rest on the shoulders of these men and women who have overall responsibilities for the organization and development of institutional programs of teacher education. As various study groups representing the academic disciplines and areas of specialized interest bring in their reports of new findings and new needs in relation to school curriculum, there is added responsibility to the administrative leadership of teacher-education programs to be aware of these new insights and new materials in order that they may be plowed back into the preparatory studies of teachers. At one time in our history it may have been possible, although certainly not desirable, for the leadership in teacher education to feel confident from year to year with a well-organized program without facing the responsibility for continual revision. The changes in the temper of our life have changed all this, and we must now face up to the need for continuing change.

Obviously, institutions of higher education are not able to develop their curriculum in a vacuum, and this underlines the necessity of close professional relationships with all aspects of education. This requires knowledge of the program and plans of the elementary and secondary schools. It requires close knowledge of frontier thinking in the various subject disciplines. The opportunity for developing these lines of communication exists on every campus, but unfortunately, in many institutions there has been, traditionally, a chasm between the subject-matter professors, the professional educators, and those responsible for planning teacher-education offerings. In recent years progress has been made in bridging this gap, and, hopefully, the AACTE has played and will continue to play a role in developing a recognition that the preparation of teachers is an institution-wide responsibility.

The association also, through its clearinghouse function, helps to disseminate information to member institutions regarding studies and projects being carried out in the learned societies and among individual professors of the several disciplines which may have direct bearing on the content of the curriculum for prospective teachers. In these lines of communication, developing in many ways, lies the hope of great improvement in teacher education.

The institution of higher education itself has a basic responsibility to provide a setting that will encourage its faculty members, both those in the academic disciplines and those in the professional field of education, to seek out new arrangements and new content for teacher preparation. The American Association of Colleges for Teacher Education has a very real responsibility to encourage this type of institutional environment which makes curriculum change and experimentation possible. Not only must there be a climate favorable to this effort, but there must be real administrative recognition of the need for the necessary study and research. This means that research funds and salaries for secretarial and research assistance must be made available, and finally, that the need for free time from regular class commitments to carry out these important activities must be recognized.

The colleges and universities that prepare teachers have a long history of cooperative relationships with public schools and public school systems. As the education of teachers increases quantitatively and becomes more complex, these relationships become more important. The recent annual conferences of the National Commission on Teacher Education and Professional Standards have underlined the desirability of closer relationships between elementary and secondary school teachers with the scholars in higher education. The progress toward developing greater understanding of the roles of teachers at the various levels of education must continue. At the same time, college and university professors should develop greater understandings of the needs of the classroom teacher—the kind of information and knowledge and skills required by the young teacher as he or she prepares for a career in teaching. Here lies a whole area of understanding and insight, one which becomes critically important when we talk about curriculum experimentation. What is needed is a two-way relationship based on mutual respect and understanding. The colleges and universities that prepare teachers are in a position to encourage the attainment of this mutual respect. As all of us gain more experience in working together, further advances will be made in this important area of professional relationships.

My remarks so far have been devoted to a somewhat theoretical discussion of the role of the institution of teacher education in curriculum experimentation. Now I would like to turn attention to specific activities that have taken place through the efforts of the AACTE and its member colleges and universities. I hope that this account may be suggestive of other ways in which a combined effort of the colleges and universities may be more effectively used in the improvement of our educational offerings.

Because of its organization and activities, the AACTE has played an important role in focusing national attention on the critical role which teacher-preparing institutions play in our educational development. Because of the availability of the association, representatives from its staff and official committees have been involved on innumerable occasions in discussions with persons concerned with curriculum experiments. This has proved to be valuable to both parties. In many instances the resources of the colleges and universities have been brought to the attention of persons who might otherwise not have found them available; it has also helped to alert the colleges and universities to new ideas and new opportunities.

This involvement at the national level has suggested possible areas of cooperation that might have been otherwise overlooked if the institutions themselves had not been organized to take advantage of new ideas and new plans. Mention has already been made of the cooperation with the National Commission on Teacher Education and Professional Standards. The AACTE, in cooperation with the American Association for the Advancement of Science, established a joint commission on the teaching of mathematics and science in 1956. This action came early in the current emphasis on restudying our science and mathematics curriculums. As a forerunner of some of the later and more complete studies, the AAAS-AACTE Commission provides a prototype of cooperative relationships which will be most useful in improving the quality of American education. The reports of this commission have been widely distributed through the efforts of the parent organizations. It is interesting to note that this activity was carried on by he AAAS and the AACTE, without foundation or government support.

In 1961 AACTE cooperated with the National Association of State Directors of Teacher Education and Certification and the American Association for the Advancement of Science in their cooperative study which resulted in the preparation of *Guidelines for Preparation Programs for Teachers of Secondary School Science and Mathematics.*

In the field of social studies, the AACTE has cooperated with the National Council for the Social Studies in a joint project for revision of the curriculum of elementary and secondary teacher-education programs, aimed at improved understanding of the international dimension of our life and of its bearing on the school curriculum. This particular project is being carried on under the auspices of the National Council and the International Relations Committee of the AACTE and is still in progress, but preliminary evaluation of the activity augurs well for its final report.

The colleges and universities in the American Association of Colleges for Teacher Education have played a leading role in utilizing television in the upgrading of the education of teachers. Through the cooperation of the National Broadcasting Company, the AACTE was instrumental in introducing for the first time a nationally televised collegiate credit course aimed primarily at upgrading the education of teachers in service. "Atomic Age Physics," presented by Dr. Harvey White, reached thousands of teachers through the United States and successfully brought to them, and to interested lay people, the new understanding of developments in the field of physics and the opportunity of seeing a master teacher at work. Through subsequent Continental Classroom presentations covering the fields of "Modern Chemistry," "Algebra," "Probability and Statistics," and "American Government," the AACTE and its member institutions have made a direct contribution to the education of teachers, making widely available high-level courses which have been useful in bringing to the teachers new material useful in changing and modifying their curriculum offerings in the schools.

Finally, the meetings of the association provide opportunities through general sessions as well as in small work groups in which college and university leaders of teacher education consider the matter of experimentation. At the 1962 annual meeting of the association a number of reports were presented from academic disciplines, outlining suggestions for new approaches to the preparation of teachers in these various fields. The reports were based on the latest studies being carried on by scholars in the field. Hopefully, this will provide an opportunity for further consideration of changes in the current offerings provided to prospective teachers.

A new day is dawning in education. No longer is it possible for the several segments of American education to work at their tasks in watertight compartments. The fact that the University of Minnesota has called this National Conference on Curriculum Experimentation, representing all groups—educational, legal, and lay—which have interests in the education of our children and young people, is conclusive proof that we have numerous opportunities and responsibilities before us. Each group and agency from whom we have heard during this meeting represents resources available to the improvement of the quality of elementary and secondary school curriculums. Those of us who have responsibilities in American education should be encouraged by these developments. However, these resources, and the opportunity to use them, will be meaningless unless we develop effective procedures for coordinating our interests and efforts. The American Association of Colleges for Teacher Education, representing a large majority of the colleges and universities in this country which prepare teachers, welcomes these developments, and stands ready to assist and cooperate with other groups to the end that our schools will be organized in such a way as to provide the education that the children and youth of our nation need to meet the demands of the future.

THE ROLE OF SUPPORTING AGENCIES

part vi

Dr. Dees presents the policies which govern the activities of the National Science Foundation in curriculum improvement. At the conference, Dr. Whitmer (whose paper could not be included) explained how these policies are carried out at the operational level.

Dr. Clark tells, similarly, of the operations of the Cooperative Research Program of the U.S. Office of Education. Dr. Jarvis presents the general policies governing the activities of the U.S. Office of Education in curriculum experimentation.

Clearly these agencies play dual roles. On the one hand they support the activities of others. Someone in the field says what he wants to do—no bureaucrat tells him what he should do, or how—and, if his proposal is sound and the money is available, he is granted support for his project. On the other hand, as arms of the executive branch of the Federal government, they set policy concerning what sorts of activities to support, and propose programs and budgets for consideration by Congress.

Dr. Jackson tells us what the private foundations can do that government agencies cannot. His comments on committee projects versus pioneering individuals are very illuminating.

25 ❀ THE ROLE OF THE NATIONAL SCIENCE FOUNDATION IN COURSE CONTENT IMPROVEMENT
Bowen C. Dees* *National Science Foundation*

The National Science Foundation's basic statute was signed into law by President Truman in May, 1950. This enabling legislation was the subject of an extended series of hearings by Congress before its enactment, and further hearings during the past several years have resulted in clarification and slight modification of the foundation's mandate.

As an independent agency within the executive branch of the government, the foundation receives its support from and is responsible to the entity we call the Federal government. The fact that it is called a *foundation* means that the NSF is frequently confused with one or another of the private foundations. Clearly, the role of a federal agency does not change simply because it bears a name somewhat different from that of its sister agencies. The National Science Foundation is responsible to the President and, through him, to the people of the United States, in the same way as are

* Bowen C. Dees is Assistant Director for Scientific Personnel and Education, the National Science Foundation, Washington, D.C.

the Atomic Energy Commission, the National Aeronautics and Space Administration, and various other independent agencies of the government.

The fact that it is responsible in this way to all the people means that the National Science Foundation must necessarily adopt somewhat different policies and be guided by restrictions which do not apply to private foundations. However, the legislation under which the foundation operates is very broad, and this makes it possible for the NSF to undertake a wide variety of programs in support of science and science education.

The specific section of the National Science Foundation statute under which many of the foundation's educational programs are authorized reads: "The National Science Foundation is authorized and directed to initiate and support . . . programs to strengthen scientific research potential in the mathematical, physical, medical, biological, engineering, and other sciences . . ."

In carrying out this mandate, the foundation has developed a number of points of view and policies which I think are relevant to the topic which has been assigned me. In the first place, the foundation has developed the conviction that science education in the United States, far from being overemphasized as some people seem to think, has been suffering for a long time because of relative underemphasis. All of us at the NSF feel that it would be a mistake to overemphasize science in our educational system. Nonetheless, there is a general feeling that the efforts that have been made thus far, plus additional efforts of other kinds, are needed in order to restore a balance in our educational system which will assure the citizens of tomorrow an adequate understanding of the increasingly science-oriented world in which they will be living. Science and applied science are so much a part of our culture that it is hard to understand why we so frequently overlook the fact that literacy in science is as important as other kinds of literacy for the educated person today. In commenting on this problem on a radio program in the summer of 1961, Dr. Sterling McMurrin said that he feels science and science education require and should receive support at the current and possibly still higher levels, but that additional support in other areas of importance must also be made available. This appraisal of the situation, from the U.S. Commissioner of Education, precisely expresses our sentiments at the NSF.

Another point of view which we have developed is that there is no single approach which can cure all of the ills that beset science education in the United States. The foundation has investigated this possibility from many angles, but any one line of attack presents major difficulties and leaves much to be desired.

The problems of science education at the various levels, from the early grades through our graduate schools, are numerous and complex. Some of these problems are susceptible to relatively rapid solution; others obviously are of a kind that can be solved only over a period of years. Moreover, it is clear, because of the nature of these problems, that they require individual treatment. A massive science fellowship program or a large-scale attack through the mechanism of science scholarships—each of which is frequently suggested as the best way of solving the current problems—are on analysis found to be relatively ineffectual in solving many of the problems that we now face. Hence the NSF has been attempting to design a coordinated series of approaches to the solution of a number of these problems.

A third attitude which underlies NSF programs in science education is that we need to place most emphasis on improving the *quality* of science education. If we could improve the teaching of science at all levels of our educational system to the point where all schools were doing as good a job as the best that we now have, there would be little question that larger numbers of students would be motivated to study science—and, of these, many more than now choose to do so would undertake careers in science. Hence it is our conviction that—if we can succeed in raising the level of science instruction—the problem of assuring a sufficiently large number of scientific and engineering workers for the future will also be solved.

NSF programming in the area of science education has developed along lines which are conditioned by the points of view I have just outlined. We have long recognized the desirability of providing at least a limited number of outstanding science students with the opportunity for advanced study at those institutions where they can obtain the best possible training. Through the two major graduate fellowship programs which the NSF now administers, more than two thousand students annually are enabled to study, usually toward the doctoral degree, in institutions where they can be assured of training of a high quality. Many of these students indicate to us, in answer to a direct question, that they would like to go into college teaching when they have obtained their Ph.D. degrees. The national needs for scientists in other types of activity are such that by no means all of those who receive NSF fellowships can be expected to become professors of science in universities and colleges. Nonetheless, those who do undoubtedly constitute an important asset in the battle we are waging to improve science education.

On our college campuses, and in our secondary and elementary schools, there are many individuals who are teaching science who need additional training or who need to have their training updated in order to be able to provide the highest level of instruction of which they are inherently capable. Through a variety of programs the National Science Foundation is attempting to increase the subject matter competence of teachers at various levels; the basic purpose of these programs is to improve instruction. Many of you, I am sure, are familiar with the NSF program of summer institutes for secondary school teachers of science and mathematics. This is our largest program and one which all evidence indicates has been notably successful in raising the competence of many teachers, thereby revitalizing instruction in science and mathematics in thousands of secondary schools throughout the country. Related NSF programs are going forward along several other lines, not only for high school teachers but also for college teachers and for a few individuals concerned with science instruction at the elementary school level.

It would not be wise for me to attempt in this paper to outline in detail all the activities which the National Science Foundation has directed toward the improvement of science education. I would rather discuss the way the foundation sees its responsibilities in connection with the improvement of course content in science, mathematics, and engineering.

The foundation's efforts to improve the course content offered at various levels of our educational system emerged gradually, starting in the middle 1950s. About a decade ago,[1] a few scientists in the universities became sufficiently concerned about inadequacies in the preparation of entering students that they (as the people who really know science) determined to take a leading role in course development. Different groups came into this activity via different paths, and the overall story is a complex one. I shall attempt in this discussion only to trace the main outlines and to give, in addition, some of the basic points of view that have been developed at the National Science Foundation in connection with this activity.

As you are well aware, the immediate postwar years offered a special set of problems for all those involved in higher education in the United States, primarily because of the large number of veterans (supported under the so-called "GI Bill") who enrolled in our colleges and universities. By about 1950, however, scientists concerned with higher education were able to pause and take stock of general developments in science education.

In one of our major universities, in the early 1950s, it was discovered that nearly three-fifths of the students entering the science and engineering departments had to take remedial courses in mathematics before they could begin college work, even at the analytical geometry–introductory calculus level. After a period of asking themselves what was wrong, a number of the faculty members at this institution decided that university mathematicians and scientists had a responsibility for helping the schools in a substantial way. They came to the conclusion that those who know modern developments best, know the intricacies and structure of their subjects, should help to design courses and materials which reflect contemporary knowledge and points of view in appropriate ways. The schools, they discovered, were not teaching anything in mathematics not known before the time of Newton, despite the fact that set theory, for example, offers powerful ideas for rationalizing arithmetic and algebra. They also became convinced that the curriculum was in large measure governed by unvalidated assumptions about the levels at which pupils could learn specific things.

The result of this university's concern was the formation of a university committee to guide experimentation on school mathematics—a group which eventually devised the Beberman project supported by the Carnegie Corporation. The university was, of course, the University of Illinois.

Other groups in other institutions were beginning to concern themselves with similar problems. Biologists around the country became concerned with educational questions. Their starting point was their awareness that modern biology demands at least as keen analytical ability as mathematics or physics, plus a willingness to work with very complex systems—yet school and early college courses were so rigidly structured as not to challenge and attract many first-rate minds. Activities were begun in 1953 under the aegis of the National Academy of Sciences—National Research Council to "do" something about this problem. A project was carried on for some four years with the aid of relatively modest grants from the Rockefeller Foundation and the National Science Foundation, with the result that a series of reports was

[1] See J. R. Steelman, *Science and Public Policy*, Washington, D.C., 1947. (Report to the President.)—Editor.

developed, a few pilot operations were carried out, and an attempt was made to engender interest and activity among biologists.

Other groups in other disciplines began to show an interest in this general problem. Specifically, in mid-1956, Dr. Jerrold Zacharias and some of his colleagues in physics—at MIT and elsewhere—decided to launch a sizable attempt to prepare a completely new and integrated program of study for secondary school physics. Groups of physicists at several institutions developed draft materials which were finally merged, after much reflection and discussion, into a working outline of a new textbook designed for twelfth-grade students of physics. With support from several private foundations as well as the National Science Foundation, this group (which designated itself the Physical Science Study Committee) undertook to prepare—and test through class-room use—physically "sound" materials of all appropriate kinds: laboratory guides and materials, motion pictures for supplementing the instruction in the classroom, supplementary reading material, and teachers' guides. Although the group's work was brought to a reasonably complete point about two years ago, additional work is being carried on in the hope that feedback from the schools now using the material will—as it did in the earlier phases of the Committee's work—make it possible to improve the PSSC course even more.

In 1958, at several conferences of leading mathematicians, the problem of launching in mathematics a study somewhat akin to that already underway in physics was discussed. As a result, the American Mathematical Society, the Mathematical Association of America, and the National Council of Teachers of Mathematics nominated members to a planning committee which outlined a course of action, selected a continuing advisory committee, and persuaded Prof. E. G. Begle of Yale University to become the director of the new enterprise—which came to be known as the School Mathematics Study Group, or SMSG. Aided by a grant from the NSF, this study group began its work in the summer of 1958; since then it has developed a tremendous amount of new instructional material for both students and teachers. SMSG materials now are available for teaching mathematics in grades 4 through 12, and a number of monographs have been produced to help the teachers of mathematics to increase their understanding of mathematics. As in the case of the physics effort, it is already clear that these activities will not only generate specific and valuable products, but that they will also stimulate a broad effort among publishers to produce a new generation of textbooks and other instructional materials (written at least in part by scientists and mathematicians of outstanding qualifications), and often reflecting the carefully developed points of view exhibited in the work of the study groups.

At this conference there are speakers who are much closer than I to the actual operations of the various study groups with which the National Science Foundation has had the good fortune to be associated. It would not be appropriate for me to go into further detail concerning the history or activities of these bodies. I should nonetheless at least mention the fact that, in addition to the Physical Science Study Committee and the School Mathematics Study Group, there are several other major groups to which the National Science Foundation has made grants. One of these is the Biological Sciences

Curriculum Study, which is going forward under the guidance of Dr. Bentley Glass of Johns Hopkins University. Dr. Arnold Grobman, the staff director of this study, prepared a paper for this conference. Two groups are carrying out studies designed to improve the materials available at the high school level in chemistry: The Chemical Bond Approach Project (described at this conference by Dr. Laurence Strong of Earlham College), and the Chemical Education Materials Study. We have made grants to groups working in other fields, but the number is too extensive to list here.

As I indicated earlier, support for work in this general domain had been provided by other groups before the National Science Foundation began to make available appreciable amounts of money for such efforts. I should like to pay particular tribute to the Carnegie Corporation (represented here by Mr. Frederick Jackson) for its pioneer efforts in these directions.

I commented earlier that the National Science Foundation must of necessity observe certain "rules of the game" because of the fact that it is part of the national government. Not long after we began to make grants for course content improvement efforts, we found it desirable to put in writing certain principles which we felt should guide the foundation in administering its Course Content Improvement program. I think these nine principles are of sufficient interest to merit listing:

1. *The initiative for a study should arise from a conviction on the part of responsible scientists of high professional stature, and of competent and experienced teachers at all appropriate levels, that a serious educational problem exists in a scientific discipline or in a group of disciplines.*

2. *The Foundation must have assurance that scientists distinguished as teachers or as investigators in the disciplines concerned will be willing to give leadership, time, and effort to the proposed study.*

3. *Support should be designed to give the scientists undertaking a study freedom of action, within the pertinent subject matter area, to follow whatever paths will in their collective judgment best accomplish the basic objectives of the study.*

4. *Studies may be comprehensive or limited in scope. In any case, the group making the study must have the respect and confidence of the scientific community in the field concerned.*

5. *Support for comprehensive studies of course content in a particular discipline should not preclude concurrent support for other imaginative and thoughtful but less extensive studies in the same field, provided they conform to the general principles here outlined.*

6. *The Foundation's interest in these projects is to support studies of course content as a kind of research enterprise, including reasonable trial and testing in schools, but Foundation funds must not be used to promote the general acceptance of the new courses or materials.*

7. *Capable and experienced teachers at all appropriate levels should be asked to participate. Their participation should reflect the interest and encouragement given the task by professional scientific and educational organizations.*

8. *To insure that all instructional materials developed in these studies are of the highest quality, the Study Group should invite the cooperation of*

persons with appropriate special talents and skills (e.g., highly competent and experienced film, television producers, and technicians).

9. *The Foundation shall be consulted upon arrangements for the general distribution and disposition of all materials conceived and developed under a grant for course content improvement studies.*

Let me refer back to the sixth point listed above. The foundation and its grantees are all keenly aware of and committed to the tradition of local control of our schools. It is our joint conviction that no school system should be in any way pressured to use the materials developed through the efforts of NSF-supported study groups. However, we are also convinced that those who guide our schools are keenly interested in finding ways to improve the quality of instruction in all fields. If, therefore, the products of the study groups we support can be shown to be superior to the materials now available, we are sure they will be used. Should it become obvious that the materials produced by one or more of these groups are in fact unsuitable—or less suitable than other materials which are now available from other sources—it would be tragic if teachers, superintendents or school boards felt that they were in any sense obliged to adopt demonstrably inferior materials.

It is probably far too soon to make any general judgment as to the degree to which the various study groups now working will be successful in their goal of producing materials which are significantly better than those which have heretofore been available. The results to date have been most encouraging, however, and we are reasonably certain that real progress toward improved science education will result from the expenditures of funds on this program. We remain convinced of the soundness of the basic idea of involving scientists and mathematicians of the first rank, as well as individuals from all of the other relevant specialties, in the task of developing new instructional materials and carrying out a critical appraisal and testing of the novel approaches which result.

We shall be most interested in the findings of this conference on curriculum experimentation, and it is my hope that your deliberations will help us to determine with greater precision the role which the National Science Foundation *should* play in the nationally important area of course content improvement.

26 ❦ THE ROLE OF THE COOPERATIVE RESEARCH PROGRAM OF THE UNITED STATES OFFICE OF EDUCATION IN CURRICULUM EXPERIMENTATION
David L. Clark* Ohio State University

The Cooperative Research Program of the U.S. Office of Education is one way, and a very important way, in which the Office expresses it concern for curricular improvement in education. The program was initiated in July, 1956, with an authorization from Congress for the Commissioner of Education to "enter into contracts or jointly financed cooperative arrangements with colleges and universities and State education agencies for the conduct of research, surveys, and demonstrations in the field of education." In the past five years nearly five hundred research studies in education have begun with partial or complete support from the cooperative research program.

For our purposes I would like to look at the program in two ways: first, as I understand my primary charge, to describe the structure and operation of the program as it now exists; second, to illustrate briefly from research now being conducted under the program, the ways in which curriculum experimentation is being supported directly and indirectly by the program. In this latter respect I would like to introduce a somewhat broader definition of curriculum experimentation than, I think, has been used in the conference so far, with the possible exception of the presentation of Dr. Cronbach and Dean Cook.

Turning then, first, to the organization and structure of the Program, I would identify five component program elements:

1. Nondirected basic and applied research
2. Demonstrations or field tests
3. Special areas of research emphasis
4. Research development activities
5. Dissemination

1. Nondirected basic and applied research

This is by far the largest and most important of the activities of the program. Over 90 per cent of the program's funds and efforts are expended in this direction. The operation of this phase of the program is very simple—it is an open competitive evaluation of proposals submitted to the Office by researchers interested in studying the process of education. A Research Advisory Committee of nine members (all non-Office of Education personnel) meets three times a year to evaluate the proposals. The committee is broadly representative of the social and behavioral sciences, and committee members are appointed for staggered three-year terms. The research advisory com-

* David L. Clark at the time of the conference was Director, Cooperative Research Program, U.S. Office of Education, Washington, D.C. He is now Associate Dean, College of Education, Ohio State University.

mittee recommends action on proposals to the Commissioner, who assumes final responsibility for approving their recommendations.

The staff of the program plays no part in the evaluation of proposals. This is a rather unique arrangement which, we feel, has the important advantage of dispelling the notion that only a certain type of research, or a certain area of research, is of interest to the program. In fact, it is acceptance of the point of view that creative and fruitful research which results in new knowledge is the product of an individual or group of individuals with an idea and with the ability to conduct an investigation relating to their idea. Stated in another way, it is recognition of the fact that we don't know what it is that we don't know about education. Of secondary importance, but still significant, is the fact that this arrangement allows the research staff of the program to talk and work freely with researchers in the field at any stage in the development of their research, before or after it has been evaluated by the research advisory committee, without having ideas in one hand and money in the other.

In closing my remarks on this phase of the program, let me mention again that it is designed to support research related to education. This is a broad charge and is so interpreted by the staff of the program. The projects being supported range across the full gamut of educational problems. The long-range objective of this activity is to increase the potential of colleges and universities and state education agencies to provide new knowledge about education.

2. Demonstrations or field tests

This phase of the program's work was initiated in April, 1961. We have six such field tests now in operation. In general, these so-called "demonstrations" have three common characteristics: (1) They are grounded in research evidence; (2) they represent a translation of research into operating school or college programs; (3) they are conducted in a noncontrolled situation with a highly controlled evaluative phase involving relatively large numbers of subjects. If we can use an analogy with the natural sciences, these demonstrations are designed to be the testing of, for example, a discriminating weed killer which was proved effective in laboratory experiments and now has to be tried out on a large number of farms where such conditions as climate, soil, and the ability of the farmers to follow instructions all vary.

During 1961, demonstration proposals were accepted only in the areas of mathematics, talent, and the mentally retarded, for purely expedient reasons. Limited funds were available, these were areas in which much research had been done, and there was an existing ferment conducive to field experimentation. In 1962 this program was expanded on an openly competitive basis and integrated with the nondirected basic and applied research program, since the field tests were, in effect, nothing more than an extension of the cooperative research program's interest, bringing within its compass the engineering phase of educational research. The implications of this activity to curriculum experimentation are self-evident; as a matter of fact, our field test projects in mathematics in 1961 grew directly out of previous projects supported by the Course Content Improvement Section of the National Science Foundation.

3. Special areas of research emphasis

From time to time the Office or the Congress expresses a special interest in research in a substantive area. A current interest in the teaching of English is described in detail by Dr. Boyer Jarvis, who discusses the overall role of the Office in curriculum experimentation. In these instances, the personnel of the program stimulate interest and activity within the area: for example, the staff has now talked with over two hundred and fifty persons who are interested in research into the teaching of English. This is not to say that the staff sets out to sell preconceived notions of the research which needs to be done in English, but rather that an attempt is made to meet with members of the scholarly community to (1) see what they think needs to be done; (2) encourage them to begin work on doing it; and (3) assist them in arriving at the point of actually proposing research in the problem area. Projects submitted in these areas are thrown into open competition with all others submitted to the program, and, of course, the special area is, in due time, again integrated with the basic program.

4. Research development activities

There are three patterns through which the program tries to assist in the development of research: (1) individual research development contract; (2) conference survey; and (3) seminar study. These three have rather specific purposes and they, too, are handled under contract:

1. Individual research development contract

These contracts are designed to provide a researcher who has recently completed a significant research project with an opportunity to analyze retrospectively the work he has done and to project, as best he can, the implications of his activities for future research by himself and others.

2. Conference survey

This technique is quite similar to the conference activities of the Social Science Research Council. It is designed to stimulate research in an area where little has been done in the past, and at the same time to survey the current status of research in this field.

3. Seminar study

The seminar is designed to analyze and synthesize what has been done, and to project hypothetical research designs for further studies in an area where substantial research has already been completed. The seminar would typically involve a relatively small number of outstanding researchers for an extended period of time, that is, perhaps up to four weeks.

5. Dissemination

Finally, let me turn to the dissemination aspect of the cooperative research program and simply enumerate its parts:

1. **Listing of projects**

An annual listing of projects which have been initiated under the program is prepared. This listing includes the title of the research project, the name of the research investigator, and the institution at which the research is being conducted. It is nothing more than a bibliographic résumé of program activities.

2. **Yearly description of projects in progress**

Each year, project descriptions of all projects initiated during the previous year are prepared for distribution. These descriptions state the problem which the investigator is pursuing, the major objectives, and the general procedures. The descriptions are generally sufficient to allow an individual reading the publication to determine whether or not he wishes to follow up a particular project more intensively.

3. **Summaries of all completed projects**

Eight- to ten-page summaries of all completed projects are prepared by the program staff. These summaries cover the major findings of the studies and restate, in greater detail than the descriptions, the objectives and procedures used during the investigation.

4. **Monograph series**

Each month a research monograph, which summarizes in substantial detail one research project completed under the program, is issued. These monographs describe projects which, in the opinion of the staff, would be of wide interest, reports of which are not available through other types of publications.

5. **Documents expediting project**

Approximately seventy-five copies of each final report received by the program is distributed through the Documents Expediting Project of the Library of Congress to a group of key libraries around the country. These reports are available on interlibrary loan through libraries which are not affiliated with the documents expediting project.

6. **Microfilming project**

The Library of Congress also provides a microfilming service for cooperative research projects, and copies of final reports may be obtained in either microfilm or photocopy at varying prices, depending upon the length of the report.

This dissemination effort is restricted primarily to researchers. Although I am much concerned with the broader problems of dissemination—effecting change in schools as a result of research development and experimentation—I will state simply that no program to achieve this end exists and that one is needed desperately in education.

Examples of research efforts

Let me turn finally to the types of curriculum experimentation being supported under the program. First, let me point out what we are not doing. This is a research program and we are not supporting the development of curricula or curriculum materials. A move in this direction has been made. It is described by Dr. Jarvis and it holds out at least the possibility of extending to the humanities the exciting and productive efforts of the Course Content Improvement Section of the National Science Foundation. What, then, is the contribution of this program to curriculum experimentation? For simplicity's sake, here is one way of classifying our efforts:

1. Learning theory and other supporting studies
2. The scope of the curriculum
3. The sequence of the curriculum
4. The process of teaching

Learning theory and other supporting studies

This may represent the cooperative research program's greatest contribution. This category includes the myriad psychological investigations of the characteristics of the learner and the teacher—their behavior, growth, and development—which complement, the meaningful curriculum development, investigations of the logical structure of course material. I would like to digress at this point for just a moment to present a model for the classification of research activities which grew out of the Social Science Research Council conference at Cornell which Dr. Cronbach mentioned in his paper. This model is useful to me in thinking about the interrelationship of types of research activities, and may help to amplify this supportive role in curriculum experimentation which I feel is so vital.

A proposed categorization of research activities

Types of research activity	Examples
1. Basic Scientific Investigation (content indifferent)	Structural linguistics
2. Basic Scientific Investigation (content relevant)	Language development in young children
3. Investigation of Educationally Oriented Problems	Comparison of phonic and word-sight methods of teaching reading
4. Classroom Experimentation	Experimentation with program for teaching reading to third graders
5. Field Testing	Preparation of curricular materials—field testing of the program
6. Demonstration-Dissemination	Marketing

This I believe is a quasi-linear sequence which tends, although obviously with many exceptions, to proceed from (1) to (6). Our emphasis in this conference has clearly been on (6) with some reference to (4) and (5). We cannot ignore the real danger that (6) is completely dependent on (1) to (5) if it is not a simple rearrangement of parts in a closed system of knowledge. A large proportion of the studies being conducted under the cooperative research program are of the types named in steps 1 to 5 and are making a major contribution to curriculum experimentation, although they might not be quickly identified as curriculum projects if one were to refer to the type of efforts described so far in this conference as curriculum experimentation.

The scope and sequence of the curriculum and the process of teaching

As you would expect, there are a large number of studies in each of the areas of scope, sequence, and process which are being conducted under the cooperative research program. These studies are directly related to curriculum improvement, and for our purposes it will perhaps be sufficient to illustrate two kinds of investigations which are going on in each of these categories. The following brief listing will give you a picture of their diversity:

1. Scope

The development of a conceptual system for dealing with problems of curriculum and instruction—John I. Goodlad, University of Chicago.

The development of designs for curriculum research—Jerome Bruner, Harvard University.

2. Sequence

Abilities of first-grade pupils to learn mathematics in terms of algebraic structures by means of teaching machines—Evan R. Keislar, University of California, Los Angeles.

A modern mathematics program as it pertains to the interrelationship of mathematical content, teaching methods, and classroom atmosphere (the Madison project)—Robert B. Davis, Syracuse University.

3. Process

Use of case histories in the development of student understanding of science and scientists—William W. Cooley, Harvard University.

The effects of direct and indirect teacher influence on learning—Ned A. Flanders, University of Minnesota.

Summary

The Cooperative Research Program of the Office of Education is playing, and I believe will continue to play, a highly significant role in curriculum improvement in this country. Because of its broad research charge it is a meeting place in which psychologists and learning theorists and scholars and practitioners can work together in attempting to unearth new knowledge about the *how, what,* and *when* questions which President Wilson has presented at this conference.

27 ❀ THE PRIVATE FOUNDATIONS
Frederick H. Jackson* Carnegie Corporation of New York

The curricular development projects being discussed at this conference represent an interesting and significant development in the recent history of American education. They are one of the important manifestations of a rekindling of interest on the part of college and university subject-matter professors in education at the secondary and elementary levels. This move-

* Frederick H. Jackson is Executive Associate, Carnegie Corporation of New York, New York City.

ment is, I believe, one of the half-dozen most important developments to appear on the educational scene since World War II.

For a generation or more, there was almost complete isolation between those concerned with the teaching of various subjects in the schools and the college and university specialists in these subjects. The high school biology, English, or mathematics teacher had little or no contact with college and university professors of these subjects. We can leave to the historian the reasons for this cleavage, as well as the reasons for the increasing cooperation which has emerged between school people and university subject-matter people during the past decade.

Everyone who is interested in the health and vitality of American education will applaud this development. The older attitudes of hostility, misunderstanding, and mutual recrimination between the professors and the teachers are becoming a thing of the past. A much better appreciation of the roles of each of these groups in the world of education is slowly appearing.

One of the characteristics of the curricular development projects we are discussing here is youth. The oldest is less than ten years of age. The first subject to undergo this type of experimentation was mathematics. The physics curriculum was examined shortly afterwards. In the sciences, the biology curriculum was studied next, and finally chemistry. In the meantime, the teaching of foreign languages has been undergoing significant modification. A major program is under way in English under the auspices of the College Entrance Examination Board. And finally, voices are being heard in the social studies bemoaning the fact that they are now virtually the only subject-matter area in which little or nothing is afoot.

The question may well be raised as to whether every field should undertake curriculum revision programs. It is evident that some fields have undertaken them with great enthusiasm, while others have appeared to have moved with reluctance. It has seemed to me that curriculum revision programs should be undertaken when there is a clear feeling, in the field, that the present curriculum is outmoded. Rapidly moving and changing fields will require more curricular revision than fields where the rate of development is slower. Physics and mathematics may call for almost continual attention; history and English may require a hard look once a decade.

The strategy of the curriculum reformers has differed from subject to subject. As far as I am aware, every significant effort to redesign the high school or elementary school curriculum currently in process is the joint effort of scientists or scholars, on the one hand, and classroom teachers on the other. In mathematics, various individuals and groups have made independent, and sometimes competitive, efforts to product new courses of study for the senior high, the junior high, and the elementary school levels. In physics, one group has produced one new course. In biology, a single group is sponsoring three new versions of a high school course. In chemistry, there are two separately organized attempts to rethink the high school offering. The Carnegie Corporation's experience has been primarily with curricular experimentation in the field of mathematics. I would like to tell you a little about how we became interested in the field and how we set about making grants for it.

But first I would like to tell you a bit about the organization itself and its philosophy of giving. In 1961, the Carnegie Corporation celebrated (very quietly) its fiftieth anniversary. Its assets are in excess of 225 million dollars and its annual income (which is spent each year) amounts to approximately ten million dollars. Its total staff is about thirty, of whom eight or nine are the officers concerned with the grant-making process. A foundation such as the Carnegie Corporation is one of the few institutions in our society which is in a position to keep itself free to act quickly and flexibly in support of the talented individual, the man with an idea, or the institution which wishes to undertake an experimental program. It is one of the relatively few sources of venture or risk capital for education experimentation in our society.

And now back to mathematics. How does a foundation decide to concentrate on a certain field, such as mathematics, at a given time? How does it go about entering a new area? To begin with, the subject is by common agreement one of the most important in the curriculum. Its usefulness to ordinary citizens needs no demonstration, and it is, of course, a necessary prerequisite for comprehending the worlds of science and technology.

The officers became aware in 1954 that mathematics might be on the threshhold of some important changes. From their reading in the field and from talking with mathematics professors and teachers, they learned that the subject had grown tremendously in the twentieth century. Whole areas of mathematics, currently very important, were unknown in 1900. The officers became convinced that this was a field in which something useful could be done. They weren't sure what, but they wanted to explore it.

A staff member was assigned to the task. Meanwhile, the president mentioned the subject at a trustees meeting. The trustees agreed that it was important. The officer who was exploring the field soon discovered that some leading mathematicians and high school teachers were strongly of the opinion that there was a need for reshaping the mathematics curriculum in our secondary schools.

The testimony of these men and women was impressive. The next step which the corporation took was to commission a study of the state of mathematics teaching. This provided strong corroboration of the need for a thorough study of the secondary school curriculum. Meanwhile, the officer involved was continuing his task of becoming acquainted with the professors and teachers who saw the need most clearly. At the same time he was letting it be known in these circles that the Carnegie Corporation would be receptive to significant ideas for constructive action. Such ideas were soon forthcoming, and the corporation was launched upon a new program.

The important thing to note is that the new program was not dreamed up in our offices on Fifth Avenue. It developed out of extensive give-and-take between foundation officers and forward-looking professors and teachers. It involved exploratory efforts which covered the length and breadth of the country and involved many individuals with many differing views.

The first grant in this program was made to a group of teachers in University High School, at the University of Illinois, who were working in cooperation with members of the University mathematics department. The second grant was to a Commission on Mathematics of the College Entrance

Examination Board. This group was composed of university mathematicians and secondary school teachers. The Illinois group and the college board group have each worked out their own prescriptions for curricular reform. They have by no means come up with identical answers. There has been healthy competition between them. Individual professors and teachers favor the program of one over that of the other, but nearly everyone in mathematics respects the dedicated efforts of both groups in producing responsible new programs. Needless to add, the Carnegie Corporation had no idea when the grants were made, what the conclusions and recommendations would be. The much more extensive program of the School Mathematics Study Group has made good use of the work of both the Illinois and the college board groups.

Both of these grants illustrate well the threefold criteria we use in measuring proposals. First and of prime importance, the caliber of the men involved was first rate. Second, the proposals themselves were carefully planned and well worked out, and there was an excellent chance that other individuals and institutions would benefit from the programs. Finally, the sponsoring institutions, the University of Illinois and the college board, were intensely interested in the programs and pledged their fullest cooperation and backing.

As the work of redesigning the curriculum at the senior high school level proceeded, it became apparent that experimentation was needed in the junior high and elementary school grades as well. The first step the corporation took in this direction was to support John R. Mayor and his associates at the University of Maryland in their efforts to produce new materials for grades 7 and 8. Writing groups were assembled and sample text materials were produced. These have been revised in the light of classroom use and are being tried out in a number of schools. In 1960–1961 some fifteen thousand seventh- and eighth-grade students studied these materials.

Reference to the elementary grades in an article on the state of mathematics teaching in the United States by Marshall Stone, distinguished professor of mathematics at the University of Chicago, led to the corporation's asking Professor Stone in 1957 to explore this area. A series of grants for the improvement of the teaching of mathematics at the elementary school level followed. Some of these Professor Stone had recommended, others not. The first and by far the largest was for the support of the Arithmetic Project at the University of Illinois, directed by David A. Page. Professor Page is attempting to provide a modernized curriculum for grades 1–6. Catherine Stern has long worked productively to improve the teaching of elementary school mathematics and has published materials on structural arithmetic for grades 1 and 2. A grant from Carnegie Corporation, made in 1958 and renewed in 1960, is enabling Dr. Stern to push forward the preparation of materials for other elementary grades. In the meantime, the activities of a mathematical logician and a mathematician at Stanford University in the elementary school field came to the corporation's attention. Patrick Suppes and Newton Hawley have been experimenting in teaching geometry, sets, and variables to primary school children. Grants from the corporation have enabled them to push on more rapidly with their work, which is being tried out in schools throughout the country.

The role of supporting agencies | **214**

Few psychologists in the United States have paid much attention to the teaching and learning of mathematics. A grant was made to enable experimental psychologist Robert Gagne of Princeton University to investigate how children learn algebra. Professor Gagne and his students are also working cooperatively with the University of Maryland junior high school mathematics program.

Since 1955, our investment in the improvement of the teaching of mathematics has been slightly under 1½ million dollars. More than a year ago the corporation decided to begin tapering off the number of grants we would be making in mathematics. This was in line with our policy of staying with a field for a reasonable length of time and then investing our funds in other lines of activity. The entrance of the National Science Foundation into the mathematics field with sums of money vastly greater than ours virtually ensured that the work begun under our support would be carried on. This enabled us to withdraw somewhat earlier than would otherwise have been the case.

I believe I am correct in saying that never in our history has so much energy, talent, and money been invested in improving the teaching of basic subjects in the high school curriculum. While a limited amount of this activity has been supported by the private foundations, the vast majority of the support has come from governmental sources—the National Science Foundation, for mathematics and the sciences; and the Office of Education, for foreign languages. The task is hardly begun, however, for, with the exception of mathematics, the elementary school curriculum has scarcely been touched. Many subjects at this level are in need of the same vigorous shaking up that the high school subjects have been receiving in recent years. As the elementary and secondary curricula are revised, it will become increasingly apparent that much of what formerly was taught at the undergraduate level will also need drastic revision. Ultimately, the effects of the ripple begun at the high school level will be felt from kindergarten through the Ph.D. programs. In a given subject, such a stem-to-stern renovation program will take at least a decade. And by then, in the rapidly changing fields, the task will need to be started again. Thus it would appear that curricular revision programs at one or another level, and in one or another field, should continue to occupy scientists, scholars, teachers, and foundations (private and public) in the foreseeable future.

If this analysis is correct, some individuals will argue that a permanent agency (or agencies) dedicated to curriculum modernization is called for. Indeed, such an organization has been proposed. What is the case for such a development? (Here I should note that I am neither advocating such an agency nor opposing it, and that I am speaking as an individual and not as a representative of the organization for which I work.) Until the current wave of curricular revision programs came along, this type of activity was done by the left hands of busy individuals, when it was done at all. All the efforts now under way are one-shot efforts. The proponents of a permanent agency point to the continuing need for activities of this kind, and argue that society must find a way of institutionalizing the process of curriculum modernization.

The best way of doing this, they claim, is by creating an agency for which this would be the prime responsibility.

If this were done, it would have to be done with great care and in such a way as to insure that various segments of the educational community would have confidence in the quality and the objective of such an enterprise. At a minimum, this would mean the establishment of a board of trustees made up of respected and trusted leaders from the schools and the universities, and a director in whom all had confidence. With such leadership, the group might devote itself initially to one or two areas of curricular modernization. Every effort would have to be made to assure that these enterprises were carefully and successfully accomplished, for on them the reputation of the new agency and its future usefulness would depend.

Some have argued that such a development might lead to a monopoly in educational modernization. Although this is a possibility, it does not appear to be a very likely one. The new organization should pledge itself to look at various approaches and not to back what might be taken to be the only path to curricular reform in a subject. It should consult widely, both before and while undertaking a particular investigation. If it appeared to develop monopolistic tendencies, there is ample precedent for believing that a rival organization would in time appear on the scene. The traditional pluralism so prevalent in American society can, I believe, be counted on to keep any such organization from gaining a stranglehold on the modernization process. If a new agency concerned with educational modernization were to appear, it should not be until after the question as to its advisability and feasibility is carefully considered by knowledgeable educators. Such a venture would represent a significant departure and should not be undertaken lightly.

28 ❀ THE ROLE OF THE UNITED STATES OFFICE OF EDUCATION IN CURRICULUM EXPERIMENTATION
J. Boyer Jarvis* United States Office of Education

On almost every hand in our country today there is an increasing recognition of the need for improvement in American education. In his message to Congress on American education, President Kennedy said:

Our progress as a nation can be no swifter than our progress in education. Our requirements for world leadership, our hope for economic growth, and the demands of citizenship itself in an era such as this all require the maximum development of every young American's capacity.[1]

* J. Boyer Jarvis was Special Assistant to the United States Commissioner of Education, Department of Health, Education, and Welfare. He is now Assistant to the President and Director of the Summer School, University of Utah.

[1] 87th Congress, 1st Sess., H.R. Document no. 92, "American Education—Message from the President Relative to American Education," Feb. 20, 1961, p. 1.

While the President sought primarily to gain congressional support for the Administration's education legislation, he also expressed the need for "a new standard of excellence in education."

In his advocacy of greater Federal participation in meeting the costs of education, Secretary Ribicoff has repeatedly stressed the importance of strengthening and improving American education.

When he assumed his duties as United States Commissioner of Education, Dr. McMurrin asserted:

Although the quality of our education has improved considerably over the past few years—from elementary school through college—it is not as good as it should be. Too often we fail to elicit from both our students and teachers their best efforts. We must have greater rigor at all levels in order to achieve the proper ends of education and guarantee excellence in our society.[2]

Concern for improving education exists in virtually every element of our national life. It is expressed not only by government officials and by leaders in education, but also by businessmen, teachers, and parents.

Without becoming involved in the problem of financing, let me say that the quality of our education can be improved in two ways: first, by attracting to the classrooms of America, at all levels, a corps of teachers who are *all* as well educated, as competent, and as dedicated as the top 10 per cent of the present body of American teachers; second, by a continuing critical review of the curriculum. It is assumed that such a review involves extensive research and experimentation, perhaps even trial and error.

If I understand correctly, the purpose of this conference is really to take an inventory of a number of relatively new developments in curriculum content, design, and administration. This is certainly a timely thing to do, and I join in the hope that this exchange of ideas and information will contribute significantly to the improvement of the curriculum in American schools.

Dr. Rosenbloom has asked me to address myself to the role of the United States Office of Education in curriculum experimentation. As most of you know, the traditional role of the Office has been to collect and disseminate information relating to education. Much of this information has dealt with the status of the curriculum and with curriculum development at various levels. Typically, this information is obtained by means of questionnaires circulated to "the field" and compiled and analyzed by specialists on the Office staff. Two recent Office of Education publications illustrate this kind of activity. *Curriculum Responsibilities of State Departments of Education* is a report on the status of current practices in the several States. It deals with such matters as supervision, textbook selection, the organization of and the techniques used in curriculum development and improvement, and the nature of curriculum research being conducted under the auspices of state departments of education. *Organized Occupational Curriculums in Higher Education* contains information relating the number of students enrolled in various technical and craftsman-clerical courses in two-year and four-year colleges and technical institutes. Now in preparation is a nationwide survey

[2] From a prepared statement at press conference in Washington, Apr. 4, 1961, p. 3.

of offerings and enrollments in high school subjects. While surveys of this kind may have considerable value as indicators of certain practices related to the curriculum, they are not themselves studies of the content of the curriculum.

Illustrative of Office of Education publications which do address themselves, at least in part, to curriculum content are the following:

Youth Physical Fitness: Suggested Elements of a School-centered Program
Social Studies in the Elementary School Program
Social Science Requirements for Bachelor's Degrees

The series *New Dimensions in Higher Education* also touches upon some aspects of the curriculum.

Another way in which the Office has been involved over the years in curricular matters relates to the consultative activities of Office specialists who customarily have participated in numerous professional meetings, conducted conferences, and visited state departments of education.

An important new direction for the U.S. Office of Education was established by Congress in 1954, when it approved legislation (Public Law 531, 83d Congress) authorizing the Office to make cooperative research contracts with colleges, universities, and state educational agencies. Since its inception, the cooperative research program has supported several hundred research projects. Many of them have dealt with various aspects of curriculum experimentation or reform. Since Dr. David L. Clark, director of the cooperative research branch, has already described this activity in detail, I shall add only that Commissioner McMurrin has a very great interest in supporting an increasing number of research projects in the substantive areas of the curriculum—projects planned and carried out under the direction of individuals with primary competence in the substantive areas.

Passage of the National Defense Education Act in 1958 has taken the Office of Education into still other programs that are related to the curriculum. Title III of the NDEA has made it possible for substantial gains to be made throughout the country in strengthening elementary and secondary school offerings in science, mathematics, and modern foreign languages. According to the 1960 *Annual Report* on the National Defense Education Act:

In the fields of science and mathematics the quality of instruction is being upgraded, and new courses are being added as a result of the purchase of badly needed equipment and instruction materials. In the preparation of project applications, local schools often have had their staffs participate in extensive curriculum evaluation, which has led to the modernization of science and mathematics courses in terms of content, sequence, and grade level.

In mentioning recent improvement in the curriculum of both science and mathematics, I am well aware of the extent to which such improvements have been influenced, or at least made possible, by the activities and grants of the National Science Foundation. Not only has the foundation made important contributions to curriculum development through its support of the

Physical Science Study Committee, the School Mathematics Study Group, the Biological Sciences Curriculum Study, the Chemical Bond Approach Project, the Chemical Education Materials Study, and other projects, but it has also helped to raise the quality of education through its extensive support of NSF institutes for teachers of science and mathematics. Apparently there have been some instances where schools have not entirely succeeded in combining the advantages of equipment purchased with the aid of National Defense Education Act funds with the advantages of teachers trained at NSF institutes. Where such failures of coordination occur, they are most regrettable.

I am happy to say that a very satisfactory working relationship exists between the officers and staffs of the U.S. Office of Education and the National Science Foundation. Commissioner McMurrin and a group of Office of Education staff members have met with Dr. Alan T. Waterman and some of his associates to discuss ways in which these two Federal agencies can work together to help raise the quality of American education.

Improvement in modern foreign languages is encouraged through Title VI, as well as Title III, of the National Defense Education Act. The research and studies program inaugurated and supported under Title VI is already having a noticeable and encouraging effect in the improvement of modern language instruction—on the college level, as well as in the elementary and secondary grades. Dr. A. Bruce Gaarder, Head of the Research and Studies Unit in the Language Development Section of the Office of Education, made a very interesting report to this conference on some of the curriculum experiments being supported through Title VI of the National Defense Education Act. Title VI also authorizes language institutes to provide advanced training, particularly in the use of new teaching methods and instructional materials, for individuals engaged in, or preparing to engage in, teaching, supervising, or the training of teachers of any modern foreign language in the elementary or secondary schools. These institutes, most of which have been held during the summer, are making a notable contribution toward raising the language competence of the enrollees.

Several other provisions of the National Defense Education Act also have some relevance to curriculum. The National Defense Fellowship Program—authorized under Title IV—gives support to new and expanded graduate school facilities, in order to encourage a wider geographical distribution of such facilities throughout the nation. Title VII was designed to support research and experimentation in more effective utilization of television, radio, motion pictures, and related media for educational purposes.

Title VIII was designed to help alleviate the manpower shortage by assisting the states to provide, through area vocational education programs, training of less-than-college grade for youth, adults, and older persons, including instruction for apprentices, designed to fit them for useful employment as highly skilled technicians in recognized occupations requiring scientific knowledge, as determined by appropriate state authorities, in fields vital for the national defense. It is evident that major innovations are needed in the curriculum of vocational education if the nation's needs for modern technicians are to be met with any degree of adequacy. In view of this need, an advisory panel appointed at the request of the President, convened to review and evaluate the current Vocational Education Act, and made recommendations for improving and redirecting that program.

In considering the role of the U.S. Office of Education as it relates to curriculum experimentation and development, I should like to refer to a letter dated February 7, 1961, addressed to Senator Hubert H. Humphrey by Prof. Paul C. Rosenbloom. In this letter, which Senator Humphrey placed in the *Congressional Record* of March 3, Dr. Rosenbloom urged that the course content improvement programs in science and mathematics, which are supported by grants from the National Science Foundation, become the model for corresponding programs in the social sciences and the humanities, with Federal grants for their support to be administered through the Office of Education. I am sure that many of you have long before now entertained the same idea. It has been expressed many times, but in no case that I know of has it been advanced more effectively than it is in Dr. Rosenbloom's letter. Commissioner McMurrin also hopes to see the U.S. Office of Education do for other basic subjects what the National Science Foundation has done, and is doing, for science and mathematics.

The first concrete move of the Office in the direction of curriculum content improvement has become known, at least among the staff of the Office, as "Project English." Its beginnings, during the fiscal year 1961–1962, were limited to research and demonstration projects financed through the cooperative research program, and to two or three curriculum development centers. Although much preliminary planning took place within the Office of Education, formal establishment of "Project English" had to await action by Congress on the 1962 budget appropriation for the Department of Health, Education, and Welfare. Now the project is a reality, administered under the direction of Mr. Ralph C. M. Flynt, Assistant Commissioner for Research and Statistics. I understand that a small group of distinguished leaders and scholars in the English teaching profession was asked to serve as advisory panel for this project. It is hoped that with their wise assistance the project can be focused upon the major problems which must be understood and solved if widespread and substantial improvement in the English curriculum is to be achieved. In this connection, the importance of adequately prepared teachers should be stressed again. The addition of English institutes for teachers was among the amendments to the National Defense Education Act proposed by the administration. As you know, Congress finally voted to continue this legislation without amendment for the next two years.

I think it is highly probable, if "Project English" can be launched successfully, that efforts will be made in the next session of Congress to provide the Office of Education with authority and funds to support curriculum improvement projects in all basic subjects other than science and mathematics. Commissioner McMurrin includes among the basic subjects the study of politics, history, and philosophy, which "is essential to the quality and character of our culture," and the cultivated appreciation of great literature, art, and music, which is a basic element of genuine national strength.

The policies which Dr. Harry Kelly and his associates have applied so successfully in administering the course content improvement activities of the NSF should govern similar projects administered by the Office of Education:[3]

1. Federal funds may be used for research and development, for production, experimentation, and dissemination of information, but not to propagandize for any particular curriculum.

2. Federal funds may not be used in any way which can be construed as pushing a particular curriculum on the schools.

3. Participation by any institution or teacher in any project supported by the program must be entirely voluntary.

4. Any materials produced with Federal support must make their own way on their own merit. Final decisions on what use will be made of such material must be left to the local educational authorities.

A related approach to the improvement of quality of the curriculum, which is being considered in the Office of Education, concerns the possibility of some Federal participation in the support of selected educational research, experimental, and demonstration centers in various parts of the country. Such centers would be locally controlled and would combine the resources of highly competent research scholars, intelligent and imaginative educational administrators and teachers, and capable and sensitive interpreters and implementers of successfully demonstrated curricular innovations. It is assumed that the centers would operate in friendly competition with each other under policies such as those stated above. Very likely, centers of this type could be most easily developed under the auspices of a great university, but that is not the only possibility worthy of consideration.

The Educational Research Council of Greater Cleveland is an example of a community-based agency, supported by public-spirited individuals and business firms in cooperation with twenty subscribing school districts. This organization, now in its third year of operation, has successfully introduced a modern, integrated mathematics curriculum extending from kindergarten through the twelfth grade. In addition, Dr. George H. Baird, executive director of the council, believes that it has begun to solve such problems as:

1. How to reduce the time lag between research findings and their actual implementation in the classroom, particularly in large groups of schools.

2. How to achieve and organize close cooperation among widely varying types of schools.

3. How to raise standards in education by gaining acceptance of new curriculum designs.

In concluding these comments on the role of the U.S. Office of Education in curriculum development, I want to emphasize Commissioner McMurrin's great personal interest in having the Office address itself to the major problems confronting American education. No longer can the Office afford to dissipate its resources—including its cooperative research funds—on trivial projects which may be of passing interest to a few individuals but which do not deal with the main stream of American education. As Dr. McMurrin

[3] See Supplement 5, this volume—Editor.

said in his statement of May, 1961, to Congressman Fogarty's subcommittee of the House Committee on Appropriations:[4]

> The task facing the leaders of American education is to so organize and administer our educational institutions that the best interests of every individual will be served and that this process will at the same time contribute to the fundamental quality of our culture and add genuine strength to our national character. We must make sure that the maximum cultivation of the individual's intellectual, moral, artistic, and spiritual capacities that make of him a genuinely free person yields also the protection and perpetuation of those institutions that are essential to a free society.
>
> The schools should not be expected to do everything. Their primary task is the achievement and dissemination of knowledge and the cultivation of the intellect. It is only when this task is firmly established as the central purpose of a school that it will produce effectively those results in personal and civic character that we rightly expect of it.

Let us never forget that the ultimate aim of American education—including all of our experimenting with the curriculum—is the development of individuals whose personal competence and commitment are dedicated to the general welfare of free men in a free society, and to the strength of this nation as the responsible leader of the free world.

[4] Hearings before the Subcommittee of the Committee on Appropriations, House of Representatives, 87th Congress, 1st Sess. Subcommittee on Departments of Labor and Health, Education, and Welfare and Related Agencies Appropriations. John E. Fogarty, Rhode Island, Chairman.
Comments on the Present Condition of American Education, p. 5.

THE ROLE
OF GOVERNMENT

part

vii

Senator Randolph and Representative Thompson tell with engaging frankness about the problems of getting educational legislation passed. They and their colleagues must interpret the common will before they can act. If common will is to be anything more than common apathy, the public must know what the problems are, why they are important, and what can be done about them. People who are concerned with the making of public policy in education will find their addresses instructive.

Dr. Fuller speaks of the responsibility of state and local governments. If we are to maintain our basic policy of local control, the communities must assume their share of the responsibility.

29 ❊ THE ROLE OF CONGRESS IN CURRICULUM DEVELOPMENT
Frank Thompson, Jr.,
United States Representative, New Jersey

It is a great pleasure for me to be able to participate in this conference, and I am sincerely honored to appear in the company of such a distinguished group of educators, scientists, and statesmen.

I must confess at the outset that when I received the invitation to participate I was tempted to depart from the precise subject of the conference's concern and discuss in detail a subject with which I have been very closely concerned—the legislative struggle to provide Federal aid for education. Had I yielded to this temptation I might have been able to give you some insights into the legislative process and some idea of the many forces and counterforces that acted upon members of Congress during their consideration—or perhaps lack of consideration—of President Kennedy's school bill. I might even have chided you—that is, the generic "you," teachers and educators—for not making a greater individual effort to have your voices heard. It was a tantalizing thought, but I resisted.

I have been asked to discuss the role of the national legislature—specifically, the viewpoint of the House of Representatives—with respect to curriculum experimentation. Phrased this way, my assignment really amounts to an exercise in abstract theory. The House acts as a "body" in a metaphysical sense only. To think of the House as having a role ignores the fact that it is composed of 437 members having different backgrounds and predispositions, and responding to different influences. Even among those standing together on a given proposition, there may be as many different points of view represented as there are voters. My personal beliefs as to the responsibilities of Congress in this area might even be shared by a considerable number of my colleagues, but I suggest to you that with curriculum experimentation, as with many other subjects of national importance, there is likely to be an awesome disparity between what Congress "ought" to do and what can actually be accomplished through the political processes.

Let me interject one thought at this point. Don't be thrown off by my use of the words "political processes." I have often deplored the fact that education becomes entangled with politics, but to some extent it is unavoidable and even necessary. A wide variety of interests is represented in Congress, and it is the function of the legislative process to arrive at some synthesis of these interests. What I have deplored is the type of disingenuous partisanship that is often displayed when major legislation comes to the Congress from the White House.

A proper discussion of what *might* be accomplished in Congress would probably require individual analysis of each legislator and a good deal of speculation after that. Perhaps I can serve best in this program, therefore, by attempting to give you my *personal* views as to where congressional interest might be focused and my own assessment of what it may be possible to accomplish.

Although any suggestion of congressional interest in what is being taught in in our schools is likely to stir up complaints against "Federal interference," there is very frequently a vital relationship between school curricula and subjects that are of undisputed Federal concerns. The most dramatic contemporary example of this relationship, I suppose, is the connection between the teaching of mathematics, engineering, and science, and the requirements of national defense. Congress gave express recognition to this relationship in the National Defense Education Act of 1958:

The Congress hereby finds and declares that the security of the nation requires the fullest development of the mental resources and technical skills of its young men and women. . . . The defense of this nation depends upon the mastery of modern techniques developed from complex scientific principles. . . . The national interest requires . . . that the Federal Government give assistance to education for programs which are important to our defense.

The same sort of relationship exists in more subtle measure with respect to such areas of Federal interest as unemployment, juvenile delinquency, health, and even cultural development. Thus, questions of Federal interference aside, a congressional committee concerned with one of these subjects would not, in my opinion, be overextending its authority by expressing an interest in related elements of school curricula.

Let me suggest some possible lines of inquiry.

Unemployment

Automation is a fact of economic life, and, before long, a relatively few machines will be doing work that was previously done by numberless humans. How will general school curricula have to be adapted to meet such technological changes? What will we require in the way of vocational curricula? Entirely new skills may have to be developed during the student's formative years to prepare him for a world in which cybernetics may have replaced industrial relations as an important branch of learning. Some reassessment of curricula may even be required in view of the increased leisure time that will come with automation.

Juvenile delinquency

The House of Representatives recently passed a bill authorizing the Secretary of Health, Education, and Welfare to assist the states in experimenting with methods for controlling and preventing juvenile delinquency. How can school curricula be developed to attain these ends? Can potential or incipient delinquency be identified in the early school years? If it can be, should there be special curricula for such children?

Cultural development

In many areas—New York City, for example—the educational progress of children of immigrants or non-English speaking citizens may be hindered by their unfamiliarity with American culture. Can this problem be solved by changes in school curricula? I understand that the Higher Horizons program in the New York schools is presently concerned with this very problem.

Other areas of curriculum development appropriate for congressional inquiry might include educational television, university extension education, and foreign student and teacher exchange programs. Indeed, the range of potential inquiry is limited only by one's imagination.

Another possible focal point for congressional interest is suggested by Mr. Paul R. Hanna's recommendation for the establishment of a national commission for curriculum research and development. Such a commission would supplement and support other efforts in this field by conducting basic research projects and making the findings available to public and private groups concerned with education. Although Mr. Hanna proposed a nongovernmental agency, privately financed, such a commission might well be created by act of Congress, thus giving it official recognition and status.

While contemplation of the *potential* might well stir the academic blood, politicians are likely to be much less sanguine about curriculum experimentation. Education wanders in the halls of Congress like a sacred cow. It is surrounded by as many taboos as mother and the home, and many congressmen feel that to lay a hand on its wrinkled flank is to risk political perdition.

Furthermore, a congressman's vote on any particular proposal may be influenced by many different factors. He may have a burning faith in the merit or lack of merit of the idea proposed. He may be subject to the pressures of a strong lobby. He may reflect strong feeling, pro or con, among his constituency. He may trade his vote for support on a completely different proposal in which he has a particular interest. The sponsor of the bill may be a close friend or a bitter enemy. Or he may just be afraid to give a potential campaign opponent any opportunity to make fun of him before the voters. You can imagine what the reaction might be in an unreconstructed rural area if a skillful candidate commented derisively on his opponent's vote to spend 5 million dollars for experimentation in foreign language curricula. It is likely that a good part of the audience would think of Paris, France, only as a place where the boys went to sin when World War I was over.

Like it or not, these are the kinds of realities that must be taken into account when one considers the possibility of accomplishing something in Congress. The very title of this conference—National Conference on Curriculum Experimentation—would be likely to put many members on their guard, if they were not already predisposed because of religious issues or some notions of Federal "control." "Experimentation" suggests newness, and novelty always breeds controversy. Furthermore, if a proposal to create a national commission did not immediately raise the suspicions of the states'-righters, it would very likely be received with obdurate boredom, since every session of Congress sees dozens of bills to create national commissions. Only last week the House dealt a bloody death to a bill to create a Federal advisory council on the arts—and who can really be opposed to the arts?

This is not pure speculation on my part, and I would like to give you a case study to prove my point. Early in 1961 the administration's school bill was introduced in both the House and the Senate. The general scheme of the proposal was that the Federal government would make grants to the states to be used, for the most part, for teachers' salaries and school construction. A complex allocation formula was worked out, and the states were, with one exception, left free to use these funds for the stated purposes in whatever percentages they desired. Section 109 of the bill was entitled "Special Educational Projects." I think it would be worth while to read this section:

Each state education agency shall set aside from the sums allocated to it . . . an amount equal to 10 per centum of the sums so allotted to it for the fiscal year beginning July 1, 1961, for paying part of the costs of pilot, demonstration or experimental projects of local educational agencies designed to meet public school programs or to develop or evaluate public school programs of a special or unique nature, including but not limited to:

1. Remedial or special instructional programs or services for pupils having special language or adjustment problems;

2. Programs or services for adapting curriculums to the needs of deprived or disadvantaged pupils;

3. Programs or services for pupils from in-migrant or unusually mobile families;

4. Programs for coordinating the school system planning and programs in the area served by the local education agency, with the planning and programs of other public or private nonprofit agencies dealing with problems related to the alleviation of the same deteriorated or depressed areas and of the families and children residing therein;

5. Programs for developing new types of elementary or secondary instruction or programming;

6. Programs for developing multipurpose use of elementary and secondary school facilities;

7. Programs to stimulate improvements in construction, design or location of elementary and secondary school facilities;

8. Programs to encourage and stimulate educational excellence, including programs for exceptionally gifted children.

One other section of the bill should be mentioned at this point. Under the provisions of Section 110, a state making application for an allotment was required to set forth the criteria and procedures it would use in approving local special educational projects coming within Section 109.

The enumerated projects in Section 109 quite clearly included curriculum experimentation in a wide range of subjects, and I think that most people would agree that the types of projects mentioned are most desirable and necessary. Such projects, in my view, are to the field of education what basic research is to the sciences. This section of the bill would have enabled local school districts to initiate and maintain projects that might otherwise have failed for lack of funds. Some sixty-six million dollars would have been available for these purposes annually had the bill passed in its original form.

Despite these noble purposes, Section 109 quickly became a subject of controversy. A few minor imperfections were pointed out by those in favor of the proposal. For instance, there was some suggestion that the enumeration of certain projects would act to exclude other projects; one state official suggested that it should be made clear that state agencies as well as local agencies might engage in such projects. Then more serious objections were raised. Some said that the bill should merely *permit* the states to use 10 per cent of their allotment for special projects rather than *require* them to do so. Others said that it appeared that the Federal government would be approving and disapproving these projects. For these reasons, Section 109, it was argued, was inconsistent with Section 103, which was an express prohibition against Federal interference. Those in favor of Section 109 suggested means of satisfying these objections. We would, as the Senate did in the bill they passed, make the 10 per cent permissive, and state clearly that the projects were subject to the approval of the states only. The chairman of the House subcommittee that held hearings on the bill repeatedly indicated his desire to delete Section 109 entirely, and thus make the bill a "states' rights" measure from start to finish.

These were only the objections that were raised publicly—the respectable objections. Others came out in the infighting. For example, there was some Southern opposition to Section 109 because it was felt that it might result in special projects for Negroes. I even heard one member object on the grounds that Section 109 would result in Civil Service status for teachers. I am still unable to fathom the arcane logic behind that one.

As a result of these pressures and the desires of the proponents of the bill to avoid any suggestion of Federal control or interference, Section 109 was deleted from the bill, never to reappear in any of the subsequent proposals.

The fate of Section 109—if not the fate of the school bill itself— dramatically highlights the chief obstacle to far-reaching legislative action with respect to curriculum experimentation—that is, the bugbear of Federal control or Federal interference. It is my personal belief that the argument is, for the most part, an appeal to a rather primitive, unthinking emotional reaction. This is especially so when it is used against such proposals to provide aid for school construction or teachers' salaries as were found in the administration's bills. Indeed, if the question could be discussed rationally, I believe that many people would agree that some type of Federal involvement might even be desirable. One need only refer to statistics showing the number of young men rejected for military service for failure to pass the intelligence examination, to build a case for nationally established minimum requirements in achievement and curricula.

In fairness, I must admit it is understandable that one who is seriously worried about Federal control might be especially concerned when it comes to *revising* curricula. The typical argument—and I have literally hundreds of letters in my files to bear this out—is that we don't want some bureaucrat in Washington telling us what our children should be taught. But however one feels about the merits of this argument, it is an argument that must be contended with by anyone who would have Congress take an active and comprehensive role in curriculum experimentation.

It is true that agencies of the Federal government have, with the blessings of Congress, made progress in this field. Dr. Bowen C. Dees of the National Science Foundation and Mr. A. Bruce Gaarder of the Office of Education have already given you some idea of the extremely important work that is being done. The National Defense Education Act is itself testimony to the possibility of overcoming the control objection. I would suggest, however, that it may be somewhat easier to gain Congressional acceptance for programs concerned with scientific and language curricula than it would for programs concerned with the social sciences, history, and the humanities. Linguistics, mathematics, and the physical sciences are much more readily thought of as objective disciplines, and consequently there is less fear of brainwashing than there is with respect to the interpretive studies. Furthermore, as I indicated earlier, the relationship between the sciences, especially, and national defense, is dramatic and appealing. But, as Dr. Dees has indicated in his remarks, even the National Science Foundation is extremely sensitive to "the tradition of local control of our schools," and has promulgated what he called "rules of the game" to avoid encroachment upon this tradition.

What, then, *can* be done in Congress to further the cause with which this conference is concerned?

The first and easiest answer is to continue to encourage the work of the National Science Foundation and the Office of Education. This task should be undertaken by the legislative committees that have responsibilities in these areas. It should not be left to the appropriations committee, where scrutiny of course development and curriculum experimentation programs is accomplished by challenging the budget items for these purposes. This sort of scrutiny may be very necessary, but it is an imperfect means of improving the substantive content of such programs. Consider, for example, the appropriations committee hearings last spring on the National Science Foundation's budget. When the subject of course-content improvement came up, the committee members seemed most concerned with the costs of putting together a new physics textbook and the possible windfall that might result to private publishing companies who would save the costs of developing

The role of government

new materials. This is entirely appropriate for that committee, but it should not be the sole evidence of Congressional interest. A legislative committee concerned with the substantive content of this program, for instance, might well conclude that it was desirable to provide this sort of indirect subsidy to book publishers. It could have the dual effect of giving wider distribution to new ideas and of eliminating powerful oppositions from publishers who, because of the costs involved, might otherwise be reluctant to see new materials developed. The development of scientific curricula and the NSF's work in this area should be the subject of completely separate hearings by the science and astronautics committee. Similarly, the education and labor committee, of which I am a member, might take a greater interest in comparable work being done by the Office of Education. Specific legislation would not be required. A demonstration of sympathetic interest by a powerful standing committee might serve the purpose equally well.

This suggests the second function that Congress can perform: that is, to provide a basis for promoting curriculum experimentation by conducting studies, by providing a public forum for those who are most informed, and by directing public attention to the need for such programs. The mere introduction of legislation provides a rallying point for supporters of a certain viewpoint, and there is generally very little opposition to holding hearings or conducting staff studies even in areas where there is no hope of enacting legislation. Hearings provide an ideal means of collecting the most recent and informed thinking on a subject, and of familiarizing both the Congress and the public with the issues and personalities that are involved. By conducting special studies, our committees can provide raw information that may not be readily available elsewhere. For example, one of the subcommittees of the House education and labor committee leaves this week for the Soviet Union to study the system of higher education in that country. This project could produce extremely valuable source material for those educators who are engaged in developing college curricula.

I sincerely hope that I have not painted too pessimistic a picture of the role of Congress in curriculum experimentation. At least, I am confident that it is not an unrealistic one. The proponents of worthy legislation soon learn that the legislative process is infinitely more complex than a reading of Article I of the Constitution might indicate. They learn also that to accomplish worthy ends they must be fully attuned to both the complexities and the realities of that process. The national government has been involved in education since the beginning of American history, but progress comes slowly. New ideas may have to be sold, resold, and sold again, before enough support is mustered to put them in the statute books. More than ten years ago, for example, Congress passed legislation providing for financial aid to school districts that were overcrowded because of unusual Federal activity in the vicinity. That was Federal aid to education. In the following decade, many proposals were introduced to broaden Federal assistance. Only a month ago the latest of these was defeated in the House of Representatives. But throughout this time we have compiled a substantial record, and we have conveyed our message to a public that is beginning to respond in force. Curriculum experimentation may be anathema to many congressmen today, and so the role of Congress may be limited at present. But those of us who favor such programs—those of us who believe that a dynamic and enlightened system of education is essential, not only to our physical security but also to the preservation and growth of our culture—are confident of ultimate success, and confident it won't be long in coming.

30 ❀ THE ROLE OF GOVERNMENT IN EDUCATION
Jennings Randolph, *United States Senator, West Virginia*

It is doubtful that anyone in this room is unfamiliar with the famous declaration of the Ordinance of 1787, in which the Congress of the Confederation stated that:

Religion, morality, and knowledge, being necessary to good government and the happiness of mankind, schools and the means of education shall forever be encouraged.

Since that time there has been a steadily increasing involvement of the Federal government in education, a participation which now embraces every major department of the executive branch and every level of education from elementary school to postdoctoral research. Since 1777, when the national government initiated instruction of military personnel, there have been some forty-five major programs enacted in aid to specialized and general education as well as research.

In the Eighty-seventh Congress alone, sixteen different measures involving substantial Federal assistance to educational, scientific, and cultural affairs were either acted upon by one of the bodies of Congress or reported by a Congressional committee. These ranged in scope from the School Assistance Act of 1961, offering aid for school construction and teachers' salaries, which was passed by the Senate with a vote of forty-nine to thirty-four, to the very constructive measures introduced in the House by Representative Frank Thompson, which would have established a Federal advisory council on the arts and a system of state grants for the establishment of development programs in the arts.

There is no question, therefore, that the Federal role in education, and in related scientific and cultural activities, is a massive and diverse one. Nor is there any question in my mind but that this role is amply justified by the "general welfare" clause of the Constitution, the intent of the founders, and the needs of modern society.

There will doubtless continue to emerge from some quarters—at the occasion of every Federal advance in this area—the claim that education is solely a state and local responsibility and that Federal aid inevitably leads to Federal "control." This cliché, and the regrettable religious controversy were, of course, the chief obstacles to enactment of general aid-to-education legislation in the House this session. Regardless of how outworn the argument and how completely the history of such legislation fails to substantiate the fears of Federal control, it still carries a strong appeal to many. Apparently, however, the opponents of general aid to education are able to quell their anxieties concerning Federal control when the issue is one of aid to so-called Federally "impacted" areas—many of which are communities that have lobbied intensively in Washington to acquire the Federal installations that are now presumed to be such a burden.

However, this is secondary to the issue on curriculum experimentation—a topic that is central not only to this conference, but also to the future of the American educational system. As Professor Robert Ulich of Harvard stated a decade ago:

Prolongation of school age is in itself not a blessing, but may even be a curse to civilization unless there goes together with the prolongation a revolutionary rethinking of the total program and a restructuring of the total educational system from the secondary school upwards.

I would concur with Professor Ulich's statement as far as it goes, but I would extend this injunction to the elementary school as well.

The need for such "rethinking" and "restructuring" was recently dramatized for me when I encountered a reference to a study of elementary school geography conducted by John D. McAulay of Pennsylvania State University. Professor McAulay discovered that over the twenty-year period covered by his inquiry, there was a lag of ten years between the formulation of new generalizations by professional geographers and the acceptance of such principles in the textbooks; there was an additional lag of a decade before these materials were introduced in the public school curriculum.

If this condition still prevails—as it doubtless does in many, if not most, school systems despite the greater articulation between university scholars and public school teachers—it would point toward very serious limitations in our traditional methods of local and state determinations of curriculum. And it becomes a "clear and present danger" to the function of public education when it is viewed in the light of such a comment as that of Dr. Bentley Glass regarding the doubling time of scientific knowledge as approximately ten years.

It would be reasonable to conjecture, also, that in such fields as physics and the life sciences—where, I believe, the growth of knowledge has been particularly rapid in recent decades—this lag between discovery and the diffusion of new principles is even greater than in geography.

Even such presumably reliable absolutes—in the minds of some—as the teaching of English and the classical languages seem to be not immune to the impact of new knowledge and new insights regarding the process of learning. Still, I am informed, the significant developments of descriptive grammar and scientific linguistics of the past few decades have as yet impinged but little upon elementary and secondary teaching of English.

And consider this statement regarding the teaching of classical languages, from the Committee on Secondary Schools of the American Council of Learned Societies (*ACLS Newsletter,* vol. 9, no. 9, p. 9, November, 1958):

With respect to the classics, the panel agrees with the Steering Committee of the Foreign Language Program of the Modern Language Association that "an ancient language can be learned most efficiently if a modern foreign language has first been approached as speech" and therefore recommends that, contrary to practice, a modern language be studied before Greek or Latin.

This view would probably be considered rank heresy by most teachers of Greek and Latin today, and most assuredly by my own Latin teacher of forty years ago.

I regret that I was not able to attend your earlier sessions and hear the reports on some of the curriculum experiments that are in progress throughout the country. This is a seminal and immensely exciting field and one which holds much for the future of American education.

It is a field to which the Congress is not insensitive in its own deliberations on aid to education, though, in view of the deletion by the House education and labor committee of the provisions of Senate *1021* for curriculum experimentation, perhaps I had best qualify that statement. My very able Congressional colleague, Representative Thompson, has the burden of explaining the House actions, and I shall therefore restrict my comments to the functioning of the Senate Committee on Labor and Public Welfare and its Subcommittee on Education.

In passing, it may be of interest to you to learn that among the nine members of our Subcommittee on Education there are three of us who have had experience in teaching: Senator Wayne Morse of Oregon, the Chairman, who has had a distinguished background as a professor of law, and was a former law student and professor at the University of Minnesota; Senator Ralph Yarborough of Texas, who was an instructor for several years in the public schools of that state; and I, who taught public speaking and journalism for a number of years at Davis and Elkins College, West Virginia, and at Southeastern University in Washington. It may fairly be stated, therefore, that, in addition to including other able and highly educated members, the subcommittee has a substantial proportion of members with the professional background for receptivity to the problems of our educational system, the community of scholars, and the teaching profession.

Regarding the more specific question of curriculum experimentation, we of course incorporated into the School Assistance Act of 1961 provisions prescribing that each state set aside 10 per cent of its allotment for this purpose and for other special projects.

However, more directly related and heavily oriented toward curriculum questions is the National Defense Education Act, which was extended by the Congress for two years. The principal function of this program was and is to strengthen the curriculum, particularly in the areas of science, mathematics, and foreign languages. During the Senate committee hearings on this measure in May, 1961, much testimony was devoted to curriculum problems, with considerable emphasis upon the need to broaden the curriculum support to include American history, government, economics, and sociology.

It is unfortunate that Federal assistance has not been extended to these areas, but that is largely the result, in this instance, I believe, of the initial justification of the bill in terms of the limited conception of national defense. Though Federal support for a strengthened curriculum in other subjects is just as essential to the long-term security and development of America as the development of physics or foreign-language teaching, it is more difficult to justify such support in terms of immediate national defense needs.

This brings me to the larger question of Federal support throughout the structure of knowledge and through all the modern branches of inquiry. Though not immediately bearing upon curriculum problems, this question most assuredly has long-range implications for such a conference as this.

Perhaps the best index of Federal activity in this field is given in the *Federal Funds for Science* bulletin number 9, published by the National Science Foundation. Total funds for research in all sciences—and this refers to research only, not research and *development*—in the fiscal year 1959 is recorded as 1.39 billion dollars. The physical sciences, as would be expected, are the largest recipients, to the amount of seven hundred and sixty-five million dollars; the life sciences follow with four hundred and twenty million dollars; the social sciences with thirty-one million dollars; and the psychological sciences with twenty-four million dollars. "Other sciences," a category including space sciences, operations research, etc., received one hundred and fifty million dollars.

For the fiscal year 1961, there is an estimated 2.3 billion dollars, the figures not yet having been completely tabulated for an increase of approximately 65 per cent. The physical sciences received the bulk of the increase with a total amount of approximately 1.5 billion dollars; the life sciences, .68 billion dollars; the psychological sciences, .4 billion dollars; the social sciences, .4 billion dollars; and "other sciences," .3 billion dollars. Presumably, the category of space sciences, in view of the increased activity in this area, is no longer tabulated in "other sciences."

If you will bear with me while I relate a few more figures, I would like to extend the implications of these remarks as they apply to universities and the academic community. Of the total Federal funds obligated to research in the fiscal year 1960, approximately 39 per cent was devoted to basic research, that is, the type of research directed toward the increase of knowledge within a particular field without reference to the practical application of such knowledge. The physical sciences averaged 31 per cent basic research funds; the life sciences, 34 per cent; the psychological sciences, 41 per cent; and the social sciences, 24 per cent. In comparison with the investment of private industry in basic research (perhaps 5 to 8 per cent of its total research and development expenditures), this represents, of course, an extremely high ratio, and is probably sufficient to maintain an adequate "capital reserve" in scientific knowledge.

Of the total Federal funds obligated to basic research in the fiscal year 1960, 44 per cent was distributed to educational institutions, 30 per cent to Federal agencies, 14 per cent to profit organizations, and 12 per cent to foundations and other groups. Many university administrators are, of course, delighted by this distribution. Yet I suggest that the very fact of this Federal cornucopia holds threatening implications for the balanced development of knowledge within our academic community and ultimately for the intellectual and cultural life of America.

You ladies and gentlemen, who live more intimately with the problem than I, doubtless know that no Federal grant covers the full cost of research, and even less so when it is distributed on some sort of matching basis. The difference between the Federal grant and the actual cost of research must, therefore, be drawn from other sources of university revenue. With the heavy preponderance of Federal funds going to the physical and life sciences, this consequently means an inevitable weakening of support by the universities themselves of the social sciences, the psychological sciences, and the humanities—those stepchildren of a modern industrial society which have traditionally carried a major share of the burden of transmitting our cultural heritage from one generation to the next.

Acknowledging that the bare figures are not an adequate index of the proportion of research activity among the various fields, because of the inordinate expense of so much of the research in the physical and biological sciences as compared to the psychological and social sciences, there still exists a disproportionate emphasis on the former. This imbalance is, of course, accentuated by the exigencies of national security, but it is not created by them. It stems primarily from a shortsighted utilitarian cast of our society. And with regard to Congressional resistance toward Federal support of the social sciences, it emerges partly from the uninformed suspicion on the part of some members of Congress that the social scientists "want to tell us how to live."

Both of these problems must be addressed by the academic community. We cannot long skimp on behavioral studies and the humanities without soon feeling the effects in the tone and quality of life in America. The correction of such imbalances cannot be initiated by the Congress, for we do not possess the expert, the professional and detailed knowledge of where the inadequacies exist. The initiative for action of the sort implied must come from the academic, scientific, and school spokesmen.

I have seen some of the reports of the work conducted under grants from the National Science Foundation by the Biological Sciences Curriculum Study at Boulder, Colorado. This valuable work fully justifies the statement by your chairman, Dr. Paul Rosenbloom, that "a modest program conceived with imagination may be more valuable than a much more costly program of a routine nature." Such studies, conducted by the other major scientific and academic societies as well, should lead to the sort of "rethinking" and "restructuring" of which Professor Ulich spoke.

But it would seem to me that we would still need some agency in the nature of a national advisory council on education to bring these findings into relation to one another, and through advice and persuasion give more rigorous attention to a coherent curriculum that meets certain national minimal standards. Of course, I am aware of the vigilance with which state and local authorities guard their rights in the field of curriculum planning. And I do not suggest that these rights be overridden by any national authority. However, it does seem to me that the national scientific and academic societies and the Federal government have a responsibility to bring the local agencies—through every voluntary means possible—up to national standards consistent with the needs of a rapidly changing technology and the increase in scientific knowledge. I would hope that the relevant Congressional committees might receive the benefit of your counsel and that of your respective professional societies in the continuing future. For, although the record of

Congress on educational legislation this past session was hardly encouraging, the issue is not closed and I can assure you that many of us are determined to achieve affirmative action in the future.

In closing, I would refer to a general curriculum problem and one which embraces many of the more detailed issues of your conference—that is the need for the attainment of a point of view which can encompass the new and altered scope of change in life. This, I believe, is the central task of the schools today. One aspect of this problem was discussed by the eminent Austrian theoretical physicist, Hans Thirring, in his article "Education for the Age of Science" in the *Bulletin of the Atomic Scientists* in September, 1959. Dr. Thirring expressed the hope that there might be included in our primary and secondary school curriculum an "ABC of elementary wisdom."

We have conveniently assumed that wisdom is the peculiar attribute of age. In this respect we have shown little advance over the doctrine of the Athenian philosopher, Solon, who taught that wisdom is to be achieved only through suffering—possibly because our traditional education has forced men to suffer before achieving wisdom. Dr. Thirring believes that this need not be. He writes:

According to the definition of wisdom which I am proposing, even a young person, driven by all the passions and impulses of his age, and without being a marvel of virtue or self-sacrifice, might be called wise if he fulfills these conditions:

First, to possess the knowledge and good will for a better understanding of, and insight into, himself and his fellow men.

Second, to be able to assign the proper values to the various human issues, duties, and responsibilities.

Third, to be trained to understand man's natural inclination to overestimate the issues lying within the range of his limited mental perspective.

These may seem ambitious aims to establish for primary and secondary schools, but I would venture to say that if the foundation for such a perspective is not laid during the relatively flexible and plastic years of youth, it is seldom achieved thereafter. There are few of us who radically alter our intellectual and spiritual garments after passing into adulthood.

Now, this is not to suggest that the schools should merely attempt to inculcate a set of socially acceptable and humanitarian attitudes. Far be it from that. The kind of wisdom, the kind of excellence, which our society calls for now is not to be achieved by shortcuts or "life adjustment courses." On the contrary, the quality of mind most in need today is that which is fostered by discipline in the basic methods of inquiry and techniques of problem solving. Only when a student feels at home with the basic structure of investigative methods and problem solving will he welcome the challenge of novel conditions and achieve competency in meeting them. I would suggest, therefore, that we attempt to break through the ancient argument of "student-centered" versus "subject-matter-centered" teaching. The "problem" embraces student, subject-matter, and—I might add—teacher, as well.

In its practical applications this should mean that we would teach science as a *process* of inquiry rather than as the products of inquiry; we would teach art as the creation and appreciation of objects rather than as their identification and labeling; and we would teach history as a pattern of inquiry and a process in time rather than as an aggregate of facts.

Many people of late—laymen as well as scholars and teachers—have posed the problem in terms of a choice between quantity and quality, a choice between equality and excellence. We have no choice. We *must*—if our civilization is to survive and persevere—have both. We *must* have a generally informed citizenry capable of making intelligent decisions on matters of the public good. And we *must* have the highly trained specialists as well as the men and women of broad-gauge learning that our modern complex society demands.

In this regard, we may bear in mind the remark of Epictetus when commenting upon the fall of Athenian democracy as caused by the education of the few: "The state says that only free men will be educated; God says only educated men will be free."

31 THE ROLE OF GOVERNMENT IN CURRICULUM RESEARCH AND EXPERIMENTATION
Edgar C. Fuller* *Council of Chief State School Officers*

The papers presented at this conference have made it clear that our primary interest is how to achieve the changes in public school courses of study that are indicated by modern society and defined through curriculum research and experimentation. The roles of local, state, and national governments are my immediate subjects, but these roles cannot be considered alone. Most individual citizens, and public and private groups of all kinds, are interested in schools, and they express their interest privately as well as to governments. What happens to the curriculum is not the concern of only a few, but is properly the concern of everyone who cherishes the freedom of the individual and the welfare of the nation.

This conference has as its stated first purpose a definition of the national interest in curriculum research and development. Its second and third purposes deal with the exchange of information; and the fourth, with establishment of lines of communication among individuals and groups responsible for policies affecting curriculum changes. I would like to comment on these, with emphasis on systems of interaction that bring curriculum changes and the policies underlying them in public elementary and secondary education.

1. National interest

It seems to me that it is impossible to define the national interest in curriculum research and development, in a fundamental sense, any differently than one would define the local or the state interest in curriculum research and

* Edgar C. Fuller is Executive Secretary, Council of Chief State School Officers, Washington, D.C.

development. The best education for local purposes can scarcely be improved upon for state purposes, and good local and state education includes national responsibilities in education.

The three levels are so interdependent that I find myself unable to separate educational purposes according to the level of government. Most of these purposes are achieved, if at all, at the local level where teacher and pupil meet. Since teaching is not an exact science capable of exact measurement, the results of curriculum research and development must be implemented through a balanced curriculum in a setting almost as broad as society itself. Every individual and every group may influence what is taught. The national interest is served along with state, local, and individual interests when the teaching process is most effectively insuring the learning and personal development of the pupil.

I realize that there is a national interest in education. It has been indicated by Ralph Tyler, Paul Rosenbloom, and others. But we are dealing specifically with the impact of the curriculum on the pupil, not with the original *source* of the information that is taught. Let us assume the maximum attention to the national interest; let us assume increased activity by national groups of all kinds, and even by the Federal Government, to express the national interest at all levels of the curriculum; let us assume all conceivable broadening of subject matter necessary to insure the country's safety and, as Tyler put it, "to satisfy the public interest." What Tyler and Hanna and others are really talking about is how to implement at the local level changes in the curriculum that are believed to emphasize the national interest more than does the present curriculum. To a large extent I join with them in their purposes, but the establishment of curricular centralization and control through power, prestige, and money at the national level is not the way it seems to me the results should be accomplished. They should be, and can be, accomplished by giving some real attention to facilitating the process of curriculum reform at the local and state levels. Someone needs to go ahead to prepare the way to do this where the schools and the children are.

Either the local and state professional and legal authorities will evaluate and accept or reject curriculum changes, or national forces eventually will impose them. Most of us choose the local and state way. We should prepare ourselves to benefit from institutionalized curriculum research, and welcome it, while improving state and local administration provisions to earn state and local educational governments and professional leaders their right to the last word on what is used in the schools.

The teacher-pupil relationship is the point at which we evaluate the effectiveness of learning and of personal development in terms of numerous interrelated purposes, and this is the place where freedom must be maintained within a broad framework of policies. This is the place where neither government nor Madison Avenue should attempt to prescribe details. The national interest in education, like the state and local interest, requires better local and state provisions for education; better teachers, administrators and board members; and serious evaluation of outside efforts to establish new courses of study in local schools.

This is not to say that courses of study and methods of teaching, as well as administrative practices, organization, finance, and other external characteristics of school systems do not need to be modernized. They do. The point is that curriculum improvement calls for careful observance of procedures in locating and trying new proposals to make certain that changes bring more gain than loss. Efforts to achieve improvements should be intensified, but along lines that will bring constructive change, even though the results may appear to be slower than might be desired. Our system of education, which I believe history proves has been organized and operated in the national interest, requires more forbearance than national systems of education in other countries where educational content is prescribed and the public schools are centrally administered.

2. Interactions in curriculum development

The respective roles of local, state, and Federal government in curriculum development can be defined in general terms. At the local level, final judgments should be made on details of the content of teaching, and conditions conducive to effective teaching should be maintained in each classroom. But there are decisions of policy concerning support of the teaching process, financially and otherwise, that must be made at higher levels of government. The making of provisions to ensure, as far as possible, that the general purposes of education will be achieved for all pupils is a function of the state. The state has the responsibility for setting minimum standards of instruction as well as for housing, organization, finance, transportation of pupils, and all the *externa* that must be dealt with in order to have effective teaching.

The role of the Federal government should be primarily one of stimulation, assistance, and service, even when it pays part of the cost. This is more important in dealing with the curriculum than with the *externa*, because curriculum development is necessarily more local in nature than activities further removed from the teacher-pupil relationship. Curriculum changes that lie within the scope of their authority can be made quickly by local educators and school boards, but as we move to the county, the state, and the nation, curricular proposals from both private and public sources should become increasingly optional to those who teach in local schools.

What are the differences between the content of teaching and the necessary but external characteristics of educational administration? Consider the use of television in formal education. This is primarily an administrative innovation involving teaching methods. Educational television calls for more flexibility in buildings, time schedules, and staff assignments, along with changes in methods of teaching.

The real issues in educational television rarely revolve about content. The producers are usually glad to accept the content developed by teachers they trust. What pleases such teachers pleases them. Television producers naturally tend to emphasize the presentation of shows and perfection of production details, even though they may be sensitive to the educational content. They can scarcely be expected to understand fully the educational import of what appears on the television screen. Teachers in the schools, therefore, have special responsibilities concerning what to present on television, using it only when it is superior to other methods of presentation in terms of pupil

The role of government | 238

learning and personal development. They have a responsibility to accept or reject, on the basis of ends achieved in teaching rather than on administrative convenience.

Questions concerning the fundamental interactions between teachers and the public are also posed by our topic. Implementation of the results of curriculum research and experimentation should take place in full view of the fact that the public schools belong to the people. We surely can provide acceptable ways for anyone to enjoy a reasonable opportunity to assist in the improvement of what schools do. The basic criterion governing influence should be the extent to which proposed changes would help us to achieve the purposes of our system of education. This is not to say that the curriculum should be developed through popular votes of the electorate. Neither should what is taught be *unilaterally* determined by organized professional groups, academic specialists, right-wingers or left-wingers, career critics, special friends of the schools with axes to grind, commercial suppliers, philanthropists, publicists, politicians, interest groups such as business or labor, individuals willing to supply large funds to promote pet ideas, or even local, state, or national governments. Yet all these, and others, can be of assistance in the process.

The welfare of education requires that ways be found to discover and to use good ideas and practices from all sources. Even a crackpot whose ideas are usually impracticable may occasionally start a train of thought and action that will be useful in curriculum development. In Harold Benjamin's delightful satire *The Saber-Tooth Curriculum*, a major subject of the paleolithic curriculum was fresh-water fish-grabbing with the bare hands. When the glaciers melted and the rivers became muddy, the tribe almost starved. Then a queer character, long exiled for his eccentricities, made a crude net to catch fish. The old curriculum was designed strictly for living in a land of clear water; it remained for an eccentric to adjust the fresh-water curriculum enough to adapt fishing to muddy waters. Even some activities called curriculum research and experimentation are uncomfortably reminiscent of courses in fresh-water fish-grabbing with the bare hands, but the processing of these is the price of sifting possible contributions from all sources.

Curriculum innovators such as foundations, foundation projects, universities, and the Federal government will succeed best if they continue to recognize, as most have, the desirability of local selection among alternative proposals for curriculum changes. The interactions involved in convincing teachers are admittedly complex, but the challenge should be fully accepted as one of professional persuasion rather than prescription. Local and state officials who have legal power to prescribe should not abandon persuasion as soon as they suffer their first feelings of impatience. An early and complete involvement of teachers and administrators in experimentation for the purpose of improving their own work will usually make official acceptance a mere formality.

Those who would be innovators in this field, then, would do well to accept the full implications of our system of public education in regard to change. They should be prepared to submit their innovations, without seeking by salesmanship to establish acceptance before trial, to the crucible of practical testing in the teaching process at the local level. That which is good will take hold and grow, too slowly for the most impatient, but nevertheless fast enough so that teaching content and processes will improve.

The people have determined the framework of policy within which the professionals operate. The local board can, and occasionally does, alter the recommendations of the professionals and substitute ideas of its own. Most states use only a little of their undoubted legal power to prescribe curricula, thus preserving local freedom of choice. Since sputnik there has been much pressure on states to fix more academic requirements, especially in high schools, and the trend toward such requirements continues. But legal mandates do not always accomplish the desired results, even when specific subjects are required. A vague legal mandate, such as to teach the evils of alcohol, has little more effect than to leave the professionals to do what they will.

During the past decade the tempo of research and experimentation has increased, and so has acceptance of changes. There is an attitude of open-mindedness and willingness to try new content and new methods which in most schools has quickened curriculum adjustments. Nevertheless, prospective innovators are often frustrated unnecessarily by the lack of prompt and careful consideration of their proposals. It should be possible to improve conditions for implementing curriculum changes in ways that would be beneficial to all concerned. I shall mention one promising possibility in this direction, with a word on its governmental and professional background.

3. A more adequate process for making choices

All citizens outside the school must be fully accepted in one sense, and fully guarded against in another, in the development of curriculum in the schools. They are often far removed from the teaching process and their differing views often cancel each other. Every school administrator knows the tremendous pressures that can be brought directly at the local level to change the curriculum to fit special viewpoints.

The American people maintain some thirty-five thousand operating local school districts in fifty state systems of education over which the Federal government has no direct Constitutional authority in education. Federal Constitutional requirements which are applicable to the whole society make strong impacts, as in the case of school segregation, but state or local school systems need not accept Federal programs of education. Federally subsidized programs are optional, whether they are legally justified under the welfare clause of the Constitution or incidental to the exercise of other Federal powers.

Legal power for formal change of the curriculum is restricted to state governments, and to the local school boards, to the extent that they have powers delegated under state laws. Sweeping reforms have to be acceptable to both these legal authorities, and to some extent to the professionals in the school, although lesser changes can be achieved by professionals alone. Such decentralization seems to imply the responsibility to give all individuals and groups, public and private, full and fair opportunity to influence the curriculum, even while insisting that they must prove the worth of their ideas in terms of their impacts on pupils.

Can we not meet this responsibility better in the thousands of local school districts and in the fifty states? It seems to me that the sifting could be vastly facilitated at the local level by a widespread and planned combination of in-service education of teachers and programs of curriculum development. This has quite often been done, but organized curriculum reexamination has not become part of the teaching obligations of all or even a majority of teachers. It has never been given a real trial. Such a pattern could accelerate improvement within the framework of educational policy and experience, protecting against undue influence while improving opportunities for innovators to be heard.

When I say this challenge has never really been taken seriously, I mean that the administrative arrangements that would have to be made at the local level to facilitate curriculum change have never been supported on a wide scale. Of course, teachers are now overworked and lack time to organize and work on curriculum to the necessary extent. There would have to be a 10½- or 11-month school year, perhaps, for most teachers in a majority of districts. There would have to be administrative and clerical help and money for consultants from universities, from national curriculum groups, from other school systems, and elsewhere. Costs might increase 5 or even 10 per cent. For rural schools special arrangements would have to be made.

In such a program, the state department of education should properly exercise all administrative chores broader than those feasible for the local district, and in general it should facilitate the movement throughout the state. All prospective innovators, no matter how influential or ambitious, should be retained on a consultant basis and assured of prompt consideration. Modernization of the curriculum and the in-service training of teachers within such traditional American patterns of control should be more than worth the price.

Not long ago it was common practice to attempt to impose curricular changes upon teachers through inspection and supervision. Teachers resented this approach. They also resented the so-called experts who indulged in it. Teachers developed attitudes of resistance to innovations, even those proposed by state or local supervisors or superintendents who presumably had been teachers. It is interesting to note that whenever community pressure groups sought to use the schools for their special purposes, however, the supervisors and administrators joined the teachers in their reluctance to accept changes. Fortunately, both state and local inspection and supervision have been largely transformed into service and assistance to teachers in recent years, a trend that makes the combination of curriculum development and in-service training of teachers increasingly practicable.

Favorable developments in other directions make such action more feasible than it was a few years ago. For instance, recent programs of curriculum development have often brought teachers and specialists in subject matter and methods together in cooperative efforts. Such projects have been discussed in this conference. Well-planned action programs of this kind operate successfully in the present educational climate. The legal authorities are also involved, and thus problems of content, methods, and administration are beginning to be considered together. This paves the way for constructive change.

Another development favoring combination of curriculum improvement and in-service education at the local level is the discovery that new curriculum developments at a central place, or in a particular school, cannot be easily transferred to other schools where the teachers have not participated in the process. There is growing recognition that diligent but relatively gradual development of the curriculum, in terms of both content and method, is the most effective way to modernize it. For all their values, most university courses in education fail to improve substantially the actual work of teachers. Teachers should work more to improve their own teaching. Reexamination of the curriculum by teachers organized according to grade level or subject matter will draw consultants from universities and other sources of practical help, and at the same time provide a forum where innovators can be heard close to the point where their suggestions can be used.

Where the pattern of combining in-service education and curriculum development is followed, the legal agencies for education are likely to cooperate. This pattern should promote a more reasonable use of innovations, utilize lay and professional experts without permitting them to prescribe, and permit the more frequent adoption of ideas and programs from foundations, governmental agencies, scholars, scientists, teachers, and other citizens when they are suitable for use in the schools. The test of suitability should not be in the source of the ideas or practices, but rather in whether their adoption will facilitate learning. Local leadership, with state assistance, can open the way for cooperation in curriculum improvement from all sources, including public and private national sources, without violating the integrity of the teacher-pupil relationship.

4. Communications

The implications for communication among private individuals and groups concerned with curriculum research and development should be clear. There should be no barriers to communication that might prevent acceptance, after appropriate consideration and experimentation, of any innovations that deserve adoption. In this field, state departments of education are the largest comparatively unused resource. They represent the state, in which is centered the legal authority for public education. They are in constant communication with schools. They are gaining in professional stature, and will become, I believe, increasingly important in implementing improvements in public schools.

Local, state and federal policies

I would like to summarize by paraphrasing only slightly the adopted policies of the Council of Chief State School Officers which delineate the respective roles of local, state, and Federal governments in curriculum development. In other areas, especially finance, teacher qualifications, and other matters of administration, their respective responsibilities are of course different.

The local school administrative unit, which is legally more a political subdivision of the state than a part of municipal government, has primary responsibility to plan and operate the education program. Within its legal authority, it should exercise all functions necessary for the satisfactory operation of schools, *including determination of the nature and scope of the curriculum.*

The state is responsible for determining the extent and quality of the educational services to be provided by its foundation program of state aid to schools, and for assisting local boards of education to assume their responsibility to provide these and additional services. The primary function of the state department of education, in relation to local administrative units, is to provide educational leadership, planning, research, and advisory services.

The Federal government should provide educational services of such a character, and performed in such a manner, as to insure that the administration and operation of the education program in each state will remain the primary responsibility of the state. This requires that all Federal participation shall be conducted in cooperation with the regularly constituted state education agencies. The Federal government should furnish consultative services and should promote and carry on research in all major fields of education.

The criteria for establishment and change of the curriculum, so far as local, state and national governments are concerned, are being well met by the groups that have reported here. The Minnesota National Laboratory and the projects of the U.S. Office of Education, the National Science Foundation, the Carnegie Corporation, and others are not being criticized by implication. Rather, these, and others, find implementation their greatest problem, and this paper concerns facilitation of implementation. With a state-local system of the kind I have suggested, their frustrations would be lessened and the temptation to call on national power instead of persuasion would largely disappear. Then the refusal to accept unsuitable suggestions would no longer lay the schools open to the too common current charge that their teachers and administrators are old fogies when they do not blithely assume that whatever is new is better than what they have.

SUPPLEMENT ❧ INTRODUCTION

The materials in this supplement complete the materials presented formally at the conference in various ways.

We have included, following a list of contributors to this volume, a fairly complete listing of curriculum projects supported by various agencies as of December, 1961, and some recent information on "Project English."

This is followed by various proposals for national mechanisms for curriculum research and development, both governmental and non-governmental.

We have included a detailed description of the Minnesota National Laboratory and its activities as an illustration of what can be done on the state level.

Finally, we have included some pending legislation, and the President's message on education, transmitted to Congress in February, 1962.

SUPPLEMENT 1 ❧ THE CONTRIBUTORS TO THIS VOLUME

Harold B. Allen	Professor of English, *University of Minnesota,* and 1961 President, *National Council of Teachers of English*
Melvin W. Barnes	Superintendent of Schools, Portland, Oregon
Kenneth R. Beittel	Professor of Art Education, *Pennsylvania State University*
Carolyn E. Bock	Professor, Classics Department, *Montclair State Teachers College, Montclair, New Jersey*
David L. Clark	Associate Dean, College of Education, *Ohio State University.* Formerly, Director, Cooperative Research Program, *United States Office of Education*
Walter W. Cook	Dean, College of Education, *University of Minnesota*
Lee J. Cronbach	Professor of Education and Psychology, *University of Illinois*
Bowen C. Dees	Assistant Director for Scientific Personnel and Education, *National Science Foundation*
Luther H. Evans	Director, Project on Automation and Education, *National Education Association*
Gilbert C. Finlay	Professor of Education, College of Education, *University of Illinois*
Edgar C. Fuller	Executive Secretary, *Council of Chief State School Officers, Washington, D.C.*
A. Bruce Gaarder	Chief, Language Research Section, Language Development Branch, *United States Office of Education*

Supplement 1 | **244**

Eli Ginzberg	Professor of Economics and Director of Conservation of Human Resources, *Columbia University*
Arnold B. Grobman	Director, Biological Sciences Curriculum Study, *University of Colorado*
John H. Haefner	Professor of Social Studies Education, *State University of Iowa*
Marguerite V. Hood	Professor of Music Education, *University of Michigan*
Frederick H. Jackson	Executive Associate, *Carnegie Corporation of New York*
J. Boyer Jarvis	Special Assistant to the United States Commissioner of Education
Edwin Moise	James Bryant Conant Professor of Education and Mathematics, *Harvard University*
Paul R. O'Connor	Associate Chairman, Chemistry Department, *University of Minnesota*
Thornton Page	Professor of Astronomy, *Wesleyan University*, and Chairman, *AAAS Cooperative Committee on the Teaching of Science and Mathematics*
Edward C. Pomeroy	Executive Secretary, *American Association of Colleges for Teacher Education*
Jennings Randolph	United States Senator for West Virginia
Paul C. Rosenbloom	Professor of Mathematics, *Institute of Technology, University of Minnesota*, and Director, *Minnesota School Mathematics Center*
Rosedith Sitgreaves	Associate Professor of Education, *Teachers College, Columbia University*
Robert C. Stephenson	Executive Director, *American Geological Institute, Washington, D.C.*
Laurence E. Strong	Professor of Chemistry, *Earlham College, Richmond, Indiana*, and Director, *Chemical Bond Approach Project*
Frank Thompson, Jr.	Representative in Congress for New Jersey
Gordon B. Turner	Vice President, *American Council of Learned Societies*
Ralph W. Tyler	Executive Director, *Center for Advanced Study in Behavioral Sciences, Stanford, California*
William Van Til	Chairman, Department of Secondary Education, *New York University*

245 | *The contributors to this volume*

SUPPLEMENT 2 ✽ CURRICULUM PROJECTS SUPPORTED BY THE COOPERATIVE RESEARCH PROGRAM OF THE U.S. OFFICE OF EDUCATION
July 1, 1956–September 30, 1961

Project no.	Project title and duration	Investigator and location
009	A Block Teaching Project, Integrating Humanities and Social Science *September, 1957–August, 1959*	Arthur Kreisman *Southern Oregon College Ashland, Oregon*
011	A Program of Education for Alaska Natives *January, 1957–December, 1958*	Charles K. Ray *University of Alaska College, Alaska*
145*	Effects of a Comprehensive Opportunity Program on the Development of Educable Mentally Retarded Children *February, 1957–June, 1959*	Drexel Lange, Lloyd L. Smith, and James B. Stroud *Iowa State Department of Public Instruction Des Moines, Iowa*
275	Problems of Adjustment of Indian and Non-Indian Children in the Public Elementary Schools of New Mexico *August, 1957–July, 1960*	Miles V. Zintz *University of New Mexico Albuquerque, New Mexico*
297	The Identification and Classroom Behavior of Elementary School Children Each of Whom Is Gifted in at Least One of Five Different Characteristics *September, 1957–August, 1959*	Frederick B. Davis and Gerald S. Lesser *Hunter College New York, New York*
333	Development of Community Centered Programs in Junior Colleges *January, 1958–August, 1959*	James W. Reynolds *University of Texas Austin, Texas*
382*	Development of a Program for Educable Mentally Retarded Children in Rural Schools *April, 1958–September, 1959*	Philip A. Annas *Maine State Dept. of Education Augusta, Maine*
385	Vocational Education in Public Schools as Related to Social, Economic, and Technical Trends *June, 1958–November, 1959*	John K. Coster, Norbert J. Nelson, and Frank J. Woerdehoff *Purdue University Lafayette, Indiana*
403	A Project in the Teaching and Development of an Integrated Physics-Algebra Course at the Ninth-grade Level *April, 1958–March, 1959*	Alexander Calandra *Washington University St. Louis, Missouri*

* Projects marked with an asterisk are available on microfilm and in photocopy.

Project no.	Project title and duration	Investigator and location
454	The Development of a Conceptual System for Dealing with Problems of Curriculum and Instruction July, 1958–June, 1960	John I. Goodlad University of Chicago Chicago, Illinois
551	Teaching High School Students a Critical Approach to Contemporary National Issues December, 1958–June, 1962	Donald W. Oliver Harvard University Cambridge, Massachusetts
614	Effects of Special Training on the Achievement and Adjustment of Gifted Children March, 1959–August, 1960	Nellie D. Hampton Iowa State Teachers College Cedar Falls, Iowa
629	The Development of a Research Design to Investigate the Functional Understandings of Technicians as Bases for Curriculum Planning in Technical Education April, 1959–August, 1960	George L. Brandon Michigan State University East Lansing, Michigan
639	A Basic Research Program on Reading July, 1959–June, 1962	Harry Levin Cornell University Ithaca, New York
642	An Evaluative Study of Psychological Research on the Teaching of Mathematics March, 1959–June, 1959	Philip H. DuBois Washington University St. Louis, Missouri
647	Analysis of the Curricular Offerings in Several Independent Liberal Arts Colleges July, 1959–January, 1961	Earl J. McGrath Teachers College, Columbia University New York, New York
715	Evaluation and Follow-up Study of Thayer Academy's Summer Advance Study Program in Science and Mathematics July, 1959–June, 1960	William W. Cooley Harvard University Cambridge, Massachusetts
727	The Development of Mathematical Concepts in Children September, 1959–August, 1962	Patrick Suppes Stanford University Stanford, California
761	Self-Directed Study: An Experiment in Higher Education at the University of Colorado September, 1959–February, 1961	Howard E. Gruber University of Colorado Boulder, Colorado
816	Systematic Observation of Verbal Interaction as a Method of Comparing Mathematics Lessons December, 1959–June, 1961	E. Muriel J. Wright Washington University St. Louis, Missouri
896	Use of Case Histories in the Development of Student Understanding of Science and Scientists April, 1960–August, 1961	William W. Cooley Harvard University Cambridge, Massachusetts

Curriculum projects supported by the Cooperative Research Program

Project no.	Project title and duration	Investigator and location
922	A Comparison of Especially Designed Art Activities with Traditional Art Activities as Used with Mentally Retarded Children and Youth *June, 1960–September, 1961*	Norris J. Haring *University of Maryland* *College Park,* *Maryland*
923	Effects of Special Training on the Achievement and Adjustment of Gifted Children *May, 1960–January, 1962*	Nellie D. Hampton *Iowa State Teachers* *College* *Cedar Falls, Iowa*
969	Effectiveness of Educational Audiology on the Language Development of Hearing-handicapped Children *January, 1961–December, 1965*	Joseph L. Stewart *University of Denver* *Denver, Colorado*
1015	Training in Problem Solving *October, 1960–September, 1961*	Horacio J. A. Rimoldi *Loyola University* *Chicago, Illinois*
1020	Characteristics of Teachers Which Affect Students' Learning *August, 1960–October, 1962*	Paul C. Rosenbloom *University of* *Minnesota* *Minneapolis,* *Minnesota*
1038	Selection and Training Programs for Vocationally Talented Pupils *September, 1960–August, 1961*	W. Donald Walling *Rutgers University* *New Brunswick,* *New Jersey*
1090	Abilities of First-grade Pupils to Learn Mathematics in Terms of Algebraic Structures by Means of Teaching Machines *August, 1960–August, 1961*	Evan R. Keislar *University of* *California* *Los Angeles, California*
1193	An Evaluation of the Madison Project Method of Teaching Arithmetic in Grades 4, 5, and 6 *July, 1961–January, 1963*	William F. Bowin *New York State Education Department* *Albany, New York*
1449	Training in Problem Solving *October, 1961–November, 1962*	Joseph R. Devane and Horacio J. A. Rimoldi *Loyola University* *Chicago, Illinois*
"A"	The Development of Designs for Curriculum Research *September, 1959–January, 1960*	Jerome Bruner *Harvard University* *Cambridge,* *Massachusetts*
D-005	Experimental Teaching of Mathematical Logic to Talented Fifth and Sixth Graders *August, 1961–September, 1963*	Patrick Suppes *Stanford University* *Stanford, Colifornia*
D-009	Accelerated and Enriched Curriculum Programs for Academically-talented Students (Mathematics) *October, 1961–December, 1965*	Miriam L. Goldberg and A. Harry Passow *Teachers College,* *Columbia University* *New York, New York*

Project no.	Project title and duration	Investigator and location
D-022	A Modern Mathematics Program as It Pertains to the Interrelationship of Mathematical Content, Teaching Methods, and Classroom Atmosphere (The Madison Project) September, 1961–October, 1962	Robert B. Davis Syracuse University Syracuse, New York

SUPPLEMENT 3 ❋ CURRICULUM PROJECTS IN SCIENCE EDUCATION*

Supporting agency	Project title	Investigator and location
National Science Foundation	Elementary School Science Project	Stanley P. Wyatt & J. Myron Atkin University of Illinois Urbana, Illinois
National Science Foundation	Elementary School Science Project	Stephen P. Diliberto University of California Berkeley, California
National Science Foundation	Biological Sciences Curriculum Study	Arnold Grobman University of Colorado Boulder, Colorado
Atomic Energy Commission & Ford Foundation	Seconday School Biological Film Series	Robert S. Leisner American Institute of Biological Sciences Kansas City, Missouri
Harvard University	New Harvard Introductory Course in Biology	George Wald Harvard University Cambridge, Massachusetts
National Science Foundation	Chemical Education Material Study	J. A. Campbell Harvey Mudd College Claremont, California
Crown-Zellerbach Foundation & National Science Foundation	Chemical Bond Approach Project	Laurence E. Strong Earlham College Richmond, Indiana
Fund for the Advancement of Education	Education Program	Robert L. Silber American Chemical Society Washington, D.C.

* For further information on science education projects, see *Science Education News*, December, 1962, published by the American Association for the Advancement of Science, 1515 Massachusetts Avenue, N.W., Washington 5, D.C.

249 | Curriculum projects in science education

Supporting agency	Project title	Investigator and location
Manufacturing Chemists' Association	Manufacturing Chemists' Association Program	William E. Chace *Manufacturing Chemists' Assn.* *Washington, D.C.*
National Science Foundation	National Committee for Fluid Mechanics Films	Ascher H. Shapiro *Massachusetts Institute of Technology* *Cambridge, Massachusetts*
American Geological Institute	Teaching Resources Development Program of the American Geological Institute	Robert L. Heller *American Geological Institute* *Washington, D.C.*
National Science Foundation & Carnegie Corporation of New York	Suppes Arithmetic Project	Patrick Suppes *Stanford University* *Stanford, California*
National Science Foundation	Geometry Project	Newton S. Hawley *Stanford University* *Stanford, California*
Carnegie Corporation of New York, National Science Foundation, & University of Illinois	University of Illinois Arithmetic Project	David A. Page *1207 West Stoughton* *Urbana, Illinois*
Carnegie Corporation of New York	The Structural Arithmetic Project	Catherine Stern *12 W. 96th Street* *New York, New York*
Holzer Foundation, Sloan Foundation, U.S. Office of Education, & others	Madison Project	Robert B. Davis *Syracuse University* *Syracuse, New York*
None	Algebra for Grade 5	W. W. Sawyer *Wesleyan University* *Middletown, Connecticut*
Carnegie Corporation of New York	WFF'N PROOF Games and Mathematical Logic	Layman E. Allen *Center for Advanced Studies in Behavioral Sciences* *Stanford, California*
American Association for the Advancement of Science	Pilot Study on the Use of Special Teachers in Mathematics in Grades 4, 5, and 6	John R. Mayor *American Association for the Advancement of Science* *Washington, D.C.*
None	Ball State Teachers College Experimental Program	Charles Brumfiel *University of Michigan* *Ann Arbor, Michigan*

Supporting agency	Project title	Investigator and location
Carnegie Corporation of New York & School Mathematics Study Group	University of Maryland Mathematics Project	John R. Mayor *University of Maryland College Park, Maryland*
National Science Foundation	School Mathematics Study Group	E. G. Begle *Stanford University Stanford, California*
University of Illinois & Carnegie Corporation of New York	University of Illinois Committee on School Mathematics Project	Max Beberman *1208 West Springfield Urbana, Illinois*
College Entrance Examination Board & Carnegie Corporation of New York	Commission on Mathematics	Julius H. Hlavaty *College Entrance Examination Board New York, New York*
Ford Foundation & National Science Foundation	Committee on the Undergraduate Program in Mathematics	Robert J. Wisner *Michigan State University Oakland Rochester, Michigan*
National Science Foundation, Ford Foundation, Fund for the Advancement of Education, & Alfred P. Sloan Foundation	Physical Science Study Committee	Jerrold R. Zacharias *Educational Services Incorporated Watertown, Massachusetts*
American Institute of Physics & American Association of Physics Teachers	Education Projects in Physics	W. C. Kelly *American Institute of Physics New York, New York*
National Science Foundation	Commission on College Physics	Walter C. Michels *Bryn Mawr College Bryn Mawr, Pennsylvania*
Various industries and foundations of industries	The Science Manpower Project	Frederick L. Fitzpatrick *Teachers College, Columbia University New York, New York*

Ford Foundation grants: science and engineering program

Grant to	Purpose
California Institute of Technology Pasadena, California	To revise and update course in introductory college physics
Marine Biological Laboratory Woods Hole, Massachusetts	Postdoctoral program to train biologists in marine systematics
Case Institute of Technology	To improve performance as regional and national center of excellence in science and technology

251 | *Curriculum projects in science education*

Grant to	Purpose
Cornell University Ithaca, New York	For expansion of faculty and facilities
Stanford University Stanford, California	To strengthen advanced training in chemical engineering and materials science

National Science Foundation grants: science teaching equipment development program

Anthropology

Graphic Aids for Teaching Basic Anthropometry. Exact reproductions of human bones showing measurement points, slides depicting measurements of skeletal materials, inexpensive anthropometric instruments. College. June, 1962. R. F. G. Spier and Dale R. Henning, Department of Sociology and Anthropology, University of Missouri, Columbia, Missouri.

Kinship Models. Kit for three-dimensional models of kin groups, marriage systems, kin terminologies. College. April, 1962. Edward A. Kennard, Department of Anthropology, University of Pittsburgh, Pittsburgh 13, Pennsylvania.

Museum of Man: Basic Slide Collection for Anthropology Courses. Collection of 350 35-mm slides illustrating ethnographic materials, descriptive booklet. College. Completed. Jack Conrad, Department of Sociology and Anthropology, Southwestern at Memphis, Memphis, Tenn.

Biology

Models of Structural Relationships in Human Anatomy. Models of difficult-to-understand areas—larynx, inguinal canal, pineal region, brain. College, medical school. June, 1962. John Franklin Huber, Department of Anatomy, School of Medicine, Temple University, Philadelphia, Pa.

Teaching Aids for Embryology and Comparative Anatomy. Pig embryo, dissectible models of skulls. Secondary, college. December, 1962. Louis E. DeLanney, Department of Zoology, Wabash College, Crawfordsville, Indiana.

Individual Laboratory Kits for High School Biology. Fruit fly, bacteriology, cell study kits. Secondary. Completed. Norman Molomut and Leo Gross, Waldemar Medical Research Foundation, 16 Sintsink Drive, East Port Washington, Long Island, New York.

Working Model of Human Circulatory System. Elementary, secondary, college. Completed. Thomas I. Marx, Engineering Division, Midwest Research Institute, 425 Volker Boulevard, Kansas City 10, Missouri.

Student Ophthalmoscope. Elementary, secondary, college. Completed. Thomas I. Marx, Engineering Division, Midwest Research Institute, 425 Volker Boulevard, Kansas City 10, Missouri.

Students' Warburg and Other Respirometer Apparatus. Secondary, college. July, 1962. Thomas I. Marx, Engineering Division, Midwest Research Institute, 425 Volker Boulevard, Kansas City 10, Missouri.

Stereophotomicrography and Other Methods for Teaching Submacroscopic Anatomy. Techniques for preparing tissues to make 3-dimensional photographs showing relationships not observable with ordinary methods. College, medical school. July, 1962. T. Walley Williams, Department of Microanatomy, and Charles C. Boyer, Department of Gross Anatomy, Medical Center, University of West Virginia, Morgantown, West Virginia.

Laboratory Exercises for Study of Forest Microclimates. College. Completed.

Frank W. Woods, School of Forestry, Duke University, Durham, North Carolina.

X-ray Circuit Model. Secondary, college. Completed. Lloyd M. Bates, Department of Radiological Science, School of Hygiene and Public Health, Johns Hopkins University, 615 North Wolfe Street, Baltimore 5, Maryland.

Portable Direct-reading Transistorized Cardiotachometer with Photoelectric Sensor Unit. College, medical school. July, 1963. John M. Lagerwerff, 6960 Encino Avenue, Van Nuys, California. (Grantee: Rosemount Aeronautical Laboratories, University of Minnesota.)

Graphic Methods for Teaching Physiology. Functional models of respiratory system, circulatory system, muscle action, knee jerk, optic-nerve distribution, eyeball muscles; small-animal respirator. Secondary, college. May, 1962. Fred E. D'Amour, Department of Zoology, University of Denver, Denver, Colorado.

Biology Teaching Aids. Student kits in immunology and biochemistry; experiments in mammalian genetics and transplantation. Secondary, college. June, 1962. Freddy Homburger, Bio-Research Institute, Inc., Cambridge 41, Massacusetts.

Inexpensive Electronic Equipment for Quantitative Physiological Studies. Kits and assembled models of stimulator, amplifier for bioelectric responses, paper-drive recorder, electric kymograph. Secondary, college. April, 1962. George P. Fulton, Department of Biology, Boston University, Boston, Massachusetts.

Instruments for Studying Physiological Phenomena. Secondary. September, 1962. Norman N. Goldstein, Jr., Engineering and Sciences Extension, University of California, Berkeley, California.

Classroom Plant Growth Chambers. Secondary, college. July, 1962. F. W. Went, Missouri Botanical Garden, 2315 Tower Avenue, St. Louis 10, Mo.

Chemistry

New Atomic, Molecular, and Crystal Models as Demonstration and Laboratory Aids in Chemistry. Secondary, college, graduate. Completed. R. T. Sanderson, Department of Chemistry, State University of Iowa, Iowa City, Iowa.

Integrated Set of Instrument Building Blocks. Modular units which illustrate instrumental principles and can be interconnected to form complex analytical instruments. Secondary, college. June, 1963. Edward N. Wise, Department of Chemistry, University of Arizona, Tucson, Arizona.

New Types of Christiansen Filters. Plastic-glass filters for study of light; inexpensive spectrophotometer. Secondary, college. Completed. Louis Auerbach, Science Department, Newtown High School, Elmhurst 73, New York. (Grantee: New York University, New York, New York.)

Apparatus for Chemical Analyses and Preparations on the Micro- and Semi-micro Scale. Secondary, college. April, 1965. John T. Stock, Department of Chemistry, University of Connecticut, Storrs, Connecticut.

Components for Student-built Instruments for Instrumental Analysis. College. June, 1962. Galen W. Ewing, Department of Chemistry, New Mexico Highlands University, Las Vegas, New Mexico.

Multi-purpose Analytical Chemical Instrument Employing Operational Amplifiers. College, graduate. September, 1962. Charles F. Morrison, Jr., Department of Chemistry, Washington State University, Pullman, Wash.

Electronic Instrumentation for Quantitative Chemistry. College, graduate. June, 1962. Charles N. Reilley, Department of Chemistry, University of North Carolina, Chapel Hill, North Carolina.

Quantitative Molecular Models Representing Molecular Charge Distribution. College, graduate. September, 1963. Karl H. Illinger, Department of Chemistry, Tufts University, Medford, Massachusetts.

Equipment and Experiments for Teaching Instrumental Analysis. Secondary, college. June, 1962. Frederick D. Tabbutt, Department of Chemistry, Reed College, Portland, Oregon.

Multi-purpose Instrument for Quantitative Chemical Measurement. College, graduate. September, 1963. Donald D. DeFord, Department of Chemistry, Northwestern University, Evanston, Illinois.

Symmetry Models of the Principal Space Groups. Graduate. July, 1962. Lyman J. Wood, Department of Chemistry, Saint Louis University, St. Louis, Missouri.

Earth Sciences

Groundwater Flow Models. College, graduate. July, 1962. John W. Harshbarger, Department of Geology, University of Arizona, Tucson, Arizona.

Aeronautical Engineering

Supersonic Streamline Visualization. College, graduate. January, 1962. Vincent P. Goddard, Department of Aeronautical Engineering, University of Notre Dame, Box 1414, Notre Dame, Indiana.

Small Hypersonic Wind Tunnel for Studying Hypersonic Gas Dynamics. College, graduate. June, 1962. John A. Fox, Department of Mechanical Engineering, University of Rochester, Rochester 20, New York. (Grantee: Pennsylvania State University, University Park, Pa.)

Lecture Demonstration Equipment in Aerodynamics. Secondary, college, and graduate. June, 1962. Erik Mollo-Christensen, Department of Aeronautics and Astronautics, Massachusetts Institute of Technology, Cambridge 39, Mass.

Inexpensive Supersonic Wind Tunnel. Secondary, college. Completed. Gabriel D. Boehler, Department of Aeronautical Engineering, Catholic University of America, Washington 17, D.C.

Educational Smoke Tunnel. Secondary, college. March, 1962. Robert S. Eikenberry, Department of Aeronautical Engineering, University of Notre Dame, Notre Dame, Indiana.

Chemical Engineering

Laboratory Equipment for Instruction in Advanced Control and Process Dynamics. College, graduate. September, 1962. Bernet S. Swanson, Department of Chemical Engineering, Illinois Institute of Technology, Chicago 16, Illinois.

Apparatus for Flow System Chemical Reaction Rate Phenomena. College. July, 1962. H. B. Kendall, Department of Chemical Engineering, Ohio University, Athens, Ohio.

Flexible Optical Analogue of Automatic X-ray Monitor and Control Systems. College. September, 1963. George A. Parks, Department of Mineral Engineering, Stanford University, Stanford, California.

Civil Engineering

Electronic Analog Teaching Aid for Mathematics, Science, and Engineering. Secondary, college, and graduate. Completed. Paul R. DeCicco, Department of Civil Engineering, Polytechnic Institute of Brooklyn, Brooklyn 1, New York.

Vortex Tank Tunnel, Visual Pipe Network, Dynamic Model, and Portable Vibrator Simulator. College. Completed. Raymond R. Fox, Department of Civil Engineering, George Washington University, Washington 6, D.C.

Transparent Flexible Models for the Observation and Demonstration of Internal Deformation Patterns. College. March, 1963. Raymond J. Stith, Department of Civil Engineering, University of Dayton, Dayton, Ohio.

Modeling Techniques for Teaching Structural Design. College. July, 1963. Robert J. Hansen, Department of Civil and Sanitary Engineering, Massachusetts Institute of Technology, Cambridge 39, Mass.

Demonstration Equipment for Structural Engineering. College, graduate. September, 1962. E. H. Gaylord, Department of Civil Engineering, University of Illinois, Urbana, Illinois.

Pneumatic Loading Device for Pure Deviatoric Loading of Soils. Graduate. August, 1962. Yehuda Klausner, Department of Civil Engineering, Wayne State University, Detroit 2, Michigan.

Electrical Engineering

Laboratory Aids for Electrical Engineering. Demonstrations of current-vs-voltage characteristics, voltmeters responding to varied properties and wave forms, and transformer connections, rectifier circuits and filter circuits. College. January, 1962. Clifford M. Siegel, Department of Electrical Engineering, University of Virginia, Charlottesville, Virginia.

Development of a Prototype Systems Laboratory Employing Electrohydraulic, Hydraulic, and Hydro-mechanical Components. College, graduate. June, 1962. H. E. Koenig and H. R. Martens, Department of Electrical Engineering, Michigan State University, East Lansing, Michigan.

Phasor Display Device for Displaying Amplitude and Phase of Sinusoidal Voltage as Directed Line on Oscilloscope. College. July, 1962. George B. Hoadley, Department of Electrical Engineering, North Carolina State College, Raleigh, North Carolina.

Digital Analog Controller for Sampled Data Systems. College, graduate. June, 1962. Paul M. DeRusso, Department of Electrical Engineering, Rensselaer Polytechnic Institute, Troy, New York.

Inexpensive Digital-to-Analog Converter for Curve Plotting with Small Digital Computers. College. January, 1962. George W. Hughes, Department of Electrical Engineering, Purdue University, Lafayette, India.

Magnetic Network Demonstrator. College. May, 1962. Neal A. Smith, Department of Electrical Engineering, Ohio State University, Columbus 10, Ohio.

Computer Techniques to Teach Statistical Methods and Random Process Theory. College, graduate. July, 1963. Granino A. Korn, Department of Electrical Engineering, University of Arizona, Tucson, Arizona.

Magnetic-Disc Memory Oscilloscope. College. July, 1962. Wallace L. Cassell, Department of Electrical Engineering, Iowa State University, Ames, Iowa.

Industrial Engineering

Punched-tape Numerically Controlled Machine Tool for Instructional Use. College, technical school. Completed. Frank W. Tippitt, Department of Industrial Engineering, Southern Methodist University, Dallas, Texas.

Portable Force Platform for Measuring Bodily Movements. College. September, 1962. J. W. Barany, Department of Industrial Engineering, Purdue University, Lafayette, Indiana.

Waiting Line Simulator. College, graduate. September, 1962. Scott Tabor Poage, Industrial Department, Arlington State College, Arlington, Texas. (Grantee: Oklahoma State University, Stillwater, Oklahoma.)

Mechanical Engineering

Transparent Overlay Visual Aids for Teaching Engineering Graphics. College. Completed. H. M. Neely, Department of Mechanical Engineering, Kansas State University, Manhattan, Kansas.

Control System Analog for Teaching Closed Loop Control Theory. College. September, 1962. Leslie M. Zoss, Department of Mechanical Engineering, Valparaiso University, University Place, Valparaiso, Indiana.

Equipment for Obtaining Contours of Fluid Membrane by Use of Monoscopic

Photogrammetric Technique. College, graduate. June, 1962. Alphia E. Knapp, Department of Mechanical Engineering, University of Illinois, Urbana, Illinois; and Frank J. McCormick, Department of Applied Mechanics, Kansas State University, Manhattan, Kansas.

Multi-purpose Tester for Demonstrations and Investigations of Shock and Vibration Phenomena. College, graduate. September, 1962. Ali Seireg, Department of Theoretical and Applied Mechanics, Marquette University, Milwaukee, Wisconsin.

Apparatus and Experiments in Magneto-Gasdynamics. College, graduate. June, 1963. A. B. Cambel, Department of Mechanical Engineering, Northwestern University, Evanston, Illinois.

Energy Conversion Devices. Solar solid-state electric, and plasma-diode devices. College. July, 1962. Robert A. Gross, Department of Mechanical Engineering, Columbia University, New York 27, New York.

Combined Shock Tube, Shock Tunnel, Light Gas Gun, and Hot Shot Wind Tunnel Apparatus. College, graduate. June, 1963. E. K. Parks and R. E. Petersen, Department of Mechanical Engineering, University of Arizona, Tucson, Arizona.

Experiments and Demonstration Apparatus for Dynamic Systems, Automatic Control, and Materials Courses in Mechanical Engineering. College. August, 1962. J. L. Shearer, Department of Mechanical Engineering, Massachusetts Institute of Technology, Cambridge 39, Massachusetts.

Multi-functional Machine for Materials Testing and Processing Experiments. College. December, 1962. Nathan H. Cook, Department of Mechanical Engineering, Massachusetts Institute of Technology, Cambridge, Massachusetts.

Analog Materials for Studying the Plastic Flow of Metals. College, July, 1962. Milton C. Shaw, Department of Mechanical Engineering, Carnegie Institute of Technology, Pittsburgh 13, Pa.

General Engineering Laboratory Equipment and Procedures. College. July, 1963. Edward F. Obert, Department of Mechanical Engineering, University of Wisconsin, Madison, Wisconsin.

Experiments in Heat Transfer and Fluid Dynamics. College. January, 1963. Fred Landis, College of Engineering, New York University, University Heights, New York, New York.

Materials Engineering

Aids for Demonstrating Atomic and Molecular Relationships in the Study of Properties of Engineering Materials. College. Completed. George N. Beaumariage, Jr., Department of Engineering, Sacramento State College, Sacramento, California.

Projection Slides for Use in Teaching Materials Science. 200 slides illustrating metallurgical microstructures. College. June, 1962. John C. Shyne, Department of Materials Science, Stanford University, Stanford, California.

Nuclear Engineering

BF$_3$ Pile Oscillator for University Nuclear Training Reactors. Graduate. May, 1963. Albert L. Babb, Professor of Chemical Engineering and Supervisor, Nuclear Reactor, and William E. Wilson, Jr., Associate Nuclear Reactor Engineer and Assistant Supervisor, Nuclear Reactor, University of Washington, Seattle 5, Washington.

General

Memo-Activity Camera. 16 mm camera which automatically records time on each frame. Graduate. October, 1962. H. G. Thuesen, Department of Industrial Engineering and Management, Oklahoma State University of Agriculture and Applied Science, Stillwater, Oklahoma.

Meterless Potentiometer Null-point Indicator. Secondary. Completed. Herbert Horky, Association of Laboratory Teachers, 68 Trinity Place, New York, New York.

Lecture-Table Thermometer and Voltmeter. Secondary, college. Completed. F. B. Dutton, Science and Mathematics Teaching Center, Michigan State University, East Lansing, Michigan.

TOPS (Tested Overhead Projection Series of Lecture Experiments). Film strips, overlay transparencies, and special apparatus for experiments in biology, chemistry, and physics. Secondary, college. January, 1962. Hubert N. Alyea, Department of Chemistry, Princeton University, Princeton, New Jersey.

Equipment for Producing Stereograms. Secondary, college, and graduate. July, 1963. David D. Donaldson, Assistant Professor of Ophthalmology, Harvard University Medical School, Cambridge, Massachusetts.

Mathematical Sciences

Teaching Aid for Analog Computer Instruction. College. Completed. Karl Kammermeyer, and James O. Osburn, Department of Chemical Engineering, University of Iowa, Iowa City, Iowa.

University of New Mexico Educational Computer Kit. Kit for constructing a relatively inexpensive digital computer with internally stored program. Junior high and high school. June, 1962. R. K. Moore, Department of Electrical Engineering, University of New Mexico, Albuquerque, New Mexico.

Mechanical Analog of Binary Adder of Digital Computers for Teaching Demonstrations. Secondary, college. Completed. Scott Tabor Poage, Industrial Engineering Department, Arlington State College, Arlington, Texas. (Grantee: Oklahoma State University, Stillwater, Oklahoma.)

Inexpensive Digital Computers and Logical Building Blocks. Secondary, college, and graduate. June, 1962. Allen L. Fulmer, Department of Science and Mathematics, Oregon College of Education, Monmouth, Oregon.

Teaching Devices for Sampling Statistics. College, graduate. Completed. Robert W. Heath, Department of Systems Engineering, University of Arizona, Tucson, Arizona.

Formal Deductive and Symbolic Logic Teaching Equipment. Secondary, college. October, 1962. Stanley J. Bezuszka, S.J., Department of Mathematics, Boston College, Chestnut Hill 67, Massachusetts.

Individual Manipulative Materials for Use in Teaching Arithmetic. Elementary. August, 1962. Joseph N. Payne, University School and School of Education, University of Michigan, Ann Arbor, Michigan.

Meteorology

Laboratory and Demonstration Equipment for Meteorological Instruction. Demonstration of radiation characteristics of the atmosphere and atomic vortices, lecture demonstrations, laboratory experiments and observational equipment for elementary meteorology. Secondary, college. December, 1962. H. Neuberger, Department of Meteorology, Pennsylvania State University, University Park, Pa.

Physics

Modern Laboratory Demonstrations and Experiments in Optics. College. July, 1962. John Strong, Department of Physics, Johns Hopkins University, Baltimore 18, Maryland.

Ripple Tank as Analog for Quantitative Radiation Studies. College, graduate.

Completed. Nelson L. Walbridge, Department of Physics, University of Vermont, Burlington, Vermont.

Apparatus for Use with Overhead Projectors in Physics Lectures. College. December, 1961. Walter Eppenstein, Department of Physics, Rensselaer Polytechnic Institute, Troy, New York.

Adaptation of Electronic Planetarium to Production of Sound-Color Motion Pictures Illustrating Satellite Motion, Gravitation, and Celestial Mechanics. Secondary, college. January, 1962. Harry F. Meiners, Department of Physics, Rensselaer Polytechnic Institute, Troy, New York.

Demonstration and Laboratory Apparatus for College Physics. Equipment and instructions for 48 experiments covering a wide range of topics. College. Completed. Robert Resnick and Harry F. Meiners, Department of Physics, Rensselaer Polytechnic Institute, Troy, New York.

The Fluorescent Lamp—a Teaching Device. Secondary, college. Completed. Isador Auerbach, John Jay High School, Brooklyn, New York. (Grantee: New York University, New York, New York.)

Apparatus for Experiments on Momentum in Introductory Physics Courses: (1) Loss of Energy in Captive Collisions; and (2) Falling Sand on Scale. Secondary, college. Completed. T. N. Hatfield, Department of Physics, University of Houston, Houston, Texas.

Apparatus for Demonstrating Simple Harmonic Motion, Its Relation to Circular Motion and Vibratory Motion, and Formation of Sine Curve from This Motion. Secondary, college. January, 1962. Morris B. Abramson, Physical Science Department, Flushing High School, Flushing 54, New York. (Grantee: Queens College, Flushing 67, New York.)

Equipment for Undergraduate Physics Experiments. Experiments in the areas of mechanics, wave motion, statistics, and kinetic theory, electromagnetism, and atomic physics. College. In progress. E. M. Hafner, Department of Physics and Astronomy, University of Rochester, River Campus Station, Rochester 20, New York.

Apparatus Drawing Project. Drawings and construction directions for 50 pieces of apparatus for lecture demonstrations and student laboratory. College. In progress. Robert G. Marcley, American Institute of Physics, 335 East 45th Street, New York 17, New York.

Basic Mass Spectrometer. Secondary, college. Completed. John W. Dewdney, Department of Physics, Dartmouth College, Hanover, New Hampshire.

A "Mossbauer Effect" Apparatus for Advanced Undergraduate Physics Laboratory. College. June, 1962. J. Richard Haskins, Department of Physics, Gettysburg College, Gettysburg, Pa.

An Electron-Optical Bench for Student Experiments. College. July, 1962. Henry E. Breed, Department of Physics, Rensselaer Polytechnic Institute, Troy, New York.

Atomic and Nuclear Experiments in Undergraduate Laboratories. College. September, 1963. George E. Bradley and Jacob DeWitt, Department of Physics, Western Michigan University, Kalamazoo, Michigan.

Apparatus for Measuring Relativistic Variation in Mass of Electrons. College. June, 1963. John W. Dewdney, Department of Physics, Dartmouth College, Hanover, New Hampshire.

Psychology

Inexpensive Timer, Memory Drum, and Psychogalvanometer. Secondary, college. Completed. Sister Mary John Catherine, Department of Psychology, Clarke College, Dubuque, Iowa.

Psycho-Biological Apparatus for Demonstrations and Student Research. Secondary, college. June, 1962. D. K. Candland, Department of Psychology, Bucknell University, Lewisburg, Pa.

Projection Color-Mixer. Secondary, college. June, 1962. Lorrin A. Riggs, Department of Psychology, Brown University, Providence 12, Rhode Island.

Inexpensive Device for Classroom Demonstrations and Student Laboratory Measurements in Audition. College. In progress. Neil R. Bartlett, Department of Psychology, University of Arizona, Tucson, Arizona.

National Science Foundation grants: course content improvement studies

General

Conference on Elementary School Science. Report presenting guidance for schools in planning science programs. 1958. Completed. National Science Teachers Association, 1201 Sixteenth Street, N.W. Washington 6, D.C.

Conference on Secondary School Science. Report presenting guiding principles for schools in planning science courses. 1959. Completed. National Science Teachers Association, 1201 Sixteenth Street, N.W., Washington 6, D.C.

Feasibility Study on Elementary and Junior High School Science. Regional conferences to investigate the need for and characteristics of major efforts to improve content and materials for elementary and junior high school science. 1960. Completed. American Association for the Advancement of Science, 1515 Massachusetts Avenue, N.W., Washington 5, D.C.

Short-vacation Lecture Series on Science for High School Students. 1958. Completed. Alfred Mirsky, Rockefeller Institute, 66th Street at York Avenue, New York 22, New York.

Films for Elementary School Science. Kinescoped 30-minute presentations by scientists. 1959. Completed. Greater Washington Educational Television Association, Raleigh Hotel, Washington 4, D.C.

Interdisciplinary Study on Films and Television in Science Education. Elementary, secondary, college. 1959. In progress. Advisory Board on Education, National Academy of Sciences-National Research Council, 2101 Constitution Avenue, Washington 25, D.C.

Motion Pictures on the International Geophysical Year. Elementary, secondary, college. 1956. Completed. U.S. Committee on the International Geophysical Year, National Academy of Sciences-National Research Council, 2101 Constitution Avenue, N.W., Washington 25, D.C.

"Horizons of Science" Film Series. Ten 20-minute films presenting reports by scientists. Elementary, secondary, college. 1959. Completed. Horizons of Science, Educational Testing Service, 20 Nassau Street, Princeton, New Jersey.

Conference on Science for Non-Science Majors. College. 1961. In progress. R. G. Hoopes, Michigan State University Oakland, Rochester, Michigan.

Anthropology

Educational Resources in Anthropology Project. Source book and other aids for teachers of introductory college courses. 1959. In progress. David G. Mandelbaum, Department of Anthropology, University of California, Berkeley 4, California.

Motion Pictures on African Bushmen. College. 1959. In progress. J. O. Brew, Peabody Museum, Harvard University, Cambridge 38, Mass.

Motion Pictures on Indian Cultures in Western America. Secondary, college. 1960. In progress. S. A. Barrett, Department of Anthropology, University of California, Berkeley 4, California.

Motion Pictures on American Archaeology. College. 1961. E. Mott Davis, Department of Anthropology, University of Texas, Austin 12, Texas.

Biology

Committee on Educational Policies in the Biological Sciences. Elementary, secondary, college. 1954–58. Completed. Division of Biology and Agriculture, National Academy of Sciences-National Research Council, 2101 Constitution Avenue, N.W., Washington 25, D.C.

Laboratory Source Book for Courses in Plant Pathology. College. 1959. In progress. Arthur Kelman, Department of Plant Pathology, North Carolina State College, Raleigh, North Carolina. (Grantee: American Phyto-pathological Society.)

Laboratory Experiments in General Physiology. College. 1959. Completed. H. W. Davenport, American Physiological Society, 9650 Wisconsin Avenue, N.W., Washington 14, D.C.

Laboratory Experiments in Human Physiology. College. 1961. In progress. Charlotte Haywood, American Physiological Society, 9650 Wisconsin Avenue, N.W., Washington 14, D.C.

New Introductory College Course in Biology. 1960. In progress. George Wald, Biological Laboratories, Harvard University, Cambridge 38, Mass.

Laboratory Course in Instrumentation for Bio-Medical Sciences. College, graduate school. 1960. In progress. K. S. Lion, Department of Biology, Massachusetts Institute of Technology, Cambridge 39, Mass.

Study of Curricula in Wood Science and Technology. College. 1960. In progress. B. A. Jayne, Society of Wood Science and Technology, School of Natural Resources, University of Michigan, Ann Arbor, Michigan.

College of the Air Television Course on "The New Biology." College. 1961. In progress. Learning Resources Institute, 860 Fifth Avenue, New York 19, New York.

Television-Film Series on the Biology of Viruses. Secondary, college. 1959. Completed. National Educational Television and Radio Center, 10 Columbus Circle, New York 19, New York. (Grantee: University of California.)

Films to Visualize Anatomical Structure in Depth. 1961. Secondary, college. In progress. R. D. Frandson, Department of Veterinary Anatomy, Colorado State University, Fort Collins, Colorado.

Film Series on "Living Biology." Secondary, college. 1960. In progress. Roman Vishniac, 219 West 81st Street, New York 24, New York. (Grantee: Yeshiva University.)

Films on the Biology of Slime Molds. Secondary, college. 1959. Completed. R. T. Porter, School of Education, State University of Iowa, Iowa City, Iowa.

Short Motion Pictures on Microbiology. College. 1959. Completed. Donald M. Reynolds, Department of Bacteriology, University of California, Davis, California.

Motion Pictures on Movement of Moisture in Wood. College. 1960. In progress. W. N. Harlow, State University of New York School of Forestry, Syracuse University, Syracuse, New York.

Film Lectures on "The Promise of the Life Sciences." 1960. Completed. J. B. Holden, U.S. Department of Agriculture Graduate School, Washington 25, D.C.

Films on Developmental Anatomy of Vertebrates. 1961. In progress C. M. Flaten, Audio-Visual Center, Indiana University, Bloomington, Indiana.

Chemistry

New Introductory Course in College Chemistry. 1958. Completed. D. H. Andrews, Department of Chemistry, Johns Hopkins University, Baltimore 18, Maryland.

Conference on Undergraduate Curricula in Chemistry. 1960. Completed. B. R. Willeford, Jr., Department of Chemistry, Bucknell University, Lewisburg, Pa.

Conference on Chemistry for Non-Science Majors. College. 1960. Completed. W. B. Cook, Department of Chemistry, Montana State College, Bozeman, Montana.

Laboratory Program for Organic Chemistry. College. 1960. Completed. Melvin I. Newman and W. N. White, Department of Chemistry, Ohio State University, Columbus 10, Ohio.

New Approach to the Teaching of Analytical Chemistry. College. 1961. In progress. B. E. Gushee, Department of Chemistry, Hollins College, Roanoke, Virginia.

Development of Modern Analytical Chemistry Courses. College. 1961. In progress. H. A. Laitinen, Department of Chemistry, University of Illinois, Urbana, Illinois.

Films on the Use of Models of Atoms, Molecules and Crystals in Teaching Chemistry. Secondary, college. 1959. Completed. R. T. Sanderson, Department of Chemistry, State University of Iowa, Iowa City, Iowa.

Film Demonstrations for Courses in General Chemistry. Secondary, college. 1960. In progress. Andrew G. Patterson, Department of Chemistry, Yale University, New Haven, Connecticut.

Engineering

Study of Engineering Education. College. 1961. Completed. John S. McNown, Dean, School of Engineering, University of Kansas, Lawrence, Kansas.

Evaluation of Technical Institute Education. College. 1961. In progress. Bonham Campbell, Department of Engineering, University of California, Los Angeles, California.

Graphics for Scientific Engineering Curricula. 1961. In progress. Paul M. Reinhard, Department of Engineering Graphics, University of Detroit, Detroit, Michigan.

Study Conference on Theoretical and Applied Mechanics Curricula. 1961. Completed. Harold Liebowitz, Engineering Experiment Station, University of Colorado, Boulder, Colorado.

Materials Science Course. 1961. In progress. Robert T. Howard, Department of Applied Mechanics, University of Wichita, Wichita, Kansas.

Simple Computer Techniques. 1961. In progress. Granino A. Korn, Department of Electrical Engineering, University of Arizona, Tucson, Arizona.

Senior Laboratory in Aeronautical Engineering. 1959. Completed. Harold M. DeGroff, Department of Aeronautical Engineering, Purdue University, Lafayette, Indiana.

Chemical Engineering Curriculum Study. 1960. Completed. Donald L. Katz, Department of Chemical Engineering, University of Michigan, Ann Arbor, Michigan.

Civil Engineering Undergraduate Curricula. 1960. Completed. F. A. Wallace, Department of Civil Engineering, Cooper Union, New York, New York.

Sanitary Engineering Curricula. 1960. Completed. Rolf Eliassen, Department of Civil and Sanitary Engineering, Massachusetts Institute of Technology, Cambridge 39, Massachusetts.

Conference on Electrical Engineering Education. 1957. Completed. Gordon S. Brown, Dean, School of Engineering, Massachusetts Institute of Technology, Cambridge 39, Massachusetts.

Conference on Materials in Electrical Engineering Education. 1959. Completed. Samuel Seely and James R. Hooper, Department of Electrical Engineering, Case Institute of Technology, Cleveland, Ohio.

Conference on Systems in Electrical Engineering Education. 1961. Completed. John G. Brainerd, Department of Electrical Engineering, University of Pennsylvania, Philadelphia, Pennsylvania.

Education Aids for Mechanical Engineering. 1960. In progress. Thomas E. Jackson, Department of Mechanical Engineering, Lehigh University, Bethlehem, Pennsylvania.

Experimental Mechanical Engineering. 1960. In progress. J. G. Goglia, Department of Mechanical Engineering, North Carolina State College, Raleigh, North Carolina.

Motion Pictures on Fluid Mechanics. 1960. In progress. Hunter Rouse, Iowa Institute of Hydraulic Research, State University of Iowa, Iowa City, Iowa.

Motion Pictures on Fluid Mechanics. 1960. In progress. Lorenze G. Straub, St. Anthony Falls Hydraulic Laboratory, University of Minnesota, St. Paul, Minnesota.

Geology

Study of Curricula and Courses in the Geological Sciences. 1961. In progress. R. C. Stephenson, American Geological Institute, 2101 Constitution Avenue, N.W., Washington 25, D.C.

Mathematics

New Approaches to Elementary School Mathematics. 1961. In progress. Paul C. Rosenbloom, Department of Mathematics, Institute of Technology, University of Minnesota, Minneapolis, Minnesota. (Grantee: Yale University.)

Survey of Recent East European Literature in Mathematics. 1956. In progress. Elementary, secondary, college. A. L. Putnam, Department of Mathematics, University of Chicago, Chicago 37, Illinois.

Regional Orientation Conferences on Mathematics. Secondary. 1960. Completed. National Council of Teachers of Mathematics, 1201 16th Street, N.W., Washington 6, D.C.

Televised Instruction in Mathematics for Grades 5 and 6. 1961. In progress. Henry Van Engen, Department of Mathematics, University of Wisconsin, Madison, Wisconsin.

Experimental Motion Pictures on the Teaching of Elementary School Mathematics. 1960. In progress. David A. Page, University of Illinois Arithmetic Project, University of Illinois, Urbana, Illinois.

Films on Selected Topics in Mathematics. Secondary, college. 1958. In progress. H. M. Gehman, Mathematical Association of America, University of Buffalo, Buffalo, New York.

Experimental Undergraduate Program in Mathematics. College. 1961. In progress. K. O. May, Department of Mathematics, Carleton College, Northfield, Minnesota.

Development of Honors Courses in Mathematics. College. 1961. In progress. A. D. Wallace, Department of Mathematics, Tulane University, New Orleans, Louisiana.

Experimental Program in Algebra. College. 1961. In progress. R. J. Walker, Department of Mathematics, Cornell University, Ithaca, New York.

Meteorology

Motion Picture Series in Meteorology. Secondary, college. 1960. In progress. Kenneth C. Spengler, American Meteorological Society, 45 Beacon Street, Boston, Massachusetts.

Motion Pictures on Meteorology. Secondary, college. 1960. In progress. Kenneth C. Spengler, American Meteorological Society, 45 Beacon Street, Boston, Massachusetts.

Physics

New Approaches to the Teaching of Quantum Mechanics. College, graduate school. 1958. Completed. Alfred Landé, Department of Physics, Ohio State University, Columbus 10, Ohio.

Laboratory Performance Tests in College Physics. 1959. Completed. H. Kruglak, Department of Physics, Western Michigan University, Kalamazoo, Michigan.

Development of Laboratory and Demonstration Experiments for Introductory College Physics. 1960. Completed. Robert Resnick, Department of Physics, Rensselaer Polytechnic Institute, Troy, New York.

New Introductory Course in Physics. 1960. In progress. A. M. Fowler, Department of Physics, Washington University, St. Louis 5, Missouri.

Preparation of Source Materials on the Recent History of Physics in the United States. 1961. In progress. E. Hutchisson, American Institute of Physics, 335 East 45th Street, New York, New York.

Development of Materials for Introductory Course in Physics. College. 1961. In progress. Henry Meiners and Robert Resnick, Department of Physics, Rensselaer Polytechnic Institute, Troy, New York.

Filmed Demonstrations in Physics. College. 1961. In progress. Franklin Miller, Department of Physics, Kenyon College, Gambier, Ohio.

Adaptation of PSSC Course and Films in Physics for Use in College. 1960. In progress. J. R. Zacharias, Educational Services Inc., 164 Main Street, Watertown 72, Massachusetts.

Films for College Courses in Physics. 1961. In progress. Robert Hulsizer, Educational Services Inc., 164 Main Street, Watertown 72, Massachusetts.

Psychology

Study of Undergraduate Curricula in Psychology. 1960. Completed. W. J. McKeachie and W. J. Milholland, Department of Psychology, University of Michigan, Ann Arbor, Michigan.

Films Series on Experimental Psychology. College. 1961. In progress. J. G. Darley, American Psychological Association, 1333 16th Street, N.W., Washington 6, D.C.

For more recent information on projects supported by the National Science Foundation, see

Science Course Improvement Projects 1, Courses, Written Materials, Films, Studies, NSF 62-38, October, 1962; and Science Course Improvement Projects 2, Science Teaching Equipment, NSF 63-15, May, 1963.

SUPPLEMENT 4 ❁ PROJECT ENGLISH*

We are convinced that adequate instruction in reading and in the written and oral use of the English language is a matter of utmost importance among our national needs.—U.S. Commissioner of Education McMurrin, speaking at a Senate appropriations hearing, April, 1961

* Reprinted from *School Life: Official Journal of the Office of Education*, vol. 44, no. 3, November–December, 1961, with permission.

Project English has been launched in the Office of Education. The 87th Congress has given the Office of Education budgetary support for a project to help raise the quality of the English curriculum and English instruction. Through the combined efforts of the professional staff of the Office, Project English will seek to complement, reinforce, and strengthen the contributions being made by public schools, institutions of higher education, State departments of education, professional and scholarly organizations, private foundations, and other groups. In consultation with representatives of these agencies and groups, the Office will sponsor research studies and experiments and will contract with universities or State departments of education for the establishment of curriculum centers to plan, develop, and test new instructional materials and methods. For these sponsored, or extramural, activities in this fiscal year approximately one-half million dollars are available.

Acting in liaison with these agencies and groups, the Office will engage in the following activities:

1. Determine the status of research and experimentation and spotlight phases that need further research and experimentation.

2. Sponsor and support research and development projects through its Cooperative Research Program.

3. Serve as a clearinghouse of information on research and development, that is, information flowing from studies under the Cooperative Research Program and from the efforts of other organizations and agencies.

4. Serve as a cooperative planning center to insure the maximum impact of and continuity in the efforts of the educational community as a whole to upgrade performance in English.

In brief, Project English encourages both study and action: it seeks to discover, define, and study the problems involved in improving English instruction, and, at the same time, to put to more vigorous use the knowledge we already have about how to improve it.

During its initial stage the project will emphasize reading, composition, and related skills, since the need for improvement in these skills is nationally recognized and the congressional appropriation implies a high interest in them. Throughout the Project, however, the Office will attempt to provide financial support for the most promising proposals, including those concerned also with the teaching of literature.

Project English encompasses all levels from the kindergarten through the graduate school, though the most promising levels to examine at this time seem to be the elementary and secondary schools and probably the freshman and sophomore years of college. As has been pointed out repeatedly, one of the greatest weaknesses in the usual English program is the lack of articulation or sequence of content. Unnecessary repetition of subject matter often handicaps the student as he moves from elementary school to junior high school, to senior high school, and even into college. This is a problem which may be aggravated by the success of the Advanced Placement Program in English in hundreds of high schools and the general upgrading of content for the college-bound student.

Still another problem at these levels is the need for more preservice and in-service education of English teachers. These teachers need the kind of institutes now provided for teachers of modern foreign languages under the National Defense Education Act and for teachers of science and mathematics under programs of the National Science Foundation, but legislative proposals which would authorize such institutes in English have not been enacted into law.

A number of programs of the Office of Education in related fields will be coordinated with Project English. One of these is a major project to improve the teaching of reading in elementary and secondary schools. As a first step the Office is collecting and evaluating data on research in reading completed between 1955 and 1960 at colleges, universities, and research centers within the United States. Using these and other research findings, specialists are writing bulletins on various aspects of reading for classroom teachers, supervisors, and administrators. The Office also plans to work, as staff becomes available, in the area of supervision and the improvement of instruction for underachieving inmigrant pupils who are severely retarded in reading and language ability.

Many institutions and agencies will become directly involved in Project English through the Office of Education's Cooperative Research Program. Under this program the Office receives annual appropriations "to enter into contracts or jointly financed cooperative arrangements with universities and colleges and State educational agencies for the conduct of research, surveys, and demonstrations in the field of education." Contracts may also be made for the organizing and synthesizing of existing research findings and for conferences and seminars of research people for the purpose of stimulating research and developing research designs.

Proposals for research projects under the Cooperative Research Program must be submitted to an advisory committee of experts appointed from outside the Office by the Commissioner of Education. Before being submitted to this committee, proposals bearing on Project English will, however, be reviewed by an advisory panel of specialists in English at the elementary, secondary, and college levels. Present members of the panel are Theodore Clymer, Robert Pooley, and Albert Kitzhaber.

Project English will provide for the development of new instructional materials and methods through curriculum study centers to be established at selected universities. Three such centers are provided for by the budget for the fiscal year 1962; two more are planned for the fiscal year beginning July 1962. They will be established by contract through the Cooperative Research Program.

The study centers will provide tangible resources for the improvement of instruction. In cooperation with State and local educational leaders they may—

1. Consider the present aims and nature of the English curriculum and propose means of strengthening it.

2. Develop a pattern for teaching reading, composition, and related language skills that has a sequence based on research in human growth and development and the teaching-learning process.

3. Test promising practices and materials.

4. Make recommendations for the curriculum and develop materials adaptable to school and college programs of instruction.

The Office's attitude toward instructional practice in English is the same as it is toward other aspects of education in the United States. In Project English, as elsewhere, the Office seeks to preserve the plurality in our educational system; it does not intend to secure the adoption of a particular curriculum; rather, it hopes to stimulate throughout the Nation an enterprising attitude toward improvement by supporting diverse kinds of promising activities. Universities and State departments submitting proposals for the establishment of centers may define their areas of concern by grade level, skill, student clientele, or on any other base or combination of bases. A center may focus, for example, on language development in grades 1–6, or on reading in the secondary school, or on articulation in composition and literature between high school and college, or on teaching English as a second language to children in large cities.

Each center will have from 3 to 5 years in which to complete the task with which it is charged, but it will be expected to issue new curriculum materials as they are developed. One of the activities of a center will be to evaluate its newly prepared materials in classrooms. This field-testing activity, while a form of demonstration project, will not constitute a dissemination effort, since the authority under which the Cooperative Research Program operates does not extend to general dissemination.

Project English is under the direction of Assistant Commissioner Ralph C. M. Flynt, director of the Division of Statistics and Research Services. Other divisions of the Office are connected with the project through an interdivisional committee representing all participating units of the Office—the sections concerned with the instructional programs of elementary, secondary, and higher education; the Cooperative Research Branch; the Library Services Branch; and the sections working on language development programs of the National Defense Education Act. This committee serves in an advisory and liaison capacity.

Anyone wishing to propose a research project or to ask how to prepare his proposal should address himself to Francis Ianni, Cooperative Research Branch, Office of Education, Washington 25, D.C.

Compared to the money and effort expended in the past few years for science, mathematics, and modern foreign languages, the outlay for Project English is modest indeed. However, one might hope that with the assistance of English teachers and scholars, professional and scholarly groups, schools, colleges, and universities, private foundations, and the public in general this first concerted national effort to strengthen instruction in English will be extremely beneficial to students, teachers, and the Nation as a whole.

PROJECT ENGLISH: ITS IMPLICATIONS FOR COLLEGES AND UNIVERSITIES*
J. N. Hook**

The National Interest and the Teaching of English, published in 1961 by the National Council of Teachers of English, spells out in detail not only the importance of English to the Nation's well-being but also the grave but remediable deficiencies that now exist. Among the deficiencies are: Too many inadequately prepared teachers now in the classrooms; too small a number of qualified new teachers being graduated each year; a lack of focus, in many English classrooms, upon sequential study of language, literature, and composition; too little articulation of the teaching of English from the elementary school through the college; the slightness of the attempts to coordinate national, State, and local efforts to improve the teaching of English; and the lack of answers to many basic questions about materials and methods—questions that research can answer. "If the teaching of English is to be improved throughout the country," says this report, "bold and immediate action must be undertaken on a national scale."

* Reprinted from *Higher Education,* vol. 18, no. 6, pp. 3–7, April, 1962, with permission.
** Prof. J. N. Hook, on leave from the Department of English of the University of Illinois, is coordinator of Project English in its initial stages. From 1953 to 1960 he was executive secretary of the National Council of Teachers of English. He is the author of numerous professional articles and a number of books, including *The Teaching of High School English, Modern American Grammar and Usage,* and a just-published book, *Guide to Good Writing.*

Supplement 4 | 266

Project English, now in its beginnings, is intended by the Office of Education to correct a number of these deficiencies. It will supplement work already underway in various quarters to improve the teaching and learning of English in the Nation's elementary and secondary schools, colleges, and universities. Many studies and experiments are going forward in colleges, universities, local school districts, State departments of education, and professional organizations—so many, in fact, that one of the probable tasks of Project English will be to serve as a clearinghouse and disseminator of information. But, despite these studies and experiments, many of which are broadly significant, a systematic attack upon the whole vast problem of English instruction can hardly be hoped for except on the national level.

In his message to Congress concerning education, on February 6, 1962, President Kennedy said: "The control and operation of education in America must remain the responsibility of State and local governments and private institutions. . . . But the Congress has long recognized the responsibility of the Nation as a whole—that additional resources, meaningful encouragement, and vigorous leadership must be added to the total effort by the Federal Government if we are to meet the task before us. For education in this country is the right, the necessity, and the responsibility of all. Its advancement is essential to national objectives and dependent on the greater financial resources available at the national level."

Sterling M. McMurrin, U.S. Commissioner of Education, has spoken often of the necessity for improved teaching and learning of English and has stressed the role of the Office in sponsoring research and disseminating information, without any desire or attempt on the part of the Office to create a national curriculum.

The Office of Education is now making long-range plans for Project English in consultation with representatives of such organizations or groups as the Modern Language Association, the College English Association, the National Council of Teachers of English, organizations of principals, administrators, supervisors, and librarians, the Commission on English of the College Entrance Examination Board, and State educational agencies. The extent to which the plans become realities is contingent upon legislative action. The Congress has allocated limited funds to the project for fiscal year 1962. These are being expended on three undertakings:

1. Curriculum study centers

These centers will span several grade levels and each is designed to operate for approximately 5 years. They are intended to develop sound patterns for sequential teaching of skills and content in reading worthwhile materials, in language, and in composition, the sequence being based upon both the subject matter and what is known about child growth and development. The centers will test promising practices and materials, make recommendations concerning curriculum, and develop materials adaptable to systematic school and lower year college programs of instruction. The centers are to be funded jointly by the Office and sponsoring colleges, universities, or State departments of education. (See English Centers Established, p. 22)

2. Basic and applied research studies

Through colleges, universities or State educational agencies, individuals or groups may present proposals for research that show promise of contributing to the improvement of instruction in English on any level. A number of such proposals have already been approved by the Cooperative Research Advisory Committee. Under the law, the committee must evaluate and pass upon requests for centers, research studies, or conferences before any concrete action is taken. Proposals that are most likely to be accepted are those that show promise of improving instruction at any academic level.

3. Research planning and development

Conferences or seminars dealing with needed research in teaching English are arranged through requests submitted by responsible officers of colleges, universities, or State educational agencies.

A number of activities already in progress in or sponsored by the Office of Education will feed results into Project English. Among the many that could be mentioned are studies of reading and summaries of research in reading on the elementary and secondary levels, a detailed analysis of the characteristics of the academically able and a wider study measuring levels of talent of all sorts, a study of curricular offerings and patterns in English and other subjects in colleges and universities, and a clearing house of research in higher education.

How higher education is involved

Increasingly during the past few years, professors in academic departments have come to realize that they are deeply responsible not only for the quality of students who go out of their classrooms but also for the quality of those who come in.

Professors teach the teachers, today's and tomorrow's teachers, teachers not only in colleges and universities but also in elementary and secondary schools. Through the content of their courses and also through their attitudes and their awareness, or lack of awareness, of their contribution to American education, professors affect what is placed in the curriculum and what is done with it.

Through their research, too, professors contribute to instruction in the lower schools. Almost any type of research may have its impact, whether it reveals a better way to teach Dickens or clarifies the auditory imagery in *Bleak House*. A college or university department should be catholic enough to attract—and to respect and reward impartially—those interested in the most esoteric of scholarly problems and those especially concerned with the curriculums of the lower schools. And it should refrain from sealing them off in separate compartments, for each may learn from the other.

It is the hope of Project English that many members of college and university departments of English will become concerned in improving the teaching of their subject on other levels, if for no other reason than that the students who come to them will then be better prepared. Their contributions are vital. They cannot do the job alone, but neither can their colleagues in education and psychology. If some of today's teachers are badly prepared in either knowledge of content or knowledge of educational principles and techniques, it is because too little cooperation has existed between teachers of the subject itself and teachers of education and psychology. The Teacher Education and Professional Standards Conferences have made plain not only that such cooperation is possible but that many leaders of higher education realize it to be imperative.

How can departments of English and departments or schools of education cooperate? What can departments of English do to help improve instruction?

Let me be as specific as it is possible to be at a time when the future outlines of Project English are still being developed. I shall describe several potential lines of action, some of them similar to those already being followed, under various auspices, in foreign languages, mathematics, and science; and I shall attempt to show some of the ways in which higher education, particularly departments of English and departments or schools of education, may be involved. Some of these potentialities may not become realities; others may materialize at once.

Institutes

The foreign language program in its first years conducted a small number of institutes to instruct teachers in the use of new methods and materials. In 1962,

85 such institutes will be held, to be staffed by about 400 college faculty persons and to be attended by about 4,500 elementary or secondary teachers.

Bills now being considered by Congress would authorize similar institutes for English. The Nation has approximately 800,000 elementary teachers (almost all of whom teach the "language arts" throughout the schoolday) and 80,000 to 90,000 teachers of secondary English. Not all of these teachers would be interested in or have need for the kind of help that institutes offer. But if only 10 percent of the elementary and 25 percent of the secondary teachers enrolled in these institutes in the next 5 years, colleges and universities would have to provide summer faculty to teach approximately 100,000 additional persons on the graduate or near-graduate level.

What is taught in an institute? It is impossible to say precisely. The Commission on English of the College Entrance Examination Board stresses a "tripod" of language, literature, and composition in the 20 institutes it is sponsoring for 1962. Institutes proposed by the Office of Education for secondary school teachers of students of mixed ability or of the non-college-bound will no doubt also emphasize the tripod, but may perhaps depart in some respects from the commission's pattern.

Institutes for elementary teachers must certainly cover reading, penmanship, spelling, composition, and the relationships of these to children's varying rates of development. But they cannot ignore scholars' discoveries of new truths about language and the discrediting of old fallacies or half-truths; they cannot ignore the fact that basic principles of organization can be taught to young children; they cannot ignore the possibility that some or even most children can learn to read richer fare than they are sometimes offered.

Evening or Saturday seminars or courses

At present a fairly large number of elementary and secondary teachers who live within 50 miles or so of a college campus enroll in evening or Saturday classes to improve their teaching qualifications. If within the next few years Federal support is offered, the number may substantially increase.

In English and perhaps in some other subjects a problem exists here—a problem that will have to be resolved by consensus of colleges and local school boards or State agencies. Often an elementary or secondary teacher desperately needs more work in English but is not qualified for graduate-level courses. Since his school board wants him to earn graduate credits, he bypasses the English that he needs and wants, and enrolls in a graduate course in another discipline for which he happens to have the prerequisite. Obviously departments of English cannot legitimately dilute their graduate courses for such teachers, but they can use whatever influence they have with school boards to permit in-service credits and salary increments for teachers who enroll in the advanced undergraduate courses they would find most beneficial. Further, English departments can offer teachers in their geographical areas more of the undergraduate and graduate evening or Saturday courses they need. In some institutions the need for new or revised courses may become evident.

Fellowships and other assistance

Financial assistance available to graduate students of English has, over the years, been limited. Except for the National Defense Graduate Fellowship Program, which supports students in all basic academic fields, the Federal Government has given almost all its fellowship support to graduate students in the sciences, engineering, and public health, and of the 5,500 NDEA fellowships thus far awarded only 324 have gone to students of English or linguistics. Institutional fellowships for students of English have also been meager. In 1955–56, for example, institutions awarded only 900 fellowships, out of a total of 24,277, to students studying English. To encourage more students to prepare for teaching English in the schools or colleges, we shall need to do a great deal more to help them financially in their graduate work.

As to programs for improving the qualifications of teachers already at work in the elementary and secondary schools, the Federal Government has limited its support almost wholly to teachers of science, mathematics, engineering, modern foreign languages, and counseling and guidance. Institutes for English teachers were proposed as an amendment to the National Defense Education Act during the last session of Congress, but no action was taken. Although the Commission on English of the College Entrance Examination Board is providing $1 million for 20 institutes to be conducted this summer, there are no plans to repeat these institutes. Improvement of the qualifications of teachers now in the schools is a major problem, and programs must be developed to solve them.

Programs in teacher education

Surveys by the National Council of Teachers of English, notably those reported in 1961 in *The National Interest and the Teaching of English*, reveal wide diversity in programs for preparing elementary teachers and secondary teachers of English. Because of differing requirements for certification, some diversity is to be expected. More serious are such facts as these:

For prospective elementary teachers:

Over 50 percent of the colleges require no more than 6 semester hours of English beyond the freshman year; some colleges require no English whatever after the freshman year.

Only 5.3 percent of the colleges require work in the history and structure of the English language.

Only 30.6 percent require a course in American literature.

Only 11.2 percent require a course in oral interpretation of literature.

For prospective secondary teachers of English:

Only 17.4 percent of the colleges require a course in modern English grammar.

Only 41 percent require a course in advanced composition.

Only 21.1 percent require a course in contemporary literature, 29.1 percent a course in literary criticism or critical analysis, and 38.8 percent a course in a literary genre or genres.

Obviously, considerable strengthening of programs for preparing teachers is needed in many colleges and universities. Project English is proposing a weeklong conference on such programs as well as the establishment of a few pilot programs. But long before results from a conference or from pilot programs could become available, committees of English and education faculty members in any college or university could examine its teacher preparation program and plug some holes.

Two other needs of national dimensions must be mentioned. On the one hand, for the liberal arts graduates who majored in English but did not earn teaching certificates, expanded master of arts in teaching programs should be made available. On the other, the newly certified teachers who discover, in the June before they begin teaching, that they lack desirable work in such subjects as linguistics, literary criticism, or advanced composition should be encouraged to fill these gaps.

Special contributions of individual scholars

In the new programs in science, mathematics, and foreign languages, eminent scholars at the growing edge of each subject have turned at least a portion of their attention to the teaching of their subject at less advanced levels. Because of the depth and often the breadth of their knowledge, they are contributing to instructional materials and procedures a quality otherwise unattainable. Working with experts in child growth and development, they have given to students information and insights never before possible. But few scholars in English have shown an eagerness to be involved in such work.

It is, however, not solely the national participation of a few dozen scholars that is needed. Within his own geographical area any levelheaded scholar can exert a wholesome influence. The first step will be to sit quietly as a visitor in a number of elementary and secondary classrooms, to observe and think about what goes on and why, and to note the varied characteristics of the pupils (not all of whom have the hereditary and cultural advantages of the professor's own children). The second step must be taken with great tact. The professor must not be a faultfinder, or pose as a person who knows all the answers or as one qualified to reform the curriculum. But he may ask in honest humility and honest pride whether there is any way in which he and perhaps some of his colleagues may assist in working toward solutions of some of the problems facing the schools. The answers may be slow in coming. The idea of such cooperation is so new in some places that it shocks. But gradually such possibilities as these will evolve: "Can you meet with our teachers and show them what the 'new grammar' is about? What does modern literary criticism have to offer high school teachers? What's new in the 18th century? Can somebody tell us about the possibilities of programed instructions in English? How can we convince the non-English teachers that they have some responsibilities for encouraging linguistic decency? Can college professors help to show the community that it is impossible to teach writing well when a teacher has 175 students a day?" No Federal support, no Project English, is needed to accomplish what is urged here. Only good will, common sense, and a few days' delay in the newest interpretation of *Moby Dick* are required. However, the presence of scholars who have worked with lower schools will make possible greater and more intelligent departmental involvement in institutes, research studies, and the like.

Scholars may help too in the recruitment of promising young students as teachers of English. The shortage of qualified teachers threatens to become as acute in the colleges as on the other levels. The American Mathematics Association has a program involving a number of scholars in mathematics who visit various campuses to acquaint students with the exciting world of mathematics and with opportunities in teaching that subject. Departments of English might well emulate that program in an attempt to lead more young people into the exciting world of English.

A special Ph.D. in English

Two types of key positions have now often to be filled with inadequately prepared persons. One is the job of the teacher of methods—a word which people in academic departments regard with less horror as they become more knowledgeable about elementary and secondary schools. The other is that of supervisor of English teaching in large city or county school systems; the person in this position exerts great influence upon the curriculum and therefore upon the amount and quality of knowledge and skill that high school graduates possess. Both these positions require, or should require, teaching experience in the lower schools and a solid grounding in both subject matter and educational principles. A second-track (not second-rate!) Ph.D. program in English, preserving the traditional values and rigors of the degree but admitting the need for professional skills and knowledge as well, would enable students to qualify for both these types of positions and would thereby become a major contribution of a few large and respected universities.

Refresher seminars for college teachers

The libraries, the journals, and the meetings of professional and scholarly organizations provide opportunity for college teachers to inform themselves about what their colleagues in other colleges and universities are thinking and doing. But something more is needed: A longer, more direct, and more unhurried opportunity to exchange ideas and information, to validate or invalidate a hypothesis, to talk with others who face similar tasks in teaching and in research, to be gently guided again for a while by a wise master. A number of short seminars on various campuses, perhaps sandwiched between summer school and the fall term, could do much to make teaching and research more productive.

Using new media of instruction

New media of instruction are here, whether we like them or not, and they cannot be quietly dismissed. Educational television, teaching machines and the programs fed into those machines, scrambled textbooks, English language laboratories, team teaching, and their descendants or cousins still beyond the grayish-blue horizon may lead us either into educational caverns measureless to man—or up to peaks in Darien.

If English departments, however, do not contribute substantially to what goes into the teaching machines, the language laboratories, and so on, they will not be very happy with what comes out. Educational psychologists may know the answers to questions about stimuli, responses, and reinforcements, but very likely they know comparatively little about sentence modifiers, plus-junctures, or "Andrea del Sarto." Cooperative research by subject-matter experts, psychologists, and technicians is essential if the brave new world is to have people in it as well as machines.

The list could go on. Project English is at the beginning of what may be a long road with many turnings. It is not just a project that will help elementary schools to teach the spelling of "cat" more systematically, nor just a project that will help the high schools to decide whether and why and when "The Rime of the Ancient Mariner" should be taught.

Rather, it is a project that must dig deeply into the usual assumptions of some of us. It must answer questions that are now unanswerable. It must correlate knowledge that is not now correlated. It must disseminate knowledge. It must build an awareness that elementary, secondary, and college teachers are working together toward the same goal: An enlightened people who can interpret well the spoken and the written word, think straight, express themselves coherently, and absorb many human truths that literature reveals.

EDITOR'S NOTE: The following major projects have received grants from the U.S. Office of Education as part of Project English:

Carnegie Institute of Technology: Development of a sequential and cumulative program for the able college-bound in grades 10–12. Duration: 4 years. Federal costs: $219,995. Directors: Erwin R. Steinberg, Robert Slack.

Hunter College: Development of reading and English language materials for grades 7–9 in depressed urban areas. Duration: 4 years 11 months. Federal costs: $249,802. Director: Marjorie Smiley.

University of Oregon: A sequential curriculum in language, reading and composition for grades 7–12. Duration: 5 years. Federal costs: $250,000. Director: Albert Kitzhaber.

University of Nebraska: An articulated program in composition, grades K–13. Duration: 5 years. Federal costs: $249,472. Directors: Paul A. Olson, Frank Rice.

Northwestern University: A curriculum study center in English and related fields.

Duration: 5 years. Federal costs: $250,000. Directors: Jean H. Hagstrum, Stephen Dunning.

University of Minnesota: Preparation and evaluation of curriculum materials and guides for grades 7–12. Duration: 5 years. Federal costs: $242,949. Director: Stanley Kegler.

University of Wisconsin: A sequential English language arts curriculum for grades 7–12. Duration: 4 years. Federal costs: $200,000. Director: Robert Cooley.

Florida State University, Tallahassee: A curriculum study to develop and test approaches to a sequential curriculum in junior high school English. Duration: 4½ years. Federal costs: $202,526. Director: Dwight Burton.

University of Georgia: Developing competency in written composition in children in kindergarten through elementary school by means of curriculum materials. Duration: 5 years. Federal costs: $249,997. Directors: J. Richard Lindemann, Rachel Sutton, Mary Tingle.

SUPPLEMENT 5 ❋ A LETTER FROM PROF. PAUL C. ROSENBLOOM TO SENATOR HUBERT H. HUMPHREY regarding the National Science Foundation education programs in science and mathematics, with recommendations for the establishment of corresponding programs in the social sciences and humanities.*

National Science Foundation Programs

February 7, 1961

Dear Senator Humphrey: I should like to call your attention to two of the most effective existing programs for Federal aid to education, the course content improvement section and the visiting lectureships of the National Science Foundation. These programs demonstrate that an effective program need not be expensive, that it can be managed without interfering with local control, and that it can help all schools without raising questions of church-state relations. If you could make a wider audience aware of these points, you would clear up several popular misconceptions concerning Federal action in education.

Course content improvement

The course content improvement section now costs about $6 million annually. It supports projects for production of new curricular materials, on the school or college level, in the natural sciences and mathematics. It supports both extensive national projects sponsored by major professional organizations and projects of individuals or small teams. It often supports competing projects in the same field.

Policies

Its activities are governed by the following policies, which could serve as models for other Federal programs:

* Reprinted from the *Congressional Record*, March 3, 1961, p. 3004.

273 | A letter from Prof. Paul Rosenbloom to Sen. Hubert Humphrey

1. Federal funds may be used for research and development, for production, experimentation, and dissemination of information, but not to propagandize for any particular curriculum.

2. Federal funds may not be used in any way which can be construed as interference with local control. They may not be used in any way which can be interpreted as pushing any particular curriculum on the schools.

3. Participation by any institution or teacher in any project supported by this program must be entirely voluntary.

4. Any materials produced with Federal support must make their own way on their own merit. Final decisions on what use is to be made of these materials must be left to the local educational authorities.

These policies have been enforced with vigor and tact by Harry Kelley, Assistant Director of the National Science Foundation, and his very able staff, including Bowen Dees, Arthur Roe, Charles Whitmer, and Richard Paulson.

Support for program

This program has supported the Physical Sciences Study Committee, the School Mathematics Study Group, the Biological Sciences Curriculum Study, the Chemical Bonds Approach, and the Chemical Education Materials Study, which are the major national projects for the improvement of the teaching of physics, mathematics, biology, and chemistry, respectively. To illustrate the scope of these projects, I shall mention only that about 150,000 students are now benefited from the work of the school mathematics study group, which is in its third year of activity. The flexibility of the program of the course content improvement section is illustrated by its support of two major competing projects in chemistry, and of a very offbeat project in elementary mathematics by Hawley and Suppes at Stanford University. This section is also supporting extensive work on the improvement of the teaching of science and mathematics in the colleges.

Note that any educational institution can avail itself of the materials produced with the support of this program. The participation of both individuals and institutions in the projects mentioned above is on the basis of merit. Any individual or institution may submit a proposal to this program, which can support it if it is judged worthy by the experts in the field.

No Federal control

In brief, the Federal Government, through the National Science Foundation, does not tell any school or college what to teach or how to teach it. It merely says to any individual or team, "If you have an idea on how to improve what is taught in your field, and if our advisors in your field recommend your idea as worthy of support, we will help you try out your idea and make your results known. But you cannot use Federal funds to push your idea on anyone else."

This one modest program has done more to improve the quality of American education than any of the widely publicized multi-million-dollar programs.

Visiting lectureships

The problem which the visiting lectureship program attacks is that of making rare teaching talent available to many more students. This program illustrates again how an effective program can operate without strings.

If a professional organization such as the American Chemical Society thinks that such a program in its field is desirable and is willing to administer it, it may submit a proposal to the National Science Foundation. Note that the National

Science Foundation does not decide who should lecture to whom. It merely tells the leaders in any field, "If you want a program like this in your field and are willing to run it yourselves, we will foot the bill to the extent that our budget permits."

I have first hand experience with the visiting lectureships of the Mathematical Association of America to the high schools and the colleges, and those of the Society for Industrial and Applied Mathematics to colleges and industry. A brief description of the program to the high schools will give a clear idea of how the program works.

No costs for schools

In the fall a brochure, listing the visiting lecturers and their topics available in a given region, and an application form is sent to every high school, public and private, in that region. Any school may apply for the services of any of the visiting lecturers. If it can contribute anything toward paying the expenses of the lecturer, it is encouraged to do so, but it does not have to pay anything if it cannot. The visiting lecturer is available also for consultation with faculty or individual students.

High quality teachers

Thus this program enables schools and colleges to obtain the services of teachers which they could never dream of securing otherwise. One can appreciate something of the significance of this program if one realizes that less than 200 of the 2,000 colleges in the country can, at present, attract or hold a recent Ph.D. in mathematics from a good graduate school.

Note that an institution need not take a visiting lecturer unless it wants him, it need not take his advice, and furthermore, any advice he gives has no official standing since he speaks only as an individual.

Small cost of program

Both of the programs I have just described often increase enormously the effectiveness of such much more expensive programs as the National Defense Education Act and the National Science Foundation summer institutes. We can learn from these examples that a modest program, conceived with imagination, may be more valuable than a much more costly program of a routine nature. We can also learn that we can often improve a large program by a relatively small addition directed at the quality of instruction.

These programs should certainly be expanded to a level based on the number of meritorious proposals which have been submitted but for which the present budgets are inadequate. An even more crying need is to establish corresponding programs in the social sciences and the humanities.

Recommendations

I recommend that a course content improvement section be established within the Cooperative Research Branch of the U.S. Office of Education. It should have primary responsibility for fields not covered by the National Science Foundation. This would, as a byproduct, utilize the talents of the subject matter specialists in the U.S. Office of Education much better than their present assignments. The support should be on a level corresponding to the urgent needs in these fields.

I recommend also that a visiting lecturer program, especially directed at the social sciences and the humanities, be established. The higher education programs branch of the U.S. Office of Education may be an appropriate agency to administer such a program. The proposed Federal Advisory Council on Education (see the report of the President's Task Force on Education) may very well set up an advisory board for this program.

Sincerely yours,

PAUL C. ROSENBLOOM,

Professor of Mathematics at the University of Minnesota and Director, Mathematics Section, Minnesota National Laboratory, Minnesota State Department of Education.

SUPPLEMENT 6 ❀ NATIONAL PLANNING AND QUALITY CONTROL IN EDUCATION

From a report of The Conference on Policies and Strategy for Strengthening the Curriculum of the American Public Schools, Stanford, California, January 24–27, 1959, by Ralph W. Tyler, Director, Center for Advanced Study in Behavioral Sciences, Stanford, California.*

Statement of the problem

The current national concern with excellence in American education brings clearly to attention the importance of developing the best possible curriculum in American public schools. Many individuals, groups, and organizations are ready to work on the problem. However, it is becoming apparent that a sound, concerted effort to improve the school curriculum cannot be undertaken until several critical issues are resolved, namely:

1. How can the public school curriculum adequately represent the national interest in the objectives, the content, and the character of education, and at the same time reflect the special needs and interests of the state and of the local community? Can a proper division of activities, of responsibility, and of authority be outlined to serve as a basis for efforts at improvement?

2. There are many groups now seeking to rebuild the public school curriculum. Which ones should be encouraged, and what is the proper division of labor among them? This involves such questions as: To what extent should the curriculum be shaped by the aspirations and desires of the general public, on the one hand, and by the best thought of contemporary scholars and scientists, on the other? What are the roles of the teacher, the parent, the school supervisor, the professor of education, the psychologist, the sociologist, and the philosopher in the development of the curriculum?

3. What is an effective strategy for moving ahead on the task of curriculum improvement? What steps can be taken and what procedures can be followed that are likely to develop a more nearly adequate public school curriculum?

Recommendations

This discussion[1] led to the first recommendation of the conference, a recommendation which was unanimously adopted.

* Ralph W. Tyler, "Do We Need a 'National Curriculum'? A Conference Report," *The Clearing House: A Journal for Modern Junior and Senior High Schools*, vol. 34, no. 3, pp. 141–148. Reprinted with permission.

[1] Discussion omitted here.—Editor

1. There should be established immediately study groups for the redefinition of objectives, content, and organization of the public school curriculum and for the development of and experimentation with instructional materials for the courses thus designed. There should be at least two study groups in each subject so as to encourage original thinking and efforts rather than to restrict exploration and experimentation to a single plan.

Each study group should be composed of school teachers and college or university professors. The study groups might also include supervisors, administrators, and persons from schools of education who could bring particular kinds of competence, experience, or ideas helpful to the study undertaken. The probable priority in the establishment of study groups is: (*a*) social studies, (*b*) English, (*c*) biology, (*d*) others. The Physical Science Study Group centered at the Massachusetts Institute of Technology and the Mathematics Study Group centered at Yale are already under way with support from the National Science Foundation. The mathematics group is concerned with the subject both in elementary school and in high school. Where possible, each study group should work on the curriculum from the earliest introduction of the subject on through high school.

A second unanimous recommendation of the conference was closely related to the first.

2. There should be established one or more study groups on problems of organization of the curriculum as a whole, its sequence and grade placement, the relations among the several subjects, and the conditions required for stimulating and guiding effective learning. Whereas the primary concerns of study groups recommended in No. 1 are the development of course objectives, outlines of content, and instructional materials for a separate strand of the school curriculum, the primary tasks of the study groups recommended in No. 2 are to work on ways of relating effectively the several subjects and ways of achieving a truly sequential organization. Since these questions would involve both subject experts and psychologists, it seemed appropriate also to ask these groups to investigate conditions for effective learning of curriculum tasks.

The purposes of these two recommendations are (*a*) to bring together again scholars and scientists and school people to make use of their special knowledge and experience in curriculum planning, (*b*) to establish a means for investigation, experimentation, and evaluation of curriculum ideas, materials, and practices so that they can be tried out in schools and revised and improved on the basis of the results from trials, (*c*) to establish multiple centers so as to prevent any monopoly of curriculum thinking and to encourage several independent lines of thought and effort whose relative values can be discovered by experimentation and appraisal.

The third recommendation of the conference was not unanimously adopted. Mr. Conant opposed it and Mr. Troy was not present when the vote was taken. This recommendation was directed toward the difficulties encountered by lay boards of education and citizens generally in getting wise guidance on current educational issues where so many special interest groups are involved.

Several of the lay members of the conference said that thy were keenly aware that today most of the articulate groups seeking to give leadership to education were groups with only a partial or limited view of the total situation. The conferees who are directly involved in the administration of public schools also spoke in support of the establishment of a commission of respected, public-spirited citizens who would study the current educational situation and make recommendations regarding policies and actions for boards of education which would be recognized as a more objective and impartial view than any currently available.

Mr. Buck expressed the majority view when he said:

We greatly need at this time a commission which would study the American public school curriculum and would report to the public on (1) how the present curriculum came to be; (2) its scope—that is, what the schools can and should do and what they should not attempt; (3) what the basic aims of the public school should be, in an exposition which would clarify the conflicting aims; (4) what the functions of the major school subjects are—for example, what is history as a subject of study in the school; (5) methods of instruction, including the role of textbooks and other instructional materials.

Mr. Buck's suggestion led to a lengthy discussion and to considerable debate. Most of the conferees said that a careful study and report by a curriculum commission which would stand or fall on its own merits would have important values at this time. Particularly is there need for strong statements on the real priorities in education which schools must recognize. In response to the discussion Mr. Hazard introduced the following resolution:

We recommend an advisory committee of persons, nonrepresentative of any organization and chosen by the donor of the required funds, to study the history and status of curriculum in the public school systems of the United States and to report and publish its conclusions as to the curriculum, priorities, and means most effective to implement such curriculum and priorities in the public schools, to the end that the common knowledge and the common values conducive to individual freedom, competence, and development may be disclosed for selection by individual public school communities. The tenure of the committee should be two years of full-time work unless the committee should find that its report can be released within a shorter period of time.

SUPPLEMENT 7 ❁ A PROPOSED ORGANIZATION FOR RESEARCH IN EDUCATION

Report to the Advisory Board on Education of a Conference held at Madison, Wisconsin July 9-11, 1958*

Foreword

The Advisory Board on Education of the National Academy of Sciences–National Research Council sponsored at Easton, Maryland on April 24–26, 1958 a conference on Psychological Research in Education. In broad summary, this report concludes (1) that the levels of educational research activity and its financial support are very low; (2) that experimental psychologists interested in learning have not systematically organized, codified, or interpreted their research literature in a way that would make it easily accessible and intelligible to educators; and (3) that increased emphasis should be placed on research on human learning and on the application of research results to educational practice.

The Easton Conference did not attempt to suggest in detail the kinds of changes that might effect substantial improvement in the research foundations

* Published by the National Academy of Sciences—National Research Council, Washington, D.C., 1958. Reprinted with permission.

of education. However, the Conference did suggest that consideration should be given to the establishment of (1) a non-governmental agency for educational research, perhaps patterned after the National Academy of Sciences–National Research Council or the Social Science Research Council; (2) a federal agency concerned with educational research similar to the National Institute of Mental Health; and (3) a summer institute in the psychology of learning.

After reviewing these findings and recommendations, the Advisory Board on Education decided to call a second conference that would have as its objective the preparation of recommendations as to what specific action the Board and the Academy–Research Council should take. Discussions and recommendations developed at this second conference, held at Madison, Wisconsin on July 9–11, 1958, are summarized in the following pages.

The Academy–Research Council appreciates the thoughtful consideration given by the participants to the problems posed at the conference. Special thanks are due to Dr. T. R. McConnell, who served as chairman, and to Dr. C. R. Carpenter, who accepted the task of preparing the initial draft of the conference report.

R. M. WHALEY, *Executive Director*
Advisory Board on Education

GLEN FINCH, *Executive Director*
Division of Anthropology and Psychology

I. Summary of conference discussion and recommendations

At the invitation of the Advisory Board on Education and of the Division of Anthropology and Psychology of the National Academy of Sciences–National Research Council, fifteen scientists and educators met in Madison, Wisconsin on July 9–11, 1958, to consider questions relating to research in education. They first reviewed and discussed the report on the previous action and recommendations taken at the meeting in April at Easton, Maryland. General agreement was reached, endorsing the recommendations contained in that report, which concluded that action was urgently needed to solve many of the problems of educational research, if such research is to have the effect of improving processes involving formal education. These problems are institutional, interdisciplinary, and financial. They involve the need for increased prestige and better education for teachers, as well as improved relationships between psychologists, natural scientists, and educators.

The participants at the Madison conference recommended that the National Academy of Sciences–National Research Council work out specific plans for the establishment and incorporation of an Organization for Research in Education (ORE). It was recommended that the incorporating group should be representative of science, the humanities, and education. It should give attention to strengthening research programs in the colleges and universities, and might also provide for a central organization for special investigations.

It was further recommended that, in order to have much impact on research in education, the Organization for Research in Education should be adequately financed, in the range of ten to fifteen million dollars, for a period of about five years, although these figures should be taken merely to indicate the general scope of activity considered at the conference.

II. Background

Education must have an enduring central place in any society. In recognition of this requirement, education has been built firmly into the structure of our democratic system and into our government at all levels. Education must grow and be strengthened as our society and nation become more complex and as we assume greater responsibility in the world family of nations.

(A) Conditions and questions

Conditions now prevail which emphasize the supreme significance of education for all aspects of our national life, for our social and cultural development, and even for the survival of free democratic societies.

Crucial questions are raised as to whether or not a due and justifiable proportion of our resources, including human competencies, is being invested in educational enterprises; questions such as (1) Is the expansion of education commensurate with needs and demands of this growing nation? and (2) Are the requisite levels of quality and excellence being achieved by the network of educational forces and activities as they now exist and operate?

The conditions that evoke these important questions are the following:

1. The great and rapid expansion of our population.
2. The increasing amounts and kinds of knowledge which it is desirable and necessary for successive generations to acquire.
3. The high levels of intellectual excellence and the range and complexity of skills required by a modern technological society and an advancing culture.
4. The constantly rising standard of living and the expectation of ever-increasing improvement in living conditions.
5. The effects on societies and cultures of the development and wide use of faster means of travel and communication.
6. The growth of interdependence, especially economic interdependence, of the nations of the world.
7. The critical position of responsibility of this nation in the world power struggle.
8. The magnitude of development in the sciences, in technology, and in the arts of war.
9. The need to discover and to use new, creative, and imaginative modes of social adaptation and accommodation.

(B) Recognition of educational needs

The basic prevailing needs to expand and improve our educational enterprises are being eloquently formulated into *demands* which are heard from many sources. Citizens of the nation are aroused and express renewed concern about education. Scientists, both as distinguished individuals and as organized groups, are redefining the central roles of the educational processes. As a consequence, scientists and mathematicians are demanding of themselves and of others increased knowledge and skills to be applied in teaching and learning. Legislators are asking what should be done and how best shall it be done. Foundations are increasing their investments to assist in meeting the "crisis in education" and to aid in the "pursuit of excellence." Business and industry, generally viewed as consumers and not producers in the field of education, are currently recognizing the indispensable supportive functions of education and are expanding their own training endeavors as well as increasing their support to schools, colleges, and universities.

It would appear that requirements to expand and to improve the quality of our educational efforts are widely and clearly acknowledged. It would seem that the nation is now ready, given the effective leadership for vast changes and developments in education. Changes must be made rapidly, and there must be developments of such great dimensions as to equal revolutionary proportions.

What shall be the character of developments and improvements? To this question many different answers are given, for in the area of education everyone has an opinion and is ready to propose answers. Such opinions are usually based on limited personal experiences, coupled with limited information. Some individuals, including some educators, find their answers to contemporary educational problems in history. Others quote literary discourses and cite the views and theories of scholars, philosophers, and other "authorities." Those who are responsible for solving acute educational problems have available as aids in making decisions only relatively limited information. Generally, proposals which delineate the means and methods for expanding and advancing education are based on more or less considered opinions, because *appropriate, sufficient, and dependable evidence rarely exists* for determining what changes should be made.

However, there is now a growing recognition of the need for evidence and its use in solving educational problems. There is a pervasive faith that evidence should exist, or may be secured, that would be both appropriate and adequate for guiding the changes, directing the developments, and thus determining the improvements which should occur in education. Likewise, there is an increasing *confidence in research* as a means of securing the evidence needed to guide decisions that must be made for governing the progress of education, for advancing learning, and for developing intellectual talent.

(C) *Place of the behavioral sciences, including psychology*

When the question is asked as to which among the sciences, professions, and arts have both the competencies and responsibilities for conducting fundamental and advanced research of central importance to education, attention turns to the behavioral sciences and related professions, especially to psychology. Men in these fields have knowledge and practiced skills in the difficult methodologies and their adaptations, for the investigation of basic problems of perception, motivation, personal development, and learning. These problem areas, in turn, lie at the very heart of the educational processes. There are members of the behavioral sciences and related professions who have long used quantitative research as an approach to understanding the determinants and characteristics of human abilities, human growth and development, and of attitudinal and social behavior—knowledge of which is essential for the intelligent and wise conduct of education. Formerly, (1890-1920) those who did research in these areas also assisted importantly in the shaping of educational developments, theories, and methods. In recent years this close liaison has been largely lost, especially between practical educators and research psychologists. Nevertheless, research in the behavioral sciences has had, and continues to have, some effect on educational theories, procedures, and methods. There is indeed a vast but diffuse literature of educational and other kinds of research results related to educational issues and decisions. The value of this literature should be assessed and interpreted.

Study of the present state of affairs, however, shows that few major researchable problems of central importance to education have been completely solved. Some of the problems are only superficially defined. Often what is discovered is poorly communicated and hence not applied. There are vast areas of educational operations which remain to be tested and validated.

III. *The state of research in education*

The conferees agreed that the observed lack of application of research results reflects inadequate investments of resources, abilities, and efforts in the field. This condition should be corrected with all speed. By many standards the total national expenditure on education is very high. This expenditure is rapidly being increased. A basic enterprise of this magnitude might reasonably be expected to require and to justify a sizable expenditure for supporting research. The records show that present expenditures for fundamental research related to central problems of education are completely inadequate. Therefore, the Madison Planning Group is convinced that greatly increased financial resources must be invested in research in education.

The second main feature of the state of research for education, as noted by the Easton Conference, is the shortage of research personnel in the field. The demands made on educators, teachers, and others for solving practical day-to-day problems preclude their deep involvement in research of the types needed.

Bold and decisive action is urgently needed to spearhead developments in research for education, not alone to advance such research directly but also to give status and prestige to the field, to attract able and well trained men, to stimulate and catalyze the efforts of educational institutions, and to ensure that old and new information shall be effectively disseminated and applied.

Actions are being taken by individuals, institutions, foundations, organized groups and governmental agencies to provide for increasing the scope and quality of the research needed in education. There has been a remarkable recent increase of interest in this area of research on the part of physical, biological, and social scientists, of mathematicians, and of scholars in the language fields.

Many of these developments are coming into focus through the National Academy of Sciences–National Research Council and its associated organizations.

The Advisory Board on Education of the Academy–Research Council is in an advantageous position to take initial leadership in stimulating, planning, and projecting needed extensions of research for education and in securing the necessary broad and effective cooperation for ensuring success of such an effort.

IV. Recommendations and suggestions of the Madison planning group

(A) General recommendations

That the National Academy of Science–National Research Council take the initiative and proceed to plan in detail the establishing of a non-profit Organization for Research in Education (ORE).

(B) Interim activities

The Madison Planning Group recommends that research efforts not be delayed until the ORE can be organized and begin work. Conference and task force groups should be assembled to work on high priority problems. The first problems to be attacked are those generally sensed by national committees working in the areas of the physical and biological sciences, mathematics, and languages. Competent reviews of existing research results, the interpretation and suggested application of these to educational problems might well be undertaken immediately and before the ORE becomes active. During the winter ahead, plans should be made for a study to be conducted during the summer of 1959.

Specifically it is suggested that the sum of about $100,000 be secured and used both to implement interim programs under the National Academy of Science–National Research Council as now operating and to defray the expenses of organizing and incorporating the Organization for Research in Education.

(C) General objectives and activities of the ORE

The broad purpose of the ORE shall be to contribute, through research on central and critical problems basic to education, to the improvement and advancement of education at all levels.

To achieve this general purpose the ORE shall conduct, encourage, sponsor, and otherwise ensure adequate efforts in the following directions:

1. *Defining and clarifying problems, hypotheses, and questions that are fundamental to the improvement of education and that can be answered by research.* Particular, but not exclusive, emphasis should be placed on formal education and its intellectual goals. Recognition should be given to the fact that motivational, social, and attitudinal factors are fundamental to the development of intellectual interests and competencies.

2. *Promoting and conducting the research on methodologies of teaching and learning which is needed in education.* The provision of optimal conditions for high quality research is of critical importance, whether the research is done in a central institute, by special task groups, or in schools and universities.

3. *Fostering the recruitment and development of investigators in adequate numbers and abilities to conduct the needed research in education.* The indications are that there exists a deficit of personnel in educational research; that short-term task force projects are needed. The complex problems now known to exist unsolved and the certainty that new and important problems will emerge make such a continuing program essential to develop new research talent and to expand investigations.

4. *Ensuring the effective analysis, interpretation, and utilization of existing and accumulating research results for educational purposes.* Specific activities may be classified under two headings, as follows: direct and indirect.

(a) *Direct activities* shall include those which the ORE will plan and conduct, such as the following: sponsoring and conducting conferences and workshops; recruitment, assignment and supervision of competent task forces to solve specific problems; the award of fellowships, internships, and distinguished positions with the ORE for mature scholars and investigators; investigations done by the professional staff of ORE.

(b) *Indirect activities* shall include projects that are in line with stated objectives and are sponsored and coordinated but not conducted by ORE, such as the following: administering grants-in-aid programs; establishing academic research centers in selected universities and school systems; liaison work with operating centers not sponsored by ORE; and encouragement of the building of educational models which use and demonstrate the realistic application of patterns of significant research results.

Special emphasis should be given to sponsoring the establishment of research centers for investigating central problems of formal education where relevant research will be conducted, evaluated, tested and applied, and where the advanced training of research personnel will be done. Each such center should occupy an administrative status in its institution that would permit the participation of specialists from many cognate fields and substantive disciplines both in research and training. Clearly, effective work by men in such a center would require that they have optimal conditions, facilities and buildings for productive advanced research. Such conditions would include protection from instructional and administrative demands usually made upon such men.

(D) **Proposed organizational structure of the ORE**

The Madison Planning Group suggests that the ORE be organized along the following pattern:

1. There shall be a Board of Directors, consisting of about twelve members selected so as to be representative of the main disciplines concerned with education and with research upon its fundamental problems.

2. The Board shall have a Chairman and an Executive Committee chosen from its own membership.

3. The Board should appoint a Chief Officer to whom it would delegate broad executive powers. The Chief Officer should have general responsibilities for the program of the ORE, including the appointment of staff members, consultants, ad hoc committees, task groups, and such others as might be needed to carry out the operations of the organization.

4. The Chief Officer would appoint, with the approval of the Board, a *Standing Committee on Planning and Programs,* which would include several members of the Board. The Chief Officer would be Chairman of this Committee.

The formation and operation of the Organization for Research in Education will require the full cooperation and continuing support of established national organizations concerned with the promotion and advancement of research both in professional education and in substantive academic disciplines. Therefore, the Madison Planning Group recommends that the National Academy of Sciences–National Research Council take all necessary initial steps to secure cooperation in founding the ORE and to ensure continuing support. Such cooperating organizations should include the American Council of Learned Societies, the American Educational Research Association, and the Social Science Research Council. It is assumed that representatives of the National Academy of Sciences–National Research Council would consult, during the development of plans and their execution, with such organizations and individuals as are likely to be interested. It is also assumed that the Academy–Research Council will take cognizance of and confer with any other groups which may be formulating plans for educational research organizations similar in structure, status, or objectives to that proposed here.

The Madison Planning Group discussed at length the range, scope, and status of the ORE which would be commensurate with present needs and feasible for a new and developing organization. The Group recommends:

1. There should be an interim period of research activity, as outlined above. This, together with launching the organization, would cost about $100,000.

2. The organization should have at first a planned general program beginning in mid-1959 and covering a five-year period. There should be a build-up over the first year involving an expenditure of about one to one and one-half million dollars. This sum would be spent for activities such as those outlined in this report.

3. The Madison Planning Group developed a firm conviction that the ORE should be so financed, organized, and conducted as to provide superior and effective leadership in educational research. The total sum envisaged as being possibly adequate, and of about an amount that could be invested wisely during the first five years, was estimated to be within the range of ten to fifteen million dollars.

4. The Planning Group recognized that the success of the organization in accomplishing its mission would depend directly upon the adequacy of its staff, especially upon the abilities of the Chief Officer. There was no dissent to the proposal that the best man in the country be secured for this position. To accomplish this will require an unusual salary and other professional advantages. The building of a strong supporting staff will require similar incentives.

5. The range of research conducted should be broad and should include projects at all levels of education.

6. The Madison Planning Group recognized that the ORE and the finances used by it could serve as an important spearhead development for research, for initiating research in neglected areas, and for stimulating educational institutions to extend and deepen their own research programs.

SUPPLEMENT 8 ❧ NEA PROJECT ON INSTRUCTION*
Ole Sand**

Today in America an earnest and searching reappraisal cuts across almost all aspects of life. It is in such a time that the NEA is undertaking a two-year project on the instructional program of the public schools.

The project is one of several other major NEA efforts of this century designed to upgrade the quality of and give direction to American public education. Notable among these are the Seven Cardinal Principles of 1918, the *Purposes of Education in American Democracy* of 1938, and the current Educational Policies Commission redefinition of the purposes of American education.

The Project on Instruction serves another highly important purpose. By establishing guidelines for instruction in the years just ahead, it will also provide the content fields with methodologies for assessing developments in their areas of study.

The need for reappraisal was summarized last summer at the NEA Convention in Los Angeles by Deputy Executive Secretary Lyle W. Ashby when he said: "The organized profession has a responsibility to state its conclusions at a time when many other voices are being heard with varying definitions of what constitutes a sound program of elementary and secondary education in today's world."

The success of the Project on Instruction will rest in no small measure on the utilization of the vast skills and experience of the teaching profession. With this fact in mind, the profession has been involved in each phase and aspect of the task, including the formulation of the directions and nature of the project. Later, the profession will be involved through departmental, state, and special meetings, as well as through other means.

The fourteen-member national committee for the project is composed of teachers, administrators, and university professors. Its membership includes Melvin W. Barnes, Thomas G. Pullen, Jr., Sarah C. Caldwell, William M. Alexander, Hollis L. Caswell, Rufus E. Clement, Marion Cranmore, Carol Douglass, Robert J. Havighurst, James D. Logsdon, Philip H. Phenix, I. James Quillen, G. Baker Thompson, and Allan M. West.

The committee has decided that the project should focus upon those important issues and decisions that will make a difference in the direction and nature of public elementary and secondary education in the sixties. To this end, four publications are planned: *Education in a Changing Society, What To Teach, Organizing for Instruction,* and *A Platform for Instruction* (a final summary report).

The first, *Education in a Changing Society*, will discuss the societal forces and trends and the fundamental values that are persuasive on American education today. A group of outstanding behavioral scientists and educators, who met at a two-day seminar at NEA headquarters last October, are serving as a major data source for this publication.

The subjects of the next two publications, *What To Teach* and *Organizing for Instruction*, were chosen by the national committee, based upon their own

---

* Reprinted from the *NEA Journal*, May, 1961, with permission.
** Dr. Sand is director of the NEA Project on the Instructional Program of the Public Schools. He is on leave from Wayne State University, Detroit, where he is professor of education.

experiences and several surveys conducted by the staff of the project. In analyzing these areas of concern, the committee will:

1. Identify and clarify the concerns or issues in each area.
2. Suggest the criteria, the guiding principles, to be applied in deciding what to teach and in organizing for that instruction.
3. Indicate the evidence for the guidelines—facts from research and experience which make the guidelines valid.
4. Propose alternative decisions, giving reasons for each.
5. Suggest a course of action and/or methods of inquiry by which local schools can make their own decisions or take their own positions. On those issues where the evidence warrants, take a position.

The evidence for the guidelines will be based upon data from five sources: (*a*) societal forces and trends, including traditional and emerging values that affect American education; (*b*) the nature and content of knowledge in the various disciplines; (*c*) the nature of learning; (*d*) human growth and development; and (*e*) key practices in the two areas of concern as revealed by a questionnaire and interview study. Position papers are being prepared indicating how evidence from these data sources can be applied to the resolution of crucial instructional issues.

The project is seeking out the best evidence wherever it can be found. In some cases, it is in the classroom; in others, it is in the offices of school administrators or in the state offices of education. In still others, it is in the colleges and universities. The search will continue for the duration of the project.

In the publication, *What To Teach,* the profession will attempt to answer such questions as, "What should be taught to whom?" and "How should the 'what' be adapted to individual and group needs?"

These questions will take into consideration the perplexities of providing education at the same time and in the same school for the American youth who may become a nuclear physicist and the youngster who is skilled with his hands and may become an increasingly needed technician.

The questions may also explore the educational needs of America's thousands of so-called alienated youth—young people who somehow have lost touch with and interest in life about them. Implied here, too, are questions which explore the increasingly urgent problem, especially in big-city schools, of the dropout and the consequent waste of human resources.

What To Teach will also consider the question of *where* decisions are made—at the local, state, and national level. How does one equate local control, needs, and standards with what some educators believe to be an increasing need for national goals and/or standards? Another issue relates to the influence of tests on decisions concerning educational objectives.

It will explore questions raised by the pressure of various demands on the schools. For instance, what is the effect, particularly in the elementary school, of "pushing things down"—of teaching foreign languages or geometry at an earlier and earlier grade? What should be the school's central responsibility and what should be left to agencies outside the school? In this changing, highly mechanized life, should there be a shift in viewpoint on what is the responsibility of the schools and what is not—and is there time for all of it?

Related to this two-part question are the questions of priorities and balance. How can schools decide what is necessary to teach as contrasted with what is merely desirable? And for education for the sixties, should the humanities and the social sciences get equal treatment with mathematics and science?

In some fields of study, the basic content has been fundamentally altered in the past fifteen years; in all fields, the quantity of knowledge has increased in geometrical proportions. To mention a few large-scale studies in certain content areas, there are the American Institute of Biological Sciences Curriculum Study; the Chemical Bond Study; the Joint Project of the American Council of Learned Societies and NEA's National Council for the Social Studies; the mathematics projects at the University of Illinois, the University of Maryland, and Yale; the National Task Force on Economic Education; and the Physical Sciences Study Committee.

The basic question for the project is: How can a teacher make intelligent use of the recommendations from such a variety of sources?

Methods of inquiry and concept formation need to be re-examined. Scholars in education and in the academic disciplines have begun to reappraise what we know about learning knowledge and ways of knowing, concerns that are not new but which have taken on renewed urgency.

A Seminar on the Disciplines will be sponsored by the project at NEA headquarters June 15–17, 1961. This major seminar should assist the project to cope better with this question: "What fundamental ideas in the various disciplines and/or methods of inquiry should get into the mainstream of the instructional program of the public schools?"

To formulate guidelines for making decisions is also the major purpose of the publication, *Organizing for Instruction*. The guidelines will deal both with issues of organizing the curriculum and of organizing the school. The publication will examine a variety of organizational ideas such as departmentalization, the nongraded school, team teaching, multiple tracks, ability grouping, instructional technology, and extended school time. As with the publication, *What To Teach*, case studies will be used to demonstrate how different types of school systems make decisions and how various forces and factors bear on the process.

The final report of the project will be addressed primarily to the public—school board and PTA members and other interested citizens. In addition to summarizing guidelines for various components of the instructional program, it will take positions based on the best available evidence from experience and research and will suggest means by which local schools can take their own positions.

But the problem of transition from reports to action will remain. Not long ago, a well-known writer on education compared committee reports to the chorus in a Greek drama: Too many of them give warning of vague trials ahead without interfering with the business of the actors or of killing the suspense of the audience. Therefore, it is essential that recommendations for *action* at the national, regional, state, and local levels be forthcoming.

The project should result in recommendations to the NEA Board of Directors and Executive Committee for immediate and long-range programs for the continuing study and improvement of instruction in the public schools of America.

NEA Project on Instruction, auxiliary publications, currently available

1. *Preliminary Report* (First-look Flyer)
2. *The Scholars Look at the Schools: A Report of the Disciplines Seminar*
3. *The Principals Look at the Schools: A Status Study of Selected Instructional Practices*
4. *Current Curriculum Studies in Academic Subjects*, by Dorothy M. Fraser

Major project volumes to be published during the 1962–1963 academic year

  I. *Schools for the Sixties: Curriculum Decisions—Issues and Recommendations*
 II. *Education in a New World*
III. *Deciding What to Teach*
 IV. *Planning and Organizing for Teaching*

SUPPLEMENT 9 ❧ THE MINNESOTA NATIONAL LABORATORY*

1. General description

The Minnesota National Laboratory is an agency of the Minnesota State Department of Education. Its function is to carry out scientific experimentation and evaluation of new curricular materials. It has a central staff supported by the state, and carries out experimentation on a contractual basis for national organizations. Until now it has only had a mathematics section, the director of which is Professor P. C. Rosenbloom of the Department of Mathematics, Institute of Technology, University of Minnesota. The State Board of Education contemplates the establishment of other sections, and the appointment of directors for other fields as corresponding national projects for curriculum revision are organized and are prepared to use our facilities for educational experimentation. The Laboratory, which is also authorized by the legislature to make cooperative arrangements with other states, began its operations on September 1, 1958.

2. Organization and procedures

The Minnesota National Laboratory is part of the Division of Instruction, headed by Farley D. Bright, Assistant Commissioner, Minnesota State Department of Education. The staff of the Mathematics Section consists of:

P. C. Rosenbloom, Director
N. Rajaratnam, Test Construction
C. Kraft, Statistician
J. A. Lown, Administrator

E. O. Swanson, Testing Consultant
W. Hively, Programmed Instruction
Jean Havlish, Secretary
Donna Bourdon, Clerk Typist

There is also a state advisory committee, consisting of:

Roland C. Anderson, Professor of Mathematics, State College, St. Cloud, Minnesota
Stanley Hill, Vice President, Minnesota Mutual Life Insurance Company, St. Paul, Minnesota
Harvey O. Jackson, Curriculum Consultant, Minneapolis Public Schools
Gerhald K. Kalisch, Professor of Mathematics, College of Science, Literature and the Arts, University of Minnesota, Minneapolis, Minnesota
Ralph Berdie, Director, Student Counseling Bureau, University of Minnesota, Minneapolis, Minnesota
Kenneth O. May, Professor of Mathematics, Carleton College, Northfield, Minnesota
William R. McEwen, Professor and Chairman, Science and Mathematics, Duluth Branch, University of Minnesota, Duluth, Minnesota
Walter W. Richardson, Superintendent of Schools, North St. Paul, Minnesota
Sister Seraphim, Professor of Mathematics, College of St. Catherine, St. Paul, Minnesota
S. E. Popper, Professor of Education, University of Minnesota, Minneapolis, Minnesota

A national advisory committee is also being formed.
Participation by school and teacher is entirely voluntary, and by application.

* Reprint of bulletin issued by the Minnesota State Department of Education, revised by editor.

Application forms for such participation have been sent to every superintendent and head of private school in the state. For each experiment carried out by the Laboratory random selections are made from the population of applicants, stratified in accordance with the design of the experiment. Similar procedures are used for participation by colleges and their staffs in projects undertaken by the Laboratory.

3. Purposes

The Laboratory has, as mentioned above, the function of performing educational experimentation and evaluation of new curricular materials. It does not recommend materials for adoption. With each experiment the Laboratory publishes a detailed technical report on the basis of which school people can make their own decisions. This information is often useful also to the writers for the revision of the materials.

It is contemplated that the Laboratory will serve the national scholarly and educational community by its performance of research in curriculum development for which facilities for state-wide experimentation are useful. It is prepared to place its facilities at the disposal of research workers in other parts of the country in cooperative projects.

4. Activities 1958–1962

Most of the work done by the Laboratory so far has been under contract with SMSG (School Mathematics Study Group), a national project for the improvement of the teaching of mathematics.

In 1958–59 the Laboratory conducted a preliminary evaluation for the SMSG experimental units for grades 7 and 8, produced by the writing project at Yale during the summer of 1958. It also conducted a preliminary comparison between the conventional 9th grade course and the course produced by the University of Illinois Committee on School Mathematics, directed by Professor M. Beberman.

During the summer of 1959 the Laboratory conducted a program of summer workshops for mathematics teachers at 19 of the 28 colleges and junior colleges in the state. A total of 234 teachers completed the program of these workshops.

During the academic year 1959–60, the Laboratory conducted preliminary evaluations of the SMSG sample texts for grades 8–12. It also carried out a careful comparison experiment, pitting the SMSG 7th grade course against the conventional course. The experiment with the Illinois 9th grade course was continued.

For two years the Laboratory also conducted a feasibility study of correspondence courses for gifted students. The courses are made available to a total of 300 students per grade per year in grades 9 and 10 in Minnesota, Wisconsin, Iowa, and the Dakotas.

During the summer of 1960 the Laboratory, under a grant from the National Science Foundation to the Minnesota Academy of Science, produced at the studios of the educational television station KTCA-TV 210 half-hour films for the in-service education of mathematics teachers. These include demonstration classes with SMSG materials in grades 7–12, lectures on the mathematical background, and a course on the psychology of elementary mathematical concepts. About 150 of these films will soon be available nationally.

During the academic years 1960–62 the Laboratory continued its experimentation with the SMSG sample texts in grades 7–12 in conjunction with a study on the characteristics of teachers affecting students' learning conducted by Flanders, Torrance, and Rosenbloom of the University of Minnesota under a grant from the U.S. Office of Education. During 1960–61 the Laboratory also conducted a preliminary evaluation of the SMSG materials for grades 4–6, written during the summer of 1960.

The Laboratory also carried out for SMSG during the academic year 1960–62 a preliminary evaluation of the SMSG materials for slower students in grades 7–10, and a special experiment comparing alternative methods of handling drill. During 1960–62 there were about 200 experimental classes in grades 4–12, spread all over the state, in the program of the Laboratory.

The experimental correspondence courses for gifted students will soon be made generally available.

The Laboratory began, in June, 1961, a project to produce materials for grades K–3 under a grant from the National Science Foundation. This will be in conjunction with an investigation of the development of mathematical concepts in children conducted by Muller-Willis and Rosenbloom at the University of Minnesota under a grant from the National Institute of Health. This project will continue under the auspices of the University of Minnesota, and will be expanded to a science and mathematics curriculum project in grades K–9.

5. Plans for the future

The Laboratory will expand its central staff to include directors for fields other than mathematics, some permanent staff on test construction, and some administrative assistance. It also plans to establish mechanisms for the dissemination of information about new developments in the curriculum and in educational research throughout the state.

It will ask Minnesota to establish permanently a program of correspondence courses for gifted students, with provision for gradual extension to all parts of the curriculum. This correspondence program may be provided as a service to educational institutions and agencies in other states.

The Laboratory plans to conduct several experiments on pre- and in-service education of teachers, and on the use of new media of instruction.

In its work the Laboratory will continue to maintain a close relationship to scholars and educators in many disciplines all over the country. The school and college men in Minnesota will, we are sure, continue their excellent cooperation so that the Laboratory may contribute to the improvement of education nationally.

A panel of national scope has met and given their recommendations for the formation of a National Advisory Committee for the Laboratory. The panel felt that the objectives and scope of the Minnesota National Laboratory should be the following:

(a) To engage in projects best conducted at the state level
(b) To conduct research and exploration in matters pertaining to curriculum
(c) To carry on programs of national interest on a state-wide level
(d) To serve as a model for other states
(e) To supply information to other states

Plans are under way for a four-year evaluation experiment on a regional basis with the materials from several of the new experimental programs such as SMSG, Illinois, Ball State, and Maryland Project. This project was begun in the spring of 1961.

NOTE: In 1963 a social studies section was established with Prof. W. Gardner, of the University of Minnesota, as director.

SUPPLEMENT 10 ❄ TEXT OF SENATE BILL 2826
"Improvement of Educational Quality Act of 1962" (Introduced by Senator Wayne Morse, February 8, 1962)

A BILL To improve the quality of elementary and secondary education.
Be it enacted by the Senate and House of Representatives of the United States of America in Congress assembled, That this Act may be cited as the "Improvement of Educational Quality Act of 1962".

Title I: Improvement of quality of teaching in elementary and secondary schools

Institutes for advanced study for teachers

SEC. 101. The Commissioner is authorized to arrange, through grants or contracts, with colleges and universities for the operation by them of short-term or regular session institutes for advanced study, including study in the use of new teaching methods and instructional materials, for individuals who are engaged in teaching, or in supervising teachers, in elementary and secondary schools, in subject-matter areas in which he finds that there is a widespread need for improvement in the quality of instruction. In determining the subject-matter areas in which such advanced studies will be provided, the Commissioner shall give preference to subjects which are generally accepted as meeting college entrance requirements, and shall take into consideration the activities, in the area of advanced studies for elementary or secondary school teachers, being supported by the Office of Education, the National Science Foundation, or other agencies or departments under other Federal laws. Each individual (engaged in teaching or in supervising teachers in elementary or secondary schools) who attends an institute operated under the provisions of this section shall be eligible (after application therefor) to receive a stipend at the rate of $75 per week for the period of his attendance at such institute, and each such individual with one or more dependents shall receive an additional stipend at the rate of $15 per week for each such dependent for the period of such attendance.

Scholarship grants for outstanding teachers in elementary and secondary schools

SEC. 102. (a) The Commissioner is authorized to make scholarship grants for one year of full-time study at colleges or universities to individuals engaged in teaching in elementary or secondary schools who have demonstrated special scholarship ability and aptitude for teaching, and who show promise of being able, through such study, to make significant contributions to improvement in the quality of instruction in elementary and secondary schools. The number of such grants to be made from the sums appropriated under this section for any fiscal year shall be the number, not to exceed two thousand five hundred, specified in the Act appropriating such sums, and the number so specified shall be allocated by the Commissioner among the States, in accordance with his regulations, on the basis of the relative numbers of persons engaged as full-time certified elementary and secondary school teachers in each State in the most recent years for which satisfactory data are available to him, except that the number so allocated to each State for any fiscal year shall be at least ten. Recipients of the grants so allocated to each State shall be selected by a State commission broadly representative of elementary and secondary education, higher education, and the public, and established or designated for the purpose by the Governor of the State; each such commission shall make its selection in accordance with criteria and procedures, consistent with this section, which are developed by it and approved by the Commissioner. Teachers awarded scholarship grants under this section shall pursue full-time courses of study primarily in the subject-matter or content areas in which the recipient teaches or expects to teach. Each such teacher shall receive a stipend, as provided in regulations of the Commissioner, equal to his or her most recent annual salary as an elementary or secondary school teacher, but not to exceed $5,000, and the college or university which such individual attends shall receive a cost of education allowance of $500.

Project grants to strengthen teacher preparation programs

SEC. 103. (a) The Commissioner is authorized to make grants to colleges and universities which have programs for the preparation of individuals to teach in elementary and secondary schools, to pay part of the cost of special projects designed to strengthen such programs through improvement of course content and curriculums (including improvements in library resources needed for such programs), improvement of student teaching activities, and improvement of standards for selection of candidates for such programs and standards for continuation in and graduation from such programs. Any grant for any such project made from an appropriation under this section for any fiscal year may include such amounts as the Commissioner determines to be necessary for succeeeding fiscal years for completion of the Federal participation in the project as approved by the Commissioner.

(b) No grant shall be made under this section for any project until the Commissioner has obtained the advice and recommendations of persons who are competent to evaluate the project as to its feasibility and its pertinence to the purposes of this section, and as to the adequacy of the resources available to carry out the project.

Authorization of appropriations

SEC. 104. There are hereby authorized to be appropriated for the fiscal year ending June 30, 1963, and for each of the four succeeding fiscal years such sums as may be necessary to carry out the provisions of this title, including sums determined by the Commissioner to be necessary for administrative expenses of scholarship commissions under section 102.

Title II: Broader application of improved instructional practices

Grants to states

SEC. 201. (a) There are hereby authorized to be appropriated $50,000,000 for the fiscal year ending June 30, 1963, and for each of the four succeeding years, for making grants to State educational agencies under this section to assist in the conduct of pilot, demonstration, or experimental projects of local educational agencies designed to improve the quality of instruction in public elementary and secondary schools, and to assist in the expansion and improvement of State educational agency activities in developing, evaluating, and promoting the broader application of improved instructional practices in such schools.

(b) (1) From the sums appropriated pursuant to subsection (a) for any fiscal year, the Commissioner shall reserve such amount, but not in excess of 1.6 per centum thereof, as he may determine for allotment among the Commonwealth of Puerto Rico, the Canal Zone, Guam, American Samoa, and the Virgin Islands, according to their respective needs. From the remainder of such sums the Commissioner shall allot to each State an amount which bears the same ratio to the amount of such remainder as the population of such State bears to the total of the populations of all the States. The populations of the several States shall be determined by the Commissioner for the most recent year for which satisfactory data are available from the Department of Commerce.

(2) A State's allotment under subsection (a) for the fiscal year ending June 30, 1963, shall, to the extent not reallotted pursuant to this subsection, remain available for payment pursuant to subsection (d) for projects or activities in such State until June 30, 1964.

(3) The amount of any State's allotment under this subsection for any fiscal year which the Commissioner determines will not be required during the period for which such allotment is available for carrying out the State plan (if any) approved under this section shall be available for reallotment from time to time, on such dates during such period as the Commissioner may fix, to other States in proportion to the original allotments to such States under this subsection, but with such adjustments as may be necessary to prevent reallotment to any State of any sum in excess of the amount which the Commissioner estimates it needs and will be able to use for such periods for carrying out the State plan. Any amount reallotted to a State under this paragraph during a year shall be deemed part of its allotment under this subsection for such year.

(c) (1) Any State which desires to receive payments under this section shall submit to the Commissioner, through its State educational agency, a State plan which—

(A) provides that the State educational agency will be the sole agency for administering the plan;

(B) sets forth a program under which all funds paid to the State from its allotment under subsection (b), except funds paid pursuant to clause (D) of this paragraph, will be expended solely for pilot, demonstration, or experimental projects of limited duration, submitted by local educational agencies or by other agencies or institutions operating a public elementary or secondary school, and approved by the State educational agency, which are designed to improve the quality and effectiveness of public elementary and secondary education, including but not limited to the following types of programs (and including the acquisition of library and other materials and equipment needed for such programs):

(i) programs to encourage and stimulate educational excellence, including course content and curriculum adaptations and special accelerated programs for exceptionally gifted children;

(ii) projects to improve the effectiveness of public elementary and secondary school teachers through preservice, internship, and in-service programs;

(iii) programs for the improvement of instruction through the more effective utilization of new or improved instructional materials and equipment or through the development of improvements in the design of school facilities;

(iv) programs for developing new types of elementary or secondary instruction or programing;

(v) remedial or special instructional programs or services for pupils having language or other special educational problems;

(vi) programs or services for adapting curriculums to the needs of deprived or disadvantaged pupils;

(vii) programs for coordinating the school system planning and programs in the area served by the local education agency, with the planning and programs of other public or private nonprofit agencies dealing with problems related to the alleviation of deteriorated or depressed communities which include such area and of the families and children residing therein;

(C) sets forth the criteria and procedures, consistent with the purposes of this section, on the basis of which projects submitted by local educational agencies or other agencies or institutions under this section will be approved by the State educational agency;

(D) sets forth a program for expansion or improvement of State educational agency supervisory or related activities, including research, development, evaluation, and promotion of improved instructional practices in public elementary and secondary schools and including administration of the State plan, except that not to exceed 10 per centum of a State's allotment under this section for any fiscal year may be expended for such activities;

(E) provides that the State educational agency will make such reports to the Commissioner, in such form and containing such information, as may be reasonably necessary to enable the Commissioner to perform his duties under this section; and

(F) provides for such fiscal control and fund accounting procedures as may be necessary to assure proper disbursement of and accounting for Federal funds paid to the State, and by the State to local educational agencies or other agencies or institutions under this section.

(2) The Commissioner shall approve any State plan and any modification thereof which complies with the provisions of paragraph (1). The Commissioner shall not finally disapprove any State plan submitted under this section, or any modification thereof, without first affording the State educational agency reasonable notice and opportunity for a hearing.

(3) Whenever the Commissioner, after reasonable notice and opportunity for hearing to the State educational agency administering a State plan approved under this section, finds that—

(A) the State plan has been so changed that it no longer complies with the provisions of this section, or

(B) in the administration of the plan there is a failure to comply substantially with any such provisions, the Commissioner shall notify such State agency that no further payments will be made to the State under this section (or, in his discretion, further payments to the State will be limited to projects under or portions of the State plan not affected by such failure), until he is satisfied that there will no longer be any failure to comply. Until he is so satisfied, the Commissioner shall make no further payments to such State under this section (or shall limit payments to projects under or portions of the State plan not affected by such failure).

(4) A State educational agency dissatisfied with a final action of the Commissioner under paragraph (2) or (3) of this subsection may appeal to the United States court of appeals for the circuit in which the State is located, by filing a petition with such court within sixty days after such final action. A copy of the petition shall be forthwith transmitted by the clerk of the court to the Commissioner, or any officer designated by him for that purpose. The Commissioner thereupon shall file in the court the record of the proceedings on which he based his action, as provided in section 2112 of title 28, United States Code. Upon the filing of such petition, the court shall have jurisdiction to affirm the action of the Commissioner or to set it aside, in whole or in part, temporarily or permanently. The findings of the Commissioner as to the facts, is supported by substantial evidence, shall be conclusive, but the court, for good cause shown, may remand the case to the Commissioner to take further evidence, and the Commissioner may thereupon make new or modified findings of fact and may modify his previous action, and shall file in the court the record of the further proceedings. Such new or modified findings of fact shall likewise be conclusive

if supported by substantial evidence. The judgment of the court affirming or setting aside, in whole or in part, any action of the Commissioner shall be final, subject to review by the Supreme Court of the United States upon certiorari or certification as provided in section 1254 of title 28, United States Code.

(d) From a State's allotment for a fiscal year under subsection (b), the Commissioner shall from time to time pay to such State an amount equal to one-half of the expenditures for projects described in subsection (c) (1) (B) and for State educational agency activities described in subsection (c) (1) (D) which are carried out under its approved State plan, except that from a State's allotment for the fiscal year ending June 30, 1963, he shall pay with respect to expenditures for State educational agency activities described in subsection (c) (1) (D) an amount equal to such expenditures.

Amendments to cooperative research act

SEC. 202. The first section of the Act of July 26, 1954, entitled "An Act to authorize cooperative research in education" (68 Stat. 533, 20 U.S.C. 331) is amended to read as follows:

"(a) In order to enable the Office of Education more effectively to accomplish the purposes and to perform the duties for which it was originally established, the Commissioner of Education is authorized to enter into contracts or jointly financed cooperative arrangements with, or make grants to, public or nonprofit private universities, colleges, and other organizations with research or professional training facilities, State educational agencies, and, with the concurrence of the appropriate State educational agency, local educational agencies, for the conduct of research, surveys, and demonstrations in the field of education, including grants to public or nonprofit private universities, colleges, and other organizations with educational research facilities to pay part of the cost of the establishment and operation, when appropriate in cooperation with State and local educational agencies, of centers for the conduct of programs of research, development, evaluation and demonstration of improved instructional practices and materials in elementary and secondary schools."

Title III: Miscellaneous provisions

Definitions

SEC. 301. As used in this Act—

(a) The term "State" means a State, the District of Columbia, the Commonwealth of Puerto Rico, the Canal Zone, Guam, American Samoa, and the Virgin Islands, except that as used in section 201 (b) (1) such term does not include the Commonwealth of Puerto Rico, the Canal Zone, Guam, American Samoa, or the Virgin Islands.

(b) The term "Commissioner" means the Commissioner of Education.

(c) The term "Secretary" means the Secretary of Health, Education, and Welfare.

(d) The term "State educational agency" means the State board of education or other agency or officer primarily responsible for the State supervision of public elementary and secondary schools, or, if there is no such officer or agency, an officer or agency designated by the Governor or by State law.

(e) The term "elementary school" means a school which provides elementary education, as determined under State law.

(f) The term "secondary school" means a school which provides secondary education, as determined under State law, except that it does not include any education provided beyond grade 12.

(g) The term "local educational agency" means a board of education or other legally constituted local school authority having administrative control and direction of public elementary or secondary schools in a city, county, township, school district, or political subdivision in a State.

Payments

SEC. 302. Payments under this Act to any individual, to a State educational agency, State commission, institution of higher education, or any other organization, pursuant to a grant or contract, may be made in advance or by way of reimbursement, in such installments and at such times as may reasonably be required for expenditure by the recipients thereof, and, in the case of grants, with necessary adjustments on account of overpayments or underpayments.

Delegation of authority

SEC. 303. The Commissioner is authorized to delegate any of his functions under this Act, except the making of regulations, to any officer or employee of the Office of Education.

Federal control of education prohibited

SEC. 304. Nothing contained in this Act shall be construed to authorize any department, agency, officer, or employee of the United States to exercise any direction, supervision, or control over the curriculum, program of instruction, administration, or personnel of any educational institution or school system.

NOTE: A modification of this bill was submitted by the administration on Jan. 29, 1963, as Title III of the "National Education Improvement Act of 1963" (H.R. 3000). This legislation was also presented separately as bills H.R. 6013 and H.R. 6025.

SUPPLEMENT 11 ❋ MESSAGE FROM THE PRESIDENT OF THE UNITED STATES
Relative to an Educational Program*

To the Congress of the United States:

No task before our Nation is more important than expanding and improving the educational opportunities of all our people. The concept that every American deserves the opportunity to attain the highest level of education of which he is capable is not new to this administration—it is a traditional ideal of democracy. But it is time that we moved toward the fulfillment of this ideal with more vigor and less delay.

For education is both the foundation and the unifying force of our democratic way of life—it is the mainspring of our economic and social progress—it is the highest expression of achievement in our society, ennobling and enriching human life. In short, it is at the same time the most profitable investment society can make and the richest reward it can confer.

Today, more than at any other time in our history, we need to develop our intellectual resources to the fullest. But the facts of the matter are that many

* February 6, 1962.—Referred to the Committee on Education and Labor, and ordered to be printed. 87th Congress, 2d Session, House of Representatives Document No. 330. Reprinted with permission.

thousands of our young people are not educated to their maximum capacity—and they are not, therefore, making the maximum contribution of which they are capable to themselves, their families, their communities, and the Nation. Their talents lie wasted—their lives are frequently paled and blighted—and their contribution to our economy and culture are lamentably below the levels of their potential skills, knowledge, and creative ability. Educational failures breed delinquency, despair, and dependence. They increase the costs of unemployment and public welfare. They cut our potential national economic output by billions. They deny the benefits of our society to large segments of our people. They undermine our capability as a nation to discharge world obligations. All this we cannot afford—better schools we can afford.

To be sure, Americans are still the best educated and best trained people in the world. But our educational system has failed to keep pace with the problems and needs of our complex technological society. Too many are illiterate or untrained, and thus either unemployed or underemployed. Too many receive an education diminished in quality in thousands of districts which cannot or do not support modern and adequate facilities, well-paid and well-trained teachers, or even a sufficiently long school year.

Too many—an estimated 1 million a year—leave school before completing high school—the bare minimum for a fair start in modern-day life. Too many high school graduates with talent—numbering in the hundreds of thousands—fail to go on to college; and 40 percent of those who enter college drop out before graduation. And too few, finally, are going on to the graduate studies that modern society requires in increasing number. The total number of graduates receiving doctorate degrees has increased only about one-third in 10 years; in 1960 they numbered less than 10,000, including only 3,000 in mathematics, physical sciences, and engineering.

An educational system which is inadequate today will be worse tomorrow, unless we act now to improve it. We must provide facilities for 14 million more elementary, secondary school, and college students by 1970, an increase of 30 per cent. College enrollments alone will nearly double, requiring approximately twice as many facilities to serve nearly 7 million students by 1970. We must find the means of financing a 75-per cent increase in the total cost of education—another $20 billion a year for expansion and improvement—particularly in facilities and instruction which must be of the highest quality if our Nation is to achieve its highest goals.

The role of the Federal government

The control and operation of education in America must remain the responsibility of State and local governments and private institutions. This tradition assures our educational system of the freedom, the diversity, and the vitality necessary to serve our free society fully. But the Congress has long recognized the responsibility of the Nation as a whole—that additional resources, meaningful encouragement, and vigorous leadership must be added to the total effort by the Federal Government if we are to meet the task before us. For education in this country is the right—the necessity—and the responsibility—of all. Its advancement is essential to national objectives and dependent on the greater financial resources available at the national level.

Let us put to rest the unfounded fears that "Federal money means Federal control." From the Northwest Ordinance of 1787, originally conceived by Thomas Jefferson, through the Morrill Act of 1862, establishing the still-important and still-independent land-grant college system, to the National Defense Education

Act of 1958, the Congress has repeatedly recognized its responsibility to strengthen our educational system without weakening local responsibility. Since the end of the Korean war, Federal funds for constructing and operating schools in districts affected by Federal installations have gone directly to over 5,500 districts without any sign or complaint of interference or dictation from Washington. In the last decade, over $5 billion of Federal funds have been channeled to aid higher education without in any way undermining local administration.

While the coordination of existing Federal programs must be improved, we cannot meanwhile defer action on meeting our current pressing needs. Every year of further delay means a further loss of the opportunity for quality instruction to students who will never get that opportunity back. I therefore renew my urgent request of last year to the Congress for early action on those measures necessary to help this Nation achieve the twin goals of education: a new standard of educational excellence—and the availability of such excellence to all who are willing and able to pursue it.

I. Assistance to elementary and secondary education

Elementary and secondary schools are the foundation of our educational system. There is little value in our efforts to broaden and improve our higher education, or increase our supply of such skills as science and engineering, without a greater effort for excellence at this basic level of education. With our mobile population and demanding needs, this is not a matter of local or State action alone—this is a national concern.

Since my message on education of last year, our crucial needs at this level have intensified and our deficiencies have grown more critical. We cannot afford to lose another year in mounting a national effort to eliminate the shortage of classrooms, to make teachers' salaries competitive, and to lift the quality of instruction.

Classrooms. To meet current needs and accommodate increasing enrollments—increasing by nearly 1 million elementary and secondary pupils a year in the 1960's—and to provide every child with the opportunity to receive a full-day education in an adequate classroom, a total of 600,000 classrooms must be constructed during this decade. The States report an immediate shortage today of more than 127,000 classrooms and a rate of construction which, combined with heavily increasing enrollments, is not likely to fill their needs for 10 years. Already over half a million pupils are in curtailed or half-day sessions. Unless the present rate of construction is accelerated and Federal resources made available to supplement State and local resources that are already strained in many areas few families and communities in the Nation will be free from the ill effects of overcrowded or inadequate facilities in our public schools.

Teachers' salaries. Teachers' salaries, though improving, are still not high enough to attract and retain in this demanding profession all the capable teachers we need. We entrust to our teachers our most valuable possession—our children—for a very large share of their waking hours during the most formative years of their life. We make certain that those to whom we entrust our financial assets are individuals of the highest competence and character—we dare not do less for the trustees of our children's minds.

Yet in no other sector of our national economy do we find such a glaring discrepancy between the importance of one's work to society and the financial reward society offers. Can any able and industrious student, unless unusually motivated, be expected to elect a career that pays more poorly than almost any other craft, trade, or profession? Until this situation can be dramatically improved —unless the States and localities can be assisted and stimulated in bringing about salary levels which will make the teaching profession competitive with other professions which require the same length of training and ability—we cannot hope to succeed in our efforts to improve the quality of our children's instruction and to meet the need for more teachers.

These are problems of national proportion. Last year I sent to the Congress a proposal to meet the urgent needs of the Nation's elementary and secondary schools. A bill (S. 1021) embodying this proposal passed the Senate last year; and similar legislation (H.R. 7300) was favorably reported to the House by its Committee on Education and Labor. It offered the minimum amount required by our needs and—in terms of across-the-board aid—the maximum scope permitted by our Constitution. It is imperative that such a proposal carrying out these objectives be enacted this session. I again urge the Congress to enact legislation providing Federal aid for public elementary and secondary classroom construction and teachers' salaries.

As noted earlier, Federal aid for construction and operation of many public schools has been provided since 1950 to those local school districts in which enrollments are affected by Federal installations. Such burdens which may remain from the impact of Federal activities on local school districts will be eased by my proposal for assistance to all school districts for construction and teachers' salaries, thus permitting modification and continuation of this special assistance program as proposed in last year's bill.

A fundamental overhauling and modernization of our traditional vocational education programs is also increasingly needed. Pursuant to my message on education last February, a panel of consultants to the Secretary of Health, Education, and Welfare is studying national needs in this area. They have been asked to develop recommendations by the close of this year for improving and redirecting the Federal Government's role in this program.

Improvement of educational quality. Strengthening financial support for education by general Federal aid will not, however, be sufficient. Specific measures directed at selected problems are also needed to improve the quality of education. And the key to educational quality is the teaching profession. About 1 out of every 5 of the nearly 1,600,000 teachers in our elementary and secondary schools fails to meet full certification standards for teaching or has not completed 4 years of college work. Our immediate concern should be to afford them every possible opportunity to improve their professional skills and their command of the subjects they teach.

In all of the principal areas of academic instruction—English, mathematics, physical and biological sciences, foreign languages, history, geography, and the social sciences—significant advances are being made, both in pushing back the frontiers of knowledge and in the methods of transmitting that knowledge. To keep our teachers up to date on such advances, special institutes are offered in some of these areas by many colleges and universities, financed in part by the National Science Foundation and the Office of Education. Many elementary and secondary schoolteachers would profit from a full year of full-time study in their subject-matter fields. Very vew can afford to do so. Yet the benefits of such a year could be shared by outstanding teachers with others in their schools and school systems as well as with countless students. We should begin to make such opportunities available to the elementary and secondary schoolteachers of this country and thereby accord to this profession the support, prestige, and recognition it deserves.

Another need is for higher standards of teacher education, course content, and instructional methods. The colleges and universities that train our teachers need financial help to examine and further strengthen their programs. Increased research and demonstration efforts must be directed toward improving the learning and teaching of subject matter and developing new and improved learning aids. Excellent but limited work in educational research and development has been undertaken by projects supported by the National Science Foundation, the Office of Education, and private groups. This must be increased—introducing and demonstrating to far more schools than at present up-to-date educational methods using the newest instructional materials and equipment, and providing the most effective in-service training and staff utilization.

Finally, in many urban as well as rural areas of the country, our school systems are confronted with unusually severe educational problems which require the development of new approaches—the problems of gifted children, deprived children, children with language problems, and children with problems that contribute to the high drop-out rate, to name but a few.

To help meet all of these needs for better educational quality and development, and to provide a proper Federal role of assistance and leadership, I recommend that the Congress enact a program designed to help improve the excellence of American education by authorizing—

(1) The award each year of up to 2,500 scholarships to outstanding elementary and secondary school teachers for a year of full-time study;

(2) The establishment of institutes at colleges and universities for elementary and secondary school teachers of those subjects in which improved instruction is needed;

(3) Grants to institutions of higher education to pay part of the cost of special projects designed to strengthen teacher preparation programs through better curriculums and teaching methods;

(4) Amendment of the Cooperative Research Act to permit support of extensive, multipurpose educational research, development, demonstration, and evaluation projects; and

(5) Grants for local public school systems to conduct demonstration or experimental projects of limited duration to improve the quality of instruction or meet special educational problems in elementary and secondary schools.

II. Assistance to higher education

In the last 10 days, both Houses of Congress have recognized the importance of higher education to the fulfillment of our national and international responsibilities. Increasing student enrollments in this decade will place a still greater burden on our institutions of higher education than that imposed on our elementary and secondary schools where the cost of education per student is only a fraction as much. Between 1960 and 1970 it is expected that college enrollments will double, and that our total annual operating expenditures for expanding and improving higher education must increase 2½ times or by nearly $10 billion.

In order to accommodate this increase in enrollments, the Office of Education estimates that nearly $22 billion of college facilities will have to be built during the 1960's—three times the construction achieved in the last 10 years. The extension of the college housing loan program—with a $1.5 billion loan authorization for 5 years, enacted as part of the Housing Act of 1961—assures Federal support for our colleges' urgent residential needs. I am hopeful that the Congress will this month complete its action on legislation to assist in the building of the even more important and urgently needed academic facilities.

But I want to take this opportunity to stress that buildings alone are not enough. In our democracy every young person should have an equal opportunity to obtain a higher education, regardless of his station in life or financial means. Yet more than 400,000 high school seniors who graduated in the upper half of their classes last June failed to enter college this fall. In this group were 200,000 who ranked in the upper 30 per cent of their class, of whom one-third to one-half failed to go on to college principally because of a lack of finances. Others lack the necessary guidance, incentive, or the opportunity to attend the college of their choice. But whatever the reason, each of these 400,000 students represents an irreplaceable loss to the Nation.

Student loans have been helpful to many. But they offer neither incentive nor assistance to those students who, by reason of family or other obligations, are unable or unwilling to go deeper into debt. The average cost of higher education today—up nearly 90 per cent since 1950 and still rising—is in excess of $1,750 per year per student, or $7,000 for a 4-year course. Industrious students can earn a part of this—they or their families can borrow a part of it—but one-half of all American families had incomes below $5,600 in 1960—and they cannot be expected to borrow, for example, $4,000 for each talented son or daughter that deserves to go to college. Federal scholarships providing up to $1,000 a year can fill part of this gap. It is, moreover, only prudent economic and social policy for the public to share part of the costs of the long period of higher education for those whose development is essential to our national economic and social well-being. All of us share in the benefits—all should share in the costs.

I recommend that the full 5-year assistance to higher education proposal before the Congress, including scholarships for more than 200,000 talented and needy students and cost of education payments to their colleges, be enacted without delay.

III. Special education and training programs

(1) *Medical and dental education.* The health needs of our Nation require a sharp expansion of medical and dental education in the United States. We do not have an adequate supply of physicians and dentists today—we are in fact importing many from abroad where they are urgently needed—and the shortage is growing more acute, as the demand for medical services mounts and our population grows. Even to maintain the present ratio of physicians and dentists to population we must graduate 50 per cent more physicians and 90 per cent more dentists per year by 1970, requiring not only the expansion of existing schools but the construction of at least 20 new medical schools and 20 new dental schools.

But here again more buildings are not enough. It is an unfortunate and disturbing fact that the high costs of the prolonged education necessary to enter these professions deprives many highly competent young people of an opportunity to serve in these capacities. Over 40 per cent of all medical students now come from the 12 per cent of our families with incomes of $10,000 or more a year, while only 14 per cent of the students come from the 50 per cent of the Nation's families with incomes under $5,000. This is unfair and unreasonable. A student's ability—not his parents' income—should determine whether he has the opportunity to enter medicine or dentistry.

I recommend that Congress enact the Health Professions Educational Assistance Act which I proposed last year to (a) authorize a 10-year program of matching grants for the construction of new medical and dental schools and (b) provide 4-year scholarships and cost-of-education grants for one-fourth of the entering students in each medical and dental school in the United States.

2. *Scientists and engineers.* Our economic, scientific, and military strength increasingly requires that we have sufficient numbers of scientists and engineers to cope with the fast-changing needs of our time—and the agency with general responsibility for increasing this supply today is the National Science Foundation. At the elementary and secondary school level, I have recommended in the 1963 budget an expansion of the Science Foundation program to develop new instruc-

tional materials and laboratory apparatus for use in a larger number of secondary schools and to include additional subjects and age groups; an expansion of the experimental summer program permitting gifted high school students to work with university research scientists; and an expansion in the number of National Science Foundation supported institutes offering special training in science and mathematics for high school teachers throughout the country. The budget increase requested for this latter program would permit approximately 36,000 high school teachers, representing about 30 per cent of the secondary school teachers of science and mathematics in this country, to participate in the program.

At the higher education level, I am recommending similar budget increases for institute programs for college teachers; improvement in the content of college science, mathematics, and engineering courses; funds for laboratory demonstration apparatus; student research programs; additional top level graduate fellowships in science, mathematics, and engineering; and $61.5 million in grants to our colleges and universities for basic research facilities.

3. *Reduction of adult illiteracy.* Adult education must be pursued aggressively. Over 8 million American citizens aged 25 or above have attended school for less than 5 years, and more than a third of these completely lack the ability to read and write. The economic result of this lack of schooling is often chronic unemployment, dependency, or delinquency, with all the consequences this entails for these individuals, their families, their communities, and the Nation. The twin tragedies of illiteracy and dependency are often passed on from generation to generation.

There is no need for this. Many nations—including our own—have shown that this problem can be attacked and virtually wiped out. Unfortunately, our State school systems—overburdened in recent years by the increasing demands of growing populations and the increasing handicaps of insufficient revenues—have been unable to give adequate attention to this problem. I recommend the authorization of a 5-year program of grants to institutions of higher learning and to the States, to be coordinated in the development of programs which will offer every adult who is willing and able the opportunity to become literate.

4. *Education of migrant workers.* The neglected educational needs of America's 1 million migrant agricultural workers and their families constitute one of the gravest reproaches to our Nation. The interstate and seasonal movement of migrants imposes severe burdens on those school districts which have the responsibility for providing education to those who live there temporarily. I recommend authorization of a 5-year Federal-State program to aid States and school districts in improving the educational opportunities of migrant workers and their children.

5. *Educational television.* The use of television for educational purposes—particularly for adult education—offers great potentialities. The Federal Government has sought to further this through the reservation of 270 television channels for education by the Federal Communications Commission and through the provision of research and advisory services by the Office of Education. Unfortunately, the rate of construction of new broadcasting facilities has been discouraging. Only 80 educational TV channels have been assigned in the last decade. It is apparent that further Federal stimulus and leadership are essential if the vast educational potential of this medium is to be realized. Last year an educational television bill passed the Senate, and a similar proposal was favorably reported to the House. I urge the Congress to take prompt and final action to provide matching financial grants to the States to aid in the construction of State or other nonprofit educational television stations.

6. *Aid to handicapped children.* Another longstanding national concern has

been the provision of specially trained teachers to meet the educational needs of children afflicted with physical and mental disabilities. The existing program providing Federal assistance to higher education institutions and to State education agencies for training teachers and supervisory personnel for mentally retarded children was supplemented last year to provide temporarily for training teachers of the deaf. I recommend broadening the basic program to include assistance for the special training needed to help all our children afflicted with the entire range of physical and mental handicaps.

7. *Federal aid to the arts.* Our Nation has a rich and diverse cultural heritage. We are justly proud of the vitality, the creativity, and the variety of the contemporary contributions our citizens can offer to the world of the arts. If we are to be among the leaders of the world in every sense of the word, this sector of our national life cannot be neglected or treated with indifference. Yet, almost alone among the governments of the world, our Government has displayed little interest in fostering cultural development. Just as the Federal Government has not, should not, and will not undertake to control the subject matter taught in local schools, so its efforts should be confined to broad encouragement of the arts. While this area is too new for hasty action, the proper contributions that should and can be made to the advancement of the arts by the Federal Government—many of them outlined by the Secretary of Labor in his decision settling the Metropolitan Opera labor dispute—deserve thorough and sympathetic consideration. A bill (H.R. 4172) already reported out to the House would make this possible and I urge approval of such a measure establishing a Federal Advisory Council on the Arts to undertake these studies.

IV. Conclusion

The problems to which these proposals are addressed would require solution whether or not we were confronted with a massive threat to freedom. The existence of that threat lends urgency to their solution—to the accomplishment of those objectives which, in any case, would be necessary for the realization of our highest hopes and those of our children. "If a nation," wrote Thomas Jefferson in 1816, "expects to be ignorant *and* free, in a state of civilization, it expects what never was and never will be." That statement is even truer today than it was 146 years ago.

The education of our people is a national investment. It yields tangible returns in economic growth, an improved citizenry, and higher standards of living. But even more importantly, free men and women value education as a personal experience and opportunity—as a basic benefit of a free and democratic civilization. It is our responsibility to do whatever needs to be done to make this opportunity available to all and to make it of the highest possible quality.

JOHN F. KENNEDY.

THE WHITE HOUSE, *February 6, 1962.*

NOTE: The improvement of educational quality was discussed again by President Kennedy in his message to Congress, January 29, 1963, 88th Cong., 1st Sess., House of Representatives Document no. 54, pp. 9–10.

INDEX

Advanced Placement Program in foreign language teaching, 54, 64
Advanced Study in the Behavioral Sciences, Center for, 1959 conference, 68
Agencies, supporting, role in curriculum improvement, 209–211
Alexander, William M., 285
American Association for the Advancement of Science, role in education, 169–173
American Association of Colleges for Teacher Education, role in curriculum improvement, 193–198
American Astronomical Society, 171
American Council of Learned Societies, Committee on Secondary Schools, 175
  role in secondary education, 173–180
American Educational Research Association, 188
  role in curriculum experimentation and improvement, 187–193
American Institute of Biological Sciences, 130
American Mathematical Society, 203
American Meteorological Society, 141
"American Method" of foreign language teaching, 50
Anderson, Roland C., 288
Arnheim, Rudolph, 128
Art education, curriculum experimentation and research in, 113–128
Ashby, Lyle W., 285
Association for Supervision and Curriculum Development, role in curriculum experimentation, 181–187
Ault, H. O., 65
Automation, educational implications of, NEA project on, 2
  effect on curriculum, 224
  influence on labor force, 5
Ayres handwriting scale, 188

Baird, George H., 87, 221
Bales, Robert F., 128
Barnes, Melvin W., 285
Bates, Marston, 134
Beatley, Ralph, 84, 86
Beberman, Max, 31, 82, 85–87, 184
Begle, E. G., 31, 77, 87, 203
Beittel, Kenneth R., 125, 127, 128
Benjamin, Harold, 239
Berde, Ralph, 288
Biological education, threshold of revolution in, 129–142
Biological Sciences Curriculum Study (BCSC), 130
  Committee on Teacher Preparation, 138
  international aspects of, 139
Biology course, grade level of, 131
  high school, three versions of, 133
  testing centers for, 135
Birkhoff, G. D., 84, 86
Birthrate influence on labor force, 5
Bloom, Benjamin S., 70, 73, 157
Boehm, G. A. W., 86
Borglum, George, 54
Bourdon, Donna, 288
Brandwein, Paul, 137
Britton, Allen P., 106, 112
Brooks, Nelson, 51
Brownell, W. A., 35, 151
Brownell-Moser study of subtraction, 28
Brumfiel, Charles F., 84, 86
Bruner, Jerome S., 6, 35, 192, 211
Buber, Martin, 127
Buckingham spelling scale, 188
Burgart, Herbert J., 125, 127, 128
Burkhart, Robert C., 117, 123, 127, 128
Bush, Vannevar, 87

Caldwell, Sarah C., 285
Carnegie Foundation, role in curriculum experimentation, 211–216

Carroll, John B., 55, 56
Caswell, Hollis L., 285
Cattell, Raymond B., 128
Chappaqua, New York, experiment in foreign language teaching, 52
Chemical Bond Approach Project, 95–98, 204
Chemical Education Material Study (CHEMStudy), 99–103, 204
Chemistry teaching in high school, 95–103
Clark, David L., 218
The Classical Investigation, 1924, 58
Classics teaching, improvement in, 57–66
  progress report, 63
  recommendations, 64
Clement, Rufus E., 285
Cleveland, Greater, Educational Research Council, 221
Clymer, Theodore, 265
College Entrance Examination Board, Commission on Mathematics, 74, 212, 213
Commission on the English Curriculum, 90
Committee on the Gifted Student, 137
Committee on Teacher Preparation, 138
Conant, James Bryant, 50
Congress, role in curriculum development, 223–230
Conservation principle, 28
"Continental Classroom," television mathematics course, 76
Contributors to this volume, 244–245
Cooley, William W., 211
Cooperative Research Program of U.S. Office of Education, curriculum projects supported by, 246–249
  role in curriculum experimentation, 206–211
Couch, Arthur S., 128
Course of study, new, developing, 159
  introducing, 159
Courtis tests in measuring achievement in elementary arithmetic, 188

Cranmore, Marion, 285
Cronbach, Lee J., 35, 152
Cuisenaire blocks, 33
Curriculum, definitions of, 90
  and national economy, 1–7
  and national interest, 13
Curriculum (NCTE) Commission on English, 90
Curriculum experimentation, in art education, 113–128
  categories, 157
  design in, formulating, 160
  in earth sciences, 143–148
  in foreign languages, 49–57
  in music education, 103–113
  problems of, scientific, 150
    earth sciences, 143–148
    social, 155
    statistical, 157–163
  types of, 158
  variables in, measuring, 159
Curriculum improvement, in classics teaching, 57–66
  Palo Alto Conference on, 16
Curriculum projects, Cooperative Research Program, U.S. Office of Education, 246–249
  current, in science education, 249–263
Curriculum research, role of government in, 236–243
Curriculum Responsibilities of State Departments of Education, 217
Curriculum revision, in physics, 38–49
  psychological participation in, 20

Desberg, D., 65
Deyrup, Ingrith, 134
Dickson, James G., 139
Douglas, Carol, 285
Drop-out problem, 5
Dropouts, school project on, 2
  reasons for, 5
Dudley, Dolores D., 112
Dupree, A. H., 87

Index | 306

Earnings, relation of education to, 4
Earth science study, developing course in, 145
　grade level of, 144
　importance of, 144
　teacher training problems in, 146
　teaching resources in, 146
Earth sciences, curriculum experimentation problems in, 143–148
Easton (Maryland) Conference on Psychological Research in Education (1958), 278, 282
Education, national interest in, 12
　national planning and quality control in, 11–18
　vocational, need for reexamination, 14
　providing in classroom, 10
Educational Implications of Automation (see Automation)
Educational Research Council of Greater Cleveland, 221
Educational Services Incorporated, 38, 47
Educational Testing Service, 51
Educational theory, language of, 21
Eicholz, Robert E., 84, 86
Eight-Year Study, 192
Eight-Year-Study schools, 25
Encyclopedia of Educational Research, 189
English, current progress in teaching of, 88–94
English curriculum, NCTE Commission study, 90
　Portland, Oregon, survey, 92
　University of Michigan planning institute, 92
Evaluation, in curriculum development, 24
　meaning to curriculum developers, 24
　research in, 24, 156
　statistical problems in, 157–163
The Experience Curriculum, 89
Experimental projects, practical problems in, 163–167

Federal Extension Service, 15
Film and TV instruction, comparison with live instruction, 24
Films, built around experiments, 41
　teaching, types for physics course, 41
　use in teaching, 23
Finlay, Gilbert C., 49
Finn, James, 2
Flanders, Ned A., 211
Flynt, Ralph C. M., 220
Ford Foundation grants, science and engineering program, 251–252
Foreign language courses, evaluation and testing, 51
Foreign language laboratories, 54
Foreign language teaching, "American Method" of, 50
　audio-lingual method, 50, 60
　disc recordings for, 51
　electromechanical aids for, 52
　materials, 51
　programmed instruction in, 60
　"programmed" presentation, techniques for, 55
　six-year sequence, 51
　tape recordings for, 51
　television broadcasting for, 52
Foreign languages, curriculum experimentation in, 49–57
Foundations, private, role in curriculum experimentation, 211–216
Fowler, M., 65
Francis, W. Nelson, 92
Freibergs, Vaira, 35
Fries, C. C., 65

Gaarder, A. Bruce, 219
Gagne, Robert, 215
Galas, Evangeline, 52
Garrett, Alfred B., 171
Garry, Ralph, 55, 57
Geological Institute of America, 146
Geophysical Year, International, 146
Gifted Student, Committee on, 137
Glass, Bentley, 130, 132, 204, 231
Gogel, Kenneth, 123, 128
Gomez, Humberto, 139

Goodlad, John I., 211
Gough, Harrison G., 128
Government role, in curriculum research and experimentation, 236–243
  in education, 230–236
Griggs, Richard, 29
Grobman, Arnold, 184, 204
Guilford's Unusual Uses test, 34
Gummere, John, 65

Hall, Roy, 164
A Handbook of Research on Teaching, 189
Hanna, Paul R., 68, 225
Harlow, Harry F., 30, 35
Harris, Chester W., 127
Hartman, Frank R., 127
Hartshorn, Merrill F., 73
Hartshorn, William C., 113
Hatfield, W. Wilbur, 89
Havighurst, Robert J., 285
Havlish, Jean, 288
Hawley, Newton, 214
Hechinger, Fred, 141
Heller, Julius, 122, 128
Heller, Robert L., 147
Herrerra, José, 139
Higgins, V. Louise, 91
Higher Horizons Program in New York schools, 2, 225
Hill, S. A., 87
Hill, Stanley, 288
Hillegas composition scale, 188
Hively, W., 288
Horn, Marilyn J., 122, 128
Huddlestone, Edith M., 56
Hull, Clark, 22
Humphrey, Hubert H., 220, 273
Hurd, Paul deH., 139
Huzar, E., 65

Illinois, University of, Committee on School Mathematics, 74, 151
Illinois Arithmetic Project, 29
"Improvement of Educational Quality Act of 1962," text, 291–296

Indiana University Honors Program Abroad for High School Students, 54
Instructional Program of the Public Schools, Project on, 285–287
Interlochen (Michigan) Arts Academy, National Music Camp, 110

Jackson, Frederick, 204
Jackson, Harvey O., 288
Jarvis, Boyer, 208
Johnson, Van, 65
Juilliard School of Music, experimental curriculum, 106

Kalisch, Gerhald K., 288
Keedy, M. L., 184
Keetman, Gunhild, 113
Keislar, Evan R., 211
Kelly, Harry, 220
Kierkegaard, Soren, 127
Kitzhaber, Albert, 265
Klammer, T. P., 65
Kline, M., 87
Kolb, C. Haven, 134
Kraft, C., 288
Krumboltz, John D., 31, 35

Labor force, birth-rate influence on, 5
  distribution of, 12
  effects of technological development on, 12
  in United States, 4
Lado, R., 65
Lambert, Sam, 164
Language teaching (*see* Foreign language teaching)
Lee, Addison E., 137
Leino, Walter B., 53
Levy, H. L., 65
Lewis, Earl, 54
Lienhard, M., 127
Little, Elbert P., 184
Logsdon, James D., 285
Long, Harold M., 73
Lowenfeld, Viktor, 114

Index | 308

Lown, J. A., 288
Lynes, Russell, 113

McAulay, John D., 231
McEwen, William R., 288
McFee, June, 119, 128
Mackenzie, Gordon N., 185
McMurrin, Sterling, 67, 95, 200, 217, 220
Madison (Wisconsin) Conference on Research in Education, 278–284
Manpower and education, 7–11
Mason, Lowell, 103
Mathematical Association of America, 203
Mathematics, College Entrance Examination Board, Commission on, 74
  new programs, 73–87
  school, University of Illinois Committee on, 74
Mattil, Edward L., 127
Mauriello, Edna, 55, 57
May, Kenneth O., 288
Mayor, John R., 87, 214
Meinz, Algalee Pool, 123, 128
Meyer, W. H., 87
Minnesota National Laboratory, 149–157
  description (reprint of Minnesota State Department of Education bulletin), 288–290
Modern Language Association of America, 49, 51
Modern Language Materials Development Center, 51
Modern Language Project of the Massachusetts Council for Public Schools, 52
Moore, John, 131, 134
Morris, Charles W., 116, 127
Morse, Wayne, 232
Moser, H. E., 35
Mosteller, Frederick, 76, 86
Mueller, John H., 107, 113
Mueller, Kate Hevner, 107, 113
Mueller, Klaus, 54
Music as academic subject, 106

Music curriculum, developments in, 103–113
  experimentation in, 103–113
Music Educators National Conference, 1961, 108
  1962, 106
Music teaching, use of television and radio in, 111

National Academy of Sciences–National Research Council Madison Conference, text of report, 278–284
National Council for the Social Studies, 68
National Council of Teachers of English, 89
  Commission on the English Curriculum, 90
National Council of Teachers of Mathematics, 203
National Defense Education Act, 52, 94, 176, 218, 219, 224, 232, 270
National Education Association (NEA) Project, on Educational Implications of Automation, 2
  on the Instruction Program in the Public Schools, 1
National interest in education, 12
The National Interest and the Teaching of English, 94, 266
National planning and quality control in education, 11–18
National Planning and Quality Control in Education (conference report), 276–278
National Science Foundation, grants by, in course content improvement studies, 259–263
  in science teaching equipment development program, 252–259
  role in course content improvement, 199–205
"NEA Project on Instruction," text reprinted from NEA Journal, May, 1961, 285–287
New York City School Survey, 1911–1912, 188

Oliver, Donald, 73
Oppenheimer, J. Robert, 193
Orff, Carl, 108, 113
Organized Occupational Curriculums in Higher Education, 217
Osgood, C., 22, 34, 128
Otterbein College Film-text for French, 54

Palmer, L. R., 66
Palo Alto Conference on Curriculum Improvement (1959), 16
Penfield, Wilder, 55, 56
Phenix, Philip H., 285
Physical Science Study Committee, 16, 38–49, 203
Physics course (PSSC), content of, 42
  evaluation of, 46
  as explanatory system, 39
  grade level of, 39
  one-year, developing, 39
  materials for, 45
Physics curriculum, revision in, 38–49
Piaget, J., 22, 29, 34
Pittsburgh survey of 1907, 188
Pooley, Robert, 265
Popper, S. E., 288
Powers, James R., 184
President of the United States, message relative to educational program, 296
Price, Roy A., 73
The Process of Education, 6, 192
Professional societies, role in education, 169–198
Programming, 31
  significant features of, 32
"Project English," 95, 220
  description of, 263–266
  implications of, 266, 272
Projects, curriculum, investigators, 246 ff.
  in science education, 249–263
  experimental, practical problems in, 163–167
  (*See also* Curriculum experimentation)

Psychological background for curriculum experimentation, 19–35
Psychological participation in curriculum revision, 20
Pullen, Thomas G., Jr., 285

Quality control in education, 11–18
Quillen, I. James, 285

Rademacher, H. A., 87
Radio use in music teaching, 111
Rajaratsom, N., 288
Reichard, Joseph, 54
Reilly, J. F., 66
Research, educational, in evaluation, 24, 156
  school survey movement in, 187
  testing movement in, 187
Research in Education, A Proposed Organization for (conference report), 278–284
Review of Educational Research, 189
Ribicoff, Abraham, 217
Richardson, Walter W., 288
Roberts, Lamar, 56
Rosenbloom, Paul C., 87, 220, 228, 273
Rosselot, Lavelle, 54
Rourke, Robert E. K., 76

The Saber-tooth Curriculum, 88, 239
Sand, Ole, 1, 285
Schaie, K. Warner, 128
School adjustment movement in educational research, 187
School Mathematics Study Group, 74, 77, 151, 203
School survey movement in educational research, 187
Schreiber, Daniel, 2, 5
Schultz, Theodore, 3
Schwab, Joseph J., 138
Science education, curriculum projects in, 249–263
"Science Study Series," 47
  translated into foreign languages, 48
Science teaching, changes in, 169–173

Index | 310

Scientific problems in curriculum experimentation, 150
Secondary schools, American Council of Learned Societies Committee on, 175
Seligson, G., 66
Senate Subcommittee on Education, 232
Senton, Edwin, 73
Seraphim, Sister, 288
Shanks, Merrill E., 84, 86
Sherred, Ruth, 53
Sitgreaves, Rosedith, 154
Skinner, B. F., 35
Slaughter, Eugene E., 184
Smedslund, Jan, 28, 35
Smithers, William, 54
Snow, C. P., 186
Social problems in curriculum experimentation, 155
Social Science Research Council, 23
Social studies instruction, need for improvement, 66–73
Solomon, H., 154, 157
Speith, Herman, 140
Starr, Wilmarth, 52, 54
Statistical problems in curriculum experimentation and evaluation, 157–163
Steelman, J. R., 87
Stern, Catherine, 214
Stewart, William Ross, 123, 128
Stone, Marshall, 214
Stone tests measuring achievement in elementary arithmetic, 187
Stouffer, S. A., 157
Stratton, Julius, 129
Strong, Laurence, 204
Suppes, Patrick, 87, 214
Swanson, E. O., 288
Sweet, Waldo, 59, 66

Taylor, Calvin, 117
Taxonomy of Educational Objectives, 70, 72, 157
Teacher Preparation, Committee on, 138
Teaching machines, 23, 30, 31, 111

Technological development in industry and agriculture, 12
Technological Development Project, 2
Television broadcasting, closed-circuit, in art education, 118
  in foreign language teaching, 52
  use in music teaching, 111
ten Hoor, Marten, 107, 113
Testing movement in educational research, 187
Thirring, Hans, 235
Thomas, George B., Jr., 76
Thompson, G. Baker, 285
Thorndike, E. L., 21
Thorndike handwriting scale, 188
Toeplitz, O., 87
Tribue language scale, 188
Tulving, Endel, 35
Two Cultures and the Scientific Revolution, 186
Tyler, Ralph, 20, 71, 73, 154, 192

Ulich, Robert, 231
Underwood, Benton J., 35
U.S. Office of Education role in curriculum experimentation, 206–211
  Cooperative Research Program, 216–222

Valdman, Albert, 55
Vocational education, need for reexamination, 14
  providing in classroom, 10

Wampler, M. H., 66
Ward, R. L., 66
Warner, Lloyd, 192
Waterman, Alan T., 219
Wayne State University Modern Language Audio-visual Project, 54
Weisman, Ronald G., 31, 35
Welch, Claude A., 134
West, Allan M., 285
West, Edith, 73
White, Harvey, 197
White, Stephen, 49

Wood, William, 54
Woods Hole Conference of 1959, 22, 192
Woody arithmetic scale, 188

Yarborough, Ralph, 232
York, Roy, Jr., 113

Zacharias, Jerrold R., 43, 203